T0394570

THE BOUNDARY BETWEEN GRAMMAR AND LEXICON

CURRENT ISSUES IN LINGUISTIC THEORY

AMSTERDAM STUDIES IN THE THEORY AND HISTORY
OF LINGUISTIC SCIENCE – Series IV
ISSN 0304-0763

General Editor
JOSEPH C. SALMONS
University of Wisconsin–Madison
jsalmons@wisc.edu

Founder & General Editor (1975-2015)
E.F.K. KOERNER †
Leibniz-Zentrum Allgemeine Sprachwissenschaft, Berlin

Current Issues in Linguistic Theory (CILT) is a theory-oriented series which welcomes
contributions from scholars who have significant proposals that advance our understanding of
language change and comparative linguistics, including issues of structure and function.
CILT offers an outlet for meaningful contributions to current diachronic linguistic debate.
A complete list of titles in this series can be found on *benjamins.com/catalog/cilt*

Volume 368

Brent de Chene

The Boundary between Grammar and Lexicon
Evidence from Japanese verb morphology

THE BOUNDARY BETWEEN GRAMMAR AND LEXICON

EVIDENCE FROM JAPANESE VERB MORPHOLOGY

BRENT DE CHENE
Waseda University

JOHN BENJAMINS PUBLISHING COMPANY
AMSTERDAM & PHILADELPHIA

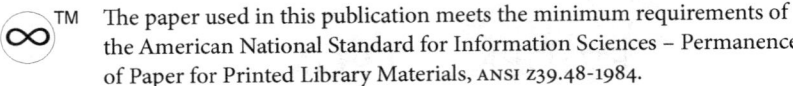

TM The paper used in this publication meets the minimum requirements of
the American National Standard for Information Sciences – Permanence
of Paper for Printed Library Materials, ANSI z39.48-1984.

DOI 10.1075/cilt.368

Cataloging-in-Publication Data available from Library of Congress:
LCCN 2024047354 (PRINT) / 2024047355 (E-BOOK)

ISBN 978 90 272 1912 1 (HB)
ISBN 978 90 272 4626 4 (E-BOOK)

John Benjamins Publishing Company · https://benjamins.com

To my teachers, Steve and Theo

Table of contents

Preface

This book is a defense of weak lexicalist or "split" morphology, according to which the traditional domain of morphology divides into syntactic and presyntactic subdomains. Those two subdomains will be seen to correspond well with inflection and derivation as ordinarily conceived, although the fundamental fact of a division between the syntactic and the presyntactic is independent of just how precise the correspondence with inflection and derivation is. Specifically, I will argue that while inflection is the phonological realization of syntactic terminal elements, at least some derivation has properties that militate against such a treatment. If so, we might do well to keep in mind the possibility that inflection and derivation, in spite of their obvious similarities, are fundamentally different phenomena, as is apparently true of their correlates in languages that have neither of them — roughly, free grammatical words and compounding, respectively.

The book's database is the verbal morphology of Japanese and the closely related Ryukyuan languages. Japanese verbal morphology is an appropriate testing ground for hypotheses about the properties of inflection and derivation because it is relatively rich in suffixes of both kinds. As an example, consider the form *to-g-ar-as-ase-rare-ta* 'was made to sharpen (it)'. The first three suffixes of that form, *-g-*, *-ar-*, and *-as-*, all create verb stems of determinate transitivity or event-type status, transitive (causative), intransitive (inchoative), and transitive, respectively. Strikingly, the second and third suffixes override the transitivity status of their base, so that at each of the three stages *to-g-*, *to-g-ar-*, and *to-g-ar-as-*, only the outermost suffix of the stem counts in determining its transitivity. This is unexpected on the hypothesis that the suffixes in question realize syntactic elements, since, in a syntactic construction, the meaning of each of the parts should be reflected in the meaning of the whole. The remaining suffixes, *-ase-* (Causative), *-rare-* (Passive), and *-ta* (Perfect) conform to this expectation, each composing with its base to produce a predictable interpretation, and are naturally understood as syntactic. I will propose that the contrasting properties of derivational and inflectional suffixes just illustrated are to be explained by the hypothesis that, while (stems and) inflectional affixes have listed or lexical representations, (roots and) derivational affixes do not. It will then be only stems and inflectional affixes that are subject to composition by the syntactic computational system. With inflectable stems lexically listed, but inflected forms syntactically generated, the boundary between lexicon and syntax will coincide with the boundary between derivation and inflection.

Consideration of the distributional and interpretive properties of verbal suffixes occupies Chapters 1 through 4 of the book. Chapters 5 through 8 constitute an extended case study of morphophonological reanalysis and regularization supporting the conclusion that stems and inflectional affixes, but not roots and derivational affixes, are subject to reanalysis of their underlying phonological shape. This generalization, like the contrast between the interpretive properties of inflectional and derivational suffixes seen above, follows naturally from the hypothesis that while stems and inflectional affixes have listed representations, the subconstituents of stems, roots and derivational affixes, do not. The book thus provides evidence from both the syntactic and the phonological branches of the grammar that the morphological units with listed representations are stems and inflectional affixes, with the further implication that the boundary between the listed and the generated falls at the boundary between derivation and inflection.

A note is in order on the book's intended readership. Ideally, I would hope to attract at least the passing attention of any linguist with a serious interest in morphology or morphophonology. At the same time, it must be said that the density of the Japanese and Ryukyuan data in Chapters 2 through 8 means that the text will be easier going for linguists with some prior knowledge of Japanese. I believe, however, that the book's main lines of argumentation can readily be followed without immersion in all the details of the data.

Much of the book's text is based on articles that have been published over the last ten years, and I am grateful to the publishers for permission to reuse the relevant material. The following is a relatively detailed accounting of the sources of individual chapters and sections, referring to articles recorded in the reference list at the end of the volume; in the text itself, I have kept direct reference to earlier work to a minimum. Chapter 1 and the beginning of Chapter 2 are mostly new; Section 2.3 incorporates material from de Chene 2022a, but is based for the most part on de Chene 2020a. Chapter 3 is a substantial expansion of de Chene 2017. Chapter 4 for the most part hews closely to de Chene 2022b. In Chapter 5, Sections 5.2 and 5.7 incorporate material from de Chene 2020b and de Chene 2019, respectively; the remainder of the chapter is largely based on material from de Chene 2016. Chapter 6 corresponds quite closely to de Chene 2019. Chapter 7 combines material from de Chene 2016 and de Chene 2020b, with material from de Chene 2014 introduced in Section 7.4; Section 7.8 is new. Chapter 8 is for the most part based on those elements of de Chene 2020b not incorporated into earlier chapters. The material of the short concluding Chapter 9, finally, is new. Throughout, analyses of individual phenomena have been updated, new material has been added, and earlier material has been regrouped and reorganized. The overarching claim that the distributional and interpretive data of Chapters 1 through 4 and the morphophonological data of Chapters 5 through 8 lead to the same conclusion regarding the division between the lexically listed and the freely generated, a conclusion that places derivation and inflection on opposite sides of that boundary, is presented here for the first time.

As a graduate student at UCLA many years ago, I had the good fortune to study under two inspiring teachers whose approaches to morphology and morphophonology were both mutually reinforcing and, in productive ways, complementary. Having now completed this book, I am struck and humbled by the degree to which it reflects the deep influence of both of them, far beyond the concrete citations of their work that it contains. Among the many things I learned from Theo Vennemann genannt Nierfeld, who left UCLA in the middle of my graduate career, was always to ask what generalizations speakers have actually made, in particular concerning morphophonology, and Chapters 5 through 8 are an exercise in applying that principle, using ongoing and completed change as the central evidence. Among the many things I learned from my doctoral advisor Stephen R. Anderson, who arrived at UCLA in the middle of my graduate career, was how to draw the distinction between inflection and derivation, and the present book could be viewed as an extended exposition of my version of his answer to that question. It gives me great pleasure to dedicate this book jointly to Steve and Theo.

I am indebted as well to many other people whose feedback and support have been invaluable in developing the ideas that have gone into this book. Prominent among them are the anonymous referees for (in chronological order) *Journal of East Asian Linguistics*, Steve's festschrift *On Looking into Words* (Language Sciences Press), *Gengo Kenkyu, Journal of Japanese Linguistics* (twice), *Diachronica*, and *Word Structure*, whose comments reliably resulted in significant improvements in the articles whose contents have been reused and reworked here; the same is true for the two scholars who reviewed the book manuscript for John Benjamins. For comments on conference presentations relevant to the book's contents, I am indebted to Kunio Nishiyama, Junko Ito, Armin Mester, Yoko Sugioka, and Masahiro Yamada, among others. For native speaker judgments on Japanese, the majority of them with respect to the data of Chapter 4, heartfelt thanks go to Sachiko Fujii, Takayuki Fujii, Kikuo Maekawa, Yuji Nishiyama, Masanobu Sorida, Yoko Sugioka, and Hideaki Suzuki. I am grateful to Masahiro Yamada for discussion of the material of Chapter 2 and to Yoko Sugioka for discussion of some of the material of Chapter 4. My former student Takayuki Ikezawa deserves special mention for sparking the discussion that led to the idea for the paper that became the kernel of Chapter 3; several of the formulations in that chapter were later sharpened as the result of online discussion with Dmitri Zelensky. Regarding the material of Chapter 5, I would like to express my appreciation to the National Institute for Japanese Language and Linguistics (NINJAL), formerly known in

English as the National Language Research Institute, and to Takuichiro Onishi in particular for allowing me to view unpublished results of the preparatory survey for the *Grammar atlas of Japanese dialects* and for helpful correspondence on related matters. I am also grateful to NINJAL for permission to use the Chunagon corpus search tool and to Kikuo Maekawa for guidance in that regard. For discussion relating to the material of Chapter 5, I thank Masae Matsuki and Takayuki Ikezawa. The material on Korean in Chapter 7 represents distillation of a larger body of work in connection with which I have benefited from discussion with and/or assistance from Sang-Cheol Ahn, Adam Albright, Jieun Bark, Ricardo Bermúdez-Otero, Jae-Woong Choe, Sukhoon Choo, Youngah Do, Yoonjung Kang, Yunjin Nam, Andrew Nevins, and Kevin Tang. Charles De Wolf graciously served as a sounding board for a number of ideas that are reflected in the book. I am deeply grateful to the CILT series editor Joseph C. Salmons for his comments on the manuscript and to him and the entire CILT editorial board for giving the project a vote of confidence at a point when my own feelings about it were still somewhat tentative. Finally, Anke de Looper and Ineke Elskamp of John Benjamins have been unfailingly responsive and supportive guides to the production process. None of the above individuals, it goes without saying, are responsible for any of the remaining shortcomings of the book.

Inflectional category names

The list below introduces the labels used in this book for the major inflectional categories of Japanese and Ryukyuan languages and identifies the forms they represent by giving the corresponding Tokyo Japanese (consonant-stem) and Shuri Okinawan suffixes. The Tokyo and Shuri suffixes are cognate except in the Conclusive and Adnominal, where the Shuri forms descend from combinations of the Adverbial suffix with inflected forms of *wor- 'be'. The dagger next to a Tokyo suffix indicates that it is obsolete or obsolescent. Chapter 2 deviates from the terminology of the list in that "Conditional" is used in place of "Provisional" for Dunan; in Chapter 8, Japanese Volitional forms, which expressed inferential meaning into the early modern period, are referred to as Inferentials. Terminological uniformity between Japanese and Shuri has not been enforced for the last three categories, those characterized by *t*-initial suffixes, where the terms used for Shuri are given first, followed in parentheses by the terms used for Japanese (and, with the substitution of "Past" for "Perfect", Dunan). With the exception of "causative" and "passive" in the body of Chapter 4, the names of affixally marked Japanese and Ryukyuan inflectional categories are capitalized throughout the book. Such names are not capitalized, however, when they are used in more general meanings ("imperative interpretations", "potential expressions", "negative existential verb").

	Tokyo	Shuri
Adverbial	-i	-i
Conclusive	-u	-(j)u-n
Adnominal	-u	-(j)u-ru
Provisional	-eba	-ee
Conditional	†-aba	-aa
Volitional	-oo	-a
Imperative	-e	-i
Prohibitive	-u-na	-una
Negative	-ana-	-an
Passive	-are-	-arir-
Causative 1	-ase-	-as-
Causative 2	†-asime-	-asimir-
Potential	-e-	-----

Perfect Adverbial (Conjunctive)	-te	-ti
Perfect Conclusive (Perfect)	-ta	-ta-n
Perfect Adnominal (Perfect)	-ta	-ta-ru

On the transcription of Japanese

In the main text, including footnotes, Japanese and Ryukyuan forms other than proper names are given in a phonological transcription in which consonants correspond to those of *Kunreisiki* romanization (with the palatal semivowel transcribed *j* for Ryukyuan languages) and vowel length is represented by gemination. Japanese proper names of all kinds are given in Hepburn romanization without the macrons that can be used to distinguish /oo/ from /o/ and /uu/ from /u/ (although in Section 4.5, macrons are used in the names of two early modern literary works and their authors). The reference list contains only Hepburn romanization, apart from names that are conventionally romanized otherwise. Macrons are used to mark length in /oo/ and /uu/ in transcribed Japanese article and book titles; outside such titles, macrons are elided except when necessary to render accurately a non-Japanese title. Gemination is used in the reference list to show length in recent loanwords (*fiirudo, foneemu, sentaa, apuroochi*); as is customary, /ii/ is transcribed *ii* everywhere.

CHAPTER 1

The syntactic nature of inflection

1.1 Introduction: The boundary between grammar and lexicon

In linguistic description, there is no more fundamental distinction than that which divides what speakers record in memory from what they generate freely — divides, that is, the lexicon from the grammar. Similarly, in differentiating linguistic models or frameworks, there is probably no more fundamental parameter than the placement of the boundary between lexicon and syntax. The lack of consensus among grammarians on this basic point, however, is striking; almost every logically possible position concerning the division between grammar and lexicon can be observed in current literature. At one extreme, the position that the lexicon (or similar list) contains only morpheme-sized pieces — roots and affixes — and that all morpheme combinations result from syntactic computation is a fundamental tenet of the framework of Distributed Morphology (DM; Halle and Marantz 1993, 1994). At the other, Construction Grammar (e.g. Goldberg 1995) and similar frameworks deny the existence of any generative computational system, treating all syntactic structures as instantiations of listed constructions. Intermediate positions, while assuming a syntactic component, treat stems or words as lexically listed or lexically derived rather than as syntactically constructed.

This book shows that two distinct strands of research on Japanese and Ryukyuan verbal morphology converge on a unified conclusion concerning the boundary between grammar and lexicon, namely that while inflection is the phonological realization of syntactic terminal elements and thus falls squarely on the grammatical side of the boundary, the regularities of derivational morphology cannot be so treated and are appropriately expressed as redundancy rules over lexically listed stems. I will also argue that inflection, in addition to being (post)syntactic in this sense, must be "piece-based" (morpheme-based, with inflectional affixes having listed representations) rather than "process-based" (rule-based, with inflectional affixes resulting from phonological rules applying to stems) — in Stump's (2001: 1) terms, "lexical" rather than "inferential". The evidence for these conclusions comes on the one hand from the distributional and interpretive properties of inflectional and derivational affixes themselves and on the other from the phenomenon of morphophonological reanalysis, which is seen to target stems and inflectional affixes, but not roots and derivational affixes.

The remainder of this chapter is structured as follows. Section 1.2 introduces basic morphological terminology and situates the position to be taken here on the relation of morphology to syntax in the spectrum of views on that subject to be observed in current literature. Section 1.3 answers a number of criticisms that have been directed at the concept of "split" or "weak lexicalist" morphology, according to which inflection is syntactic but derivation is not. Section 1.4 then argues that because the clearly syntactic elements of one language may correspond to the inflectional elements of another, syntax and inflectional morphology, if they were distinct grammatical components, would largely have to duplicate each other's content. By the same token, if inflectional affixation were the output of rewrite rules operating on a lexical category augmented by the full set of morphosyntactic features necessary for the creation of an inflected word form, those rules would need to duplicate hierarchical relationships that have independent syntactic motivation. A survey of the attested types of inflectional features and operators in Section 1.5 reveals that the only subtype whose syntactic status might be doubted, that of "inherent" inflection as typified by verbal tense and nominal number, in fact appears to be unambiguously syntactic. Section 1.6, finally, previews the content of the following chapters.

1.2   Background: Morphological concepts and frameworks

Morphology is typically defined as the theory of the internal structure of words and of how that structure is represented and/or generated. On a traditional conception, the atoms of morphology are morphemes, where the morpheme is in principle the minimal linguistic unit that pairs sound and meaning (Bloomfield 1933:161ff.). Morphemes may be divided into the lexical and the functional or grammatical depending on whether the associated meaning is concrete or abstract; they are also free or bound depending on whether they may occur as independent words or not. An affix is a bound grammatical morpheme, while a root is any lexical morpheme, free or bound.

Affixes are traditionally divided into inflectional and derivational types, where the core function of inflectional affixes is to mark morphosyntactic features that are subject to manipulation by syntactic operations such as agreement and case marking, and the core function of derivational affixes is to create new lexical items, in particular, new items of the major lexical categories noun, verb, and adjective. In many languages, a full inflected word thus typically consists of a root, often acategorial, followed first by a derivational affix, often with identifiable semantic content, that fixes the lexical category and renders the combination inflectable, and then by an inflectional affix that limits the syntactic contexts in which the inflected word may be used. In such a case, the combination of root and derivational affix is called an (inflectable) stem. Abbreviating "derivational affix" as "DA" and "inflectional affix" as "IA", the resulting word structure is thus as in (1), where the affixes are represented as suffixes.

(1)   [[[Root] DA $_{Stem}$] IA $_{Word}$]

For example, the Latin root *am-* 'love' underlies a noun stem *am-ōr-* 'love (n.)' and a verb stem *am-ā-* 'love (v.)'; as typical inflected forms built on those stems, the genitive singular of the former is *am-ōr-is* 'of love', and the first person plural present tense form of the latter is *am-ā-mus* 'we love'. In addition to word-forming inflectional affixes like *-is* and *-mus*, there are stem-forming inflectional affixes, illustrated by the *-v-* that forms the perfect stem *am-ā-v-* seen in *am-ā-v-imus* 'we loved'. This point is worth noting in the present context because the Passive and Causative (and sometimes Negative) suffixes of Japanese, which are inflectional on both syntactic/semantic and morphophonological criteria, are sometimes characterized without argument as "derivational" (Iwasaki 2013: 81), apparently on the basis that they are stem-forming.

     Contemporary theories of morphology vary along a number of dimensions, among them the relationship that is envisioned between morphology and syntax and whether affixation is treated as piece-based or process-based (see Harley 2015 for a review). Here, for expository purposes, I will first separate out asyntactic or strongly lexicalist morphological theories, those that postulate no interaction between morphology and syntax except for, typically, insertion of fully inflected words into syntactic structure. I will then use comparison with two prominent frameworks that treat some or all morphology as syntactically determined to situate the position to be taken in this book concerning the relation between the two fields.

     Asyntactic theories of morphology have in common that any and all internal structure that is attributed to words is established presyntactically, typically in the lexicon. This structure and speaker knowledge of it can be taken to be either declarative (i.e. formulated in terms of redundancy rules over listed representations), on the one hand, or procedural or generative, on the other (on this distinction, see e.g. Pollard and Sag 1987: 209). A very wide range of grammatical frameworks incorporate theories of morphology that are asyntactic in this sense, among them correspondence-based frameworks such as The Parallel Architecture (Jackendoff 1997, 2002) and Autolexical Syntax (Sadock 1991), unification-based frameworks such as Head-Driven Phrase Structure Grammar (Pollard and Sag 1994) and Lexical-Functional Grammar (Bresnan et al. 2016), Lexical Morphology and Phonology (Kiparsky 1982) and its successor Stratal Optimality Theory (Kiparsky 2015), Paradigm Function Morphology (Stump 2001, Bonami and

Stump 2016) and Network Morphology (Brown and Hippisley 2012), and Word and Paradigm Morphology (Blevins 2016).[1]

Among linguists working in the syntactocentric framework that goes back to Chomsky 1955, there is a robust tradition of treating at least part of morphology as the phonological realization of syntactic elements (see e.g. Baker 1988, 1996), and at least since the introduction into syntax of the operation Agree (Chomsky 2000), this treatment has been an integral part of the Minimalist Program (Chomsky 1995). Self-identified schools of morphology that take this stance, however, have been fewer in number. The most prominent of these is DM, which, as noted above, treats all morpheme combinations as the result of syntactic computation, including the formation of inflectable stems from the combination of roots and derivational affixes. DM is also characterized by postsyntactic insertion of phonological material ("Vocabulary Items" or VIs) into syntactic terminals ("late insertion") on the basis of a Subset Principle (Halle 1997: 428) that requires the inserted VI to be specified for a (proper or improper) subset of the features of the target terminal and prioritizes candidate VIs specified for a greater number of matching features over those specified for a lesser number. Another framework that treats some morphology as syntactic is A-Morphous Morphology (Anderson 1982, 1992; below, AM), and it will be useful for us to understand the similarities and differences between DM and AM. For that purpose, I will focus on the question of what morphology is deemed syntactic in the two frameworks and the question of what morphological units are taken to have listed representations.

One major difference between DM and AM is that while the former, as we have seen, takes all morphology to be syntactic, the latter accords that treatment only to that morphology realizing properties that participate in what appear to be unambiguously syntactic processes, where the latter are characterized (Anderson 1992: 83) as processes that operate over phrasal domains. Anderson (1992: 82–83) divides such properties into those, typified by structural case, that are assigned on the basis of an element's structural position ("configurational properties"), those participating either as triggers ("inherent properties") or as targets ("agreement properties") in processes of agreement, and those that characterize a full phrase but are realized on individual words of that phrase ("phrasal properties"). This characterization of what is syntactically relevant quite clearly excludes the traditional domain of derivational morphology, and Anderson, correspondingly, takes derivational relationships to be a matter of the lexicon. Regarding the formal

---

1. The framework of Chomsky 1995, in which inflected forms are freely generated presyntactically but subject to feature checking in the syntax, is not asyntactic in the same sense as the frameworks just reviewed because inflected forms are in the end chosen as the result of syntactic operations.

device by means of which such relationships are captured, both the possibility of unidirectional generative rules and the possibility of redundancy rules of the type introduced in Jackendoff 1975 are entertained (see Anderson 1992: 185–186); for concreteness, I will identify the AM treatment of derivational morphology with that of Jackendoff 1975.

A second major difference between DM and AM is that while DM treats individual affixes as realizing individual syntactic terminals, AM treats affixes as the result of rewrite rules that may also perform operations like deletion and feature change, and for which the addition of affixal material is thus only one possibility among several. The DM treatment of inflection, in other words, is piece-based, while that of AM is process-based; the former assumes that affixes have listed representations, while the latter assumes that they do not. This difference between DM and AM is crucially tied to a difference in the two theories' conception of syntactic terminals: DM assumes a syntax in which many inflectional features constitute syntactic terminals of their own (Halle and Marantz 1993: 112), while AM assumes rather that inflectional features are collected on the corresponding lexical category terminal, making those terminals parallel to the "complex symbols" of Chomsky 1965 (see Anderson 1992: 92, 101).

It is now possible to specify concisely the position on the relation of morphology and syntax that will be argued for in the present book. Assuming with DM and AM that inflection (at least) is the postsyntactic phonological realization of representations developed by the syntax, I will claim concerning the two points of contrast I have identified between those two theories that DM is correct in granting listed representations to inflectional affixes and that AM is correct in denying them to derivational affixes. The resulting theory is much like DM with respect to inflection, but rejects DM's syntactic derivation of stems from roots plus derivational affixes in favor of a lexicon of stems whose internal structure is captured by Jackendovian redundancy rules. Adapting DM's slogan "Syntactic Hierarchical Structure All the Way Down" (Halle and Marantz 1994: 276), that framework might be characterized as involving "Syntax down to the Stem" (below, "SdS"). In Table 1, the three frameworks DM, SdS, and AM are first identified by the property that sets them apart from all asyntactic theories of morphology, namely that they treat inflection as syntactic. They are then differentiated by whether they grant listed representations to inflectional and to derivational affixes.

The second column of the table records the fact that, with respect to inflection, SdS, like DM and as opposed to AM, is a piece-based theory. Given the principle, associated with DM, that grammar contains only a "single generative engine" (Marantz 2005: 429; see also 443–444), the content of the third column, which records whether each theory is piece-based with respect to derivation, is also a proxy for whether derivation is syntactic or not: if (roots and) derivational

Table 1. The treatment of inflection and derivation in three frameworks

	Inflection syntactic	Inflectional affixes listed	Derivational affixes listed
DM	+	+	+
SdS	+	+	−
AM	+	−	−

affixes have listed representations, those representations will have to be combined by the grammar, and syntax is the only mechanism available for doing so. If, on the other hand, roots and derivational affixes do not have listed representations, the results of combining them (i.e. stems) will have to be listed rather than generated. We will see below that both evidence involving the distributional and interpretive properties of Japanese verbal suffixes and evidence involving morphophonological reanalysis and regularization lead to the conclusion that, as shown in the SdS row of Table 1, stems and inflectional affixes have listed representations, but roots and derivational affixes do not.

On the above account, SdS, like AM, is a weak lexicalist theory, one on which derivational formations are unanalyzable, atomic units from the point of view of the syntax, but inflectional formations are not. Equivalently, those frameworks exemplify the "split morphology" hypothesis (Perlmutter 1988), on which morphology divides into presyntactic and (post)syntactic subparts. The weak lexicalist position, while perhaps intuitively natural in view of the well-known differences in regularity between inflection and derivation, is underrepresented in current thinking about morphology: Part IV of Hippisley and Stump 2016, for instance, introduces six contemporary morphological frameworks, but none of them is weak lexicalist. The same is true for the even greater number of frameworks covered in Audring and Masini 2019 (Part II). It is also the case that weak lexicalism, typically under the label "split morphology", has been subject in the morphological literature to certain criticisms, and before proceeding, it will be useful to examine some of those criticisms and to show that, when the idea of split morphology is properly understood, they are not well-founded.

1.3   Objections to split morphology

Perhaps the most basic possible objection to splitting morphology into the lexical and the syntactic, attributed by Lieber (1980:11) to an unpublished manuscript by Steven Lapointe, is that "a theory of grammar in which all morphology is confined within a single component, namely the lexicon, is more constrained, and therefore more desirable than a theory in which derivational morphology is lex-ical and inflectional morphology syntactic". Against that argument, I suggest that its presupposition that "morphology", taken as the union of derivation and inflec-tion, constitutes a natural class of phenomena may not in fact be well-founded. If it is not, there is no reason to expect derivation and inflection to be treated in a single grammatical component.

To appreciate this suggestion, it is useful to ask what the correlates of deriva-tion and inflection are in languages that have neither of them — in languages, that is, that lack affixation or have only a very limited amount of it. A well-known example of such a language is Vietnamese (Nguyễn 1987), which lacks inflection and has derivation only to the extent that certain recurrent compound members approach the status of derivational affixes. What takes the place of derivation in such a language, it seems clear, is compounding; what takes the place of inflec-tion is function words or grammatical "particles". Compounding and grammati-cal particles, however, have little or nothing to do with each other: compounding is a lexeme-creation mechanism, and grammatical particles are realizations of syntactic terminals. If derivation is lexeme-creation and inflection is the realiza-tion of syntactic terminals, then, they may have as little intrinsic connection as do compounding and particles. The fact that they both involve affixation may be a relatively superficial similarity, and the reason, apart from that commonality, that they might appear to constitute a unified system may be that they interact with each other in more obvious ways than compounding and grammatical par-ticles do.

Other objections that have been raised in the literature against the split mor-phology hypothesis are based on an artificially strict interpretation of that hypoth-esis and can be shown to be ill-founded when a more realistic version of it is adopted. In particular, Anderson's (1982: 587) formulation "Inflectional morphol-ogy is what is relevant to the syntax" has suggested to some observers that the hypothesis should be evaluated by first determining on independent grounds which morphology is inflectional and which is derivational and then verifying whether or not all and only the inflectional morphology as so identified is syn-tactically relevant. Thus Siddiqi (2014: 351) writes, "In the end, there is no satis-factory definitional distinction between derivation and inflection, which seems to doom the Split Morphology Hypothesis." This is a non sequitur, however; the split morphology hypothesis does not require that inflection and derivation be given watertight definitions in advance. On a maximally general interpretation, in fact, it requires only that both syntactic and nonsyntactic morphology exist. Ander-son's formulation goes beyond that minimal claim to the proposal that the crite-rion of syntactic relevance, suitably characterized, provides a well-defined basis for reconstructing the traditional distinction between inflection and derivation. This does not mean, however, that that criterion will necessarily mirror the traditional distinction in every case. In the end, the syntactic relevance criterion implies, it is syntactic theory that must draw the crucial distinction: the morphology that a properly constrained syntactic theory will account for is "inflectional", and the morphology that it will not account for is "derivational" or "lexical".

Siddiqi (2014:352), continuing, claims that not only is the split morphology hypothesis "theoretically untenable", but that it is "empirically incorrect" as well. His reference here is to work by Booij (1993, 1996) arguing that the attested occurrence of inflected forms in the nonhead position of compound and derived stems, contrary to the apparent prediction of the split morphology hypothesis that inflection should always appear outside such stems, falsifies that hypothesis and requires all morphology to be produced lexically. The impossibility of arguing from the occurrence of [A B]$_B$ to the lexical status of A, however, is shown by the grammaticality in English and related languages of compounds of the form [XP N]$_N$ ("phrasal compounds").[2] These are illustrated, in some cases following Lieber (1992:11), in (2).[3]

(2) a.   a [what-can-you-do]$_{CP}$ expression
     b.   a [don't-order-me-around]$_{TP}$ look
     c.   a [stay-at-home]$_{VP}$ mom
     d.   a [hard-to-read]$_{AP}$ book
     e.   an [off-the-rack]$_{PP}$ dress
     f.   a [floor of the birdcage]$_{NP}$ taste

Just as the split morphology hypothesis does not require a prior definition of inflection and derivation, then, neither does it entail that inflected forms can never occur internal to derived or compound stems. Rather, we may conclude, the question of what feeding relationships obtain among syntax and the various subtypes of morphology should be separated from the split morphology hypothesis, where the latter is understood first as the claim that both syntactic and nonsyntactic morphology exist and second as the additional claim that that division correlates well with the traditional distinction between inflection and derivation.

---

2. Booij is in fact fully aware of this implication of the existence of phrasal compounds; as he writes in a closely contemporaneous article (1992:57), "Once we have to allow for a loop from the syntactic component back to the morphological component in order to account for phrasal nonheads of compounds, inflection could also be located in the syntactic component, and yet feed the morphological component."

3. The phenomenon of phrasal nonheads in derived stems, as in *stick-to-it-iveness* and *one-up-manship* (Bauer 1983:164), is far more marginal.

In the present section, I have argued that there are no principled objections to the split morphology hypothesis as so understood. In the next, I proceed to arguments that, corresponding to positive specifications in Table 1 for that table's first two parameters, inflection must indeed be (a) syntactic and (b) piece-based.

1.4   The syntax/inflection duplication problem

Haspelmath (2011: 32) notes that linguists often assume, with Dixon and Aikhenvald (2002: 6), that "Morphology deals with the composition of words while syntax deals with the combination of words" and that "[t]he (grammatical) word forms the interface between" the two subfields. Haspelmath calls this stance into question, however, on the grounds that linguists have never identified a cross-linguistically reliable concept of grammatical word, and that in the absence of such a concept there is no defensible distinction between morphology and syntax.

A similar argument leading to the conclusion that, cross-linguistically, (inflectional) morphology cannot cogently be differentiated from syntax is suggested by the fact that the word, the presumptive domain of morphology, varies from roughly morpheme-sized in isolating languages to roughly sentence-sized in poly-synthetic languages. If syntax and (inflectional) morphology are distinct fields, then, it appears that there will be a great deal of overlap between their respective contents. More concretely, uncontroversially syntactic elements in one language sometimes not only correspond one-to-one with inflectional elements in another, but display identical hierarchical relations in the two languages. This phenomenon can be illustrated by comparison of Japanese with English. Consider first the English example (3).

(3)   She will not be made to sing.

Setting aside the subject DP and "infinitival" *to*, and treating *make* as the realization of a functional head Causative, a plausible structure for (3) is that given in (4).

(4)

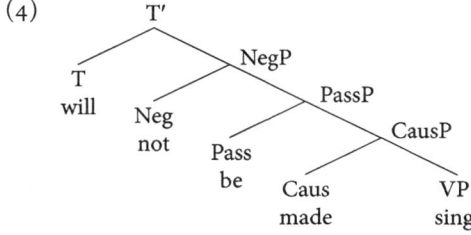

It seems clear that (3) is built in the syntax from the five heads T(ense), Neg(ative), Pass(ive), Caus(ative), and V(erb), plausibly by means of an operation Merge (Chomsky 1994) that, roughly, combines two elements and projects one of them. Further, the hierarchical order of the five heads is for the most part the result of general principles: the argument-structure-affecting heads Pass and Caus are predictably closer to the verb stem than Neg and T, whose scope includes the full argument structure, and the relation Pass > Caus as well reflects semantic and syntactic scope. The relation T > Neg, finally, probably represents the unmarked option cross-linguistically, although there are languages that display the reverse hierarchical order (see Cinque 1999: 137).

The Tokyo Japanese equivalent of (3) is (5), a plausible structure for which is given in (6).

(5)   *utaw-ase-rare-na-i* (~ *utaw-as-are-na-i*)

(6)

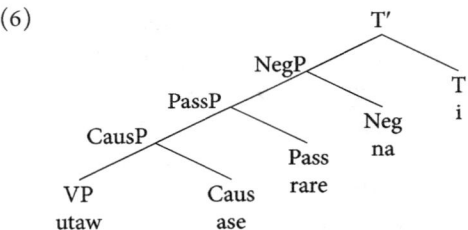

(5) is by all indications a single word: it is not interruptible; it constitutes a single accentual domain; and, as we will see in Chapter 5, its three verbal suffixes (Caus, Pass, and Neg) are all in principle subject to a morphophonological rule that applies only at verb stem boundary (its tense suffix -*i*, on the other hand, is adjectival). If syntactic and morphological computation are separate, then, (5) will be formed presyntactically in the morphology. The hierarchical relationships in (6) are identical to those of (4), however, and there is no reason to believe that the principles that determine those relationships are any different in the two cases.[4] Insisting that (5) be derived presyntactically, then, will require that presyntactic computation duplicate syntactic computation over a wide range of selectional and scopal relationships.

We have seen that cross-linguistic considerations strongly suggest that syntax and inflectional morphology cannot be two independent grammatical modules,

---

4. The hierarchical relationship of Caus and Pass is essentially fixed in Japanese, in accordance with the cross-linguistic tendency to prohibit passive morphology under causativization (see Hyman 2003: 278 (note 26), where the observation is attributed to Judith Aissen). Some speakers, however, accept a combination like *nagur-are-sase-* (punch-Pass-Caus) with the "noninterventive" interpretation 'allow (him) to be punched'.

with inflection being treated as presyntactic. The Japanese data of (5)–(6) also provide an argument that inflectional affixation, in addition to being syntactic, must be piece-based rather than process-based. The reason is that, for interpretive purposes, the scopal relations embodied in the hierarchical structure of (6) must be established in narrow syntax, the computation to LF. If so, treating the affixes of (5)–(6) as the output of phonological rewrite rules rather than as morpheme-sized "pieces" would mean that the order of those rewrite rules would have to recapitulate precisely a set of hierarchical relations that are also represented syntactically (for this argument against AM, see Halle and Marantz 1993: 112–113). If the data of this section are representative, then, it would appear that arguments based on the need to avoid duplication between syntax and inflectional morphology are sufficient to establish positive specifications for both of the first two parameters of Table 1. Unless we are willing to countenance theories of syntax and inflection that substantially duplicate each other's content, that is, we are forced to conclude that both result from a single structure-building component, and that the question of how much of the material that component generates is incorporated into the word is a language-specific and relatively superficial parameter.

1.5   The subtypes of inflection

Within the set of morphosyntactic features that appear to be relevant to syntax, it is possible to distinguish between those that are fully determined by syntactic context, such as structural case and features assigned by processes of agreement, and those that are free from such determination, such as number in nouns and tense in verbs. As observed by Booij (1993: 30), who calls the former "contextual" and (following Anderson) the latter "inherent" inflection, this distinction has been recognized by many scholars; in the framework of Chomsky 1995, for example, it appears as the distinction between formal features that, semantically, are [−Interpretable] and those that affect meaning and are thus [+Interpretable].

It seems fair to say that the syntactic status of the features of contextual inflection is uncontroversial, at least in general terms; as just observed, such features are in fact purely syntactic in the sense that they have no semantic interpretation (although they are of course interpreted phonologically). The features of inherent inflection, however, have been to some extent controversial in this regard, with some scholars taking their semantic interpretability as a reason to assign inherent inflection a status intermediate between derivation and contextual inflection and to conclude, accordingly, that the derivation/inflection distinction is in fact a continuum (see Booij 1993: 30–31 and references cited there). In this context, it is important to point out that in English, at least, verbal tense and nominal number, two of the most widely cited examples of inherent inflection, can both be shown to be unequivocally syntactic, in the sense of constituting the phonological realization of syntactic elements that are independent of the corresponding stems. For instance, it is well-known that tense in English is realized at some distance from the verb with which it is interpreted in negatives (*Jim didn't sing*), questions (*Did Jim sing?*), and a number of other constructions. Similarly, in a sentence like (7), where interpretively there are two instances of *sing*, the position hosting the one phonological occurrence of that verb stem is in an anaphoric relationship with the position occupied by *do*, and that relationship excludes the inflectional material that is associated with the two stems.

(7)   Jim sings even better than his father did.

Regardless of precisely what derivation is envisioned for (7), as long as we assume that there is an identity condition on establishment of the anaphoric relationship in question and that that identity condition must be satisfied in the syntax, it will follow that tense is represented separately from the verb stem on which it is ultimately realized. For instance, if a PF-deletion analysis of (7) is adopted, the terminal elements of that sentence's syntactic representation will be roughly as in (8).

(8)   Jim sing [−Past] even better than his father sing [+Past]

After spellout, the point in a derivation at which the phonologically relevant elements of the derived structure are transferred to the phonological component (Chomsky 1995: 229), the phonological matrix of the second occurrence of *sing* will be deleted under identity of the two terminals, and the phonological matrix of *do* will be inserted in its place. Specifications of tense and agreement will then either be realized as affixal material, trigger phonological adjustments to the stem, or both, as in the case of [do [+Past]], which is realized as /di-d/.

   We may note in this connection that while it is common to question the proposition that a past tense form like *sang* involves a phonologically null past tense suffix (Anderson 1992: 62–63, Stump 2001: 10, Blevins 2016: 43), the above considerations make it clear in what sense that proposition is true. In the syntax, *sang* is [sing [+Past]]. Further, it is uncontroversial that the [+Past] of that representation has no realization as an overt affix. In the phonology, on the other hand, the [+Past] of [sing [+Past]] is reflected by the operation of a rule that changes the [ɪ] of the base form *sing* to [æ]. What is an "item" or discrete element in the syntax, then, corresponds in the phonology to a process. On this view, there is no incompatibility between the "item" and "process" accounts of the past tense of *sing*; each of the two interpretations is applicable in its own domain, and the two are thus complementary rather than conflicting.

What a sentence like (7) shows for tense, examples like those of (9) show for the inherent nominal category of number.

(9)   a.   Jim has a black cat, and Sue has two white ones.
      b.   My brother is stronger than all of yours put together.

In (9a), *cat* and *one* are in an anaphoric relationship to the exclusion of the plural suffix *-s*. A parallel analysis can be offered for (9b) if *yours* (with zero plural suffix) in such cases is a portmanteau of *your* and *one*, as suggested by the equivalence of *yours* (singular possessum) and the *one belonging to you/the one you have*. In any case, the anaphoric relationship in which *brother* is the antecedent clearly excludes the representation [+Plural] that must be present for interpretive purposes in *yours*.[5] The representation of number in (9), like the representation of tense in (7), must thus constitute an independent syntactic terminal. If the data of (7) and (9) is representative, then, inherent inflection would appear to be just as syntactic as contextual inflection, in the sense of constituting the phonological realization of syntactic terminal elements.

The domain of inflection is typically taken to be exhausted by the contextual and inherent types just discussed. But a glance at the Japanese example (5)–(6) reveals three suffixes, those of the Causative, the Passive, and the Negative, which will be seen below to group with inflection on all relevant criteria, but which, rather than realizing either contextual or inherent morphosyntactic feature specifications, represent operators (functions) of various types. The Causative suffix, for example, is (in the terms of Chomsky 1995 and subsequent work) a type of "little v" that contributes a causative meaning, introduces an external argument with the semantic role "Cause" (typically an agent), and assigns accusative case. It seems unquestionable that operators of this sort are syntactic objects, and thus that they conform to the generalization that inflectional affixes represent the phonological realization of syntactic terminals.

In this section, we have seen that inflectional affixes can be divided into those that realize contextually determined features like those of structural case and agreement, those that realize inherent features like tense and nominal number, and those that realize operators like those of the Causative and Negative. Only with respect to the affixes of inherent inflection has any doubt arisen about the syntactic status of those elements, and I have argued that if English data are representative, inherent inflection is in fact no less syntactic than that of the other two categories. Below, then, I will assume that these three types of affix represent

---

5. (9b) is based on Spanish data from Ojeda 1982 reported by Sadock (1995: 334). While expression of the plurality of a possessum is suppressed in English genitives (*all of yours/*yours's, all of mine/*mines*), this is not the case in Spanish (*todo-s lo-s tuyo-s* 'all those (m.) of you (sg.)').

the phonological realization of syntactic terminal elements, a process that I will take to be governed by Halle's Subset Principle, noted above in Section 1.2. While I thus adopt DM's principle of late insertion as regards inflectional material, nothing below depends on whether or not that principle applies as well to inflectable stems (see Halle and Marantz 1993: 172 (note 10)). In the following section, I outline the plan of the remainder of the book.

1.6   Preview of Chapters 2 through 9

Deviations from one-to-one correspondence between morphosyntactic features and segmentable morphs are often cited as problems for a morpheme-based account of inflection (see e.g. Anderson 1992: 51ff.). Consistent with sentence (5) above, deviations of this sort are relatively rare in Japanese, and this tendency extends for the most part to the related Ryukyuan languages as well. In the case of Dunan, spoken on Yonaguni Island at the western end of the Ryukyus, however, it has been claimed that the language's verbal morphology is not naturally amenable to a morpheme-based treatment and is probably best analyzed by assuming a lexicon of fully inflected forms (Yamada et al. 2015, Pellard and Yamada 2017). After an introductory discussion of the phenomenon of cumulative exponence and the processes of morphological and phonological fusion, Chapter 2 takes up the case of Dunan, providing both a fully articulated analysis of the Dunan verb based on segmentation into morphemes and the application of phonological rules and a set of principles on the basis of which the crucial points of that analysis could be acquired by learners. In the end, then, Dunan does not provide a counterexample to the syntactic and piece-based account of inflection proposed in the present chapter.

Chapters 1 and 2 deal only with inflection, a domain regarding which, as shown in Table 1, the basic claims of SdS do not differ from those of DM. Chapters 3 and 4 take up derivation, with respect to which the claims of those two frameworks diverge sharply. The starting point of Chapter 3 is the claim (Harley 2008: 39, Marantz 2013: 106) that Japanese suffixes that create transitive and intransitive verb stems are instances of little v, causative and inchoative, that attach to roots and that the verb stems themselves are thus syntactic constructions. That chapter argues that the formation of Japanese transitive and intransitive verb stems cannot in fact be analyzed as syntactic, beginning with the observation that when two derivational stem-forming suffixes occur in sequence, a phenomenon not previously discussed, the outer suffix cancels or overrides the properties of the inner one rather than composing with it semantically.

Chapter 4 considers a challenge to the thesis of Chapter 3 in the form of claims (Miyagawa 1984, 1989, 1998) that the Japanese syntactic Causative suffix *-(s)ase-* may form "lexical" causative stems (i.e. ordinary transitives) when no other suffix is available to do so. If this were the case, it would imply that both types of causative must be treated in the same grammatical component and suggest that, by extension, the same is true of inflectional and derivational morphology in general. Chapter 4 shows that the causative formative *-ase-* that appears to have both syntactic and lexical uses in fact represents two suffixes, syntactic *-(s)ase-* and lexical *-(a)se-*, that are distinct in both their morphophonological behavior and their phonological form. It then considers a wide range of examples that have been identified in the literature as "lexical *-(s)ase-*", arguing that these are in fact either lexical *-(a)se-* or syntactic *-(s)ase-*. Chapter 4 concludes with a summary of results to that point.

In Chapter 5, the focus shifts to the phenomenon of morphophonological reanalysis and to the book's main example of that phenomenon, the reanalysis of the set of Japanese verbal inflectional suffixes that alternate depending on the consonant/vowel polarity of the stem-final segment. The chapter begins by noting that while at least four observationally adequate analyses of these alternations have been proposed in the literature, each of those analyses makes different claims about which forms are regular and which are irregular and thus generates distinct predictions about what changes should be observed if irregular forms are eliminated in favor of regularized substitutes. It then argues that ongoing change in Japanese dialects shows that speakers have adopted an analysis of the suffixes according to which (a) their underlying representations coincide with consonant-stem suffix alternants and (b) regular vowel-stem alternants are produced by a rule inserting *r* intervocalically at verb stem boundary ("Analysis A"). The chapter closes by considering alternative interpretations of the ongoing changes adduced as evidence for Analysis A and arguing that they fundamentally misconstrue the nature of those changes.

The process of regularization under Analysis A remains incomplete in almost all Japanese dialects. The closely related Ryukyuan languages, however, include a number of dialects in which regularization has gone to completion, with virtually all exceptions to Analysis A eliminated. This is true in particular for the Shuri dialect of Okinawan, the best documented of all Ryukyuan varieties. Chapter 6 considers the evidence for the adoption of Analysis A in Ryukyuan languages. Concentrating to begin with on Shuri, it first shows that comparative, internal, and philological evidence converge in showing that that dialect descends from an ancestor with the same contrast between vowel-stem and consonant-stem inflection that characterizes Japanese, a fact not readily apparent on inspection. It then traces the course of regularization under Analysis A through the written records of the 16th through 18th centuries, a process that eventually triggered the reanalysis of vowel-stems as *r*-stems, and argues that in large part, this history can be inferred to hold for Northern Ryukyuan (Amami and Okinawan) in general. The chapter concludes by examining the southern or Sakishima languages Miyako, Yaeyama, and Dunan (Yonaguni), showing that while Yaeyama and Dunan display unmistakable evidence for the adoption of Analysis A, such evidence is lacking in Miyako.

The ongoing and completed regularization documented in Chapters 5 and 6 appear to establish that, as claimed in Chapter 5, Analysis A is the descriptively adequate analysis of the set of alternations it covers. If so, it should be possible to show why Analysis A should have been chosen by speakers from the set of observationally adequate alternatives — that is, to approach the level of explanatory adequacy (Chomsky 1964a, 1964b) for that analysis. This task is particularly pressing because, as will be seen, the choice of Analysis A appears to defy the widespread assumption that morphophonological analyses are chosen so as to maximize phonological or morphological predictability. Chapter 7 first reviews a number of possible hypotheses about morphophonological analysis that are counterexemplified by the choice of Analysis A. It then proposes two principles of evaluation, both of which are argued to be necessary in accounting for that choice. The first of those principles appeals to the concept of type frequency and is motivated by accounts of completed or ongoing reanalyses in Portuguese and Korean; the second appeals to a principle requiring minimization of the phonological distance between the input and output of a rule and is motivated by an account of an ongoing reanalysis in Modern Greek.

A problem complementary to that of what principles dictate the choice of Analysis A from among the available alternatives is that of what factors inhibit the adoption of that analysis in situations where its preconditions would seem to be satisfied, but the regularizations it predicts are not observed. Chapter 8 starts from the observation that while the *r*-Epenthesis rule of Analysis A is naturally understood as a generalization of the *r*-zero alternation of three suffixes which have displayed it since the 10th century or before, the *r*-epenthetic suffixes of other categories do not appear until the 18th. It then shows that this time lag is illuminated by Kyushu dialects, where adoption of Analysis A is blocked by retention of the bigrade stem alternation, which in most dialects was leveled in the 17th century. It is proposed in explanation of this "bigrade blocking" effect that the order in which alternations become subject to regularization is constrained by the phonological distance between alternants, and this principle is shown to account as well for the relative chronology of leveling in two further contemporaneous Japanese cases.

Chapter 9, finally, first notes that while the distinction between inflection and derivation is often characterized as a continuum, the results of Chapters 1 through 8 reveal a clear-cut boundary between those domains that appears on both the syntactic and the phonological sides of the grammar. It then raises the question of whether the book's conclusions, based for the most part on Japanese data, can be expected to apply cross-linguistically. Citing the case of a Modern Greek suffix sequence with characteristics parallel to the Japanese suffix sequences treated in Chapter 3, it suggests that there is reason for optimism on that point.

CHAPTER 2

An apparent challenge: Morphosyntactic and phonological fusion

2.1 Introduction

The morpheme-based account of inflection argued for in Chapter 1 has sometimes been seen as disconfirmed or called into question by deviations from the ideal of one-to-one correspondence between elements of form and elements of meaning in inflected words. Such deviations, that is, have been taken to suggest that the morph is not a "minimal sign" (Anderson 1992: 54, Blevins 2016), that morphology is not a matter of morphemes (Anderson 1992: Chapter 3), and, along with other considerations, that the theory of inflection must be inferential (process-based) rather than lexical (morpheme-based) (Anderson 1992: 71, Stump 2001: 9–12). This line of argument, however, is vulnerable to the potential existence of deviations from a one-to-one relationship between morphs and meanings above the level of the word: because of the implausibility of process-based accounts of syntactic combinations, the occurrence of such deviations across word boundaries would show that they do not entail a process-based account of inflection either. Haspelmath (2011: §3.10) argues that a number of representative deviations from a one-to-one relationship between morphs and meanings do in fact occur in syntactic combinations; for example, he notes that the English definite article has a zero exponent in possessive phrases (*the/Ø Jim's book), and that compound tenses like the English perfect (have + past participle) involve a many-to-one correspondence between morphs and meanings.

Cumulative exponence (Matthews 1972: 65ff.), the expression by a single segmentable morph of multiple units of meaning, is perhaps the most widely discussed of the deviations from one-to-one morph-to-meaning correspondence, and is typically taken as the defining property of the "fusional" morphological type. In this chapter, I first show that cumulative exponence is observed across word boundaries and, insofar as it cannot be accounted for phonologically, demonstrates the existence of morphosyntactic fusion, the postsyntactic fusion of distinct syntactic terminals (Halle and Marantz 1993: 116). It follows that, when multiple syntactic terminals are involved, cumulative exponence within the word may also be attributed to morphosyntactic fusion and thus does not threaten a morpheme-based account of inflection. I then turn to the Ryukyuan language

Dunan, where apparent indeterminacy of segmentation has led to the claim that a morpheme-based analysis of verbal morphology is inappropriate, and argue that that claim is not well-founded.

2.2   Morphosyntactic and phonological fusion

Sound change, capable of turning Proto-Romance *agosto* 'August' to French *août* [u] in roughly a millennium, can be disruptive of morphological analysis when it applies at morpheme boundaries, as we will see below. For instance, if sound change applies to a sequence of affixes X+Y, where X realizes morphosyntactic property A and Y realizes morphosyntactic property B, the result may be an element Z that realizes both A and B. In such a case, if phonetic Z is plausibly analyzed as phonological X+Y synchronically, the "fusion" of X and Y may be seen as a purely phonological phenomenon. If the segmentation X+Y is unrecoverable through phonological analysis, however, the fusion of X and Y must be seen as morphosyntactic — that is, as the post-spellout fusion of the corresponding syntactic terminal elements. Hagège (1990) and Igartua (2015: §3) provide a number of examples that suggest morphosyntactic fusion within the inflected word, cases of inflectional paradigms in which properties A and B are ordinarily expressed by separate suffixes but where, for particular values of A and B, what appears instead is a fused or "portmanteau" suffix. Crucially, the phenomenon of morphosyntactic fusion is not limited to word-internal domains, as shown by the well-known French data in Table 1, where fused combinations of preposition plus definite article are underlined.

Table 1. Preposition plus definite article combinations in French

	the street	the park	the streets
by (way of)	par la rue	par le parc	par les rues
in	dans la rue	dans le parc	dans les rues
of/from	de la rue	du (*de le) parc	des (*de les) rues
at/to	à la rue	au (*à le) parc	aux (*à les) rues

As the first two lines of the table show, prepositions and definite articles (f.sg. *la*, m.sg. *le*, pl. *les*) are normally distinct syntactic elements in French. The prepositions *de* 'of/from' and *à* 'at/to', however, fuse with *le* to produce *du* [dy] and *au* [o] respectively, and with *les* to produce *des* [de] and *aux* [o]. A phonological derivation of *au* from *à le* /alə/ via final schwa deletion, *l*-vocalization, and monophthongization might be contemplated, but such an account seems clearly out of reach for the other three cases. As is generally acknowledged, then, the fusions in question are to be understood as morphosyntactic.

A parallel case, cited by Haspelmath (2011: 57) along with the French one, involves sequences of personal pronouns in Tagalog. In Tagalog, as in other "Philippine-type" Western Austronesian languages, every clause contains one and only one "pivot" phrase with the following characteristics (Chen and McDonnell 2019: 176): (a) it is uniquely subject to relativization; (b) it is accompanied by a pivot marker; (c) it triggers affixally marked "voice" agreement on the verb. In Tagalog, the possible pivot phrases and corresponding verbal voices include those defined by the semantic roles (or macroroles) actor (agent or experiencer), patient, direction (goal or source), beneficiary, and instrument (Schachter 1987: 939–940); the main pivot markers are preposed *ang* (for common nouns) and *si* (for personal names). Personal and demonstrative pronouns do not take pivot markers but are divided into pivot and nonpivot series. Sequences of pivot and nonpivot pronouns undergo no phonological fusion, but the expected combination of 2sg. pivot *ka* and 1sg. nonpivot *ko* is replaced by the unsegmentable portmanteau form *kita*; both *ka ko and *ko ka are ungrammatical (Schachter and Otanes 1972: 81, 89).

Tagalog personal pronouns are typically second-position clitics (Schachter and Otanes 1972: 183ff.), and on the view that "clitics are not syntactic objects at all, but ... overt morphological markers of the morphosyntactic properties of phrases" (Anderson 2005: 83), it might appear that they could be treated as "phrasal affixes" and assimilated to a process-based account of inflection (see Anderson 2005: 165–176). But the pivot series pronouns are not clitics in all their uses; in particular, like other nominal phrases, they may be predicative. This is illustrated in (1), where *ikaw* is the suppletive predicative form of the 2sg. pivot series pronoun (Schachter and Otanes 1972: 79) and the pivot marker *ang* takes a clausal complement (Schachter and Otanes 1972: 62) (in the gloss, PV abbreviates "pivot", and NPV "nonpivot").

(1) Ikaw   ang mahal ko.   [movie title, 1996]
     2SG.PV PV love   1SG.NPV
     'You're the one I love.' / 'It's you I love.'

It thus seems clear that, in the general case, Tagalog personal pronouns are phrasal constituents, presumably DPs. If so, they will be treated like other DPs in the syntax, although subject to reordering after spellout. If this line of analysis is sustainable, the portmanteau form *kita*, like the contracted forms of Table 1, represents morphosyntactic fusion above the level of the word. And if morphosyntactic fusion exists above the word, there would seem to be no barrier to appealing to it word-internally as well, in particular as an account of cumulative exponence in inflection.

2.3   Fusion in Japonic: The case of Dunan

2.3.1   Background and preview

Japanese displays a handful of cases, all of them limited to verbal inflection and involving negation, in which a single morph expresses multiple meanings: Negative Adverbial *-(a)zu*, which attaches to stems, Negative Potential *-kane-*, which attaches to Adverbial forms, Negative Inferential *-mai*, which attaches to Adverbial forms (equivalently, stems) for vowel-stems and to Conclusive forms for consonant-stems, and Negative Imperative *na*, which attaches (or cliticizes) to Conclusive forms (apart from the last, all of these portmanteau morphs are to one or another degree literary). Both in terms of morph-meaning ratio and in terms of segmentability, however, the language hews for the most part quite closely to the agglutinative ideal. As a result, neither morphosyntactic nor phonological fusion is typically an issue in analyzing Japanese inflectional morphology.

The genetic affiliations of Japanese are notoriously controversial; the case for even the most likely connection, between Japanese and Korean, has recently been called into question (Vovin 2010). But Japanese proper and the Ryukyuan languages constitute together a manifest genetic unity, with the two having separated on the order of only about 1500 years ago (for discussion, see Pellard 2016). Below, I employ the term "Japonic" (attributed to Leon Serafim (Shimabukuro 2007:1)) to refer to the family consisting of Japanese and the Ryukyuan languages; an alternative usage (Frellesvig and Whitman 2008:1) takes "Japanese" to include the entire family. A simplified family tree of Japonic, where Northern Ryukyuan divides further into (at least) Amami and Okinawan, and Yaeyama divides into Yaeyama proper and Dunan or Yonaguni, is as in (2) (compare Pellard 2016:100).

(2)

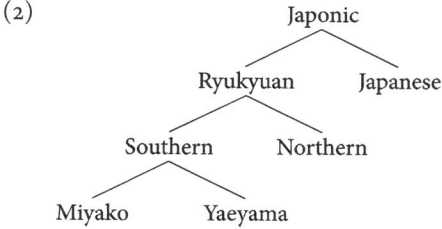

Ryukyuan may thus be considered to consist of the five languages Amami, Okinawan, Miyako, Yaeyama, and Dunan; that order corresponds to the languages' geographical distribution, proceeding from northeast to southwest.

Within Ryukyuan, there is one language whose verbal morphology, unlike that of Japanese, displays considerable phonological fusion at stem boundary. This is Dunan, the language of Yonaguni Island. As a result of this fusion, it has been claimed (Pellard and Yamada 2017: 33) that "Morpheme-based approaches are not well-suited for the analysis of Dunan's verb morphology, which rather calls for an abstractive *Word and Paradigm* approach." In the remainder of Section 2.3, I argue against that claim by providing both an analysis of the Dunan verb based on segmentation into morphemes and the application of phonological rules and a set of principles on the basis of which the crucial points of that analysis could be acquired by learners. Section 2.3.2, a prerequisite for what follows, is a discussion of the role of phonological rules and "morphomes" (Aronoff 1994) in accounting for alternations conditioned by complex morphological environments. Section 2.3.3 presents the fundamentals of the inflectional morphology of the Dunan verb, Section 2.3.4 introduces a relatively low-level set of rules that govern the resolution of hiatus at verb stem boundary, and Section 2.3.5 surveys the small number of cases in which suffixes display listed allomorphy. Section 2.3.6 then discusses the allomorphy of stems, most of which is argued to be rule-governed rather than listed. Section 2.3.7 summarizes the proposed analysis of Dunan and provides derivations for representative forms, and Section 2.3.8 explores the question of how that analysis could be attained by speakers. Section 2.3.9, in concluding, revisits the challenge that Dunan verbal morphology might appear to pose to Chapter 1's claim that inflection is postsyntactic and morpheme-based and the reasons that challenge is not in the end successful.

2.3.2   Prolegomenon: Rules and morphomes

There are multiple schools of thought concerning the conditioning of phonological form by complex morphosyntactic environments and the degree to which that phenomenon constitutes a reflection of phonological rules. With regard to Dunan, the position of Pellard and Yamada (2017: 45) on this question is clear: "a morpheme-based morphophonological approach ... would only lead to posit[ing] rules or constraints that are unnatural and lack any generality because of their lexically or morphologically restricted character." Similarly, Yamada et al. (2015: 459) assert that "Trying to account for Dunan's stem alternations with derivational rules would be rather pointless, since rules would not be generalizable but would turn out to be specific to some verb classes and suffixes, and they would thus hold no explanatory power." Yamada et al. (2015: 458–459) claim further that Dunan "stems and suffixes are arbitrarily co-indexed", that it is necessary to "[posit] a complex system with several dozens of inflectional verb classes and eight stems", that "[s]tem-shape alternation patterns are lexeme-based and follow no general (morpho)phonological rule", and that "[t]here is ... no single form or stem that

can serve as a principal part or reference form and predict a verb's paradigm".[1]
In addition to showing that Dunan verbal morphophonology yields naturally to
morpheme-based analysis, therefore, it will be an important aim below to determine how much irregularity the system actually displays, in the form of listed allomorphy (suppletion) and lexical conditioning of alternations. Among our findings
will be that none of the four claims just enumerated is accurate.

An apparent alternative to a phonological account of alternations that are
conditioned by complex morphosyntactic environments is a treatment of such
alternations as "morphomic" (Aronoff 1994). Pellard and Yamada (2017) label
many features of Dunan verbal (morpho)phonology morphomic — in particular,
stems (i.e. stem alternants, p.38), stem alternations, suffix allomorphy, and
metatony (pp.33, 46) — although they do not spell out what concrete consequences morphomic status has for the analysis of the alternations involved, apart
from the claim that those alternations are not rule-governed and thus require
extensive lexical listing of alternants (see Pellard and Yamada 2017: 45, Yamada
et al. 2015: 458). In this section, I outline the view of rules and morphemes that
I will assume in the remainder of the chapter. I begin with the issue of when a
(nonautomatic) phonological alternation is rule-governed, which I take to be an
empirical question about the phonological generalizations that speakers make.

Automatic alternations may be assumed to be rule-governed as a matter of
course, but the question of when speakers take nonautomatic alternations to be
the result of phonological rules is a complex one. There are indications both from
phonological experimentation and from language change, however, concerning
what factors are more important and what factors are probably less so. One generalization that seems clear is that alternations in which input and output differ in
only a single feature specification are more likely to be extended — that is, taken
to be rule-governed — than alternations that involve an input-output divergence
of more than one feature. This is the result obtained by Skoruppa et al. (2011)
from an artificial language experiment, and it is consonant with the large body of
research reviewed by Moreton and Pater (2012a) as well as the literature on the
subject cited by Hayes and White (2015: 290). It is also reinforced by the fact that
documented cases in which speakers extend nonautomatic alternations tend to
involve (apart from epentheses) changes of a single feature. Two cases in which
a sound change meeting that condition has been extended in a limited morphological domain are Finnish assibilation of *t* before past tense *-i* (Kiparsky 1973

---

1. Yamada (2016: 280–283) presents a somewhat more systematic view and is in particular more
receptive to the postulation of phonological rules. A further precedent for a rule-based account
of Dunan phonology is provided by the Lexical Phonology analysis of Arimoto (2001a, 2001b,
2002a, 2002b).

[1982]: 167–171) and German umlaut in adjectival comparatives and superlatives (among other contexts), as in *arm/ärmer/ärmst* 'poor (absolutive/comparative/ superlative)', a word that originally took back-vowel suffixes that did not trigger umlaut (Ringe 2006: 284). Two cases in which the rule that undergoes extension represents inversion of a sound change, on the other hand, are Portuguese lowering of *e* and *o* under stress in verbal conjugation and Korean assibilation of *t* in nominal inflection before vowel-initial suffixes (for details and references on those two examples, see Chapter 7 below).

The role of phonetic content and phonetic naturalness in determining whether an alternation will be taken as rule-governed is much less clear, as emphasized in Moreton and Pater 2012b. Overall, Moreton and Pater (2012b: 711–712) conclude that "Inductive bias, a property of the learner's pattern-detection processes, facilitates faithful acquisition of simple patterns and rejection or innovative simplification of more complex ones, but is (relatively) insensitive to their phonetic motivation." If this is so, we should be cautious about taking complex or "unnatural" conditioning as a disqualifying condition for the postulation of a phonological rule. This conclusion matches Kiparsky's (1996: 31) claim, based on the failure of type of conditioning to correlate with other diagnostic criteria, "that the conditioning of an alternation is irrelevant to its status as morpholexical versus morphophonological, and should be eliminated from the diagnostics for this distinction."

Faced with the question of whether a nonautomatic alternation is rule-governed, then, it would seem reasonable to take excessive phonological distance between input and output, but not complex morphosyntactic conditioning, as a contraindication to the positing of a rule. Let us now turn to the question of how to characterize a morphome and the related question of what kinds of analysis count as morphomic. On this point, I submit that, in order to be a theoretically significant phenomenon, morphomicity must involve the postulation of a level of representation distinct from both morphosyntactic (MS) representation and (morpho)phonological (MP) representation and mediating between the two, with MS representations mapped to morphomic representations and those in turn mapped to MP representations. A straightforward example of this kind of morphomicity is provided by Bermúdez-Otero and Luís (2016: 317–318), following Aronoff (1994: 67–70).

Spanish noun and adjective stems appear without thematic vowels before most derivational suffixes. If this state of affairs accurately reflects the lexical representations of the stems in question, those representations will have to be annotated with diacritics specifying what thematic vowel appears in environments where one is required. Aronoff's proposal is that these diacritics take the form of arbitrary lexical class specifications, so that, for example, masculine nouns are assigned by rule to class 1 unless specified otherwise, and feminine nouns to class 2. A separate set of rules then provides that class 1 nouns are rewritten as suffixed with *o* and class 2 nouns as suffixed with *a*. Bermúdez-Otero (2013) argues that in fact, noun and adjective stems are stored in the lexicon with their theme vowels, so that the lexical class specifications proposed by Aronoff are unnecessary. What is important in the present context, however, is that, under Aronoff's proposal, those specifications constitute a distinct level of representation that is at once the range of a function whose domain is a subset of MS representations and the domain of a function whose range is a subset of MP representations. As indicated, I take the existence of such an intermediate level of representation as the defining property of a morphomic analysis, so that the term "morpheme" is properly restricted to the elements of such a level — in the case just illustrated, specifications such as "class 1" and "class 2". In this connection, it should be noted that the postulation of a morphomic level of representation has been called into question in a number of cases on the grounds that it not only complicates the grammatical architecture, but obstructs the statement of significant generalizations (Bermúdez-Otero 2013, Steriade 2016, de Chene 2022a).

There is also, however, a widespread use of "morpheme" to refer to any disjunction of morphosyntactic properties that has consistent formal consequences, regardless of whether or not a dedicated morphomic level of representation is postulated. For example, there are a number of disjunctive environments whose diachronic persistence in Romance verb paradigms has attracted a good deal of attention in recent years (see Maiden 2018 and references cited there). While those environments are widely referred to as morphemes — for example, the N-morpheme, which reflects the distinction between rhizotonic and arhizotonic forms, and the L- and U- morphemes, which reflect the distinction between forms whose endings conditioned palatalization of the stem final and forms whose endings did not — it seems clear that reference to them does not presuppose a dedicated morphomic level of representation. While it is an important observation, then, that these environments are diachronically active and thus apparently psychologically real, their existence does not have the consequences for the architecture of the grammar that the postulation of a morphomic level of representation would. Rather, such environments are arguably simply conditioning — conditioning of morphophonological rules when the alternations in question are judged to be rule-governed, and conditioning of the distribution of suppletive alternants otherwise. Below, then, in postulating complex morphosyntactic environments as conditioning for some of the rules of Dunan verbal morphophonology, I will not consider those environments or the analysis involving them to be morphomic.

2.3.3   Fundamentals of Dunan verbal inflection

In introducing Dunan verbal morphology, I begin with several remarks on transcription and phonological contrast. I will assume with Uemura (1997:331), Izuyama (2012:413), and Yamada et al. (2015) that the language lacks contrastive vowel length, while noting that this question has been to some degree controversial (Takahashi 1997b:413). In representing the contrast between glottalized and aspirated voiceless stops, I will write aspiration with a superscript *h* and use plain voiceless stop symbols for the glottalized series; in this connection, it may be noted that the distribution of aspiration is restricted both syntagmatically (it occurs only word-initially) and paradigmatically (/k^h t^h/ occur, but */p^h c^h/ do not), so that aspirated stops are clearly the marked members of the opposition. I will assume that morphological segmentation and the analysis of segmental alternations can proceed independently of an account of accentual alternations, and will leave accent unmarked; for some discussion of accentual alternations in verbal inflection, see Pellard and Yamada 2017:39–41. Dunan data will be drawn from Hirayama and Nakamoto 1964, Uchima 1980, Takahashi 1987a, Takahashi 1987b, Hirayama 1988, Takahashi 1997b, Izuyama 2012, Yamada et al. 2015, Yamada 2016, and Pellard & Yamada 2017.

Table 2 illustrates the basic paradigm of the Dunan verb with the stem *dum-* 'read' (J(apanese) *yom-*).

Table 2. Dunan inflectional suffixes

Category	Suffix	Example
Negative	-anun	dum-anun
Causative	-amir-	dum-amir-
Passive	-arir-	dum-arir-
Conclusive	-un	dum-un
Adnominal	-u	dum-u
Prohibitive	-unna	dum-unna
Conditional 1	-uba	dum-uba
Conditional 2	-ja	dum-ja
Imperative	-i	dum-i
Adverbial	-i	dum-i
Conjunctive	-ti	dum-i-ti
Past	-tan	dum-i-tan
Perfect	-an	dum-i-an

The table follows in large part the presentations of Takahashi 1987b: 548ff. and Takahashi 1997b: 419, but differs from those sources and accords with Yamada 2016: 268–269 in two respects. First, it excludes the Volitional or Hortative form in -*u* (typically realized as [o:] in sentence-final position (Takahashi 1987b: 543)), which, although well-represented in works published in the 1960s through 1980s, is now obsolete, with other constructions filling the gap (Izuyama 2012: 422, Yamada 2016: 276 (note 18)). Second, it includes the stem-forming suffixes Causative -*amir*- and Passive -*arir*-. The palatal semivowel, transcribed for Japanese with *y*, is written *j* in transcriptions of Dunan and, below, in transcriptions of other Ryukyuan languages as well.

The category name "Conclusive" translates Japanese *syuusikei* (-*kei* 'form'); Conclusive forms head finite, sentence-final clauses. The category names "Adnominal" and "Adverbial" translate *rentaikei* and *ren'yookei*, respectively; while both Dunan forms have multiple uses (see Takahashi 1987b: 543ff.), the names reflect the fact that Adnominal forms typically head clauses that modify NPs (relative clauses) and Adverbial forms typically head nonfinal conjunct clauses. I will assume that, in their central uses, these three categories reflect the position of the verb in syntactic structure rather than expressing any modal or aspectual content and are in that respect roughly parallel to the structural cases nominative, accusative, and genitive.

The forms of Table 2 are divided into four groups. The suffixes of the first three groups begin, respectively, with *a*, *u*, and *j/i*, and those of the fourth group have in common that they are added to the Adverbial form rather than to the stem.[2] The only respect in which the representations of the table are phonologically abstract is that Perfect /dum-i-an/ is realized as *dumjan* as the result of a rule that will be discussed immediately below; the sequence *i-a* in that form is underlined to show that it is subject to hiatus resolution.

That the final *n* of the Negative, Conclusive, Past, and Perfect suffixes of Table 2 is in fact a Conclusive morpheme is shown by the forms of Table 3, which displays the contrast between Conclusive and Adnominal forms in both the Nonpast and the Past when the verb is, respectively, Affirmative and Imperfect, Negative, and Perfect.[3] Table 3 thus also shows that the Negative suffix is -*anu*-, the Past suffix is -*ta*-, and the Perfect suffix is -*a*-. Further, it shows that the Conclusive form *dumun* of Table 2 contains a suffix -*u*-, which I will identify with the

---

2. The alternative of treating *i* as an unsegmentable part of the Conjunctive, Past, and Perfect suffixes would require complication of several of the rules to be postulated below.

3. For the most part, the segmentations of Table 3 follow Yamada et al. (2015: 461–462), for whom, however, what I have called Conclusive -*n* is an Indicative suffix, and Adnominal -Ø and -*ru* are Participial.

-*u* of Adnominal *dumu* and take to be a realization of the feature complex [−Neg −Perf −Past]. Finally, I postulate a [−Past −Perf] Adnominal suffix -Ø corresponding to the Adnominal suffix -*ru* that appears elsewhere — that is, in [+Past] and in [+Perf] forms. Below, I will in principle assume the segmentations of Table 3, but in citing examples, will typically suppress the morpheme boundary before Conclusive -*n*. Negative -*anu*- and Perfect -*a*-, as well as those suffixes in combination with Past -*ta*-, may also be followed by either of the Conditional suffixes (Yamada et al. 2015: 461), but I will omit those forms here.

Table 3. Dunan Conclusive and Adnominal forms

		[−Past]	[+Past]
[−Neg −Perf]	Con	dum-u-n	dum-i-ta-n
	Adn	dum-u-Ø	dum-i-ta-ru
		[−Past]	[+Past]
[+Neg]	Con	dum-anu-n	dum-anu-ta-n
	Adn	dum-anu-Ø	dum-anu-ta-ru
		[−Past]	[+Past]
[+Perf]	Con	dum-i-a-n	dum-i-a-ta-n
	Adn	dum-i-a-ru	dum-i-a-ta-ru

2.3.4 Hiatus at verb stem boundary: A first pass

A recurrent theme in the account of Dunan verbal morphophonology presented below will be the treatment of hiatus at verb stem boundary. In this section I present the most general set of rules that deal with this phenomenon, rules that are plausibly understood as repair mechanisms whose function is to enforce compliance, within the inflected word, with constraints that also hold (with minor exceptions) morpheme-internally. I start, then, by briefly surveying the occurrence of hiatus within morphemes and the processes by which earlier occurrences thereof have been eliminated.

Of the nine possibilities for hiatus afforded by Dunan's three vowels, only two, *ai* and *ui*, occur freely within a morpheme (*ai* 'indigo' (J *ai*), *ui* 'above' (J *ue*), *ui* 'melon' (J *uri*)). An earlier length contrast has been lost, so that (letting Japanese historical *kana* spellings stand in for ancestral forms) a pair like *i* 'cooked rice' < *ipi* (J *ii*) and *i* 'picture' < *we* (J *e*) are homophones (see the word list of Takahashi 1987a). Inherited and derived Vu sequences have been eliminated by assimilation of V to *u* and shortening: *su* 'tides, current' (< *siu*) < *sipo* (J *sio*), *su* 'pole' (< *sau*) < *sawo* (J *sao*), although unassimilated *au*- 'blue' < *awo*- (J *ao*-) is a well-known exception. *ia* and *ua*, finally, have been eliminated by desyllabification of the high vowel. This is particularly clear for *ua*, as shown by adjective stems like *dwa-* 'weak' (< **dua-*) < *yowa-* (J *yowa-*) and *kʰwa-* 'hard' (< **kua-*) < *kowa-* (J *kowa-* 'stiff'); an example for *ia* is provided by *mjangi* 'gift' < *miage*, originally a compound (J *miyage*).

Given the situation morpheme-internally, it would not be surprising if there were processes functioning to resolve hiatus at verb stem boundary. Table 4 illustrates all nine possibilities for V+V at stem boundary using the suffixes Perfect *-an*, Prohibitive *-unna*, and Adverbial *-i* from Table 2 and the vowel-final allomorphs of *ba(r)-* 'break' (J *war-*), *mu(r)-* 'serve (food)' (J *mor-*), and *ugi(r)-* 'receive' (J *uke-*), which will be treated in Section 2.3.6.3.

Table 4. Hiatus at verb stem boundary in Dunan

	-an		-unna		-i	
ba(r)-	ba-an	[ban]	ba-unna	[banna]	ba-i	
mu(r)-	mu-an	[mwan]	mu-unna	[munna]	mu-i	
ugi(r)-	ugi-an	[ugjan]	ugi-unna	[uginna]	ugi-i	[ugi]

Note that Perfect *-an* appears to be added directly to this vowel-final allomorph, without the intervention of the Adverbial suffix. This is unexpected on the basis of the forms of Tables 2 and 3, and I propose an explanation for the discrepancy immediately below.

As Table 4 makes clear, of the nine VV sequences, only /ai/ and /ui/ survive unaltered: V_iV_i sequences undergo shortening (descending diagonal), *u* deletes after any vowel (middle column), and high vowels desyllabify before *a* (bottom left form and the one above). These changes are codified in the rules of (3) through (5). Those rules typically apply at verb stem boundary, but, as shown by the Perfect form *dumjan* /dum-i-an/ from Table 2, their environment must be more general than that. Here and below, I represent the morphological boundary in question by an unlabeled right bracket.[4]

---

4. Apart from not appealing to morpheme boundary, Yamada's (2016:280) (27) 3. coincides with rule (3); his (27) 2. represents half of rule (5), that portion applying to *u*.

(3) Shortening $V_i \rightarrow \emptyset \:/\: V_i] \:\_\_$

(4) *u*-Deletion $u \rightarrow \emptyset \:/\: V] \:\_\_$

(5) Desyllabification $\begin{matrix} V \\ [+\text{high}] \end{matrix} \rightarrow [-\text{syllabic}] \:/\: \_\_ \:] \: a$

While rules (3)–(5) would be justified on the basis of the input-output relations of Table 4 alone, they gain further plausibility, as we have already noted, from the fact that their results mirror the situation observed morpheme-internally, where *ai* and *ui* are the only VV combinations that occur freely.

There is one further rule that needs to be postulated in connection with stem-boundary hiatus. Consider the two Perfect forms reported by Izuyama (2012: 423) for the verb *mui(r)*- 'burn (i)', *mwan* and *mun*, the second involving a Perfect suffix *-u-n* that will be discussed in Section 2.3.5 (here and throughout, "(i)" and "(t)" in glosses abbreviate "(intransitive)" and "(transitive)", respectively). As with the verbs of Table 4, it is the vowel-final allomorph of *mui(r)*- that appears in the Perfect. As a result, the two forms cited appear to be phonological /mui-an/ and /mui-un/, again assuming that Perfect *-an* is added directly to the vowel-final stem allomorph. As is immediately clear, however, the medial *i* of those representations is not reflected in the attested forms, which follow from inferred intermediate representations /mu-an/ and /mu-un/ by rules (5) and (3) (or (4)), respectively. It is thus necessary to assume a rule deleting intervocalic *i* that will feed rules (3)–(5):

(6) Intervocalic *i*-Deletion $i \rightarrow \emptyset \:/\: V \:\_\_ \: V$

Rule (6), motivated on the basis of deletion of a stem vowel, also provides an explanation for the failure of the Adverbial suffix to appear in the Perfect forms of Table 4. This is because, assuming the presence of that suffix, those forms will have the phonological representations /ba-i-an/, /mu-i-an/, and /ugi-i-an/, respectively. Since by the same token, the two Perfects of *mui(r)*- 'burn' noted above will be phonological /mui-i-an/ and /mui-i-un/, it is clear that rule (6), if it takes the form stated, must be allowed to apply iteratively.

Variation in the shape of stems and suffixes that is due to rules (3) through (6) will of course not have to be recorded in any form in lexical entries. Cases in which multiple allomorphs of a single stem or suffix do have to be lexically listed exist as well, however, and the next section deals with the listed allomorphy of suffixes, along with cases in which suffix choice is conditioned by individual stems. The suffixes treated are those of the Conditional, the Perfect, and the Causative.

2.3.5   Suffixal allomorphy

In addition to the Conditional suffixes *-uba* and *-ja* of Table 2, there is a Conditional suffix alternant *-iba*, which occurs only after vowels. *-iba* is thus in complementary distribution with both *-uba* and *-ja*, which occur, following a verb stem, only after consonants.[5] *-iba* is considered an allomorph of *-uba* by Hirayama and Nakamoto (1964), Takahashi (1987b), Takahashi (1997b) (for all of whom *-uba* and *-iba* are alternate forms of the "Zyooken A" suffix), Yamada et al. (2015), and Yamada (2016). There is reason to believe, however, that this is an oversimplification, and that *-iba* shares semantic properties with *-ja*. Notably, forms suffixed with *-iba* and *-ja*, but not those suffixed with *-uba*, can be used as weak imperatives (the "Meirei A" and "Meirei B", respectively, of Hirayama and Nakamoto 1964 and Takahashi 1987b).[6] I will therefore assume that the semantic range of *-iba* covers both that of *-uba* and that of *-ja*, so that *-iba* is not an allomorph of either *-uba* or *-ja* to the exclusion of the other. This judgment can be captured formally under the assumption of late insertion of phonological material, introduced in Chapter 1. Inflectional affixes will be morphosyntactic feature complexes in the lexicon and in the syntax, phonologically realized at spellout by rules of exponence that insert phonological forms into those feature complexes (syntactic terminals). In the present case, we will need both a feature that represents what *-uba* and *-ja* have in common and a feature that represents how they differ. Call these two features "[Conditional]" and, in rough accord with examples cited by Izuyama (2012: 447–448), "[Realis]". The rules realizing the three Conditional suffix allomorphs may then be written as in (7).

(7)   a.   [+Cond −Real] ↔ uba / C __
      b.   [+Cond +Real] ↔ ja / C __
      c.   [+Cond] ↔ iba

As noted in Section 1.5, I assume that exponence is governed by the Subset Principle (Halle 1997: 428), according to which (a) every feature specified in the rule must be present in the terminal that is the target of insertion, and (b) rules matching in more features take precedence over rules matching in fewer features. In accordance with (b), rules (7a) and (7b) will apply before rule (7c), and *-iba* will be, formally speaking, the default realization of the specification [+Cond].

---

5. Additionally, according to the data of Yamada et al. (2015: 461), the Conditional 2 suffix is *-ja* after Past *-ta-* and Perfect *-(j)a-*, but *-rja* (my segmentation) after Negative *-anu-* and Perfect *-(j)u-*; the Conditional 1 suffix is *-ba* in all four cases.

6. This imperative use of Conditional forms is also observed throughout the Yaeyama dialect area as well as in Okinawan (Hirayama and Nakamoto 1964: 139–140), and has a parallel in Tokyo Japanese V-*(r)eba* (with final rise) "why don't you V?"

The Yaeyama dialects of Iriomotejima and the surrounding islands, to the east of Yonaguni, make clear what the history of the three alternants of (7) must be, since, with one partial exception, those dialects uniformly have a single Conditional form in -iba (Iriomote Sonai, Hatoma, Kuroshima, Hateruma) or -iwa (Kohama) regardless of the stem-final segment (see Hirayama et al. 1967: 174–190); the exception is that the suffix is -eba in Hateruma after polysyllabic stems in $h < s$. In Dunan, -iba, while remaining unchanged after a vowel, must have progressed from -iwa through ia to ja after a consonant, a development that mirrors the change -eba > -jaa observed in many Japanese dialects (see the *Grammar atlas of Japanese dialects*, Kokuritsu Kokugo Kenkyujo 1989–2006 (below, GAJ), maps 126–131). Dunan -iba and -ja, then, appear to reflect an original Conditional suffix of the shape *-eba (J -eba), suggesting that -uba is secondary; on this hypothesis, it is unsurprising that it is precisely -iba and -ja that display a weak imperative interpretation. The origin of -iba/-ja in *-eba is confirmed by the Conditional of s-stems: bagas- 'boil (t)' (J wakas-) has the Conditional baga-iba, which must descend from *bagas-eba (cf. Hateruma bagaheba), since stem-final s remains before *i (Adverbial bagas-i). We will return to the Conditional of s-stems below.

The relation between the postvocalic Conditional suffix -iba and the postconsonantal suffixes -uba and -ja is suppletive, in that all three alternants must be listed, but no lexical conditioning is involved. In the case of Perfect -a- and -u- (below, -an and -un), in contrast, there is clearly a degree of lexical conditioning, although the distinction between the two suffixes appears for the most part to be semantically conditioned.

As Yamada et al. (2015: 460 (note 4)) and Yamada (2016: 284–287) observe, the distribution of -an and -un correlates at least in part with the agentivity of the verb. In one direction, this correlation is in fact highly reliable: of the 80 or so verbs recorded in the word list of Takahashi 1987a as having Perfects in -un, virtually all are clear unaccusatives, verbs taking a nonagentive subject. The correlation with unaccusativity raises the possibility that the two Perfect suffixes are semantically distinct, perhaps along the lines of the "have" perfect auxiliaries (German *haben*, French *avoir*, etc.) and the "be" perfect auxiliaries (German *sein*, French *être*, etc.) of European languages, with the semantics of the latter but not the former involving a state resulting from the action of the verb. The proposal that the two suffixes are semantically distinct is also consistent with Izuyama's (2012: 423–424) observation that for a subset of verbs, the two forms coexist and contrast in meaning, a phenomenon that can be seen as parallel to the variable unaccusativity that is documented in European languages for certain types of verbs (Sorace 2000). If this proposal is on the right track, Perfect -an and -un, rather than constituting a case of allomorphy, will represent two distinct morphemes.

Table 5. C-stem and historical V-stem inflection in Tokyo, Hirara, and Dunan

	C-stem inflection ('write')			*V-stem inflection ('arise')			
	Suffix	Tokyo	Hirara	Dunan	Suffix	Tokyo	Hirara	Dunan
Imp	-e	kak-e	kak-i	kʰag-i	-ro	oki-ro	uki-ru	ugir-i
Vol	-au	kak-oo	kak-a	kʰag-u	-u	oki-yoo	uki-Ø	ugir-u
Adv	-i	kak-i	kak-ï	kʰat-i	-Ø	oki-Ø	uki-Ø	ugi < ugi-i
Neg	-anu	kak-ana-	kak-an	kʰag-anu-	-nu	oki-na-	uki-n	ugir-anu-
Caus*	-asime-	kak-asime-	kak-asïmi-	kʰag-amir-	-sime-	oki-sime-	uki-sïmi-	ugi-mir-

* A second Causative suffix, -as- (J C-stem -as(e)- ~ V-stem -sas(e)-), is said by Hirayama and Nakamoto (1964:123) to be frequent in the Adverbial form in Dunan, but their only example involves a C-stem verb, and I am not aware of any evidence for the shape of the suffix in Dunan after historical V-stems.

I have suggested that verbs forming Perfects in -un are reliably unaccusative. The converse implication, that unaccusatives form Perfects in -un, appears to be subject to two types of counterexample. To begin with, there are isolated lexical exceptions; thus nk- 'become full' has the Perfect ntjan (Hirayama and Nakamoto 1964:112, Takahashi 1987a:18). A far more systematic class of apparent counterexamples is constituted by unaccusative ar-stems such as nar- 'become', atar- 'strike (i)' and agar- 'become light', which appear to invariably have Perfects in -an. The lack of ar-stem un-Perfects, however, can be attributed to phonological rules that we have already seen. Specifically, a Perfect form of the shape /Xa-i-un/ will reduce to [Xan] as a result of the application of Intervocalic i-Deletion and u-Deletion (rules (6) and (4) above). The Perfects of unaccusative ar-stems, then, appear in the end to be consistent with the idea that the choice of Perfect suffix depends in principle on the unaccusativity of the verb.

The last suffix to be taken up in this section, that of the Causative, needs to be seen in the context of the set of suffixes that, historically, alternate depending on the consonant/vowel polarity of the stem-final segment. Table 5 displays consonant-stem (C-stem) and historical vowel-stem (V-stem) inflection for five inflectional categories in Tokyo Japanese, Hirara Miyako (Karimata 1997a, 1999), and Dunan; for comparative purposes, the table includes Dunan Volitional forms. The forms of that table show that (a) all three dialects display reflexes of the same C-stem suffixes, with the reinterpretation of the Negative suffix as an adjective-stem formant shown by the Tokyo form and the reinterpretation of the Causative suffix as r-final shown by the Dunan form representing the only nonphonological developments (the alternation of stem-final *g* with *t* seen in the Dunan Adverbial *kʰati* is due to a rule that will be discussed in the next section); (b) Tokyo and Hirara show reflexes of the same V-stem suffixes, with nonphonological developments in the Tokyo Volitional as well as the Tokyo Negative suffix; (c) Dunan, in contrast, shows no reflex of distinctive V-stem inflection for the first four categories, inflecting the representative example 'arise' by adding C-stem suffixes to an *r*-final stem (with loss of *r* before Adverbial *-i*, as illustrated in Table 4). There is a single exception to this statement for the Negative suffix, namely the Negative of *kʰu-* 'come', which is *kʰu-nu-*, preserving the old C-initial allomorph of the suffix that is reflected in Tokyo *oki-na-* and Hirara *uki-n*. The historical process leading toward replacement of V-stem inflection by *r*-stem inflection in Dunan and many other Japanese and Ryukyuan dialects will be investigated in detail in Chapters 5 and 6.

A more systematic exception than *kʰu-nu-* to the generalization that Dunan has eliminated the distinction between C-stem and V-stem inflection is the Causative suffix, where historical V-stems like *ugi-* < *oki-* 'arise', rather than adding the C-stem suffix alternant *-amir-* to a stem that has been augmented by *r*, retain a V-stem alternant that, like those of Tokyo and Hirara, differs from its C-stem counterpart in lacking initial *a* and thus takes the shape *-mir-*.[7] Since the *a*-zero alternation is (apart from the *-nu-* of *kʰu-nu-*) specific to the Causative suffix, the allomorph *-mir-*, restricted to the environment "i] _", will need to be lexically listed alongside the default form *-amir-*. Two further wrinkles in the morphology of the Causative as reported by Yamada (2016) are that (a) the Causative of 'come', *kʰur-amir-*, does involve *-amir-* added to an *r*-final stem allomorph and (b) the small number of stems in *-ui(r)-* (notably *ubui(r)-* 'remember', *mui(r)-* 'burn (i)', *mui(r)-* 'sprout, bud') take *-amir-*, but add that suffix to their V-final allomorph. This results in forms like /ubui-amir-/, which undergoes rules (6) and (5) above to surface as *ubwamir-*. If stem-final *r* is in place for these stems at the time the Causative suffix is realized phonologically, however, the choice of *-amir-* rather than *-mir-* will follow. We will return to Causative forms in Sections 2.3.6.3 and 2.3.7.

---

7. The most detailed source of information on Dunan Causatives that I am aware of is Yamada 2016; earlier sources (e.g. Hirayama and Nakamoto 1964, Takahashi 1987b) tend to characterize the Causative suffix, like those of the Negative and the Passive, as added to the *Mizenkei* ('Irrealis form'), and to characterize the *Mizenkei* of historical vowel stems as ending in *ra*, thus predicting (in our segmentation) **ugir-amir-* for the Causative of 'arise', parallel to Negative *ugir-anu-* and Passive *ugir-arir-*. In addition to the data of Yamada 2016, citations of Causatives formed with the short suffix alternant *-mir-* on the original vowel-final stem can be found in Hirayama 1988 (p.375) and in the GAJ (maps 118 and 121).

The Dunan Causative suffix, then, involves a clear case of listed allomorphy. In general, however, as Table 5 shows, Dunan displays a good deal less listed allomorphy in response to the consonant/vowel polarity of the stem-final segment than do more conservative dialects like Tokyo and Hirara.

The three cases considered in this section appear to constitute the major examples in which Dunan verbal suffixes display lexically listed allomorphy or conditioning by individual stems. If so, suffixal irregularity in Dunan is quite limited. In the following sections, I take up stem alternations. Essential to the account I propose will be distinguishing between the phonological relation of stem alternants to each other and the morphosyntactic environments in which those alternants occur. It will become clear that, while the relevant morphosyntactic environments are complex for some alternations, the phonological relations among stem alternants are both simple and general. This will mean that, just as in the case of suffixes, there is only a limited amount of lexically listed stem allomorphy.

2.3.6 Stem alternations

2.3.6.1 *Velar-final stems*

With one exception that we will examine below, Dunan stem alternations affect only stem-final segments, of which there are 13, 11 consonants and two vowels. Dunan's eleven stem-final consonants can be divided into three groups according to whether they alternate and if so, how. The six stem-finals *b t d c m n*, first of all, are nonalternating in all environments (see e.g. Hirayama and Nakamoto 1964: 111). By comparison with Tokyo Japanese, where six of nine stem-final consonants alternate in forms with *t*-initial suffixes as a result of the changes known as *onbin*, or Shuri Okinawan, where all stem-finals except *t* and some occurrences of *r* alternate with zero under the same conditions, the nonalternating status of the majority of Dunan stem-final consonants is striking.[8]

The second group of stem-final consonants with regard to alternation pattern consists of the three velars *k g ŋ*. Before the Adverbial suffix -*i* these become dentals, with nasals denasalizing and nonnasals devoicing. Stem-final *ŋ* thus alternates with *d*, while *k* and *g* both alternate with *t*, as we saw for *g* in Table 5. Assuming features [dorsal] and [coronal], the rule for the alternation of stem-final velars can be written as in (8), where "[Adv]" represents the set of morphosyntactic features that are realized by the Adverbial suffix. The paradigm of velar-final stems is illustrated with *k ʰag-* 'write' in Table 6.

---

8. The absence of *onbin* alternations in *t*-suffixed forms is characteristic of the Sakishima languages generally (Karimata 2015: 133).

(8) Velar Dentalization

$$\begin{bmatrix} + \text{dor} \\ <-\text{nas>} \end{bmatrix} \rightarrow \begin{bmatrix} + \text{cor} \\ -\text{nas} \\ <-\text{voi>} \end{bmatrix} / \_\_]\,[\text{Adv}]$$

Table 6. The inflection of velar-final stems

Negative	-anun	kʰag-anun
Causative	-amir-	kʰag-amir-
Passive	-arir-	kʰag-arir-
Conclusive	-un	kʰag-un
Adnominal	-u	kʰag-u
Prohibitive	-unna	kʰag-unna
Conditional 1	-uba	kʰag-uba
Conditional 2	-ja	kʰag-ja
Imperative	-i	kʰag-i
Adverbial	-i	kʰat-i
Conjunctive	-ti	kʰat-i-ti
Past	-tan	kʰat-i-tan
Perfect	-an	kʰat-i-an

To the extent that all velar-final stems alternate in the same way, no information about the alternations in question will need to be included in the lexical entries of individual verbs. There is one fact about the inflection of velar stems that is not reflected in Table 6, however. This concerns how they combine with Perfect -un. The stems *sag-* 'bloom' (J *sak-*) and *kʰarag-* 'dry (i)' (J *kawak-*), in keeping with their status as unaccusatives, form their Perfects with -un rather than with the Perfect suffix -an that is illustrated in Table 6; the stem *tʰudug-* 'reach, arrive' (J *todok-*), similarly, allows -un in addition to -an. The Perfect forms for those stems are, respectively, *satun* (Yamada et al. 2015: 458), *kʰaratun*, and, in addition to *tʰudutjan*, *tʰudutun* (Takahashi 1987a). Since the stems of the *un*-Perfects have undergone Velar Dentalization, it is immediately clear that those forms, like velar-stem *an*-Perfects, must involve the Adverbial suffix, even though no reflex of that suffix appears on the surface. The question of how the Adverbial suffix comes to be absent from forms like *satun* and *kʰaratun* will be taken up below, in our discussion of *r*-stems.

Above, we have seen that stems ending in six of Dunan's eleven stem-final consonants are entirely nonalternating, and that stems ending in three more consonants undergo only Velar Dentalization. We may note further that after these nine stem-final consonants, suffixes, apart from the exceptions treated in Section 2.3.5, have a constant shape as well. With respect to morphological structure, Pellard and Yamada (2017: 32) contrast Japanese, which they characterize as almost canonically agglutinative, with Dunan, which they claim "cannot easily be treated in the same way". In fact, the Dunan paradigms of stems ending in nonalternating or velar consonants are, apart from the Perfect, impeccably agglutinative; it is only the paradigms of *r*-stems, *s*-stems, and stems ending in the vowels *a* and *u* that are exceptional in this regard. Stems ending in those four segments may be characterized informally as displaying "fused" rather than agglutinative paradigms, in the sense that many of their forms undergo deletion of the stem-final segment and reduction of the vowel sequences that arise from the juxtaposition of vowel-final stem allomorphs and vowel-initial suffixes. It is to stems showing such fused paradigms that we now turn. I will pursue an approach to the relevant alternations that maximizes phonological predictability and consequently requires considerable extrinsic ordering of rules, but will note at the end of Section 2.3.8 that the essential claims of this chapter are also entirely consistent with a range of analyses that treat some of the alternations in terms of morphologically conditioned readjustment rules, with decreased dependence on rule ordering.

2.3.6.2 *Vowel-final stems*

Dunan *a*-stems and *u*-stems, first of all, correspond to Japanese *w*-stems, specifically to *aw*-stems and to *ow*- and *uw*-stems, respectively. Japanese stem-final *w* reflects Proto-Japonic **p*; in Dunan, no trace of that stem-final consonant remains. Because of the conversion of historical *i*-stems and *e*-stems to *r*-stems that we observed in Section 2.3.5 and the fact that the two verbs in which stem-final *p* was originally preceded by a front vowel have become consonant-stems in Dunan (*nd-* < **ip-* 'say', *bir-* < **wep-* 'become intoxicated'), *a*-stems and *u*-stems exhaust the set of Dunan vowel-final stems, and may be referred to simply as V-stems.

The crucial fact about the inflection of V-stems is that they undergo a stem-boundary hiatus-resolution rule that deletes the first of two back vowels and is thus distinct from rules (3)–(5) above:

(9) Back Vowel Truncation $\begin{matrix} V \\ [+back] \end{matrix} \rightarrow \emptyset / \underline{\quad}] \begin{matrix} V \\ [+back] \end{matrix}$

This is shown in Table 7, where, as before, vowel sequences that undergo hiatus resolution are underlined, with, in addition, strikethrough identifying the stem vowels that are deleted by rule (9) (below, "BVT"). The sample stems are *sima-* 'put away, finish (doing)' (J *simaw-*) and *madu-* 'go astray' (J *mayow-*).

Table 7. The inflection of V-stems

Negative	-anun	sima-anun	madu-anun
Causative	-amir-	sima-amir-	madu-amir-
Passive	-arir-	sima-arir-	madu-arir-
Conclusive	-un	sima-un	madu-un
Adnominal	-u	sima-u	madu-u
Prohibitive	-unna	sima-unna	madu-unna
Conditional	-iba	sima-iba	madu-iba
Imperative	-i	sima-i	madu-i
Adverbial	-i	sima-i	madu-i
Conjunctive	-ti	sima-i-ti	madu-i-ti
Past	-tan	sima-tan	madu-tan
Perfect	-an	sima-an	madu-an

The first three forms of *madu-*, those with *a*-initial suffixes, show that BVT reduces /u+a/ to *a*, in contrast to rule (5), which reduces /u+a/ to *wa*. The following three forms of *sima-*, those with *u*-initial suffixes, show that BVT reduces /a+u/ to *u*, in contrast to rule (4), which reduces /a+u/ to *a*.

The Perfect forms of Table 7, which surface as *siman* and *madwan*, respectively, appear to pose two analytic questions, that of why the Adverbial suffix *-i-* fails to appear in them and that of why the underlined vowel sequences do not undergo BVT. The answer to the first question is that the *-i-* of underlying /sima-i-an/ and /madu-i-an/ is deleted by rule (6), Intervocalic *i*-Deletion, and the answer to the second is that Intervocalic *i*-Deletion applies after BVT, counterfeeding it — that is, producing forms that meet its structural description but do not undergo it. As we saw in the discussion of Table 4, the output of Intervocalic *i*-Deletion, instead of being subject to BVT, undergoes rules (3)–(5). Assuming the ordering BVT > Intervocalic *i*-Deletion, then, there is a phonological explanation for the Perfects *siman* and *madwan*. The failure of the Adverbial suffix to appear in the Past forms *simatan, madutan*, on the other hand, poses a problem for which there is no obvious phonological solution, given the minimal contrast with Conjunctive *simaiti, maduiti*. When we note that the Adverbial suffix appears before Conjunctive *-ti* in all verbs, and before Past *-ta-* in all verbs except those whose relevant stem allomorph ends in a vowel, it becomes clear that we must postulate the category-specific hiatus-resolution rule (10).

(10) Past Tense *i*-Deletion   i → Ø / V] __ [Past]

As we will see immediately below, rule (10) applies in the paradigms of *r*-stems and *s*-stems in addition to that of vowel-stems. The origin of that rule can be explained by the hypothesis that the Past suffix was originally -*utan* rather than -*i-tan*, a hypothesis that receives support internal to Dunan from the synchronically irregular paradigm of 'come', which shows Adverbial *s-i* and Conjunctive *s-i-ti*, but Past *s-utan* (Takahashi 1987b: 565). In several neighboring Yaeyama dialects, regular verbs inflect in parallel fashion; thus Hatoma and Kuroshima show Adverbial *tur-i*, Conjunctive *tur-i-ti*, and Past *tur-uta* for *tur-* 'take' (Hirayama et al. 1967: 188, 178), and *hak-utan* is reported for the Past of 'write' in Hateruma (Aso 2015: 430). Historically, then, the lack of any vowel preceding Past -*tan* postvocalically — specifically, in the paradigm of V-stems, *r*-stems, and *s*-stems — will be the result of deletion of *u* after a vowel at stem boundary, as in rule (4) above, and the presence of *i* preceding Past -*tan* postconsonantally will be the result of a subsequent reanalysis of the remaining Past forms in -*utan* as based on the Adverbial, in accordance with the parallel analysis of the Conjunctive and the Perfect.

2.3.6.3 *r-stems*

A significant part of the paradigm of *r*-stems has already been observed above: Table 4 illustrates the fact that stem-final *r* undergoes deletion in the Perfect, the Prohibitive, and the Adverbial, and Table 5 shows that, in contrast, it is retained in the Negative and the Imperative (as well as in the obsolete Volitional). Table 8 shows the full paradigm of the three *r*-stems that were illustrated in Table 4, *bar-* 'break', *mur-* 'serve (food)', and *ugir-* 'receive'; as above, vowel sequences that are subject to hiatus resolution are underlined; these occur in the Prohibitive, the Perfect, and in the Adverbial and Conjunctive of *ir*-stems.

The deletion rule for stem-final *r* is clearly not phonologically conditioned, as shown most clearly by the contrast between Adverbial /bar-i/ [bai] and Imperative /bar-i/ [bari] (where Imperative -*i* < *-*e* (see Table 5)). Stem-final *r* is lost in three morphologically defined environments, before the Adverbial suffix (i.e. in the last four categories of Table 8), before the Prohibitive suffix, and before the Causative suffix when preceded by *i*. The required rule may thus be written as in (11).

(11) *r*-Truncation   r → Ø / <i> __] [[Adv] ∨ [Proh] <∨ [Caus]>]

Historically, the presence of the disjunct [Adv] in (11) is the result of loss of *r* before *i and the fact that the Adverbial is the only suffix that began with that vowel. The likely explanation for the disjunct [Proh] is slightly more complex.

Table 8. The inflection of *r*-stems

Negative	-anun	bar-anun	mur-anun	ugir-anun
Causative	-amir-	bar-amir-	mur-amir-	ugi-mir-
Passive	-arir-	bar-arir-	mur-arir-	ugir-arir-
Conclusive	-un	bar-un	mur-un	ugir-un
Adnominal	-u	bar-u	mur-u	ugir-u
Prohibitive	-unna	ba-unna	mu-unna	ugi-unna
Conditional 1	-uba	bar-uba	mur-uba	ugir-uba
Conditional 2	-ja	bar-ja	mur-ja	ugir-ja
Imperative	-i	bar-i	mur-i	ugir-i
Adverbial	-i	ba-i	mu-i	ugi-i
Conjunctive	-ti	ba-i-ti	mu-i-ti	ugi-i-ti
Past	-tan	ba-tan	mu-tan	ugi-tan
Perfect	-an	ba-an	mu-an	ugi-an

The change *ru* > *n* / _ *n* (a prominent feature of colloquial Tokyo Japanese) is not obviously common in Yaeyama dialects; for Prohibitives, Hirayama et al. (1967: 171, 185) report only *tunna* < *turuna* 'don't take (it)' for Kabira and *minna* < *miruna* 'don't look' for Kohama. If we can nevertheless assume that this development took place in Dunan, and that the original form of the Prohibitive suffix was -*una* (see Nakamoto 1990: 467), it will have created an alternation in that suffix between -*nna* (e.g. *ba-nna* < *bar-una*) for *r*-stems and -*una* for other stem types. Given that *r*-stems constitute more than 60% of the verbal lexicon (see de Chene 2020a: 275), it will then not have been surprising if the *nn* ~ *n* alternation was leveled in favor of *nn*, resulting in the observed Prohibitive suffix -*unna* and leaving *r*-stem Prohibitives with the truncated stem allomorph resulting from the change *ru* > *n*. Presence of the disjunct [Caus] in (11), finally, will allow *ubwamir-*, the Causative of *ubuir-* 'remember', to be derived from /ubuir-amir-/, as proposed in Section 2.3.5. The Causatives of *ir*-stems other than those ending in *uir*, however, require separate treatment, and will be dealt with in Section 2.3.7 below.

For the Perfect, Table 8 shows only the suffix -*an*. Many *r*-stems, however, form their Perfects in -*un*, as illustrated in Section 2.3.4 by the alternative Perfect *mun* of *muir-* 'burn (i)'. These *r*-stem *un*-Perfects, particularly those based on *ir*-stems (the vast majority) provide important evidence about the morphophonology of Perfect forms. Remember first that we took the application of Velar Dentalization in *satun* (*sag-* 'bloom') as evidence that the Adverbial suffix must be present abstractly in that form. *satun*, that is, derives from /sag-i-un/, just as *kʰatjan*, the Perfect of 'write', derives from /kʰag-i-an/. The difference between the two cases is that whereas the vowel sequence of /kʰag-i-an/ will correctly reduce to *ja* by Desyllabification (rule (5)), the vowel sequence of /sag-i-un/ must not undergo *u*-Deletion (rule (4)), which would, after the application of Velar Dentalization, predict *satin*. The same difference between *an*-Perfects and *un*- Perfects can be illustrated with *r*-stems. As we saw in Table 4, the Perfect /ugi-i-an/ of *ugir*- 'receive' surfaces as *ugjan*. /ugi-i-un/, the Perfect of *ugir*- 'arise', however, surfaces as *ugun*.

It might appear, then, that we need a rule deleting *i*, whether that vowel is the Adverbial suffix or part of the stem, before Perfect -*un*. A handful of monosyllabic *ir*-stem *un*-Perfects, however, suggest a slightly different analysis. Specifically, consider the Perfects /hi-i-un/ and /ni-i-un/ of *hir*- 'go' (and its segmental homophone *hir*- 'become cold' (J *hie*-)) and *nir*- 'cook (i)' (J *nie*-). After the application of Intervocalic *i*-Deletion, these surface as *hjun* and *njun*, forms that apparently derive from a process that desyllabifies, rather than deletes, *i* before -*un*, although the resulting semivowel will have to be deleted in the vast majority of cases. These processes of desyllabification and semivowel deletion appear to be conditioned by a single suffix, Perfect -*un*, and so manifestly lack generality. They interact, however, with processes that do display generality, namely Velar Dentalization and *r*-Truncation, and failure to postulate them would force complication of both those rules and the principles determining the morphological composition of inflected forms. If *satun*, for example, were to be derived from /sag-un/ rather than from /sag-i-un/, Velar Dentalization would have to apply before Perfect -*un* as well as before the Adverbial suffix, and the principle that Perfect forms contain the Adverbial suffix would have to be made sensitive to the identity of the Perfect suffix. Similarly, if we wished to derive *ugun* from /ug-un/ (< /ugir-un/) rather than from /ugi-un/ (< /ugi-i-un/ < /ugir-i-un/), we would need to say that before Perfect -*un*, but in no other environment, *r*-stems undergo deletion not only of their stem-final consonant, but of the preceding vowel as well. I will therefore adopt the two rules in (12), ordered after Intervocalic *i*-Deletion, as a treatment of the vowel sequence /i+u/ resulting from suffixation of Perfect -*un*.

(12)   Hiatus Resolution before Perfect -*un*
   a.   i → j   / C __] [un [Perf]]
   b.   j → Ø / [σ₁C __] [un [Perf]]

The preceding consonantal environment of (12a) will be unnecessary if rules (12) follow Intervocalic *i*-Deletion, but I include it for parallelism with (12b), in which the preceding environment is required. (12b) is written so as to delete *j* before -*un* after a consonant in Perfect forms with polysyllabic stems; preconsonantal *n* in stems like *nkir*- 'sink (i)', Perfect *nkun* (Takahashi 1987a) counts as syllabic for the purposes of that rule. Because Perfects of compounds with second member *hir*-

'go' fail to undergo (12b) (*hansi-hir-* 'remove, unfasten', Perfect *hansi-hjun*; *sui-hir-* 'take (someone) along with', Perfect *sui-hjun* (Takahashi 1987a)), we must assume that the sequence $\sigma_1 C$ in (12b) contains no V-boundary. Correspondingly, the Perfect *tʰintjun* (Takahashi 1987b: 212) for the stem *tʰintir-* 'shorten, shrink' (cited as transitive) suggests that that stem is reduplicated and does contain an internal V-boundary.

2.3.6.4   *s-stems*

In examining the V-stem paradigms of Table 7, we found that they included both instances of hiatus that were resolved by BVT, rule (9), and instances of hiatus that were resolved by rules (3)–(5) subsequent to deletion of intervocalic *i*. In contrast, Table 8 showed that hiatus in the paradigm of *r*-stems, that arising from deletion of intervocalic *i* as well as that arising from deletion of stem-final *r*, is always resolved by rules (3)–(5). The paradigms of *s*-stems are like those of V-stems in requiring reference both to BVT and rules (3)–(5). In Table 9, as in Tables 7 and 8, all vowel sequences subject to hiatus resolution are underlined, and vowels that undergo BVT are shown with strikethrough; the stems illustrated are *bagas-* 'boil (t)' (J *wakas-*), *utus-* 'drop (t)' (J *otos-*), and *hus-* 'dry (t)' (J *hos-*) (for the paradigm of the last, see Takahashi 1987b: 557 and Yamada 2016: 269). Sample surface forms are Negative *baganun, utanun, hwanun* and Conclusive *bagan, utun, hun*.

Table 9. The inflection of *s*-stems

Negative	-anun	baga-anun	utu-anun	hu-anun
Causative	-amir-	baga-amir-	utu-amir-	hu-amir-
Passive	-arir-	baga-arir-	utu-arir-	hu-arir-
Conclusive	-un	baga-un	utu-un	hu-un
Adnominal	-u	baga-u	utu-u	hu-u
Prohibitive	-unna	baga-unna	utu-unna	hu-unna
Conditional	-iba	baga-iba	utu-iba	hu-iba
Imperative	-i	baga-i	utu-i	hu-i
Adverbial	-i	bagas-i	utus-i	hus-i
Conjunctive	-ti	bagas-i-ti	utus-i-ti	hus-i-ti
Past	-tan	baga-tan	utu-tan	hu-tan
Perfect	-an	bagas-i-an	utus-i-an	hus-i-an

The distribution of vowels marked with strikethrough in Table 9 shows that hiatus resulting from deletion of stem-final *s* is resolved by BVT only when two conditions are met: the second vowel must be *a*, and the stem must be polysyllabic. In other cases, hiatus resulting from deletion of stem-final *s* is resolved by rules (3)–(5). There must thus be two rules deleting stem-final *s*, one ordered before and one after BVT. In accordance with the observations just made, the first rule may be stated as in (13).

(13) *s*-Deletion Before *a* $s \rightarrow \emptyset / [_{\sigma_1} C_{\sigma_0} V \_\_] a$

The second *s*-deletion rule applies before all *u*-initial suffixes and, among *i*-initial suffixes, before those of the Imperative and the Past (on the Conditional, see Section 2.3.7 below). It can thus be written as in (14).

(14) *s*-Truncation $s \rightarrow \emptyset / \_\_]$ [u ∨ [Imp] ∨ [Adv] [Past]]

With *s*-stems, we come to the end of our survey of Dunan stem-types. There are also at least seven verbs that display one or more kinds of irregularity (de Chene 2020a: 274–275), but I will omit the relevant details here. In the next section, I consolidate and summarize the analysis that has been developed above.

2.3.7   Readjustment, rule ordering, and derivations

There are two combinations of stem-type and inflectional category for which, given the representations we are assuming, the rules postulated above will not produce the correct forms. These are the Causatives of the great majority of *ir*-stems and the Conditionals of *s*-stems. Let us consider those two cases in turn.

As noted in Section 2.3.6.3, the Causative *ubwamir-* of *ubuir-* 'remember' will be correctly derived from /ubuir-amir-/ by the rules we have postulated, given that *r*-Truncation, rule (11), applies before the Causative suffix when stem-final *r* is preceded by *i*. Following the account first sketched in Section 2.3.5, the derivation will proceed /ubuir-amir-/ → /ubuiamir-/ → /ubuamir-/ → *ubwamir-*, with Intervocalic *i*-Deletion and Desyllabification (rules (6) and (5)) applying after *r*-Truncation. By the same token, however, our rules would predict **ugjamir-* rather than the observed *ugimir-* for the Causative of *ugir-* 'arise'. The allomorph *ugi-* of *ugimir-*, then, cannot be the result of rule (11). This conclusion is confirmed by the observation that, given our assumption that the Causative suffix is *-mir-* after stem-final *i* and *-amir-* otherwise, the stem allomorph *ugi-* must be in place before exponence (phonological realization) of suffixes in order to condition the choice of *-mir-*. (11), on the other hand, applies after BVT (rule (9)), counterfeeding it, and BVT presupposes that suffixes have already been phonologically realized.

A parallel situation arises in the Conditional of *s*-stems. According to the rules of exponence (7), the Conditional allomorph *-iba* will appear only after vowels. In order to generate a Conditional form like *bagaiba* (*bagas-* 'boil (t)'), then, the stem allomorph *baga-* must be in place at the point when suffixes are phonologically realized. Consequently, that allomorph cannot be due to the *s*-Truncation rule (14) because, like *r*-Truncation, *s*-Truncation must apply after BVT.

DM recognizes a class of "readjustment rules", morphologically conditioned rules governing cases of allomorphy that cannot be attributed to the independently motivated phonology (see e.g. Halle and Marantz 1993:124 or Harley and Noyer 1999:5). I will assume the readjustment rules in (15) to account for the two cases of stem allomorphy just noted, whose crucial characteristic is that the derived allomorph is presupposed by rules of suffixal exponence (other conceivable treatments would obviate the need for rules (15) by recapitulating historical developments or complicating the representations of suffixes).

(15)   Readjustment
    a.   *Xir-* → *Xi-* / __ [Caus] (condition: X does not end in *u*)
    b.   *Xs-* → *X-* / __ [Cond]

Let us now consider the ordering relationships that obtain among the phonological rules that we have postulated. The rule *s*-Deletion Before *a* feeds BVT, which in turn is counterfed by *r*-Truncation and *s*-Truncation. Both of those consonant-deletion rules feed Past Tense *i*-Deletion, and *r*-Truncation feeds Intervocalic *i*-Deletion as well. Intervocalic *i*-Deletion feeds both hiatus resolution before Perfect *-un* and the general hiatus resolution rules (3)–(5). Finally, the two rules (12) of hiatus resolution before Perfect *-un* are in a bleeding and counterbleeding relationship with *u*-Deletion, rule (4); as noted in the discussion of Section 2.3.6.3, it is the former that must apply to intermediate representations like /sat-i-un/ (*sag-* 'bloom') and /ugi-un/ (*ugir-* 'arise'). Inserting Velar Dentalization at the head of the list, the rules we have postulated may thus be ordered as in (16). Parenthesized abbreviations are those used in the derivations displayed below; the last three rules, (3)–(5) above, are grouped together in those derivations under the label "GHR" (General Hiatus Resolution).

(16)   a.   Velar Dentalization (VD, (8))
    b.   *s*-Deletion Before *a* (*s*-Del, (13))
    c.   Back Vowel Truncation (BVT, (9))
    d.   *r*-Truncation (*r*-Trunc, (11))
    e.   *s*-Truncation (*s*-Trunc, (14))
    f.   Past Tense *i*-Deletion (Past *i*-Del, (10))
    g.   Intervocalic *i*-Deletion (V_V *i*-Del, (6))
    h.   *i* → *j* before Perfect *-un* (*i* → *j*, (12a))
    i.   *j*-Deletion before Perfect *-un* (*j*-Del, (12b))

      j.   Shortening

      k.   *u*-Deletion

      l.   Desyllabification

Tables 10 through 12 display derivations involving the rules of (16). The initial row "Spellout" of those tables shows the linear sequence of morphemes resulting from syntactic operations, with stems represented in their phonological underlying forms. After rows displaying the results of readjustment and exponence of suffixes, each applicable phonological rule is identified by its letter within (16) and the abbreviation given there. Inflectional categories are abbreviated Neg(ative), Cau(sative), Ad(verbial), Cnc (Conclusive), Cnd (Conditional), Pt (Past), and Pf (Perfect).

      Table 10, to begin with, shows the derivation of representative *s*-stem and *r*-stem forms. Its first three columns illustrate that loss of stem-final *s* may be due to readjustment, to *s*-Deletion before *a*, or to *s*-Truncation, while the fourth shows that *s*-Deletion before *a* does not apply to monosyllables. The last two columns of the table contrast two *r*-stem Causative forms with regard to whether loss of stem-final *r* is due to readjustment or to *r*-Truncation.

Table 10. Derivations I: *s*-stem and *r*-stem forms

Stem gloss	'boil (t)'	'drop (t)'	'boil (t)'	'dry (t)'	'arise'	'burn (i)'
Spellout	bagas-Cnd	utus-Neg	bagas-Cnc	hus-Neg	ugir-Cau	muir-Cau
Readjustment	baga-Cnd				ugi-Cau	
Exponence	baga-iba	utus-anun	bagas-un	hus-anun	ugi-mir-	muir-amir-
b. *s*-Del		utu-anun				
c. BVT		ut-anun				
d. *r*-Trunc						mui-amir-
e. *s*-Trunc			baga-un	hu-anun		
g. V_V *i*-Del						mu-amir-
j.-l. GHR			baga-n	hw-anun		mw-amir-
Output	[bagaiba]	[utanun]	[bagan]	[hwanun]	[ugimir]	[mwamir]

The derivations of Table 11 illustrate Past Tense *i*-Deletion and how that rule is fed by *r*-Truncation and *s*-Truncation.

      Table 12, finally, illustrates the derivation of Perfect forms. Its first two columns show the Perfects of the segmentally homophonous stems *sag-* 'tear', a transitive, and *sag-* 'bloom', an unaccusative. In response to that difference, the Perfect suffix is realized as *-an* in the first case and *-un* in the second, thereby

Table 11. Derivations II: Past forms

Stem gloss	'get lost'	'become'	'go'	'boil (t)'	'drop (t)'
Spellout	madu-Ad-Pt	nar-Ad-Pt	hir-Ad-Pt	bagas-Ad-Pt	utus-Ad-Pt
Exponence	madu-i-tan	nar-i-tan	hir-i-tan	bagas-i-tan	utus-i-tan
d. *r*-Trunc		na-i-tan	hi-i-tan		
e. *s*-Trunc				baga-i-tan	utu-i-tan
f. Past *i*-Del	madu-tan	na-tan	hi-tan	baga-tan	utu-tan
Output	[madutan]	[natan]	[hitan]	[bagatan]	[ututan]

Table 12. Derivations III: Perfect forms

Stem gloss	'tear (t)'	'bloom'	'arise'	'go'	'become'	'soak (t)'
Spellout	sag-Ad-Pf	sag-Ad-Pf	ugir-Ad-Pf	hir-Ad-Pf	nar-Ad-Pf	kir-Ad-Pf
Exponence	sag-i-an	sag-i-un	ugir-i-un	hir-i-un	nar-i-un	kir-i-an
a. VD	sat-i-an	sat-i-un				
d. *r*-Trunc			ugi-i-un	hi-i-un	na-i-un	ki-i-an
g. V_V *i*-Del			ugi-un	hi-un	na-un	ki-an
h. i → j		sat-j-un	ugj-un	hj-un		
i. *j*-Del		sat-un	ug-un			
j.-l. GHR	sat-j-an				na-n	kj-an
Output	[satjan]	[satun]	[ugun]	[hjun]	[nan]	[kjan]

determining the further course of the derivation. The third and fourth columns show the Perfects of polysyllabic and monosyllabic unaccusative *ir*-stems. The fifth illustrates that failure of unaccusative *ar*-stems to show *un*-Perfects can be attributed to hiatus resolution following loss of intervocalic *i*. The sixth, finally, shows the Perfect of a transitive *ir*-stem, with Perfect suffix *-an* and hiatus resolution due to Desyllabification, rule (5).

In closing this section, I identify several crucial properties of the analysis just summarized. First, that analysis involves no representational abstractness at the level of the morpheme: apart from a small number of cases of listed allomorphy (the Conditional and Causative suffixes plus a few irregular verbs), each stem and suffix has a unique phonological representation that coincides with an actually occurring phonetic alternant thereof. Second, while the *r*-Truncation and *s*-Truncation rules display disjunctive morphological conditioning and several additional rules refer to individual inflectional categories, the main hiatus resolution rules, BVT and the rules (3)–(5), are purely phonological, apart from the fact that they are written to apply at morpheme boundary. Further, rules with and without morphological conditioning are interspersed in the ordering, showing that the set of rules is not divisible into morphological and purely phonological blocks. Third, although I have postulated a rather large inventory of rules, the derivational depth displayed by individual inflected forms is for the most part limited: it is only Perfects (as in Table 12) and the Causatives of *uir*-stems (illustrated in Table 10) that require the application of more than two rules. In sum, apart from its dependence on rule ordering, the analysis offered above can be seen as a relatively surface-oriented account of Dunan verbal morphophonology. In the next section, I argue that that analysis also has the property that its basic tenets follow from a small number of general principles.

2.3.8   Motivation for the analysis

In attempting to identify principles that would result in the choice of an analysis for Dunan verbal morphophonology along the lines of that proposed above, I begin by postulating a guideline for the choice of phonological underlying representations (URs), one that can be characterized as conservative and relatively uncontroversial.

(17)   In the absence of evidence to the contrary, the UR of a morpheme M is the maximally informative alternant of M.

There are multiple ways in which alternants of a given morpheme M may differ in informativeness. Perhaps most obviously, if there is segmental or featural material that one alternant includes but another lacks, the alternant that includes that material will be more informative than the alternant that lacks it. For example, when a stem-final consonant alternates with zero, as *r* and *s* do in Dunan, (17) will choose as underlying an alternant that manifests the alternating consonant over one that does not.

An alternant may also be more informative than another by virtue of preserving a contrast that the other alternant neutralizes. For example, in the environment preceding the Adverbial suffix, the Velar Dentalization rule (8) neutralizes the contrast between stems that otherwise end in *k* or *g* and (nonalternating) *t*-stems, and between stems that otherwise end in *ŋ* and (nonalternating) *d*-stems. For stems that have both velar-final and dental-final alternants, then, (17) requires that the velar-final alternant be underlying. Finally, (17) will choose the unique alternant of a nonalternating morpheme as underlying, given that the maximally informative alternant is naturally characterized as that with respect to which there exists no alternant that is more informative.

Let us assume further that, if inflected forms are transparently segmentable for some stem classes but not for others, speakers will base their analysis of the morphemic composition of those forms on the segmentable cases. Since that analysis will be realized by the syntax, it will then necessarily apply to the less transparent cases as well, given that syntactic structure cannot plausibly be made sensitive to the identity or phonological characteristics of individual stems or stem classes. For example, if speakers decide on the basis of a subparadigm like Adverbial *dumi*, Past *dumitan*, Perfect *dumjan* (*dum-* 'read') that the Adverbial suffix is a constituent of Past and Perfect forms, that suffix will also be present in the Past and Perfect of a subparadigm like *mui, mutan, mwan* (*mur-* 'serve (food)'), even though no trace of it appears on the surface. Since Dunan verb forms are transparently segmentable for stems ending in any of the nine consonants *b m t d n c k g ŋ*, there will be no ambiguity, given this principle, about the morphemic makeup and thus the phonological underlying shape of forms that are not transparently segmentable, namely (a proper subset of) the forms of V-stems, *r*-stems, and *s*-stems. Once phonological underlying shapes are known, the remaining analytic task is determination of the function that converts them into the observed phonetic shapes. As indicated above, I have been guided in formulating the proposed rules by the principle of appealing to phonological conditioning when possible and to morphological conditioning only when necessary. In closing, however, I observe that analyses that make more extensive use of morphological conditioning are also possible. Since the alternations in question are free of lexical conditioning, however, attributing them to the properties of individual lexical entries will not be a plausible strategy.

It was noted at the end of the previous section that the analysis of Dunan verbal morphophonology proposed above is concrete in representational terms, since the vast majority of stems and suffixes have unique phonological representations that coincide with occurring alternants. At the same time, however, that analysis could be considered abstract as regards its rules and rule interactions, given its postulation of two distinct strata of hiatus resolution mediated by consonant deletion rules that feed the rules of the later stratum but counterfeed the rule of the earlier one, BVT (rule (9)). If the goal is to reduce this apparent abstractness, the most effective analytic adjustment will be to abandon the idea that BVT is phonologically conditioned and treat it as a readjustment rule parallel to the two rules of (15). As a consequence, it will also be necessary to treat as a matter of readjustment the results of *s*-Deletion before *a*, which feeds BVT in the analysis proposed above. The readjustment rule replacing BVT for vowel stems will have the form XV- → X- and will apply in the first six morphological categories of the conjugation tables above; the generalization that these are just the categories with back-vowel suffixes will be deemed accidental rather than linguistically significant. The readjustment rule replacing *s*-Deletion before *a* will have the form $\sigma_1 C_o V s$- → $\sigma_1 C_o$- and will apply in the first three categories of the conjugation tables; again, the generalization that these are just the categories with *a*-initial suffixes will not be captured. Further transfer of rules from the phonology to the readjustment rules is also conceivable. *r*-Truncation and *s*-Truncation could be treated as readjustment rules with minimal reformulation. Similarly, Past Tense *i*-Deletion could be taken to be conditioned by stem type rather than by a preceding vowel and assigned to the readjustment rules. Crucially, however, none of these reassignments will alter the essential nature of the account proposed above, namely its basis in the segmentation of inflected forms into stems and affixes against the background assumption that inflectional affixes are the realizations of syntactic elements.

2.3.9   Conclusion

At first sight, Dunan might appear to pose a challenge to the piece-based view of inflection that was argued for in Chapter 1. Certainly it has been seen that way by those who have claimed that an account of Dunan verb morphology involves lexical listing of "whole inflected forms (minimally, principal parts)" for each verb, so that "roots, stems, and affixes are only *post hoc* abstractions over existing full forms." (Pellard and Yamada 2017: 46). And there is no question that morpheme boundaries are indeed not readable off surface forms in all cases. For example, given the Negative *baganun* and the Conclusive *bagan* of *bagas*- 'boil (t)', there is no way in advance of phonological analysis to know that while the underlined vowel originates in the suffix in the first case, it originates in the stem in the second (see Table 9).[9] Above, however, we have seen that, in the end, a morpheme-based account of the Dunan data is eminently achievable. In fact, it is only within that kind of account that it is possible to state phonological generalizations like those embodied in the hiatus resolution rules (3)–(5), which we have seen to hold morpheme-internally with minor exceptions and thus to be substantially surface-true. The lesson of Chapter 2, then, is that neither morphosyntactic nor phonological fusion constitutes an insuperable barrier to a syntactic and morpheme-based account of inflection.

---

9. The difficulty of segmenting surface forms pretheoretically is illustrated by fluctuating and mistaken segmentations of surface forms in published sources. For example, the Past *madutan* /madu-i-tan/ of *madu*- 'go astray' is segmented *mad-utan* by Takahashi (1987b: 559, 1997b: 419), thus attributing to a suffix a vowel that belongs to the stem, and the Perfect *madwan* /madu-i-an/ of the same verb is segmented *madw-an* in Takahashi 1987b, but *mad-wan* in Takahashi 1997b.

CHAPTER 3

The nonsyntactic nature of verbal derivation

3.1 Introduction

As summarized in Table 1 of Chapter 1, the grammatical framework proposed in this book treats inflection as syntactic and morpheme-based, but denies that a parallel treatment of derivational morphology is possible. Chapter 1 set out the rationale for a syntactic and piece-based treatment of inflection, and Chapter 2 defended that treatment against a putative counterexample involving phonological fusion in a Ryukyuan language, arguing at the same time that morphosyntactic fusion is not a cogent challenge to it either. The present chapter, shifting the focus to derivational morphology, takes up a Japanese test case for the nature of derivation, the structure of transitive and intransitive verb stems, and presents several kinds of evidence that that structure is not the result of syntactic computation. I begin with a brief survey of the range of options available for the treatment of derivation.

In early generative grammar, there was effectively no alternative to a transformational account of derivational morphology, as typified by English deverbal nominals like *criticism, refusal,* and *destruction* — an account, that is, on which a noun phrase like *their criticism of the movie* is derived from a sentential representation corresponding to *They criticized the movie.* This situation changed decisively with the publication of Chomsky's (1970) *Remarks on nominalization,* which argued that this transformational account of deverbal nominals was untenable. The negative nature of Chomsky's conclusion, however, gave succeeding commentators a great deal of latitude in drawing out its implications. Because Chomsky suggested treating *destroy* and *destruction* as manifestations of a single lexical item whose lexical category was determined by the context into which it was inserted, a DM account on which both the verb and the noun involve an acategorial root selected by a category-determining little v or little n has a reasonable claim to represent the most faithful realization of Chomsky's original idea (Marantz 1997, Harley and Noyer 2000:350, Embick 2021). On the other hand, Jackendoff (1975:641) writes concerning the proposal of an acategorial lexical item that "Since Chomsky gives no arguments for this particular formulation, I feel free to adopt here the alternative theory that *decide* and *decision* have distinct but related lexical entries." The theory of lexical redundancy rules that he develops pursuant to this idea is sharply distinct from the syntactic account of derivational morphology proposed by DM. Finally, the most widely adopted response to Chomsky's argument against a transformational account of deverbal nominals (see e.g. Scalise 1984: 24) was to postulate a set of word-formation rules — in effect, a second generative component of the grammar — operating internal to the lexicon, a proposal that was pioneered by Halle (1973). We will return below to these three possible responses to Chomsky's (1970) observations.

3.2   Background and preview

In recent years, Japanese stem formation has been cited repeatedly (Harley 2008: 39, Harley 2012: 346, Marantz 2013: 106–109) as illustrating the DM claim that syntax is root-based — the claim, that is, that along with functional morphemes, the atoms of syntactic computation are roots rather than (inflectable) stems or (inflected) words (Embick and Marantz 2008: 5). Specifically, it has become widely accepted (Marantz 2013: 106) that the Japanese suffixes that create transitive and intransitive verb stems are instances of little v, causative and inchoative, that attach to roots and thus that the verb stems themselves are syntactic constructions — much like, say, the combination of a verb stem with a tense element or a main verb with an auxiliary. As we will see below, there are also variants of this account of Japanese transitivity suffixes that take advantage of the distinction between little v and Voice introduced by Pylkkänen (2002, 2008).

Below, I argue that in fact, Japanese stem formation cannot plausibly be treated as syntactic, and that it thus provides suggestive evidence against a syntactic treatment of derivational morphology more generally. Perhaps the most decisive data is provided by sequences of derivational suffixes, which have not previously figured in the discussion: while a single (in)transitivizing suffix per stem might appear consistent with treatment of that suffix as the realization of a syntactic object, sequences of such suffixes display properties that militate against such a treatment. Specifically, in a sequence of derivational suffixes, only the properties of the outermost suffix are manifested, those of inner suffixes being masked or overridden. I will refer to this situation below by saying that sequences of derivational suffixes combine not by composition, but by cancellation. Correspondingly, the order of derivational suffixes may be sensitive to the identity of individual roots, two suffixes appearing in one order with some roots but in the opposite order with others, with no systematic effect on interpretation. This is only possible because inner suffixes are interpretively inert.

There are also arguments against a syntactic treatment of Japanese stem formation that do not depend on the properties of suffix sequences. One is that transitivizing and intransitivizing suffixes, causative and inchoative little v on a DM account, do not in fact have constant meanings, but in the general case express relative degree of transitivity, as when a verb of receiving and a verb of giving, both syntactically transitive in the sense of taking agentive subjects and assigning accusative case, are formed on a common root and differentiated by being marked with intransitivizing and transitivizing suffixes, respectively. A final characteristic of derived stems that shows that they are not syntactic constructions is their semantic instability over time. In all of these respects, derivational suffixes contrast sharply with the suffixes of inflection, which compose with each other semantically, show no lexical conditioning of suffix order, display constant meanings, and exhibit diachronic stability in combination with stems. Below, Section 3.3 introduces the Japanese system of stem formation, and Sections 3.4 through 3.7 argue that, as just sketched, its properties preclude a syntactic treatment. Section 3.8 discusses the phenomenon of featural override as a general characteristic of derivational morphology, Section 3.9 revisits the spectrum of possible responses to Chomsky 1970, and Section 3.10 draws out an apparent implication of root-based syntax.

3.3   Data

3.3.1   Suffixes and alternations

Of the nine Japanese consonants that occur as the final segment in verb stems, all except *n* (final in the single stem *sin-* 'die') can be shown to be suffixal in some cases. Such consonantal suffixes occur in the form -C- after a vowel and in the form -aC- after a consonant, as illustrated in (1)–(8). Here and throughout, stems are cited without inflectional material when the focus is on stem-internal structure; representations of both roots and suffixes abstract away from low-level rules that delete *y* before front vowels and *w* before nonlow vowels.

(1) a. kim-ar-   'be decided' (cf. kim-e- 'decide')
     b. utu-r-   'be transferred, reflected' (cf. utu-s- 'transfer, reflect')

(2) a. sam-as-   'cool (t)' (cf. sam-e- 'cool (i)')
     b. utu-s-   'transfer, reflect' (cf. utu-r- 'be transferred, reflected')

(3) a. kuy-am-   'rue, regret' (cf. kuy-i- 'regret')
     b. ita-m-   'be painful; get damaged' (cf. ita- 'painful')

(4) a. yur-ag-   'swing (i)' (cf. yur-e- 'swing (i)')
     b. yawara-g- 'soften (i), subside' (cf. yawara-ka- 'soft')

(5) a.   muk-aw- 'proceed toward' (cf. muk- 'face')

    b.   uruo-w- 'become moist' (cf. uruo-s- 'moisten')

(6) a.   uk-ab-   'float, ride on the water' (cf. uk- 'float, rise to the surface')

    b.   koro-b-   'fall down' (cf. koro-gar- 'roll, tumble')

(7) a.   wak-at-   'divide (t), separate (t)' (cf. wak-e- 'separate (t)')

    b.   ta-t-   'cut off' (cf. ta-y-as- 'eradicate', ta-y-e- 'die out')

(8) a.   yuw-ak-   'bind' (cf. yuw- 'tie up; dress (hair)')

    b.   nozo-k-   'peer into; be partially visible' (cf. nozo-m- 'look out on')

The adjective stem formant -(a)si- displays the same alternation, as illustrated in (9).

(9) a.   kuy-asi- 'causing chagrin, regret' (cf. kuy-i- 'regret')

    b.   suzu-si- 'cool, refreshing' (cf. suzu-m- 'cool off, refresh oneself')

It should be noted that the *a* that alternates with zero in the above examples is probably in all cases originally a root-final vowel that has been stranded on the right side of the root boundary by phonological change, specifically deletion of the root final in root stems and coalescence of the root final with a vocalic suffix in *e*-stems. This can be illustrated with the root *yur(a)* 'swing, sway', which supports at least the five verb stems in (10).

(10) a.   yur-   'swing (i/t)'

     b.   yur-e-   'shake (i), sway'

     c.   yur-ag-   'sway, waver' (= (4a))

     d.   yur-as-   'cause to sway/oscillate'

     e.   yur-amek- 'waver, flicker'

That the original form of the root in question is *yura* is shown by the adverbial forms *yurayura* and *yura-ri* (*to*) 'in a swaying or wavering manner'. That root has been subject to deletion of its final vowel in the root stem (10a) and to coalescence with a vocalic suffix *-i- in the *e*-stem (10b), however, so that in the verb stems of (10) the root appears in the truncated form *yur-*.[1]

It would be possible to take the root to be *yura* in the stems of (10) as well as in the adverbial forms cited. The underlying forms of (10a) and (10b) would then be /yura-Ø-/ and /yura-e-/ or /yura-i-/, with the observed stems derived

---

1. The hypothesis of a derivational suffix *-i- is due to Unger (1977), pursuant to work by Ono (1953), who, however, derives inflected forms directly from roots and identifies the suffix in question with Adverbial -*i*. Unger takes *-i- to derive from *-gi-; variations and developments of his proposal may be found in Whitman 2008 and Frellesvig 2008.

by phonological rule, and (10c)–(10e) would be segmented *yura-g-*, *yura-s-*, and *yura-mek-*, respectively. Under a generalized version of that proposal, consonantal suffixes could be consonant-initial in all of their occurrences, with no need to assume the preconsonantal *a*-zero alternation seen in (1)–(9) above. In place of that alternation, however, it would be necessary to postulate a postconsonantal *a*-zero alternation, as illustrated by the stems *na-r-* 'sound (i)' (cf. *na-k-* 'weep') and (under the proposed segmentation) *na-ra-s-* 'sound (t)'. In the absence of compelling evidence for adopting the more abstract analysis characterized by vowel-final roots and derivation of suffixal *-e-* by reduction of underlying vowel sequences, I will assume the more conventional segmentation (Jacobsen 1992, Volpe 2005, Matsumoto 2016) under which the suffixes *-∅-* and *-i-* have resulted in the reanalysis of originally vowel-final roots as consonant-final. Because *a* is not the only vowel that occurred root-finally, this decision will result in suffix allomorphy additional to that arising from the *a*-zero alternation. Thus, for example, the suffix *-(a)s-*, documented in (2) above, will also have allomorphs *-os-* and *-us-* that result from reanalysis of originally *o*-final and *u*-final roots as consonant-final. This is illustrated in (11) below, where (11a) reprises (2a).

(11) a.   sam-as- 'cool (t)'   (cf. sam-e- < *sama-i- 'cool (i)')
      b.   ok-os-   'raise, rouse' (cf. ok-i- < *oko-i- 'get up, occur')
      c.   tuk-us- 'exhaust'   (cf. tuk-i- < *tuku-i- 'become exhausted')

Further, there are suffixes *-(a)re-* (intransitive) and *-(a)se-* (transitive) that have not been treated above. In order to simplify the classification of suffix pairs in the following section, these will be collapsed with *-(a)r-* and *-(a)s-*, respectively, resulting in suffixes *-(a)r(e)-* and *-(a)s(e)-* in which the alternation between *e* and ∅ in the final position is conditioned by the identity of the root.

Finally, it should be noted that in addition to the suffixes of the form *-(a)C-* illustrated above, there are also a number of suffixes that might seem to invite analysis into multiple parts but in fact arguably function as units, parallel to cases such as Latin noun-forming *-tiōn-*, which represents a combination of the two suffixes *-ti-* and *-ōn-* (Buck 1933:312). Consider in this context paired inchoative and causative verb stems of the form X-*mar-* and X-*me-*, illustrated in the (b) and (c) examples of (12) below.

(12) a.   sizu-ka   'quiet, calm'
      b.   sizu-mar- 'become calm'
      c.   sizu-me-   'make calm'
      d.   sizu-m-   'sink (i)'
      e.   sizu-m-e- 'sink (t)'

The X to which -*mar*- and -*me*- attach is often characterized as an adjective stem, but (12b) and (12c), where X is a root with stative semantics, show that that characterization is marginally too restrictive. Crucially, (12) also provides an argument against segmenting paired inchoative and causative -*mar*- and -*me*- into -*m-ar*- and -*m-e*-: while the root *sizu*- supports a stem in -*m*-, namely (12d) *sizu-m*- 'sink (i)', the meaning of *sizu-mar*- and *sizu-me*- in (12b) and (12c) indicates that those stems are derived directly from the root rather from *sizu-m*-. On the other hand, causative *sizu-m-e*- 'sink (t)' in (12e) does appear to be derived from *sizu-m*-, so that (12) displays a minimal pair for the distinction between -*me*- and -*m-e*-. All five stems of (12) are attested in Old Japanese in essentially their modern meanings (see the entries of Omodaka et al. 1967), so that the presumed reanalysis of -*m-ar*- and -*m-e*- sequences as the compound suffixes -*mar*- and -*me*- must be dated to the prehistoric period.

There are other suffixes that, similarly, appear to represent the fusion of what must once have been discrete elements. This is true, first of all, for *n*-initial -*nar*-/-*ne*- (*kasa-nar*-/*kasa-ne*- 'pile up (i/t)' (cf. *kasa* 'bulk, size')) and -*naw*- (*tomo-naw*- 'accompany' (cf. *tomo* 'companion')), whose second elements coincide transparently with established suffixes, but whose -*n*- is not to my knowledge identifiable with any known morpheme. The suffixes -*gar*- 'show signs of; put on an air of' and -*mek*- 'show signs of', which attach freely to nouns as well as to a variety of bound stems, are other clear candidates for such a "fusional" analysis. The same is true of transitivizing -*(a)kas*- (*obiy-akas*- 'threaten' (cf. *obiy-e*- 'take fright'); *hane-kas*- 'splash (t)' (cf. *hane*- 'splash (i)')). The existence of such compound suffixes underlines the need to be sensitive to the danger of overparsing suffixal material.

3.3.2   Isoradical relations

Among noncompound Japanese verb stems, many are unsegmentable — that is, monomorphemic, at least synchronically. A significant number of others are segmentable into a root and a suffix, but are the only verb stems built on the root in question. This is true, for example, of many stems in -*r*-, including both examples with a long history, such as *sibu-r*- 'falter; avoid' (10th c.; cf. *sibu* 'astringent taste', *sibu*- 'astringent; sullen; austere'), and examples of more recent origin, such as *sabo-r*- 'skip work or school, loaf on the job' (1925; cf. *sabo*, truncated form of *sabotaazyu* (from French) 'go-slow strike').[2] In other cases, as exemplified in (10) above, a single root may underlie as many as five verb stems.

---

2. Here and below, dates attached to lexical items represent first attestations as per the *Nihon kokugo daijiten* (Nihon kokugo daijiten dainihan henshu iinkai/Shogakukan kokugo jiten henshubu (eds.) 2000–2002 (below, NKD)).

There is, however, a widespread conception of the Japanese verbal lexicon, or at least its most systematic subpart, as a collection of roots each of which supports precisely two stems, one, roughly speaking, transitive and the other intransitive. This is the conception encouraged by the pairwise lists of Jacobsen (1982, 1992), Volpe (2005), and Matsumoto (2016) and by the use of the term "transitivity pair" throughout works like Kageyama and Jacobsen 2016.[3] In discussing relations among isoradical stems (i.e. stems based on a common root), I will at the outset temporarily adopt this pairwise perspective, identifying what I take to be the canonical set of suffixes involved in such transitivity pairs and the set of suffix pairs that would be observed if the canonical suffixes combined with complete freedom. In this way, it will be possible to impose a simple hierarchical structure on a set of suffix pairs that is typically presented as an unstructured list, to propose a clear division between central and peripheral suffix pairs, and to identify possible but nonoccurring pairs as well as pairs that have not always been recognized in previous accounts.

To begin with, I take the set of canonical (in)transitivity suffixes to have only four members, -(a)r(e)-, -(a)s(e)-, -e-, and -Ø-, where the first is inherently intransitivizing, the second inherently transitivizing, and the remaining two flexible in that they may create either intransitive or transitive stems. It is then natural to classify suffix pairs according to whether they involve both -(a)r(e)- and -(a)s(e)- (below, Type 1), -(a)r(e)- but not -(a)s(e)- (Type 2), -(a)s(e)- but not -(a)r(e)- (Type 3), or neither of the two (Type 4). Within each of the four types thus defined, the a-zero alternation will have a determinate value, and the e-zero alternation will create subtypes.

Consider first Type 1 suffix pairs, those involving both -(a)r(e)- and -(a)s(e)-. With neither -e- nor -Ø- involved, roots will be vowel-final and suffixes consonant-initial. Depending on the e-zero alternation, we thus predict the four suffix-pair subtypes -r-/-s-, -re-/-s-, -r-/-se-, and -re-/-se-. For each of these subtypes, Table 1 displays a type number, the suffix pair itself, an example if the pair is attested, and the number of instances of the subtype that appear in Jacobsen's (1992) appendix.[4]

---

3. It must be noted that the treatment of Jacobsen (1982, 1992), which forms the basis for those of Volpe and Matsumoto, does not refer to roots as characterized above in Section 1.2 (although Jacobsen (1992:55) does use *root* in the meaning '(inflectable) stem'); where one might expect reference to roots, Jacobsen (1992:56) says simply "there is always an obvious mutual resemblance in the non-suffixed part of verbs paired together."

4. The numbers (which exclude cases that Jacobsen has parenthesized as involving compounds) should be taken as approximations; Jacobsen's judgments on the matter do not coincide in every case with my own or with those of Matsumoto (2016). The three instances of subtype 1c noted in the table appear in Jacobsen's Type XII under the heading "-Ø-/-se-" along with four that do exemplify that suffix pair (which falls outside the set we are considering here).

Table 1. Suffix pairs involving both *-(a)r(e)-* and *-(a)s(e)-*

Type	Pair	Example	Number
1a	-r-/-s-	modo-r- / modo-s- 'return (i/t)'	27
1b	-re-/-s-	kowa-re- / kowa-s- 'break (i/t)'	18
1c	-r-/-se-	no-r- 'ride' / no-se- 'let ride'	3
1d	-re-/-se-	*	0

Type 2 and Type 3 suffix pairs, since they involve *-e-* or *-Ø-*, show consonant-final roots and vowel-initial suffixes. The predicted subtypes are as in Tables 2 and 3.[5]

Table 2. Suffix pairs involving *-(a)r(e)-* but not *-(a)s(e)-*

Type	Pair	Example	Number
2a	-ar-/-e-	sim-ar- / sim-e- 'close (i/t)'	70
2b	-ar-/-Ø-	sas-ar- 'pierce (i)' / sas- 'impale'	8
2c	-are-/-e-	wak-are- / wak-e- 'separate (i/t)'	3
2d	-are-/-Ø-	*	0

Table 3. Suffix pairs involving *-(a)s(e)-* but not *-(a)r(e)-*

Type	Pair	Example	Number
3a	-e-/-as-	sam-e- / sam-as- 'cool (i/t)'	45
3b	-Ø-/-as-	wak- / wak-as- 'boil (i/t)'	38
3c	-e-/-ase-	okur-e- 'be late' / okur-ase- 'delay'	0
3d	-Ø-/-ase-	aw- / aw-ase- 'match (i/t)'	0

Jacobsen (1992) lists the Table 3 examples of subtypes 3c and 3d under subtypes 3a and 3b, respectively. As we will see in Chapter 4, however, *okur-as-* 'delay' has been almost entirely replaced by *okur-ase-*, as shown by corpus evidence, and *aw-ase-* has been a transitive counterpart of *aw-* since Old Japanese times.

---

5. Matsumoto (2016: 485) lists two pairs of Type 2d; the intransitive members are *um-are-* 'be born' and *wakat-are-* 'be divided'. I take the former, universally listed in dictionaries, as the lexicalized Passive of the corresponding transitive *um-* 'give birth to' and the latter, which is not listed even in the NKD, as the (nonlexicalized) Passive of the corresponding transitive *wakat-* 'divide'.

Type 4 suffix pairs, finally, limited to the two suffixes -*e*- and -Ø-, display only two subtypes, shown in Table 4.

Table 4. Suffix pairs involving neither -*(a)r(e)*- nor -*(a)s(e)*-

Type	Pair	Example	Number
4a	-e-/-Ø-	yak-e- / yak- 'burn (i/t)'	32
4b	-Ø-/-e-	tat- / tat-e- 'stand up (i/t)'	44

The 288 instances of the types enumerated in Tables 1 through 4 represent about 85 percent of the full set of pairs listed in Jacobsen's appendix and can thus be seen to constitute a well-defined core of regular cases.

There is, however, reason to believe that the pairwise analysis of Japanese verb stems is inadequate if one's aim is the investigation of isoradical relations — that is, the identification of sets of stems that share a common root. One problem, already referred to above, arises from the fact that a considerable number of roots underlie not two verb stems, but three or more. Consider in this connection how the isoradical set (13) is dealt with in Jacobsen's (1992) and Matsumoto's (2016) appendices.

(13) a.   dok-   'move out of the way (i)'
      b.   dok-e-   'move out of the way (t)'
      c.   dok-as-   'move out of the way (t)'

In Matsumoto's (2016) appendix, first of all, both *dok-/dok-e-* and *dok-/dok-as-* appear as transitivity pairs (items 3, 39). Listing the two pairs separately and without any indication that they are connected, however, leaves uncaptured and unnoted the fact that the two pairs are based on a single root. In Jacobsen's (1992) appendix, on the other hand, *dok-/dok-e-* appears (class II), but *dok-/dok-as-* does not. Jacobsen thus avoids duplicate listing of the root, but at the cost of leaving *dok-as-* out of his catalogue.

The treatment of the isoradical set (14) in the two appendices is similarly revealing.

(14) a.   hag-   'peel off (t), divest'
      b.   hag-e-   'peel off (i); become bare, bald'
      c.   hag-as-   'peel off (t)'
      d.   hag-are- 'peel off (i)'

The two transitive and two intransitive stems of (14) generate four potential transitivity pairs. Each of the appendices under consideration lists three of them, but not the same three. The two appendices agree, first of all, in listing *hag-e-/hag-* and *hag-e-/hag-as-* (Jacobsen types I and IX, Matsumoto items 147 and 88). Jacobsen additionally lists *hag-are-/hag-*, but classified as irregular (type XVI) and thus not segmented, although it instantiates type 2d above; Matsumoto, on the other hand, lists *hag-are-/hag-as-*, but segmented *haga-re-/haga-s-* (item 286), and thus treated as an instance of subtype 1b (for this pair, see also Jacobsen 1982: 202). Setting aside failure or inconsistency of segmentation, it is clear that the pairwise treatment of the two appendices fails to reflect the fact that there is a single root *hag-* that underlies four verb stems: both appendices list *hag-* in three different places and have duplicate listings for the stems *hag-e-* and *hag-* (i.e. *hag-Ø*) or *hag-e-* and *hag-as-* as well. In the end, then, a case of this sort tends to cast doubt on the idea that the suffix pair or transitivity pair is a meaningful unit of analysis.

A second reason that the pairwise approach is inadequate for the purpose of investigating isoradical relations is that, while it necessarily involves morphological analysis below the level of the stem, it fails to carry that analysis through to its logical conclusion. The isoradical sets (15) and (16) provide a simple illustration.

(15) a. ita-   'painful' (adjective stem)
      b. ita-m-   'be painful, get damaged' (= (3b))
      c. ita-m-e- 'injure'

(16) a. uk-   'float, rise to the surface'
      b. uk-ab-   'float, ride on the water' (= (6a))
      c. uk-ab-e- 'float (t), launch'

Both Jacobsen (1992) and Matsumoto (2016) recognize the relationship between the (b) items and the (c) items of (15) and (16), in the form of transitivity pairs *itam-Ø-/itam-e-* and *ukab-Ø-/ukab-e-*. But the equally patent relationship between the (a) items and the (b) items goes unremarked, in (15) because the (a) item is adjectival rather than verbal, in (16) because the (b) item involves the relatively uncommon suffix *-(a)b-*. The result is that neither the fact that the (c) items each display two suffixes rather than one nor the fact that the roots of the two sets are *ita-* and *uk-*, respectively, is reflected in the accounts in question. It thus seems clear that restriction of the data set to pairs of verb stems involving the canonical suffixes of Tables 1 through 4 above has the consequence that only an arbitrary subpart of the field of stem-internal structure is treated.

Further examples parallel to (15)–(16) suggest that, in the general case, Japanese verb stems involve a layer of suffixation internal to the outer layer constituted by the suffixes *-(a)r(e)-*, *-(a)s(e)-*, *-e-*, and *-Ø-* and variants thereof such as *-i-* and *-os-*. In illustration, consider the isoradical sets (17)–(19).

(17) a.   tuna   'rope'
      b.   tuna-g-   'tie together, tie up'
      c.   tuna-g-ar-   'get connected'
      d.   tuna-g-e-   'connect'

(18) a.   tuta   'ivy'
      b.   tuta-w-   'creep/move along'[6]
      c.   tuta-w-ar-   'reach; be reported'
      d.   tuta-w-e-   'report'

(19) a.   ugo-mek-   'wriggle'
      b.   ugo-k-   'move (i)'
      c.   ugo-k-as-   'move (t)'

(15)–(19) show that -(a)m-, -(a)b-, -(a)g-, -(a)w-, and -(a)k- may all occur in this inner position. There is reason to believe that the same is true of a transitivizing -r-:

(20) a.   nezi   'screw (n)'
      b.   nezi-r-   'twist'
      c.   nezi-r-e-   'get twisted'

We will see more examples of this sort in Section 3.4. It is important to note, however, that the idea of two distinct suffixal positions or slots in the Japanese verb stem is in fact only an approximation to a more complex reality. For one thing, as we will see below, the two "outer layer" suffixes -(a)r- and -(a)s- may each occur internal to the other. For another, it is clear that more than two suffixes may appear "stacked" within a single stem, as several examples below will attest.

3.4   Suffix sequences and their interpretation in DM

3.4.1   Transitivity suffixes as causative and inchoative little v

I turn now to the question of whether Japanese transitivity suffixes can be interpreted as realizations of syntactic objects and in particular to the question of the treatment of those suffixes under DM assumptions. It should be noted to begin with that, depending on what syntactic heads are assumed to occupy the domain

---

6. The connection between 'ivy' and 'creep/move along (a flat or cylindrical object)' is noted with some frequency online, although those doing so appear for the most part to assume that the noun is derived from the verb.

between the root R and the tense element T, there will be multiple options for the syntactic interpretation of transitivity suffixes. Let us therefore first survey the basic functions that must be fulfilled by the material between R and T and how those functions may plausibly be associated with syntactic heads.

If roots are acategorial, one function that must clearly be fulfilled between R and T is specification of lexical category. In the great majority of stems treated here, this will be verbalization. Another is specification of the stem's eventuality type — roughly, state, (unaccusative) process, or caused event. Finally, since external arguments such as agents and experiencers have been taken since the 1980s to be generated in a specifier position within the extended verbal projection, introduction of the external argument (and concomitant assignment of accusative case) is also a function that must be fulfilled between R and T. In the framework of Chomsky 1995, all three of these functions were taken to be fulfilled by the single head little v. Pylkkänen (2002, 2008) introduced the claim that, at least in some languages, there are two heads rather than one between R and T, with Voice, the higher of the two, responsible for introduction of an external argument, and little v responsible for verbalization and event semantics. Given two intermediate heads, there is one further possibility consistent with the plausible requirement that the head introducing the external argument be at least as high in the structure as the head recording event semantics, and that the latter be at least as high as the categorizing head. This is that the categorizing head is a dedicated categorizer, with no other function, and event semantics is associated with the higher head, that whose specifier is occupied by the external argument. We will have occasion below to refer to all three of these possible interpretations of the extended verbal projection. At the outset, however, I will frame the discussion in terms of the simplest of them, that according to which all three functions enumerated above are fulfilled by little v.

In the context of a theory of basic clause structure, Harley (2008: 39) provides a straightforward interpretation of Japanese transitivity suffixes under the assumption that little v performs all three of the functions in question: theme arguments are selected by roots, and $\sqrt{P}$ (root P) is selected by one of two event-type encoding little v elements, causative or inchoative, the first of which also selects a specifier (i.e. an external argument). Given that framework, "the inchoative/causative suffixal morphology of Japanese … is a realization of the two types of v^{o}". Marantz's (2013: 106–107) discussion of the issue is entirely parallel. Writing causative little v as "v_c" and inchoative little v as "v_i", the Harley/Marantz proposal (identified for convenience below as the DM position) is thus that transitivizing suffixes are v_c and intransitivizing suffixes are v_i, and that inflectable stems are syntactic constructions composed of roots and derivational affixes.

Because individual verb stems may be exclusively transitive, exclusively intransitive, or of flexible transitivity, and because individual suffixes may form exclusively transitive stems, exclusively intransitive stems, or both transitive and intransitive stems, there is nevertheless a degree of ambiguity inherent in this proposal. At least the following three versions, in increasing order of restrictiveness, are conceivable.

(21) a. Any suffix that forms a verb stem is a realization of v_i and/or v_c in that stem.
  b. Any suffix that forms a verb stem of determinate transitivity is a realization of v_i or v_c in that stem.
  c. Only suffixes that create exclusively stems of a specific transitivity are realizations of v_i or v_c.

On (21a), the -r- of the stem *sibu-r-*, referred to at the beginning of Section 3.3.2, would realize v_i when that stem is used in the meaning 'falter, slow down' and v_c when it is used in the meaning 'avoid doing'. On (21b), the -r- of *sibu-r-* would not realize v_i or v_c and would presumably be a transitivity-neutral verbalizer, but the -r- of *nao-r-* 'recover (from illness)' would realize v_i, since that stem is strictly intransitive. (21c), finally, would appear to be too restrictive, as illustrated by the suffix -e-, which creates transitive stems in the suffix pair subtypes 2a, 2c, and 4b (Tables 2 and 4 above) and intransitive stems in the suffix pair subtypes 3a, 3c, and 4a (Tables 3 and 4). It should be noted in this connection that there are no apparent grounds for postulating two distinct suffixes $-e_c-$ (causative) and $-e_i-$ (inchoative), and that allowing such an analysis in the absence of independent evidence would render unfalsifiable the claim that suffixes of flexible transitivity exist, since any apparent case thereof could be reanalyzed as a pair of transitivity-specific suffixes. It would appear, then, that the DM claim that transitivizing and intransitivizing suffixes are realizations of v_c and v_i must be interpreted as (21a) or (21b).

Let us return now to the isoradical set (17) and in particular to the stems (17b) *tuna-g-* 'tie together' and (17c) *tuna-g-ar-* 'get connected'. Concentrating for a moment on the suffix -g- of those stems with the aim of determining its meaning, consider the further examples (22)–(25).

(22) a. to(-isi) 'whetstone' (isi 'stone')
  b. to-g- 'whet'
  c. to-g-ar- 'become pointed'

(23) a. tumu 'spindle'
  b. tumu-g- 'spin'

(24) a.   ha(-ne) 'feather' (ne 'root')
      b.   ha-g-   'fletch (an arrow)'[7]

(25) a.   huta   'cover, lid'
      b.   husa-g- 'cover, stop up'

(25b) displays an irregular alternation, but the phonologically expected form *huta-g-* is preserved dialectically in the Kansai area (Tojo 1951:711, Hirayama et al. 1992–1994:3509, 4425) and in eastern Kyushu (Hirayama et al. 1992–1994: 4427–4428).

In all of the above examples, *-g-* attaches to a noun (or the root underlying it) that refers, broadly speaking, to a tool or instrument t, and derives a transitive verb stem whose meaning instantiates the schema 'apply t to an appropriate object' or 'make typical use of t'.[8] In (26) below, on the other hand, *-g-* attaches to a body part noun, and the semantic relationship between that noun and the resulting verb stem appears more difficult to characterize.[9]

(26) a.   mata   'crotch, fork'
      b.   mata-g-   'step over, straddle (t)'
      c.   mata-g-ar- 'straddle (i)'

Two additional stems, one phonologically irregular in Tokyo Japanese, the other obsolete, clarify that semantic relationship. The first is *katu-g-* 'carry on the shoulder' (*kata* 'shoulder'), which remains *kata-g-* over a wide geographical range in Western Japan (Tojo 1951:176, Hirayama et al. 1992–1994:1214–1217). The second is *una-g-* 'carry on the neck' (*una-zi* 'nape of neck'), attested only in the 8th and 9th centuries, according to the NKD. These two cases have in common with (26b) that the complement of *-g-* represents a body part. They can also, however, be said to have in common with the (b) examples of (17) and (22)–(25) that that complement represents a tool or instrument — specifically, a tool used for carrying or transport. If we can assume, as suggested by the most concrete meaning listed for (26c) *mata-g-ar-* in the NKD, that the prototypical meaning of the stems (26b)

---

7. One account of the history of (24b) treats the voicing of the stem final as secondary and identifies the stem with *hak-* 'put on, wear (a sword)' (see e.g. Ono et al. 1974).

8. A further candidate for this relationship is the *-na* of *kata-na* 'sword' (lit. 'single blade'; cf. *moro-ha* 'double-edged sword') and *na-g-* (*nagi-taos-*) 'mow down' (Omodaka et al. 1967:193, 512). Two cases in which the verb is obsolete are *kase* 'fetter', *kase-g-* 'support, fix in place' (see Ono et al. 1974) and *kase* 'bobbin, reel', *kase-g-* 'wind (spun thread) on a bobbin'.

9. Matsumoto (2016:494) flags the stems of (26b) and (26c) as displaying "no contrast in transitivity", but, whatever their semantic overlap, the fact that the former, but not the latter, assigns accusative case is sufficient to guarantee the contrast in question.

and (26c) was 'straddle (i/t) a horse', the meaning of -g- in (26b) *mata-g-* can be unified with the meaning 'make typical use of a tool'. Just as the shoulder or neck can be seen as a tool that can be used for carrying or transport, that is, the crotch can be seen as a tool that can be used for mounting and riding a horse or other animal.

The meaning of -g- in (17) and (22)–(26) is thus quite specific. It is also inherently transitive. Under the DM proposal that transitivizing suffixes are v_c and intransitivizing suffixes are v_i, then, -g- will be a realization of v_c. Indeed, the -g- in question would be a realization of v_c even under the narrowest interpretation of that proposal, argued above to be too restrictive, under which it applies only to suffixes that create exclusively stems of a specific transitivity.

In contemporary Tokyo Japanese, the most transparent examples of suffixal -g-, semantically and phonologically, are (17b) *tuna-g-* 'tie together' and (26b) *mata-g-* 'step over', followed, perhaps, by (22b) *to-g-* 'whet'. In all three of these cases, an intransitive stem is derived from the transitive stem in -g- by means of the suffix -ar-, one of the canonical or core suffixes discussed in Section 3.3.2. Since, under the DM interpretation of transitivizing and intransitivizing suffixes, -ar- will be a realization of v_i, the stem *tuna-g-ar-* will have the structure $[[[R]v_c]v_i]$, where "R" represents a root. (27) below reproduces the first three items of (17) and displays the structures assigned to them under the DM interpretation of suffixes (in (27a), little n is a nominalizer required under DM assumptions to derive a noun stem from a root). The structures of (27) apply to the corresponding items of the isoradical sets (22) and (26) as well.

(27) a. tuna $[[R]n]$ 'rope'
      b. tuna-g- $[[R]v_c]$ 'tie together, tie up'
      c. tuna-g-ar- $[[[R]v_c]v_i]$ 'get connected'

Given that v_c and v_i are taken to be causative and inchoative heads, however, the interpretation of the representation $[[[R]v_c]v_i]$ poses a problem for the idea that suffixes such as -g- and -ar- realize syntactic elements and that the stem *tuna-g-ar-* is thus a syntactic construction. If $[[[R]v_c]v_i]$ is constructed in the syntax, we will expect it to be interpreted compositionally, with the meaning of v_i combining with the result of composing the meaning of v_c with that of the root. In fact, there is no trace of a causative interpretation in stems like *tuna-g-ar-*; informally speaking, the inchoative interpretation of v_i cancels or overrides the causative interpretation of v_c rather than combining with it compositionally. Nor, of course, is there any trace of an external argument in structures involving *tuna-g-ar-*, in spite of the fact that v_c is taken to introduce such an argument. A minimal interpretive contrast with the structure $[[[R]v_c]v_i]$ is provided by the combination of a stem with the

Causative and Passive suffixes — schematically, [[[S]Caus]Pass]. In the latter case, of course, the complex representation is in fact interpreted compositionally, and there is no cancellation of the properties of the inner suffix by those of the outer.

In general, it seems reasonable to assume that compositional interpretation of structures generated by the syntax is automatic, so that there is no way to block the compositional interpretation of a syntactic constituent. If so, the structure $[[[R]v_c]v_i]$ will reach the interpretive interface and receive a compositional interpretation, but that interpretation will have to be discarded because it is not the actual one. Alternatively, the element v_c in the structure $[[[R]v_c]v_i]$ could be deleted in the post-spellout computation to LF or assigned a diacritic that would render it uninterpretable. Any such operation, however, would violate a widely assumed prohibition on "tampering" (Chomsky 2008:138) with previously derived structure. Harley's (2009:321) statement of the relevant principle is that "the analysis and structures proposed for a form must also be contained within the analysis of any structure derived from that form", and Pross (2019:217), citing Harley, calls this the principle of "containment". The hypothesis that $[[[R]v_c]v_i]$ is a syntactic construction thus appears to lead either to a violation of compositionality, in the sense that the predicted compositional interpretation is unusable, or to a violation of containment.

In the remainder of this section, I provide further documentation of the fact that in sequences of two derivational suffixes, the properties of the outer one cancel or override those of the inner, beginning with stems that under the DM interpretation of derivational suffixes will instantiate the configuration $[[[R]v_c]v_i]$, as in (27c). It may be noted at the outset that, far from being an idiosyncratic property of Japanese verbal stem formation, this overriding of the properties of an inner suffix by those of an outer one is entirely typical of derivational morphology, a point to which we will return below.

In addition to cases of $[[[R]v_c]v_i]$ involving transitive stems in -*g*-, there are cases involving transitive stems in -*m*- (and allomorphs thereof). These are illustrated below in the format of (27).

(28) a. tuka   [[R]n]   'hilt, handle' (originally also 'handbreadth')
      b. tuka-m- $[[R]v_c]$ 'grasp' (accusative object)
      c. tuka-m-ar- $[[[R]v_c]v_i]$ 'be captured'; 'hold on to' (dative object)[10]

---

10. The isoradical set of (28) includes *tuka-m-aw-e-* 'capture', which, although it may historically be a compound rather than a derivative (Ono et al. 1974), is a candidate for a trisuffixal stem.

(29) a. haza-ma   [[RR]n]   'gap, interstice' (< hasa-ma (ma 'interval'))
      b. hasa-m-   [[R]v_c]   'insert between'
      c. hasa-m-ar- [[[R]v_c]v_i] 'get caught between'

(30) a. kur-Ø-   [[R]v_c]   'reel in, wind'
      b. kur-um-   [[R]v_c]   'wrap by rolling'
      c. kur-um-ar- [[[R]v_c]v_i] 'be rolled up, wrapped up'[11]

There are also cases of [[[R]v_c]v_i] involving transitive stems in -r-, as we have
already seen in (20) above. (31) repeats (20) in the format of (27), and (32)–(34)
provide further examples, with (34) displaying as well a case involving transitivizing -k-. The element n_a in (33a) forms adjectival nouns, which, like other nouns
(but unlike verbs and adjectives), inflect by means of the copula.

(31) a. nezi   [[R]n]   'screw'
      b. nezi-r-   [[R]v_c]   'twist'
      c. nezi-r-e- [[[R]v_c]v_i] 'get twisted'

(32) a. mak-Ø   [[R]v_c]   'roll up, wind around'
      b. mak-ur-   [[R]v_c]   'roll up, tuck up'
      c. mak-ur-e- [[[R]v_c]v_i] 'get turned up, ride up'

(33) a. kasu-ka   [[R]n_a]   'faint, at the limits of perception'
      b. kasu-r-   [[R]v_c]   'graze (touch lightly in passing)'
      c. kasu-r-e- [[[R]v_c]v_i] 'become faint or discontinuous (printing, writing);
                                     become hoarse (voice)'[12]

(34) a. yabu-k-   [[R]v_c]   'rip (t)'
      b. yabu-r-   [[R]v_c]   'rip (t)'
      c. yabu-r-e- [[[R]v_c]v_i] 'rip (i)'
      d. yabu-k-e- [[[R]v_c]v_i] 'rip (i)'

The stems of (31)–(34) are all in common use in contemporary Japanese; a final
parallel set that is particularly transparent semantically but for which the verb
stems are essentially obsolete is *kubi* 'neck', *kubi-r-* 'strangle', *kubi-r-e-* 'die by hang-
ing oneself'.

---

11. The isoradical set of (30) includes transitive *kur-um-e-* 'lump together' (= (38c) below).
That the root was originally *kuru* is verified by the adverbials *kuru-ri* (*to*) '(turn) around,
(change) suddenly' and *kurukuru* 'round and round (rotation or winding)'.
12. The isoradical set of (33) also includes stems *kasu-m-* 'become hazy, dim' and *kasu-m-e-*
'cloud (the vision of), deceive; skim off, steal'.

Differing from (28)–(30) above only in that the suffix that occurs outside of -*m*- in the (c) item is not -*(a)r*- but adjectival -*(a)si*-, naturally interpreted as the realization of a stative little a (Marantz 2013:103), are the sets (35)–(36).

(35) a. uto- $[[R]a]$ 'distant, ill-informed'
      b. uto-m- $[[R]v_c]$ 'shun, ostracize'
      c. uto-m-asi- $[[[R]v_c]a]$ 'unpleasant, repugnant'

(36) a. nozo-k- $[[R]v_c]$ 'peer into; be partially visible' (= (8b))
      b. nozo-m- $[[R]v_c]$ 'hope for, expect'
      c. nozo-m-asi- $[[[R]v_c]a]$ 'desirable, to be hoped for'[13]

The (c) examples of (35) and (36) thus have in common with those of (27)–(34) that their structure contains a "trapped" v_c, a causative little v whose causative interpretation and external argument fail to surface. v_c may also be trapped by another v_c, as illustrated by the (c) items of (37) and (38).

(37) a. tuna $[[R]n]$ 'rope' (= 27a))
      b. tuna-g- $[[R]v_c]$ 'tie together, tie up' (= 27b))
      c. tuna-g-e- $[[[R]v_c]v_c]$ 'connect (t)'

(38) a. kur-Ø- $[[R]v_c]$ 'reel in, wind' (= (30a))
      b. kur-um- $[[R]v_c]$ 'wrap by rolling' (= (30b))
      c. kur-um-e- $[[[R]v_c]v_c]$ 'lump together'

In spite of being assigned under DM assumptions a structure that would seem to entail an iterated "causative of a causative" interpretation, that is, (37c) and (38c) are simple causatives, entirely parallel to stems that have only a single transitivizing suffix.

In the same way that the causative interpretation of v_c is trapped in the structures $[[[R]v_c]v_i]$, $[[[R]v_c]a]$, and $[[[R]v_c]v_c]$, the inchoative interpretation of v_i will be trapped in the structures $[[[R]v_i]v_i]$, $[[[R]v_i]a]$, and $[[[R]v_i]v_c]$. The first of those structures appears to be exemplified by the (c) items of (39) and (40).

(39) a. yasu-raka $[[R]n_a]$ 'quiet, peaceful'
      b. yasu-m- $[[R]v_i]$ 'rest'
      c. yasu-m-ar- $[[[R]v_i]v_i]$ 'feel rested, relax'

---

13. Having both transitive and intransitive uses, *nozo-k*- and *nozo-m*- raise the question of polysemy versus homophony and, under a DM interpretation, the issue of the choice between (21a) and (21b) above. In the present context, the important fact about (36c) is that it is based transparently on a transitive (use of) *nozo-m*-.

(40) a. yuru-   [[R]a]   'slack'
      b. yuru-m-   [[R]v_i]   'slacken (i)'
      c. yuru-m-ar-   [[[R]v_i]v_i]   'slacken (i)'

It must be remembered, however, that the isoradical set (12) has shown that the -*mar*- of R-*mar*- (R a stative root, typically coinciding with an adjective stem) may be a unitary suffix even when a stem R-*m*- also exists. (39) and (40) must therefore be judged to be only equivocal evidence for [[[R]v_i]v_i], although we will see below an example of that structure in which the two intransitivizers are clearly separate suffixes.

The (c) items of (41) and (42) are stems that under DM assumptions will have the structure [[[R]v_i]a] (in (42c), -*azi*- is an uncommon variant of -*asi*-).

(41) a. isa-giyo-   [[RR]a]   'gallant, righteous' (kiyo- 'pure')
      b. isa-m-   [[R]v_i]   'be vigorous, in high spirits'
      c. isa-m-asi-   [[[R]v_i]a]   'brave, valiant, gallant'

(42) a. mutu-goto   [[RR]n]   'intimate words' (koto 'word')
      b. mutu-m-   [[R]v_i]   'be on friendly terms with'
      c. mutu-m-azi- [[[R]v_i]a]   'friendly, intimate, harmonious (relations)'

The structure [[[R]v_i]v_c], finally, is illustrated by the (c) items of (43) and (44), where (43b)–(43c) show a suffix -*(a)g*-, seen in (4) above, that is distinct from the transitivizing -*g*- meaning 'apply (tool) to an appropriate object'.

(43) a. yawara-ka-   [[R]n_a/a]   'soft'
      b. yawara-g-   [[R]v_i]   'soften (i)' (= (4b))
      c. yawara-g-e- [[[R]v_i]v_c]   'soften (t)'

(44) a. hiso-ka   [[R]n_a]   'stealthy, secret'
      b. hiso-m-   [[R]v_i]   'be hidden, lurk'
      c. hiso-m-e-   [[[R]v_i]v_c]   'conceal, mask'

It may be noted that the configuration [[[R]v_i]v_c] would be consistent with compositional interpretation of suffix sequences if causative v_c were taken to select v_iP rather than √P — that is, if causatives were analyzed as involving an inchoative layer of structure.[14] We will return briefly to this possibility below.

---

14. If category-determining elements are identified with phase heads (Marantz 2007), lexical causatives, being monophasal, will necessarily be root-based, excluding this analysis. Harley (2008: 42–44), similarly, argues against it on the grounds that it will render impossible an account of well-known distinctions between lexical and syntactic causatives.

All six double-suffix structures just reviewed illustrate the problem identified above for the idea that Japanese transitivity suffixes are syntactic elements, namely that the members of a suffix sequence combine semantically by cancellation rather than by composition: only the properties of the outer suffix are manifested, the inner suffix being interpretatively inert. If compositional interpretation of structures generated by the syntactic computational system is automatic, as suggested above, and if syntactic computation is characterized by a principle of containment or a "no tampering" principle that disallows alterations of structures once built, this result appears to show that the claim that the suffixes in question are the syntactic elements v_i and v_c will be difficult or impossible to maintain.

3.4.2 Transitivity suffixes under a Voice-little v split

To this point, our discussion of the DM interpretation of Japanese transitivity suffixes has assumed a syntactic representation in which categorization, specification of event type, and introduction of an external argument are all functions of little v. In considering the space of analyses that is opened up by splitting little v into two heads, I will distinguish two parameters. The first is how the three functions just enumerated are distributed between the two heads. If we assume that, in terms of command relations, Head(external argument) ≥ Head(event semantics) ≥ Head(categorization), there will be two possibilities, depending on whether event semantics is associated with the higher or the lower head.[15] It should be added that "associated with" here is intended to be neutral between a conception on which event-type properties are "hardwired" into the morphosyntactic representations of particular functional heads and a conception on which those properties, while localized in particular heads, are the output of a function that also takes root meaning and/or root identity into account (cf. (15c), Oseki 2021: 11). The second parameter is which of the two heads canonical transitivity suffixes like intransitivizing *-(a)r-* and transitivizing *-(a)s-* are taken to realize. These two binary parameters determine four possible accounts of transitivity suffixes, which I will consider in turn below. Throughout, following much earlier literature, I refer to the two heads in question as "Voice" and "little v".

As already noted, under the standard interpretation of the Voice-little v split due to Pylkkänen (2002, 2008), event semantics is associated with little v (or an equivalent head), and the unique function of Voice is introduction of an external argument. Let us ask how this split will affect the argumentation of Section 3.4.1

---

15. I will not discuss the possibility that, as suggested by a juxtaposition of Pylkkänen's (2008: 84–85) (10a) and (11b), there could in fact be three distinct heads between R and T, one for each of the three functions in question.

regarding suffix sequences if we continue to assume that canonical transitivity suffixes realize little v.

We noted above that in the structures $[[[R]v_c]v_i]$, $[[[R]v_c]a]$, and $[[[R]v_c]v_c]$, the causative interpretation and external argument predicted for the stem-internal v_c by the DM analysis are "trapped" and do not surface. If external arguments are introduced by Voice rather than by little v, however, stem-internal v_c will introduce no argument, and only its causative interpretation will be trapped. The Voice-little v split, then, will render the counterfactual consequences of the proposal that transitivizing suffixes represent causative little v less dramatic, but will not eliminate them. In the same way that the three structures listed above will involve a trapped causative interpretation even under the assumption of a Voice-little v split, the three structures $[[[R]v_i]v_i]$, $[[[R]v_i]a]$, and $[[[R]v_i]v_c]$ will involve a trapped inchoative interpretation.

If we retain the standard interpretation of the Voice-little v split but assume that canonical transitivity suffixes realize Voice, the existence of the little v position will make available a way to distinguish "internal" from "external" suffixes structurally: suffixes like *-(a)g-* and *-(a)m-* may be taken as little v, so that a stem like *tuna-g-ar-* 'get connected' will have the structure $[[[R]v]Voi]$.[16] As exponents of little v, internal suffixes will realize the event-type properties of the stem as a whole, but will have no distinctive transitivity affiliation of their own. A minimally different account will take the locus of event-type semantics to be Voi rather than little v, so that the function of little v will be limited to verbalization of the root.[17] Under either of these proposals, the three verb stems based on (the root underlying) *tuna* 'rope' (cf. (27) and (37)), analyzed as in (45) under the assumptions of Section 3.4.1, will have instead the structures of (46), where I use "Voi_t" and "Voi_i" for transitivizing and intransitivizing Voice, abstracting away from the question of whether Voice codes event-type semantics as well as the presence of an external argument.

(45) a. tuna-g- $[[R]v_c]$ 'tie together, tie up'
      b. tuna-g-ar- $[[[R]v_c]v_i]$ 'get connected'
      c. tuna-g-e- $[[[R]v_c]v_c]$ 'connect'

(46) a. tuna-g-Ø- $[[[R]v]Voi_t]$ 'tie together, tie up'
      b. tuna-g-ar- $[[[R]v]Voi_i]$ 'get connected'
      c. tuna-g-e- $[[[R]v]Voi_t]$ 'connect'

---

16. This is the analysis of Oseki (2017, 2021), who assumes that Voi bears a feature [D] coding whether or not it introduces an external argument and that event type, while jointly determined by roots and functional categories, is localized in little v (Oseki 2021: 11–12).

17. Thanks to Kunio Nishiyama (personal communication) for suggesting a treatment of suffixal *-g-* in particular as a transitivity-neutral verbalizer.

Under the parameters identified at the outset of this section, there is one further analytic possibility, namely that event-type semantics is a property of Voi, but that canonical transitivity suffixes occupy little v and are thus pure categorizers. That interpretation I will set aside as unpromising.

Both of the proposals just sketched, that in which event type is a property of little v and that in which it is a property of Voi, have characteristics that could be seen as problematical. The first, in treating canonical transitivity suffixes such as -(a)s- and -(a)r- as the realization of a head that determines the presence or absence of an external argument but is unrelated to event type, abandons the widely held intuition that those suffixes at least typically code the distinction between causative and inchoative events. Correspondingly, in stems with suffix sequences, it is the inner suffix that will realize the head with eventive properties: -g- will be the exponent of an inchoative head in *tuna-g-ar-* 'get connected', but the exponent of a causative head in *tuna-g-e-* 'connect'. The second proposal, in treating little v and its instantiations such as -(a)g- and -(a)m- as pure verbalizers, introduces a novel type of suffix whose postulation could be viewed as questionable on grounds of ontological parsimony. To see this, note that under that treatment, the combination of *tuna-* and -g- as shown in (46a) is claimed to be verbal, but at the same time has no event-type properties and is incapable, without further suffixation, of undergoing verbal inflection. This seems paradoxical, however: it is unclear what content "verbal" might have in the absence of eventive properties and the ability to inflect like a verb. We will see another analysis that raises this issue in Chapter 9.

There are other problems that the two proposals in question share. The denial of distinctive transitivity properties to internal suffixes is in prima facie conflict with our observations concerning the -g- of (17) and (22)–(26), for which we documented a specific, inherently transitive meaning. Further, the thesis that verbal derivational suffixes are divided into those that realize Voi and those that realize little v will necessitate a number of arbitrary decisions, in particular as regards suffixal -r-. If only intransitivizing -r- can be Voi, for example, the -r- of *nao-r-* 'recover' (cf. *nao-s-* 'cure') will be Voi, while the -r- of *nezi-r-* 'twist (t)' (cf. *nezi-r-e-* 'get twisted') will be little v; the -r- of *sibu-r-* will be Voi when that stem means 'falter' but not when it means 'avoid' or alternatively, perhaps, will be Voi in neither case because of its semantic flexibility. It is not clear that there is any natural, nonstipulatory answer to dilemmas of this sort.

The reason that the introduction of a distinction between Voi and little v will not solve the problems for a syntactic account of transitivity suffixes identified in Section 3.4.1 even if all noncanonical suffixes are relegated to the status of simple categorizers, however, is that the problem of "trapped" interpretations that fail to surface arises within the set of canonical transitivity suffixes as well, in particular with regard to -*(a)r*- and -*(a)s*-. Consider first the partial isoradical set (47), which can be taken as suggesting that the division between internal and external suffixes itself is less than watertight.

(47) a.   aka-   'red'
      b.   aka-r-i   '(a) light'
      c.   aka-r-am-   'redden (i), blush'
      d.   aka-r-am-e-   'redden (t)'

The root *aka*- is the base for a number of derivatives that cluster around the meanings 'red' and 'light, bright'. The verb stem *aka-r*- 'become red/light', attested up to 1600, is obsolete, but is preserved in (47b), a lexicalization of that verb's Adverbial form; the transitive pendant *aka-s*- 'spend (the night); reveal' of *aka-r*- remains current, along with its lexicalized Adverbial *aka-s-i* 'proof'. (47c) appears to represent the result of suffixing -*(a)m*- to *aka-r*- and thus to be an example, if an isolated one, of an "internal" suffix occurring outside an "external" suffix. Under the DM analysis of Section 3.4.1, (47c) will involve a sequence of two v_i, but there will be no plausible analysis for that stem in any system where intransitivizing -*(a)r*- is Voi and -*(a)m*- is little v, assuming that Voi is higher than little v. (47d), finally, attests to the existence of trisuffixal stems.[18]

The occurrence of -*(a)r*- inside transitivizing -*(a)s*- is illustrated in (48), where transitive *na-r-as*- is formed by suffixation of -*as*- to intransitive *na-r*-.

(48) a.   na-k-   'make characteristic sound' (animal); 'weep' (human)
      b.   na-r-   'sound (i)' (inanimate subject)
      c.   na-r-as-   'sound (t)'

The history of the set (48) involves an Old Japanese transitive stem *na-s*- (see e.g. Omodaka et al. 1967: 522) that subsequently was totally supplanted by *na-r-as*-. A parallel case in which the replacement in question is not complete in all modern dialects (see the NKD entry for *he-s*-) is shown in (49).

(49) a.   he-r-   'decrease (i)'
      b.   he-s-   'decrease (t)' (dialectal)
      c.   he-r-as-   'decrease (t)'

(50)–(53) display further examples of -*(a)r-as*- sequences. The first three items of (50) duplicate (22) above; (50d) is a clear example of a trisuffixal stem.

---

18. It should be noted that, diachronically, the sequence *ra* of (47c) and (47d) may well be the adjectival noun formant seen in e.g. *mida-ra* 'lewd' (cf. *mida-re*- 'get disordered', *mida-s*- 'make disordered') and preserved after *aka*- in *akara-gao* 'ruddy face' (*kao* 'face').

(50) a. to(-isi)   'whetstone'
      b. to-g-   'whet'
      c. to-g-ar-   'become pointed'
      d. to-g-ar-as-   'sharpen'

(51) a. kumo   'cloud'
      b. kumo-r-   'cloud up, fog up (i)'
      c. kumo-r-as-   'cloud up, fog up (t)'

(52) a. pikapika   'shining'
      b. hika-r-   'shine (i)'
      c. hika-r-as-   'shine (t), polish'

(53) a. subesube   'smooth'
      b. sube-r-   'slide, slip'
      c. sube-r-as-   'cause to slide'

(53), like (48) and (49), is a case in which historically, a stem of the shape R-*s*- has been replaced by one of the shape R-*r-as*-: *sube-s*- is the original transitive corresponding to *sube-r*-, attested from the 10th to the 13th century in the meaning 'slip off (a garment)'.

The status of the *s*-stems of (50)–(53) requires comment. As we will see in detail in Chapter 4, there is a strong tendency for stem-final -*as*- to be replaced by -*ase*-, where the latter coincides with the C-stem alternant of the syntactic Causative suffix. Even when this change is substantially complete, however, the short variant -*as*- is preserved in certain contexts, notably before Causative -*(s)ase*-. Thus, for example, the productive Causative of (50d) is *to-g-ar-as-ase*- 'cause to sharpen', as in the following example.[19]

(54) ... B wa, ... E ni biniiru-gasa nana, hati-hon o   koonyuu s-ase-ta   ue,
      B TOP   E DAT plastic-umbr. seven, eight-CL ACC purchase do-CAUS-PF top,
      ta   no sinzya ni kasa   no kanagu bubun no   sentan o
      other GEN follower DAT umbr. GEN metal   part GEN tip   ACC
      togaras-ase-ta.
      sharpen-CAUS-PF

---

19. (54) comes from the text of a decision of the Tokyo Regional Court in the case of a member of the cult Aum Shinrikyo charged in connection with the Tokyo subway sarin attack of March, 1995. The text of a related decision has a closely parallel passage (see bit.ly/3wbzLfu, bit.ly /3QKtnW5). Category names follow the Leipzig Glossing Rules with the abbreviations PRF → PF and CLF → CL.

'B, having had E buy seven or eight plastic umbrellas, had other followers sharpen the tip of the metal section (of each of them).'

Crucially, the fact that *togaras-* is subject to productive causativization guarantees, under the principle that iteration of syntactic *-(s)ase-* is impossible, that that stem's *-as-* is a lexical suffix and not the short version *-(s)as-* of *-(s)ase-* (both the constraint against stacked causatives and the allomorphy of *-(s)ase-* will be discussed in Chapter 4). The responses of native speaker consultants indicate that, given appropriate contexts, the (c) examples of (51)–(53) are, likewise, subject to productive causativization.

The stems in *-(a)r-as-* of (48)–(53), then, illustrate that two "external" suffixes can occur in sequence, and in particular that speakers find nothing unnatural about adding transitivizing *-as-* to intransitivizing *-(a)r-*. Stems of this sort, with the structure $[[[R]Voi_i]Voi_t]$ under any proposal that external suffixes realize Voi, might be taken to involve a compositionally interpreted suffix sequence if the DM-internal arguments against an inchoative layer in causatives referred to in note 14 were set aside. In order to maintain consistency of structure, however, transitive stems of the apparent shape $[[R]Voi_t]$ would then be taken to involve zero inchoative elements, so that *nao-s-* 'cure', for example, would include an inchoativizer distinct from the one that actually occurs with the root in question, namely the *-r-* of *nao-r-* 'recover'. This does not seem like a natural or attractive proposal. From the perspective developed above, the upshot of the side-by-side existence of *na-r-as-* type transitives and *nao-s-* type transitives is that, as noted throughout Section 3.4, an internal suffix is simply irrelevant to the event type and argument structure of a stem. This point is made with particular clarity by (50d) *to-g-ar-as-* 'sharpen', in which *-g-* first creates a transitive stem *to-g-* from a noun (or the root that underlies it), *-ar-* then flips the transitivity of that stem, deriving from it the intransitive *to-g-ar-*, and *-as-*, finally, flips the transitivity value again, deriving the transitive *to-g-ar-as-*.

If there were any suffix we might expect not to occur in the internal position of a suffix sequence, it would probably be *-(a)s-*. (55), however, makes it clear that this expectation is not realized.

(55) a. aw-   'come together, meet, match (i)'
      b. aw-ase-   'bring/put together, match (t)'
      c. aw-as-ar-   'come/fit together (i)'

Whereas (55a) *aw-* and (55b) *aw-ase-* date from Old Japanese, (55c) *aw-as-ar-* is a recent innovation; all three citations of the stem in the NKD are from the 20th century. The creation of *aw-as-ar-* may have rested on sporadic reanalysis of *aw-ase-* as *aw-as-e-*; on the other hand, as we will see in Chapter 4, there is a variant *aw-as-* of *aw-ase-* that would obviate the need to appeal to such a reanalysis. A third possibility is that *aw-as-ar-* owes its existence to proportional analogy (e.g. *atumeru*: *atumaru* :: *awaseru*: X) operating on unsegmented word forms — without regard, that is, for morphological constituency. In any case, however, there is no question but that (55c) displays a suffix sequence *-as-ar-* and thus instantiates the structure [[[R]Voi$_t$]Voi$_i$] under the assumptions of the present section. (56) is a parallel set, with (56c) *kabu-s-ar-* attested from the late 17th century.

(56) a. kabu-r-   'put on (headwear); take (burden) upon oneself'
      b. kabu-se-   'put (headwear) on another; place (burden) upon another'
      c. kabu-s-ar-   'cover (i), lie over; (burden) fall on'

While (55c) and (56c) occur frequently in the contemporary language, (57c) is much rarer, to the point of being absent from most dictionaries.

(57) a. tur-   'hang (t), suspend'
      b. tur-us-   'hang (t), suspend'
      c. tur-us-ar-   'hang (i), be suspended'

The NKD, however, has two citations for (57c), one from the 18th century, one from the 20th. Like (55c) and (56c), then, (57c) illustrates that there is no restriction against sequences of transitivizing -(V)s- plus intransitivizing -ar-.

In Section 3.4.1, I argued that the violations of containment displayed by sequences of transitivity suffixes militate against interpreting them as syntactic objects — in particular, as realizations of causative and inchoative little v, as proposed by Harley (2008) and Marantz (2013). Informally speaking, we saw that, under that interpretation, the properties of the outer member of a suffix sequence cancel or override the properties of the inner one rather than composing with them, so that the latter properties are "trapped" and fail to find expression. In the present section, we have seen that that argumentation is not substantially affected by the postulation of a second verbal head between the root and the tense element. In particular, it became clear that it is not possible to avoid the conclusions of Section 3.4.1 by treating one subset of transitivity suffixes as pure verbalizers and attributing event-type and/or argument-structure properties only to the remainder. This is because even intransitivizing -(a)r- and transitivizing -(a)s-, prototypical examples of suffixes taken under DM assumptions to realize heads having event-type and/or argument-structure properties, may occur as internal suffixes and must thus be subject to cancellation. In sum, the conclusions of Section 3.4.2 reinforce those Section 3.4.1: the cancellation of the properties of an earlier suffix by those of a later one, a phenomenon we observed occurring twice within a single stem in *to-g-ar-as-* 'sharpen', renders Japanese derivational morphology an unlikely candidate for treatment in terms of natural language syntax, given the principle of containment or prohibition against tampering that is widely understood to characterize the latter.

3.5   Another case of root-specific suffix orders

The rough division of verbal derivational suffixes into "internal" and "external" groups imposes constraints on the order in which suffixes appear: suffixes such as -(a)g- and -(a)m-, for example, do not in principle appear outside suffixes such as -(a)s- and intransitivizing -(a)r-, although we saw an apparent exception to this generalization in (47c). The fact that suffix sequences are interpreted non-compositionally, with the properties of the outer suffix overriding those of the inner, however, generates the prediction that for two suffixes whose order is not determined by position class, it should not matter what order they occur in with respect to a given root. In fact, we have just seen evidence that this prediction is borne out for -(a)s- and intransitivizing -(a)r-: while those two suffixes attach directly to a root in *modo-r-/modo-s-* 'return (i/t)', *na-r-as-* 'sound (t)' is built on *na-r-* 'sound (i)', while *aw-as-ar-* 'fit together (i)' is built on *aw-as(e)-* 'put together'. This section documents another case of two suffixes whose order is not restricted by position class and is consequently a function of the individual root.

As has already been illustrated above (see (35)–(36) and (41)–(42)), many Japanese roots support both a verb stem in -(a)m- and an adjective stem formed with the suffix -(a)si-. While adjective stems in -(a)si- are not treated in the DM literature on Japanese derivation, that suffix, as suggested in connection with (35)–(36), has a natural DM analysis as a category-determining little a, where the latter is a stative counterpart of inchoative v_i and causative v_c. (58)–(59) illustrate roots to which both of these suffixes attach directly.

(58)   a.   suzu-si-   'cool, refreshing' (= (9b))
      b.   suzu-m-   'cool off, refresh oneself'

(59)   a.   kuy-i-   'regret'
      b.   kuy-asi-   'causing chagrin, regret' (= (9a))
      c.   kuy-am-   'regret; lament'

There are a number of roots supporting both stems in -(a)m- and stems in -(a)si-, however, for which the former is derived from the latter. This is illustrated in (60)–(61), where (60d) is a trisuffixal stem.

(60)   a.   kuru-w-   'go mad'
      b.   kuru-si-   'painful, uncomfortable, difficult'

    c.   kuru-si-m-   'suffer'

    d.   kuru-si-m-e-   'torment'

(61) a.   kan-e-   'be unable' (as V_2 in $V_1 V_2$ compound)

     b.   kan-asi   'sad, lamentable'

     c.   kan-asi-m-   'grieve, sorrow'

And there are roots for which, in contrast, the verb stem in -*(a)m*- serves as the base for derivation of the adjective stem in -*(a)si*-. (62) and (63), like (41) and (42), involve intransitive *m*-stems.[20]

(62) a.   ita-   'painful' (= (15a))

     b.   ita-m-   'be painful; get damaged' (= (3b), (15b))

     c.   ita-m-asi-   'pitiable, pathetic'

(63) a.   nay-e-   'weaken (i)'

     b.   nay-am-   'worry, be troubled'

     c.   nay-am-asi- 'worrisome, troublesome'

Finally, there is at least one root for which both the verb stem in -*(a)m*- and the adjective stem in -*(a)si*- contain both suffixes, in the opposite order in the two cases:

(64) a.   tutu-m-asi- 'modest, unpretentious'

     b.   tutu-si-m- 'be cautious regarding; abstain from'

    It would appear that all four patterns of suffixation illustrated in (58)–(64) constitute equivalent methods of forming isoradical verb-adjective pairs. This could only be the case, however, if, as in the examples of Section 3.4, the properties of a stem are determined exclusively by the outer member of a sequence of suffixes: if the inner member of a suffix sequence contributed to the interpretation of the whole, we would expect verbs of the form [[R]*m*] and verbs of the form [[[R]*si*]*m*], as well as adjectives of the form [[R]*si*] and adjectives of the form [[[R]*m*]*asi*], to differ systematically in meaning, contrary to fact. The occurrence of root-specific suffix orders like those documented in this section, then, can be considered a diagnostic for noncompositional interpretation of suffix sequences, with the concomitant implication that the suffixes in question cannot plausibly be viewed as syntactic elements. It should be noted that, as in the above examples,

---

20. For an English parallel to the three types (58)–(59), (60)–(61), and (62)–(63), consider *ambigu-ous/ambigu-ity* and *credul-ous/credul-ity, lumin-ous/lumin-os-ity* and *curi-ous/curi-os-ity*, and *ubiqu-ity/ubiqu-it-ous* and *duplic-ity/duplic-it-ous*.

stems of the form [[[R]si]m] and [[[R]m]asi] do typically inherit some of their meaning from the inner stems [[R]si] and [[R]m], respectively. These inherited meanings, however, are neither properties of the inner suffixes nor predictable consequences of the concatenation of those suffixes with roots, but rather idiosyncratic properties of the lexical items [[R]si] or [[R]m], parallel to the meaning 'make into a government-owned/operated business' that is idiosyncratic in *nationalize* (contrast *national*), but which is then inherited by *nationalization*.

3.6   The meaning of "intransitive" morphology

Independent of the properties of suffix sequences that have been our focus above, the interpretation of transitivity morphology in a number of cases calls into question the DM position (as in Harley 2008: 40) that transitivizing and intransitivizing suffixes realize fixed causative and inchoative meanings. As will become clear in this section, the syntactic and semantic difference between intransitivizing and transitivizing morphology is in the general case relative rather than absolute, and I will argue that this fact poses a problem for a syntactic account of the morphology in question. The relative nature of suffix semantics is illustrated by a comparison of (65) and (66).

(65) a. uk-ar-   'pass (exam), be admitted to (school)'
      b. uk-e-   'receive; undergo; take (exam), apply to (school)'

(66) a. azuk-ar- 'take on deposit, take custody of'
      b. azuk-e- 'deposit, place in someone's custody'

In (65), the morphological contrast R-*ar*-: R-*e*- codes the distinction between an unaccusative and a transitive with the basic meaning 'receive'. In (66), on the other hand, the same morphological contrast codes the distinction between a transitive with the basic meaning 'receive' and a transitive with the basic meaning 'give'. The morphologically intransitive *azuk-ar-*, we may note, has all the attributes of a transitive stem, including an agentive external argument and the ability to assign accusative case.

   If the difference between intransitivizing and transitivizing morphology is in the general case relative, and if in particular stems with intransitivizing morphology are not reliably inchoative, how should the meaning of the suffixes in question be understood? One possibility is suggested by a closer examination of the stems of (66). While both of those stems are transitive, there is reason to believe that they have distinct argument structures. In particular, while (66a) is a simple transitive, taking an agent and a patient/theme, (66b) appears to take in addition a goal argument marked by *ni*, rendering it ditransitive. Parallel to (66) in this respect is the pair (67).

(67) a.   ka-ri- 'borrow' (Western Japanese ka-r-)
      b.   ka-s- 'lend'

(68)–(69) represent a slightly different kind of transitive/ditransitive pair, one in which the verb with intransitive morphology represents the same action as the verb with transitive morphology, but carried out reflexively rather than vis-a-vis an independent goal argument (the verbs of (69) are limited in application to clothes that go on the torso, as opposed to the feet or lower body).

(68) a.   kabu-r-   'put on (headwear)' (= (56a))
      b.   kabu-se- 'put (headwear) on another' (= (56b))

(69) a.   ki-Ø-   'put on (clothes)'
      b.   ki-se-   'put (clothes) on another'

Using as diagnostic tests the ability to launch a floating numeral quantifier and the ability to appear (with and without an accompanying particle) in the focus position of a cleft sentence, Sadakane and Koizumi (1995: 11–12) argue that the *ni*-marked objects of donatory verbs such *ag-e-* 'give' are grammatical arguments and not postpositional phrases. I will take this conclusion to apply to (66b) *azuk-e-* and (67b) *ka-s-* and assume that it extends to "vestitory" verbs such as (68b) *kabu-se-* and (69b) *ki-se-*.[21] If so, both pairs of verbs might be taken to suggest that what unites inchoative/causative pairs and transitive/ditransitive pairs is that the stem with transitivizing morphology has one more argument than the stem with intransitivizing morphology.

An alternative account of the difference between intransitivizing and transitivizing morphology with the potential to cover both inchoative/causative and transitive/ditransitive pairs is offered by the gradient concept of transitivity proposed by Hopper and Thompson (1980). Hopper and Thompson (1980: 252) identify ten parameters of transitivity along which clauses may differ and show that they covary in a wide range of languages. Some of the parameters are binary (telic/atelic, affirmative/negative, realis/irrealis); others are explicitly or implicitly

---

21. Regarding the former test, it should be noted that it was originally taken as uncontroversial that quantifier float from the *ni*-marked goal argument of a donatory verb is impossible (see Shibatani 1977: 798); substantial numbers of speakers appear to share this opinion (Sadakane and Koizumi 1995: 30 (note 9)). I have recorded the same judgment from speakers born in the 1990s, and have furthermore been unable to find any naturally occurring examples of the construction.

scalar (agency or potency, affectedness and individuation of the object). For each of those parameters, a clause displaying a positive or higher value may be said to exhibit a greater degree of transitivity than a clause displaying a negative or lower value. Among Hopper and Thompson's parameters, level of agency and individuation of the object are clearly relevant to the above examples: in view of the greater degree of control that the giver ordinarily exercises compared to the receiver in a donatory situation, the agents of the (b) examples of (66) and (67) exhibit a higher level of agency than the agents of the corresponding (a) examples, and the (b) examples of (68) and (69) differ from the corresponding (a) examples precisely in differentiating the goal argument or indirect object from the agent.

Regardless of the way the difference between intransitivizing and transitivizing morphology is conceptualized, however, the fact that that difference is in the general case relative speaks in favor of lexical listing rather than syntactic derivation for the stems that display that morphology. Because crossreference between listed items is uncontroversially possible, it will be straightforward to capture the relationships we have seen in this section if stems are listed in the lexicon. If stems are derived in the syntax from combinations of roots and functional elements like v_i and v_c, on the other hand, capturing the generalization that a suffix like -(a)r- may realize v_c just in case the root it attaches to also underlies a stem with an additional argument or a greater degree of transitivity will require crossreference not between distinct listed items but between distinct derivations, clearly an undesirable consequence. If so, the semantic properties of "intransitive" morphology provide an argument against the syntactic generation of stems that is independent of the argument based on the interpretation of suffix sequences that was developed in Sections 3.4 and 3.5.

3.7   The instability of stem meaning

It was suggested in Section 3.4.1 that compositional interpretation of structures generated by the syntax is automatic, so that there is no way to block the compositional interpretation of a syntactic constituent. If so, no instance of a syntactically generated structure can idiosyncratically fail to display the compositional semantic interpretation associated with that structure. As a result, a phrase like *kick the bucket* that is demonstrably generated by the syntax will automatically have the compositional interpretation predicted by its lexical items and its syntactic structure, independently of whether it has one or more listed interpretations as well. As a diachronic corollary, we can infer that loss of the compositional interpretation of a syntactically generated constituent is not a possible change, assuming that the grammar and the lexicon have remained stable in the relevant respects. Thus, it would not be possible for *kick the bucket* to lose its compositional interpretation over time, retaining only the idiomatic one. When a phrase that was once generated by the syntax does have only a listed interpretation, it is either because the component words have dropped out of the lexicon, as is probably the case for the phrase *to plight one's troth* for most contemporary English speakers, or because the grammar no longer generates phrases of the type in question, as is the case for the phrase *till death do us part*.

What is true for manifestly phrasal constituents is true for inflected forms as well. Lexicalization (i.e. idiomatization) of *guts* in the meaning 'courage' and *balls* in the meaning 'audacity' has no effect on the status of those forms as regular plurals as long as the relevant stems and the rules for forming and interpreting plurals are diachronically stable. In Japanese, many verbal Conjunctive forms in -*te* are lexicalized as adverbs: *sitagatte, yotte* 'consequently' (*sitagaw-* 'obey', *yor-* 'be due to'), *kiwamete, itatte* 'extremely' (*kiwame-* 'reach, carry to extremity', *itar-* 'reach'). As long as the relevant verb stems remain in the lexicon and -*te* remains an inflectional suffix, however, there is no way that these idiomatic meanings can replace the compositional meanings that the forms have by virtue of their inflectional (ultimately, syntactic) status. The same is true of Adverbial forms that have been lexicalized as nouns: *nagasi* 'sink' (*nagas-* 'make flow'), *nagare* 'flow, course of events' (*nagare-* 'flow').[22]

If loss of a compositional interpretation is not a possible semantic change, assuming stability of grammar and lexicon, then demonstrating that the predicted compositional meaning of a putatively syntactic construction is in fact subject to loss over time will support the conclusion that the construction in question is not syntactic after all, since if it were, its compositional meaning should be diachronically stable. In this section, I will make this argument with respect to the Japanese lexical causative in -*(a)s-*, documenting several cases in which the construction [R[(a)s]] can be shown to have had the predicted interpretation CAUS(‖R‖) (‖R‖ the interpretation of R) originally, but later to have lost that interpretation in spite of the fact that ‖R‖ itself has remained constant.

As a first example, consider the stem *yurus-* 'allow, forgive'. In Old Japanese (see Omodaka et al. 1967), the primary meaning of this stem is 'slacken (t)', with secondary meanings 'let go of'; 'allow, comply with, tolerate'; and 'forgive,

---

22. The semantics of these nouns has been treated in the DM literature since Volpe 2005 as involving selection of root allosemes by a noun-forming suffix ("special meanings of the root triggered across the little *v* head" (Marantz 2013: 107)). The extreme semantic distance that separates many of the nouns from their corresponding verbs, however, renders implausible attribution of the nominal meanings to the respective roots (cf. Kiparsky 2020: 43). Nor is there any need to postulate a nominalizing suffix homophonous with Adverbial -*i* (Harley 2008: 50 (note 23)), any more than there is to postulate a derivational suffix /z/ deriving lexicalized *guts* and *balls*.

exempt'. *yurus-*, in other words, is historically the causative in *-(a)s-* on √yuru 'slack' (see (40) above), a root that in modern Japanese underlies the adjective stem *yuru-* 'slack', the adjectival noun *yuru-yaka* 'slack, gradual', and the verb stems *yuru-m-* 'slacken (i)' and *yuru-m-e-* 'slacken (t)'. As is clear from these four stems, the root has been completely stable semantically over thirteen centuries, and the same can be assumed for causative *-(a)s-*. In the modern language, however, the main remnants of the original primary meaning 'slacken' for *yurus-* are two lexicalized phrases (see the NKD) in which that verb denotes a psychological process of relaxation, *ki o yurus-* 'let down one's guard' (*ki* 'mind') and *kokoro o yurus-* 'come to trust' (*kokoro* 'heart'). In the lexical entry of the verb itself, in other words, the primary meaning appears to have been completely replaced by originally secondary or extended meanings, notably 'allow' and 'forgive'. If *yuru-s-* had been a syntactic construction, with the meaning 'slacken (t)' the compositional result of a semantic rule of interpretation, this replacement should have been impossible, just as we have suggested that it would be impossible for *kick the bucket* to lose its compositional meaning and retain only the idiomatic one.

A parallel case is *itas-*, which in Old Japanese is the causative corresponding to *itar-* 'reach a limit' and thus means 'bring to a limit' (Omodaka et al. 1967). In the modern language, while intransitive *itar-* has retained its original meaning, *itas-*, bleached of concrete content, is a suppletive humble variant of *se-/si-/su-/s-* 'do'. Two phrases in which *itas-* might appear to have other meanings, *hutoku o itasu tokoro* 'is my fault' and *omoi o itasu* 'direct one's thoughts', like the idioms involving *yurus-* just noted, have dedicated entries in the NKD (first attestations 1875 and 1945, respectively), indicating that the meanings in question are not part of the lexical entry of *itas-* itself. Like *yurus-*, then, *itas-* is a case in which the predicted interpretation CAUS(‖R‖) of the construction [R[(a)s]] has been lost from the lexical entry in question over time in spite of the fact that the meaning of the relevant root, as shown in each case by one or more isoradical stems, has remained constant.

In this section, we have seen an argument against the syntactic derivation of Japanese verb stems based on semantic change, using two causatives in *-(a)s-* as evidence. It goes without saying that perhaps the most common type of semantic change, the addition of idiomatic or extended meanings, does not count against the hypothesis of syntactic generation: as is well known, linguistic units of any size can be idiomatized, with the tendency to undergo idiomatization inversely proportional, roughly speaking, to length (Di Sciullo and Williams 1987:14). But loss of a putatively compositional meaning, I have claimed, does count against syntactic generation, because there is no reason to take the compositional interpretation of syntactic structure to be anything but automatic and exceptionless. In order for a compositional meaning M to be lost, the syntactic structure underlying it would first have to be exempted from compositional interpretation, with M being lexicalized at the same time; M could then be lost from the lexicon. If this sequence of events is impossible because exemptions of the required type are never granted, however, a putatively compositional meaning that is in fact subject to loss cannot have been based on a syntactic derivation in the first place.

3.8 Derivation, inflection, and featural override

In the preceding sections, we have examined the derivational suffixes displayed by morphologically complex Japanese verb (and adjective) stems. We have seen that the properties of the outer suffix of a sequence override the properties of the inner, that suffix order can be root-specific, that suffix meaning is in the general case relative rather than fixed, and that root-suffix combinations can be semantically unstable over time.

On all four of these points, inflection presents a sharp contrast with derivation. First, sequences of inflectional suffixes are interpreted compositionally, as was illustrated with (5) *utaw-ase-rare-na-i* 'will not be made to sing' in Chapter 1. Second, there are no stem-specific orders of inflectional suffixes. Thus, in contrast to the variable order of intransitivizing *-(a)r-* and transitivizing *-(a)s-* that we observed in (48c) *na-r-as-* 'sound (t)' versus (55c) *aw-as-ar-* 'come/fit together (i)', Passive *-(r)are-* and Causative *-(s)ase-* occur in the order *-(s)ase-rare-* for all stems; as was observed in note 4 of Chapter 1, when the opposite order is exceptionally permitted, it is with the expected compositional interpretation 'cause to be V-ed' (*nagur-are-sase-* 'allow (him) to be punched'). Third, while it was argued that "intransitive" morphology, rather than realizing a fixed inchoative meaning, conveys that the stem it forms is "less transitive" than some other stem formed on the same root, inflectional suffixes never have meanings that are relativized in this way. Finally, while inflectionally derived forms, wordforms and stems alike, may be lexicalized (i.e. idiomatized), they are not subject to loss of their compositional meaning in the way we documented for stems like *yuru-s-* 'forgive' as long as the elements composing them remain in the lexicon and are semantically stable. Thus *nom-are-*, the Passive of *nom-* 'drink', is lexicalized in the meaning 'be overwhelmed, overawed', but it retains as a matter of course its predicted meaning 'be drunk' as well.

Perhaps the most fundamental of the four differences between inflection and derivation just reviewed is the contrast between what I have referred to above as combination by composition and combination by cancellation. It is important to ask whether the noncompositional interaction that we have observed in sequences of Japanese derivational suffixes should be understood as an idiosyncratic property of those suffixes or whether, on the other hand, it is part of a more general phenomenon. In fact, it is not difficult to show that the phenomenon of a suffix overriding or cancelling properties of its base is not confined to the Japanese examples we have examined, but is entirely typical of derivational morphology.

To begin with, much derivation results in a change of lexical category, with concomitant cancellation not only of the lexical category of the base but of any property of the base that is specific to that lexical category. Even derivation that preserves lexical category typically alters identifiable features of the base such as [human] and [abstract]. Thus the -er of *potter, glover, jeweler* creates [+human] nouns from nouns that are [−animate] (and thus [−human]), and the -*hood* of *priesthood, childhood, sisterhood* creates [+abstract] nouns from nouns that are [+human] (and thus [−abstract]). An example involving a morphological feature with no direct semantic interpretation is the German diminutive suffix -*chen*, which creates nouns that are [+neuter] regardless of the gender of their base (Ortmann 1999:102). Scalise (1984:109–113) provides thorough exemplification from Italian that derivation can alter selectional and subcategorizational features in addition to lexical category, inflectional class, and features like [count], [animate], [abstract], and [common]. There are of course derivatives like *untie, unclear, ex-president*, and *smallish*, where there is no obvious conflict between the features of the affix and those of the base and thus no apparent phenomenon of featural override. The principle that whenever a conflict does arise, the features of the affix will prevail over those of the base (whether the latter is monomorphemic or itself the result of affixation) would appear to be exceptionless, however. In this context, the fact that the transitivity status and argument structure of a Japanese verb or adjective stem depends only on the outermost transitivity-determining suffix is exactly what one would expect on the assumption that the suffixes in question are derivational.

Inflection, in contrast, clearly does not typically involve suffixal overriding of features of the base, although the possibility of category-changing inflection must be allowed for (Haspelmath 1996). This fundamental contrast between derivation and inflection with regard to featural override is not often highlighted in the morphological literature,[23] but Lieber 1992:112 contains a very clear (if in part theory-internal) formulation of it (see also Lieber 2004:151):[24]

---

23. For example, I have been able to find no discussion of it in the 2300 pages of the *Oxford encyclopedia of morphology* (Lieber 2020).

24. A categorial signature is a set of morphosyntactic features "that are of syntactic relevance for a particular category in a particular language" (Lieber 1992:88–89).

> In derivational word formation the value for a feature of a head morpheme will supersede or override that of an inner morpheme. Features from inflectional morphemes can never override features from their bases, but can only fill in values unspecified in the categorial signatures of their bases.

In sum, it seems clear that the cancellation of the properties of an inner suffix by an outer one documented above for Japanese transitivity suffixes, rather than being in any way anomalous or unexpected, is the manifestation of a general property of derivational morphology.

3.9   Conclusion: A lexicon of stems

In Section 3.1, it was noted that there have been three main responses to the observations of Chomsky 1970 concerning derivational morphology, the root-based and syntactic account of DM, an account deriving from Jackendoff 1975 according to which most stems are listed and stem-stem relations are captured by redundancy rules, and an account whose central feature is a battery of word-formation (minimally, stem-formation) rules operating internal to the lexicon. In this chapter, I have argued that the derivational morphology of the Japanese verb and adjective cannot plausibly be treated in syntactic terms. Regarding the remaining two possibilities, there are two considerations that appear to favor stem listing over stem generation. The first is that postulation of lexicon-internal stem-formation rules would represent a violation of the "single generative engine" principle, noted in Section 1.2, which I take to be a null hypothesis concerning grammatical organization. The second is that, while the Portuguese and Korean reanalyses to be examined in Section 7.4 make it clear that, as phonological entities, stems must have listed representations, there appears to be no parallel evidence for roots. I will therefore assume that the results of this chapter are best accommodated by assuming a lexicon of stems and a set of redundancy rules defined over them. On this interpretation, knowledge of stem-internal structure, in contrast to knowledge of inflected forms and syntactic structure more generally, is declarative rather than generative.

This conclusion, particularly as it concerns Japanese transitive and intransitive verb stems, has consequences for the status of little v. The original arguments for little v were essentially syntactic in nature, involving the independence of the external argument from the immediate projection of the verb, the desirability of a binary branching analysis for dative and double object constructions, and the implications of binding facts for c-command relations in those constructions. Attribution of causative meaning to little v can be seen as a separate issue, and it is notable that when cross-linguistic data is adduced in support of that attribution (see the French and Chichewa examples in Adger 2003: 132–133), that data appears to represent syntactic constructions, so that it is less than fully clear what implications it has for the analysis of lexical causativity.

It would be possible to maintain that little v is the unique source of causativity in transitive verbs, so that *kill*, for example, has no independent existence, but is simply what results from V-to-v movement after *die* (or *dead*) is selected by little v. Consider now what effect that position would have on our understanding of Japanese *nao-s-* 'cure', given our conclusion that that stem has a listed or lexical representation. In light of the minimal contrast with *nao-r-* 'recover', it seems clear that *-s-* is the locus of causative meaning in *nao-s-*. But if little v is the only source of causativity, that fact will be unexpressible: the form of the suffix, in this case and others, will be part of a lexical stem, but its meaning will be associated with a (phonologically unrealized) syntactic object that resides outside that stem. Taking this to be an unacceptable consequence, I will assume that what is known as lexical causativity inheres in individual lexical stems and lexical suffixes, and that little v is, as far as can be presently ascertained, a purely syntactic object. If so, there will be no little v in unaccusative clauses, as originally assumed (see e.g. Chomsky 1995: 316), and thus no subdivision of little v into causative and inchoative varieties. In conclusion, while the DM interpretation of Japanese transitivity morphology appears to hold out the promise of concrete validation, in the form of overt affixal material, for a project of lexical decomposition in the syntax involving multiple subcomponents of verbal meaning, the account of the Japanese facts presented above suggests that there may in the end turn out to be little morphological support for that project.[25]

3.10   Epilogue: The implications of root-based derivation

Some readers of this chapter may have wondered if they are obliged to accept or "believe in" all the isoradical relations that have been postulated therein. The author's answer is that adoption of a Jackendovian lexicon, in which most stems are listed and relations among them are expressed by redundancy rules, makes it natural to remain agnostic on this question and to speculate that the precise inventory of stem-to-stem relations postulated varies considerably with idiolect. Advocates of a DM approach to derivational morphology are of course free to claim, in parallel fashion, that the precise inventory of roots varies with the speaker. But there remains an asymmetry between the two perspectives arising

---

25. For doubts about the syntactic evidence for lexical decomposition, see Siloni 2019.

from the fact that the basic stance of the Jackendovian approach is that in the unmarked case, stems are listed, while the basic stance of the DM approach is that in the unmarked case, stems are derived from roots in the syntax. Advocates of the latter approach are thus committed in principle to capturing isoradical relations syntactically, and if they wish to deny in particular cases that such relations obtain, they will need a criterion on the basis of which to do so. In concluding the chapter, I would like to suggest that such a criterion may be difficult to come by.

In an irony of juxtaposition, the article preceding Jackendoff's "Morphological and semantic regularities in the lexicon" in the pages of *Language* 51.3 is Theodore Lightner's (1975) "The role of derivational morphology in generative grammar". Lightner's approach to derivational morphology is diametrically opposed to that of Jackendoff and parallel to that of DM in that he is a firm advocate of synchronic root-based derivation. Leading off his article with a long list of English words containing the Proto-Indo-European root *gen- 'beget', including but by no means limited to *kindred, progeny, gonad, cognate*, and *nascent*, he claims "The important point of this example is that if the words listed above are NOT [emphasis in original] all synchronically derived from the same root, one will miss semantic and phonological generalizations right and left." In the absence of a definitive refutation, this argument suggests that once one enters on the path of synchronic root-based derivation, there may be no natural stopping point this side of the relevant protolanguage. Returning to the isoradical relations postulated in this chapter, then, the approach that is until further notice committed to them is not that which claims that stems are lexically listed, but that which claims that they are syntactically derived.

CHAPTER 4

An apparent challenge: Syntactic and lexical causatives

4.1 Introduction

Chapter 3 argued that Japanese transitivity suffixes are not syntactic elements and that the stems that contain them are lexically listed rather than syntactically derived. This conclusion appears to face a challenge from the well-known analysis (Miyagawa 1984, 1989, 1998, 2012) of the causative suffix -(s)ase- as a default form which, in addition to forming semantically regular and productively derived causative stems, can be called upon to form lexical causatives (i.e. ordinary transitives) when no other suffix is available to do so. Miyagawa's analysis, while predating DM, is entirely consistent with the DM position that there is no significant distinction between derivational and inflectional morphology, and it has a natural DM interpretation (Harley 2008: 41–42) in terms of -(s)ase- selecting vP ("high attachment") for syntactic causatives and √P ("low attachment") for lexical causatives. If it were actually the case that causative -(s)ase- could form both syntactic and lexical causatives, that fact would argue for a unified treatment of inflection and derivation in this case and, by implication, more generally.

In fact, it is not difficult to demonstrate that postulation of a causative suffix that spans the inflection/derivation boundary is not unavoidable. This is because the causative formative -ase- that appears to have both syntactic and lexical uses can be shown to represent two suffixes, syntactic -(s)ase- and lexical -(a)se-, that are distinct in both their morphophonological behavior and their phonological form. The morphological and morphophonological facts are thus consistent with the position that no causative suffix is syntactic in some cases and lexical in others, and in particular with the position that there is no "lexical -(s)ase-". In that case, however, Japanese causatives will pose no obstacle to the view that inflectional and derivational morphology are treated in distinct components of the grammar, with inflected forms generated syntactically, but stems that result from derivational processes lexically listed.

The morphological and phonological distinction between syntactic -(s)ase- and lexical -(a)se- is the topic of Section 4.2. In order to validate the implied conclusion that there is no causative suffix that spans the syntactic/lexical boundary, the following sections argue that cases of -ase- that have been identified in the literature as representing lexical -(s)ase- are in fact either lexical -(a)se- or syntactic -(s)ase-. Section 4.3 first discusses the concept of blocking and its interaction with Japanese causatives, arguing that while blocking looms large in treatments of the subject such as Miyagawa 1989 and Harley 2008, it is in the end of marginal relevance to the question of whether lexical -(s)ase- exists. Section 4.4 argues that in one set of cases where -ase- has been taken to be lexical -(s)ase-, -ase- is a diachronic development of lexical -as- and is to be identified as -(a)se-; and that in another, -ase- is indeed -(s)ase-, but is syntactic rather than lexical. Section 4.5 proposes an explanation for the tendency to replace stems in -as- by stems in -ase- documented in Section 4.4, and Section 4.6 reviews the chapter's results, ending with a discussion of how we are to understand formal similarities between derivational and inflectional morphology, in the Japanese case and in general. Section 4.7, finally, summarizes the conclusions of the first four chapters of the book in preparation for the treatment of morphophonological reanalysis that begins in Chapter 5.

4.2   Syntactic -(s)ase-, lexical -(a)se-

4.2.1   Hiatus in derivation and in verbal inflection

The demonstration that syntactic and lexical -ase- are distinct suffixes morphophonologically hinges on the differential treatment of hiatus resulting from derivational suffixation and hiatus resulting from suffixation of verbal inflectional elements. Setting aside instances of hiatus that result from phrase-level deletion of w before nonlow vowels (i u e o) and of y before front vowels (i e), hiatus is in principle disallowed at both types of boundary, but is resolved by distinct processes in the two cases.[1]

Consider first the question of hiatus at derivational boundary. As we saw in examples (1)–(9) of Chapter 3, Japanese verbal and adjectival derivational suffixes other than -e- (and -i-) alternate between an a-initial form after a consonant and a form without the a after a vowel. If, as in DM, stems are syntactically constructed, stem-internal phonology will be generative, with the alternants of derivational suffixes related to each other by phonological rule. In this context, if the longer alternant of each suffix is underlying, hiatus at derivational boundary will be resolved by deletion of suffixal a, as in (1) (below, "a-Deletion").

---

1. The rare cases in which -e- is added to a vowel-final root (mi-e- 'be visible' (cf. mi- 'see'), ko-e- 'cross, exceed' (cf. ko-s- 'cross, overtake'), which result historically from deletion of intervocalic y, show that the prohibition of hiatus at derivational boundary is not absolute.

(1)   a → Ø / V] [___

In a case like *tutu-si-m-* /tutu-asi-am-/ 'be cautious regarding; abstain from' ((64b), Chapter 3), rule (1) will apply at two locations within the same stem, showing that it cannot be characterized as applying at root boundary. If stems created by derivational suffixation are lexically listed, on the other hand, the *a*-zero alternation will be represented by a bidirectional redundancy rule of the form (2).

(2)   aC / C] [___ ↔ C / V] [___

The fact that there are no nonalternating *a*-initial suffixes, captured in the generative account by rule (1), will be the result of the rightward implication of (2); the fact that there are no nonalternating consonant-initial suffixes, captured in the generative account by the fact that suffix URs are all vowel-initial, will be the result of the corresponding leftward implication.

Now consider the question of hiatus in verbal inflection. Japanese verbal inflectional suffixes divide into two groups, those that begin with $t \sim d$ after all stems, and those that alternate between a consonant-initial form (or zero) after vowel-final stems and a vowel-initial form after consonant-final stems. No hiatus can result from addition of suffixes of the first group, but if the underlying forms of the suffixes of the second group are vowel-initial, hiatus will be occasioned by the combination of those suffixes with vowel-final stems. I will provisionally adopt here the analysis of the second group of suffixes to be argued for in Chapter 5, namely that their underlying or default forms are indeed vowel-initial, and that the regular strategy for resolving the hiatus that results from their addition to vowel-final stems is epenthesis of *r* at verb stem boundary. Assuming that epenthesis targets a position between stem and suffix, an interpretation that will be argued for in Chapter 7, the rule epenthesizing *r* may be written as in (3).

(3)   Ø → r / V $_{Vb}$] ___ [V

While *a*-Deletion, which operates stem-internally, will be a rule of the stem-level phonology, *r*-Epenthesis, which operates within combinations of stem and inflectional suffix, will belong to the word-level phonology.

4.2.2   High/low attachment analyses and the passive and causative suffixes

As we saw in Section 3.3.1, there is an intransitivizing suffix *-(a)re-* that coexists with intransitivizing *-(a)r-*. *-(a)re-* is illustrated in (4)–(5).

(4)   a.   wak-are-   'separate (i)' (cf. wak-e- 'separate (t)')
      b.   sut-are-   'go out of use' (cf. sut-e- 'discard')
      c.   tor-aw-are- 'be caught' (cf. /tor-aw-e-/ 'catch', tor- 'take in the hand')

(5) a. kaku-re- 'hide (i)' (cf. kaku-s- 'hide (t)')
     b. kobo-re- 'spill (i)' (cf. kobo-s- 'spill (t)')
     c. tao-re-   'fall over' (cf. tao-s- 'push over')

The postconsonantal alternant -*are*- of this suffix is identical to the postconsonantal alternant of the passive suffix -*(r)are*-. Furthermore, we have suggested that this postconsonantal form coincides with the underlying or lexical representation of the suffix in both cases, assuming a generative account of the *a*-zero alternation. Finally, while derivational -*are*- and passive -*are*- are morphophonologically distinct, the first undergoing *a*-Deletion and the second undergoing *r*-Epenthesis, this difference, in accordance with the observations of Section 4.2.1, is naturally seen as following from the distinction between stem-level and word-level phonology. In sum, the phonology of derivational -*are*- and passive -*are*- is consistent with treating those two suffixes as low attachment and high attachment versions of the same element, the first taking √P as a complement (except insofar as it attaches to a suffixed root, as in (4c)), the second taking vP.

Just as intransitivizing -*(a)r*- is paired with -*(a)re*-, transitivizing -*(a)s*- coexists with -*(a)se*-, again as seen in Section 3.3.1. Consider first the postconsonantal alternant -*ase*- of -*(a)se*-, illustrated in (6) (where (6b) reprises (55b), Chapter 3).

(6) a. okur-ase- 'delay' (cf. okur-e- 'be late')
     b. aw-ase-   'bring/put together, match (t)' (cf. aw- 'match (i))
     c. sir-ase- 'inform' (cf. sir- 'know')

In (6a), -*ase*- must be a derivational or lexical suffix because *okur*- is a root and not an inflectable stem, and inflectional suffixes attach only to stems. The lexical status of -*ase*- in the two remaining examples of (6) is generally held to be established by the ban on successive occurrences of syntactic -*(s)ase*- (Martin 1975:288, Kuroda 1993:8–10, Miyagawa 2012:198) that was referred to in Section 3.4.2 together with the fact that *aw-ase-sase*- 'cause to match (t)' and *sir-ase-sase*- 'cause to inform' are unproblematically acceptable (Kuroda 1993:23–24); we will return to the restriction on double -*(s)ase*- at several points below.

While one might imagine that lexical causative -*ase*- in (6) could be an instantiation of syntactic -*(s)ase*-, there are compelling reasons to doubt this proposition. If -*(s)ase*- could occur as a lexical suffix, we would expect to find lexical stems of the form X*V-sase*-, parallel to the stems of the form X*C-ase*- seen in (6). Searches of electronic dictionaries, however, yield no such verb stems, strongly suggesting that they do not exist.[2] Further, diachronic considerations make it clear

---

2. The headwords ending in the string *saseru* in the NKD are those of (a) -*sase*- itself, (b) the causative *s-ase*- of 'do', (c) four idiomatic phrases ending in (a) or (b) that have been lexicalized as units, and (d) two frozen and/or archaic expressions (smaller dictionaries show only (a) and (b)).

why this is the expected result: absent from Old Japanese (8th century), -*sase*-
is first attested in texts of the 10th century (Yamaguchi and Akimoto 2001: 899,
284–285) as the postvocalic alternant of the innovative causative suffix -*ase*- that
replaced earlier -*asime*- (Frellesvig 2010: 236–237), and has always been exclusively an inflectional suffix (in traditional Japanese grammar, an auxiliary verb).
Another phenomenon we would expect to observe if lexical -*sase*- existed is felici-
tous sequences of the form -*sase-sase*- (or -*sas-ase*-, with the alternant -(s)*as*- of the
syntactic causative suffix that is treated in Section 4.5 below), parallel to the examples of -*ase-sase*- that were cited in the last paragraph. To the best of my ability
to determine, however, such sequences are not attested.[3] In place of lexical -*sase*-,
what we do find, as predicted by the existence of lexical -*ase*- and the *a*-Deletion
rule (1) or its equivalent (2), is a postvocalic lexical causative suffix -*se*-, already
observed in (68b) and (69b), Chapter 3:

(7) a. no-se-   'place on; publish' (cf. no-r- 'get on, ride; be published')
     b. yo-se-   'bring near' (cf. yo-r- 'come near')
     c. kabu-se-   'put (headwear) on another' (cf. kabu-r- 'put on (headwear)')
     d. mi-se-   'show' (cf. mi- 'see')
     e. ni-se-   'model on' (cf. ni- 'resemble')
     f. ki-se-   'put (clothes) on another' (cf. ki- 'put on (clothes)')
     g. abi-se-   'pour over another' (cf. abi- 'pour over oneself')

It seems clear, then, that the postvocalic alternant of lexical causative -*ase*- is not
-*sase*-, but -*se*-, so that the lexical suffix has the form -(*a*)*se*-, in contrast with syntactic -(s)*ase*-. Indeed, any attempt to deny this proposition would require one to
explain why -*ase*-, alone among derivational suffixes, should be exempt from
a-Deletion; why -*se*-, alone among postvocalic derivational suffix alternants, should
have no *a*-initial postconsonantal counterpart; and why lexical -*sase*- is unattested.

We saw above that, given the stem-level rule of *a*-Deletion and the word-level
rule of *r*-Epenthesis, the fact that derivational -(*a*)*re*- ((4)–(5) above) and passive
-(*r*)*are*- coincide postconsonantally as -*are*- appeared to give a green light, at least
phonologically, to a low attachment versus high attachment analysis whereby both
suffixes would have the phonological form /are/. In this way, assuming a syntactic
treatment of derivational morphology, as in DM, derivational -(*a*)*re*- and passive
-(*r*)*are*- could be the same syntactic element even though they alternate differently.

---

3. Miyagawa (2012: 198–199) presents an example with *i-sase-sase-ta* 'made (X) make (Y)
remain' and argues that the ban on double (syntactic) -(s)*ase*- entails that the first -*sase*- thereof
must be lexical. The native speakers I have consulted about this example, however, find it anomalous. If that judgment is reliable, *i-sase*- (as suggested by its compositional semantics) is not
lexicalized, and *i-sase-sase*- is a violation of the double -(s)*ase*- ban.

Crucially, this kind of analysis cannot be extended to lexical causative *-(a)se-* and syntactic causative *-(s)ase-* in spite of the fact that the two suffixes coincide post-consonantally as *-ase-*. The reason is that not only are lexical and syntactic *-ase-* morphophonologically distinct (pace Harley 2008:36) in undergoing different alternations, the different morphophonological behavior they display cannot be attributed to the grammar. Rather, they must have distinct phonological representations, either in the lexicon or, in a DM analysis, in the vocabulary (exponent) list.

Specifically, because syntactic *-ase-* alternates with *-sase-* after a vowel, and because that alternation is morpheme-specific, the form *-sase-* must be recorded in the phonological representation of the suffix. On the analysis to be argued for in Chapter 5, *-ase-* will be the default form of the syntactic causative, and *-sase-* will appear in the suffix's lexical representation with a restriction limiting it to the postvocalic environment; the two alternants will thus be collapsible with angled brackets as <s>ase</V__>. On an alternate analysis (as in e.g. McCawley 1968), *-sase-* will be the unique UR of the suffix, and *-ase-* will be the result of a rule deleting the second of two consonants at verb stem boundary (although *t*-initial suffixes will have to be excluded in one way or another from the domain of that rule). While the form *-sase-* (and in particular its initial *s*) must thus be part of the phonological representation of the syntactic causative suffix regardless of how the *s*-zero alternation of that suffix is analyzed, it clearly cannot be part of the phonological representation of lexical *-(a)se-*. *-(a)se-* and *-(s)ase-*, then, are not potentially collapsible in the way that *-(a)re-* and *-(r)are-* might be held to be, and are irreducibly distinct suffixes.

Having established that there are distinct syntactic and lexical causative suffixes, *-(s)ase-* and *-(a)se-*, that coincide postconsonantally as *-ase-*, one might propose regarding the set of all instances of *-ase-* that, regardless of precisely which are syntactic and which are lexical, the syntactic instances may be assumed to be *-(s)ase-* and the lexical instances *-(a)se-*. It would then follow that no causative suffix has both syntactic and lexical uses, and the claim that the facts of Japanese causatives are consistent with the position that inflectional but not derivational morphology is syntactic could be seen as having been established. In view of the large number of instances of *-ase-* that have been taken (Miyagawa 1989, Harley 2008) to represent lexical use of *-(s)ase-* and thus to counterexemplify these claims, however, concluding the discussion at this point would be unsatisfying. Section 4.4 below will therefore investigate cases of putative lexical *-(s)ase-*, arguing, as indicated above, that they are in fact either lexical *-(a)se-* or syntactic *-(s)ase-*. There is one topic, however, that it will be useful to treat in advance of the consideration of putative lexical *-(s)ase-*. This is blocking, a concept that plays a central role in the argumentation of Miyagawa and Harley concerning Japanese causatives, and which is taken up in Section 4.3.

4.3   An introduction to blocking and causatives

In the most general terms, blocking is the preemption of a default by a special case, or of a rule-governed pattern by a lexically listed item. The most straightforward kind of example is illustrated by the various mechanisms for forming the English past tense, among them suppletion (*go/went*), vowel change (*give/gave*), the *t*-suffix (*bend/bent*), and the default suffix /d/. As Embick and Marantz (2008: 2) note, this case involves competition only at the level of the morpheme: while the various exponents of the past tense compete with each other, word-level **gived* does not compete with *gave*, for example, but simply fails to be generated by the grammar.

Ideally, all blocking could be assimilated to the morpheme-level variety just illustrated; this is in fact the project that Embick and Marantz (2008) pursue. Superficially, however, there are many cases of blocking that appear to involve units larger than the morpheme. Apparent competition between word-sized units, for example, is illustrated by the case with which Aronoff (1976: 43ff.) brought blocking to the attention of the linguistic community, that involving suffixation of nominal *-ity* to adjectives in *-ous*. Drawing from Aronoff's examples, *-ity* may be suffixed to *curious* (*curiosity*), but not to *furious* (**furiosity*), and this difference in suffixability correlates inversely with the availability of an unsuffixed abstract noun (**cury, fury*). The existence of *fury*, in other words, seems to block the derivation of **furiosity* from *furious*. It should be noted that the ability of *fury* to block **furiosity* is presumably dependent on the predicted synonymy of the two expressions; it is because **furiosity* would not mean anything except what *fury* does, that is, that blocking is observed (contrast the case of *pomp*, which does not block *pomposity*).

The claims of Miyagawa and Harley about blocking in Japanese causatives involve both morpheme-level and stem-level blocking. Consider first the former. Harley (2008: 40) presents the relation of transitivizing suffixes like *-s-* or *-as-*, on the one hand, and causative *-(s)ase-*, on the other, as entirely parallel to the relation of English irregular past tense formations and the default suffix /d/, as introduced above: *-(s)ase-* is the default realization of a root-selecting morpheme Harley calls v_{CAUS} and is preempted in that role by a suffix like *-s-*, which is subcategorized to attach to the roots that appear on an associated list. While this account will not cover cases in which transitivizers are added to derived stems, I will set that issue aside for present purposes. The hypothesis of *-(s)ase-* as a default transitivizer can be stated as in (8).

(8) a.   *-(s)ase-* attaches to root R if R is selected by no other transitivizer.
     b.   *-(s)ase-* does not attach to root R if R is selected by some other transitivizer.

If R_1 is selected by no other transitivizer and R_2 is selected by some other transitivizer, then, R_1-*(s)ase*- will be licensed under (8a), and *R_2-*(s)ase*- will be blocked
under (8b). With regard to (8a), Section 4.4 will argue that, as already indicated
in Section 4.2.2, there is in fact no reason to believe that -*(s)ase*- ever attaches
to roots: the postvocalic allomorph -*sase*- in particular is exclusively inflectional,
and thus attaches only to stems. If this is correct, so that (8a) is not instantiated,
the hypothesis of blocking under (8b) will be rendered vacuous, since it would
make no sense to say that a phenomenon not attested in the first place is subject
to case-by-case blocking. Section 4.4 will also show that many putative examples
of root-selecting -*(s)ase*- fail even on their own terms, given (8): in cases where
-*ase*- is an innovative variant of the transitivizer -*as*-, the latter should block -*ase*-
under (8b) if -*ase*- does indeed represent -*(s)ase*-.

Turning now to the question of stem-level blocking, it is crucial, in discussing
the claims that have been made in this area, to distinguish the various senses of
causation that can be expressed by Japanese causatives, lexical and syntactic. At
least the following five causation types, illustrated here by English examples, can
be identified:

(9) a. manipulative   Sue stopped Jim. (i.e. by physically intervening)
     b. directive   Sue had Jim stop. (i.e. by directing him to do so)
     c. inducive   Sue got Jim to stop. (e.g. by promising him a reward if he
                           did)
     d. permissive   Sue let Jim stop. (i.e. gave him explicit permission to do so)
     e. noninterventive   Sue let Jim stop. (i.e. failed to intervene to prevent his
                           doing so)

All five causation types of (9) assume an agentive causer as the causative subject.
As a result, when the causative subject is a nonagentive cause, either an inanimate
or an animate (typically human) acting inadvertently, the contrast among the
types of (9) is neutralized in favor of a single impersonal causation type. (9b) and
(9d) require an animate (typically human) causee, but this is not the case for the
other three causation types, as will be illustrated below.

Consider now the question of whether there is any blocking relationship
between the transitive member of a transitive-intransitive pair and the causative
of the intransitive member, between *tom-e-* 'stop (t)', for example, and *tom-ar-
ase-* 'cause to stop (i)'. It is well known (see e.g. Shibatani 1976:31–38, Jacobsen
2017:86–89) that for many such pairs, the transitive stem and the causative of
the intransitive display a rough complementary distribution by causation type,
with the transitive stem expressing manipulative causation and the intransitive +
causative expressing other causation types, notably directive causation. In such

cases, while the existence of the transitive stem affects the range of interpretations that can be assigned to the intransitive + causative combination, there is no blocking. When the intransitive takes only an inanimate subject, as with *wak-* 'boil (i)', it has been claimed (Miyagawa 1989:140) that a related transitive (here, *wak-as-* 'boil (t)') does block the intransitive + causative combination (*wak-ase-* 'cause to boil'). However, while *wak-ase-* is indeed incapable of expressing manipulative causation, and while directive and permissive causation are precluded by the inanimate causee, Kuroda (1993:44) points out that *wak-ase-* can express noninterventive causation ('let the water (continue to) boil'), and Chung and Shibatani (2018:142–145) note further that it can express inducive causation ('get the water to boil') as well. In the end, then, this kind of case is not distinct from that of *tom-e-* 'stop (t)' and *tom-ar-ase-* 'cause to stop (i)': a lexical transitive tends to monopolize manipulative causation, but leaves other causation types open for expression by an intransitive + causative combination.

Consider finally the case in which a lexical transitive stem occurs in an idiom. I take as an example the idiom *hakusya o kak-e-* 'spur on, accelerate (t)' (*hakusya* 'spur', *kak-e-* 'bring into action'). *kak-e-* 'bring into action' has an isoradical intransitive counterpart *kak-ar-* 'come into action', and that stem appears in an intransitive correlate of the idiom *hakusya o kak-e-*, namely *hakusya ga kak-ar-* 'accelerate (i)'. If we now ask whether, as claimed by Miyagawa (1989:126), the transitive idiom *hakusya o kak-e-* blocks the causative of the intransitive idiom, which would be **hakusya o kak-ar-ase-*, the answer is that it plausibly does. Relevant here is the fact that the subject of *hakusya o kak-e-* is typically inanimate, so that the contrast among the causation types of (9) will be neutralized, as indicated above. Even when the subject is agentive, however, the object will represent an existing process or tendency, and no contrast among causation types will be possible. There will thus be no opportunity for a division of labor between transitive *hakusya o kak-e-* and intransitive + causative **hakusya o kak-ar-ase-*. Just as *fury* is capable of blocking **furiosity* because it means everything that **furiosity* would, that is, *hakusya o kak-e-* is capable of blocking **hakusya o kak-ar-ase-* because it fully covers the predicted semantic range of the latter.

The blocking of the causative of an intransitive idiom by a corresponding transitive idiom is not an inviolable principle. For example, the transitive idiom *hara o her-as-* 'wait for a meal, get hungry' does not block the causative *hara o her-ase-* 'id.' of the corresponding intransitive idiom *hara ga her-* 'get hungry' (lit. 'belly runs low'); we will return to this example in Section 4.4.4. It is also the case that the causative of an intransitive idiom cannot cogently be claimed to be blocked by a corresponding transitive idiom when the intransitive idiom itself is not attested. Consider for example *te no hira o kaes-* 'change one's attitude abruptly' (lit. 'turn over the flat of one's hand'), for which Miyagawa (1998:69) notes the ungrammaticality of the potential alternate form *te no hira o kae-r-ase-*, based on the syntactic causative of the intransitive stem *kae-r-* that corresponds to transitive *kae-s-*. While it might appear that *te no hira o kaes-* blocks *te no hira o kae-r-ase-*, that appearance would be illusory. To support a judgment that a form F is blocked, it is not enough to (a) show that F fails to occur and (b) display a plausible blocker for F; there must in addition be a presumption that F *should* occur — reason to believe, that is, that there is some grammatical process that would be expected to generate it. The claim that *furiosity* is blocked by *fury*, for example, rests on data suggesting that, in the absence of *fury*, *furiosity* would be produced from *furious* by the relevant word-formation rule. In a case like *te no hira o kae-r-ase-*, in contrast, there is no reason to expect that form to exist in the first place, given the lack of an intransitive idiom *te no hira ga kae-r-*. If so, there are no grounds for saying that it is blocked.

In the present context, however, the crucial fact about the apparent blocking effect seen in an example like *hakusya o kak-ar-ase-* is that that effect has no bearing on hypothesis (8), even setting aside the fact that (8) presupposes suffixation to roots. The reason is that, while that hypothesis claims that the appearance of *-(s)ase-* as a lexical transitivizer will be blocked by a distinct lexical transitivizer, the *-ase-* of *hakusya o kak-ar-ase-* would be an instance of syntactic *-(s)ase-* if it did occur, like the *-ase-* of unblocked *hara o her-ase-* 'wait for a meal, get hungry' and in accordance with the principle, introduced immediately below, that *-ase-* is syntactic when suffixed to an intransitive stem that has a distinct isoradical transitive counterpart. The nonoccurrence of *hakusya o kak-ar-ase-*, then, is not a case of blocking under (8b), and the blocking effect it does illustrate, while apparently genuine, has nothing to tell us about the question of whether *-(s)ase-* functions as a default lexical transitivizer.

4.4   Reinterpreting "lexical *-(s)ase-*"

4.4.1   Distinguishing lexical and syntactic *-ase-*

In setting out to show that cases of *-ase-* that have been identified in the literature as lexical *-(s)ase-* are naturally interpreted either as lexical *-(a)se-* or as syntactic *-(s)ase-*, it is important to be clear about what criteria are available for distinguishing between lexical and syntactic occurrences of the suffix allomorph in question. Consider first morphological criteria. We have noted that the *-ase-* of (6a) *okur-ase-* 'delay' is necessarily lexical because it attaches to a root that is not also a stem. It is less straightforward to determine the status of *-ase-* when it attaches to a stem, particularly when the stem is intransitive. This is illustrated by the case of *kusa-r-ase-* 'cause to rot, discourage' (*kusa-r-* 'rot, become discouraged'; *kusa-* 'malodorous').[4] Dictionaries agree in recording a stem *kusaras-* in the relevant meaning, but, as we will see below, corpus evidence makes it clear that *kusaras-* has been entirely replaced in the contemporary language by *kusarase-*. This would suggest that there is a lexical entry *kusarase-*, where *-ase-*, as in the examples of (6) above, is a lexical transitivizer. On the other hand, dictionary entries typically gloss *kusaras-* simply as '*kusaru yoo ni suru, kusaraseru*', suggesting that the semantics of *kusarase-* may be entirely compositional. In that case, *kusarase-* could be analyzed as involving syntactic *-ase-*, and no lexical entry of that form would be necessary. For concreteness, I will follow the intuitions of the lexicographers and assume that a lexicalized stem exists in such cases, but nothing in the argumentation below will depend on that assumption. I will further assume that an instance of *-ase-* suffixed to an intransitive stem that has a distinct isoradical transitive counterpart is syntactic, as in a case like *ag-ar-ase-* 'cause to rise' (*ag-ar-* 'rise', *ag-e-* 'raise').

With regard to nonmorphological criteria for the distinction between lexical and syntactic *-ase-*, I have already noted the double causative test, which will be appealed to and discussed in Sections 4.4.3 and 4.4.5. I will also argue that cases of *-ase-* that have replaced earlier *-as-* (i.e. *-(a)s-*) represent lexical *-(a)se-*, and that, on the other hand, *-ase-* represents syntactic *-(s)ase-* when the interpretation of X-*ase-* is compositional, even if X itself is an idiomatic expression.

4.4.2   The putative complementarity of *-ase-* and other transitivizers

We saw in Section 4.3 that Miyagawa (1989, 1998) and Harley (1995, 2008) claim that *-(s)ase-* is a default transitivizer, called into service when no other transitivizer is lexically specified for a given root. Correspondingly, those authors place great emphasis on the apparent complementarity between *-ase-* and other transitivizers. Thus, taking appearance in idioms as a diagnostic of lexical status, Miyagawa (1998: 69–70) says, "if a V_{intr}-*(s)ase* has a corresponding and competing transitive verb stem, the causative verb does not participate in idiomatization, but if no transitive stem exists, the causative verb is available for idiomatization."

---

4. It has been claimed (Miyagawa 1989: 129, Harley 2008: 32) that the availability of an adversity interpretation (Oehrle and Nishio 1981) for *kusarase-* implies that the *-ase-* of that form is lexical. It is not clear why this implication should hold, however: as Oehrle and Nishio (1981: 167–168) make clear, adversity readings, like manipulative causative readings, occur only with lexical causative stems when those exist (e.g. with *otos-* 'drop (t)' but not with *otisase-* 'cause to drop (i)'), but are available to syntactic causatives when there is no isoradical transitive stem. Indeed, Oehrle and Nishio (1981: 167) state explicitly that the *-ase-* of adversity *kusar-ase-* is syntactic.

Similarly, Harley (2008: 33) claims (italics in the original) that "*Only intransitive roots with no other transitive form can behave lexically with* -sase." These formulations raise a number of questions. One is whether appearance in idioms is actually diagnostic of lexical status; it will be argued below that it is not. Another is whether an arbitrary instance of -*ase*- can be assumed to instantiate -*(s)ase*-; the existence of -*(a)se*- means that it cannot. A third, raised for idioms in particular by the co-occurrence of *hara o her-as*- and *hara o her-ase*- 'go hungry', is whether the claimed complementarity actually obtains.

There is a more general problem, however, with the idea that -*ase*- is in complementary distribution with other transitivizers. This is that lexical -*ase*- turns out to occur only in cases where lexical -*as*- is also a possibility, with the stem in -*as*- the historically prior form in all but a handful of cases.[5] Far from never facing competition from another transitivizer, then, lexical -*ase*- always faces competition from (typically preexisting) -*as*-. Section 4.4.3 documents the variation between -*as*- and -*ase*- for representative verb stems, looking at the relative strength of the two variants in the Balanced Corpus of Contemporary Written Japanese (below, BCCWJ; see reference list for link) and sketching the history of variation to the extent that it is reconstructible from the entries of the NKD.[6] Section 4.4.4 then introduces possessor-raising causatives, which show that syntactic -*(s)ase*- may be a purely formal element devoid of semantic effect and illustrate the fact that -*(s)ase*- may embed an idiomatic verb phrase, appearing as a result in a transitive idiom. Section 4.4.5 extends this line of inquiry by examining putative lexical -*(s)ase*- in a range of VP idioms, arguing that those instances that are not syntactic -*(s)ase*- are lexical -*(a)se*-.

---

5. Miyagawa (1984 [2012]: 184–185) treats this -*as*- as -*(s)as*-, a "morphological variant" of -*(s)ase*-; on this interpretation, see Section 4.4.3.

6. The BCCWJ has been accessed using the Chunagon search tool. Chunagon supports searches by lexeme and inflected form, but the associated dictionary omits some lexemes of interest here (e.g. *niow-ase*- 'hint at' (see immediately below)), and the associated morphological parser is not entirely dependable (most instances of *niow-ase*- 'hint at' are parsed as (productive) Causatives of *niow*- 'smell', but some are treated as Imperatives, Provisionals, or Realis forms (*Izenkei*) of the variant *niow-as*- 'hint at'). I have therefore conducted only searches of character strings. As representative inflected forms, I have employed the Conclusive in -*(r)u*, the Perfect in -*ta*, and the Conjunctive in -*te*. Comparison of lexeme-based and character-based searches suggests that tokens of those three categories constitute the great majority of any verb's inflected forms in the corpus, taking an inflected form to be one in which the stem is followed by an ending rather than a stem-forming suffix (as in Negatives, Passives, and Causatives) or another stem (as in compounds).

4.4.3   Verb stems: Lexical -ase- as a historical development of -as-

Of the three examples of lexical -ase- cited in (6) above, aw-ase- and sir-ase-
are attested in Old Japanese and thus predate the consolidation of the innovative
inflectional causative suffix -(s)ase- (see Frellesvig 2010: 63). The third example,
okur-ase- 'delay', however, has an entirely different history. For this stem, the NKD
records only the form okur-as-, making it clear that -ase- in okur-ase- is a relatively recent replacement for -as-. At the same time, the BCCWJ has a scant 10
instances of okur-as- (4%) over the three forms Conclusive, Perfect, and Conjunctive (below, "the forms C/P/C") as against 271 for okur-ase- (96%), showing
that this replacement is essentially complete. Since the -as- of okur-as- represents
the suffix -(a)s- of (2), Chapter 3, and the -ase- of okur-ase- the -(a)se- of (6)–(7)
above, this is a case of the diachronic substitution of -(a)se- for -(a)s-; -(s)ase-,
clearly, is not involved.

An example of lexical -ase- whose history can be sketched in a bit more detail
is niow-ase- 'hint at' (cf. niow- 'smell (i)'), for which citations in the NKD begin
in 1799. In the same meaning, however, niow-as- occurs as early as The Tale of
Genji, around the year 1000. It is evident, then, that niow-as- represents the original shape of the stem, and that variation with niow-ase- dates back only about
two hundred years. Today, niow-ase- is unquestionably the dominant form, but a
degree of variation is still observed: searching both Chinese character and hira-
gana representations of the stem, the BCCWJ contains 17 occurrences of niow-as-
(14%) and 104 of niow-ase- (86%) in the meaning 'hint at' over the forms C/P/C.
niow-ase- 'hint at' is illustrated in the dictionary example (10), and the fact that
it is subject to syntactic causativization, as in (11) (a constructed example), argues
for its lexical status.[7]

(10)   Kare wa gen'eki   intai   o   niowase-ta.
        he   TOP active play retirement ACC hint.at-PF
        'He hinted at retiring from active play.'

(11)   Ka-tyoo   wa bu-tyoo   o   aser-ase-yoo   to   omot-te
        section-chief TOP dept.-chief ACC get.anxious-CAUS-VOL QUOT think-CNJ
        kaname no syain   ni zisyoku   o   niowase-sase-ta.
        linchpin GEN employee DAT resignation ACC hint.at-CAUS-PF
        'The section chief, seeking to rattle the department chief, had a key employee
        hint at resigning.'

---

7. Here and below, category names in glosses follow the Leipzig Glossing Rules with the addition of CNC (Conclusive), CNJ (Conjunctive), and VOL (Volitional) and the abbreviation of PRF
as PF.

Let us take a closer look at the process, still incomplete, as a result of which *-as-* is being replaced by *-ase-* in *niow-as(e)-* 'hint at'. The Japanese of the 11th century will have had a contrast between [[niow] as $_V$] 'hint at' (among other meanings) and [[[niow]$_V$] ase] 'cause to smell, give off a smell', where, with the innermost brackets enclosing a root, the labeled bracket $_V$] marks the right edge of a lexical verb stem, so that an occurrence of *ase* outside that bracket represents syntactic *-(s)ase-*.[8] Starting by 1800, the tendency to replace *-as-* by *-ase-* in [[niow] as $_V$] will have produced variation between [[niow] as $_V$] and [[niow] ase $_V$] in the meaning 'hint at', variation which, as noted above, persists to this day. Even if, at some future date, [[niow] as $_V$] is entirely eliminated in favor of [[niow] ase $_V$], the structural distinction between [[niow] ase $_V$] 'hint at' and [[[niow]$_V$] ase] 'cause to smell' will remain; the latter is illustrated in (12), another dictionary example.

(12) Kanozyo wa itumo koosui   o   honoka-ni niow-ase-te   i-ru.
      She   TOP always perfume ACC   faint-ADV smell-CAUS-CNJ be-CNC
      'She always gives off a faint smell of perfume.'

If the above account is correct, explication of contemporary uses of *niow-ase-* 'hint at' as "literally, 'cause to smell'" (Miyagawa 1989: 124, Harley 2008: 22) is inaccurate: *niow-ase-* 'hint at' and *niow-ase-* 'cause to smell' involve distinct suffixes, *-(a)se-* and *-(s)ase-*, respectively, and distinct structures. Similarly, the impression that "*niow-* 'smell' lacks a simple transitive counterpart" (Miyagawa 1989: 124) is a misapprehension resulting from ongoing replacement of *niow-*'s transitive counterpart [[niow] as $_V$] by [[niow] ase $_V$] and the consequent incipient neutralization of the surface contrast between that stem and the syntactic causative [[[niow]$_V$] ase]. For comparison, in the case of *her-* 'decrease (i)', *her-as-* 'decrease (t)', *her-ase-* 'cause to decrease', an otherwise similar example in which replacement of *-as-* by *-ase-* has not taken place, the lexical transitive and the causative of the intransitive remain phonologically distinct.

We have seen that *niow-ase-* 'hint at' arose, apparently around 1800, as a variant of preexisting *niow-as-*. Under the hypothesis, stated in (8b) above, that the existence of a competing transitive stem should block lexical *-(s)ase-* (Miyagawa 1984, 1989, 1998, 2012), this is an unexpected development if, as Miyagawa and Harley assume, *niow-ase-* 'hint at' exemplifies *-(s)ase-*: the lexical causative *niow-as-* should have blocked the emergence of *niow-ase-*.[9] In fact, far from exerting

---

8. The *s*-final variant *-(s)as-* of *-(s)ase-* did not appear until the Muromachi period (1336–1573) and was not widely used until after 1600 (Yamaguchi and Akimoto 2001: 285, 358, 903–904). On this topic, see Section 4.5 below.

9. A parallel case is provided by what appears to be the incipient emergence of *tob-ase-* as a variant of *tob-as-* 'make/let fly' in the idiom L *e tob-as-* 'demote to L' (L a location). Kuroda

a blocking effect, the prior existence of a lexical causative in -as- turns out to be a necessary condition for the appearance of innovative lexical -ase-. Before supporting this claim with additional cases of the diachronic replacement of -as- by -ase-, let us ask if there are alternatives to the above account of the introduction of innovative niow-ase- 'hint at', in particular alternatives that are consistent with Miyagawa's claim that -(s)ase- may function as a lexical suffix just when there is no competing transitive stem and will be blocked by an existing transitivizer.

One possible approach is suggested by Miyagawa's (1984 [2012]: 184–185) treatment of variation between stems in -as- and stems in -ase- for idioms like *hara o her-as(e)-* 'wait for a meal, get hungry'. Miyagawa interprets this as variation between -(s)as- and -(s)ase- and proposes that in such a case, the stem in -(s)ase- is basic, with the stem in -(s)as- constituting a "morphological variant" thereof. The *her-as-* of *hara o her-as-*, in other words, will have the structure [[her] (s)ase $_V$], with the final vowel of -(s)ase- subject, I will assume for present purposes, to an optional rule of deletion. In the same way, one might assign *niow-as-* the structure [[niow] (s)ase $_V$], claiming that from the year 1000 to the year 1800, the rule deleting the final vowel of -(s)ase- applied with 100% reliability. This account, however, preserves the claim that lexical -(s)ase- will be blocked by an existing transitivizer only by recharacterizing the existing transitivizer -as- that threatens to counterexemplify the claim as a variant of -(s)ase-. Further, that recharacterization is unpersuasive: as we have seen above, *a* is the segment that alternates with zero both in lexical -as- and in lexical -ase-, so that there is no basis for the postulated *s* of [[niow] (s)ase $_V$]. Finally, as pointed out in note 8 and explained more fully in Section 4.5 below, the short variant -(s)as- of -(s)ase- did not become prominent until around 1600 and so would not have been available in the year 1000.

Miyagawa (2012: 200) presents a second explanation of the origin of *niow-ase-* 'hint at' in proposing that that verb is the result of "semantic drift" and consequent lexicalization of the homophonous syntactic causative; on this account, 'hint at' would be expected initially to have the structure [[[[niow]$_V$] (s)ase] $_V$], presumably later reanalyzed as [[niow] (s)ase $_V$]. This proposal, however, takes no account of the prior and continued existence of *niow-as-* and therefore provides no explanation for the apparent failure of blocking. Furthermore, while lexicalization of

---

(1993: 59) reports *tob-ase-* as acceptable in his own speech in addition to *tob-as-*, and offers this as a counterexample to Miyagawa's claim that the existence of a lexical causative (here, *tob-as-*) should block idiomatic uses of -ase- (the latter construed as syntactic -(s)ase-). Miyagawa (1998: 95) clearly agrees that this is a potential counterexample, and his only recourse is to question Kuroda's judgment regarding the acceptability of *tob-ase-* in the idiom. One reason that *tob-ase-* 'demote' remains marginal may be that the idiom itself appears to be a relatively recent innovation (first NKD citation 1966).

syntactic causatives is clearly possible (see Section 4.4.5 below), there will be no motivation for it if, as in this case, a lexicalized stem on the same root in the relevant meaning (i.e. *niow-as-*) already exists. In sum, it seems reasonable to conclude that, just as in the case of *okur-ase-* 'delay', the appearance of *niow-ase-* 'hint at' represents diachronic replacement of *-(a)s-* by *-(a)se-*, and that alternative explanations for *niow-ase-* lack plausibility.

Let us turn now to evidence from other verbs for the diachronic tendency in question. First of all, we should note that in the case of *niow-as(e)-*, the historical priority of *-as-* over *-ase-* is particularly clear: lexicalized *niow-ase-* 'hint at' and compositional *niow-ase-* 'give off a smell' are sharply distinct in meaning, so that little uncertainty arises about which is involved in any given case. Further, both *niow-as-* and *niow-ase-* have dictionary entries in the lexicalized meaning, with an eight-century gap between first attestations of the two stems. For other verbs in *-as- ~ -ase-* that are taken by Miyagawa and Harley to represent lexical *-(s)ase-*, the boundary between compositional and lexicalized uses is often less sharp, and the relative chronology of the forms more difficult to ascertain. Nevertheless, the tendency to replace *-as-* with *-ase-* is unmistakable, and apart from the small handful of verbs in *-ase-* that go back to Old Japanese (notably those of (6b) and (6c)), lexical *-ase-* appears always to have this history. Table 1 displays ten representative examples, nine of which are cited as instances of lexical *-(s)ase-* in Miyagawa 1989:124–129; the tenth, *hasir-as(e)-* 'cause to run', is like most of the others in appearing in idioms (*me o hasir-ase-* 'scan with the eyes'). The table records dates of first attestation as per the NKD for the stem in *-as-* and, in the minority of cases where it has a separate entry, the stem in *-ase-* as well (stems in *-ase-* without dictionary entries are bracketed). Finally, frequencies in the BCCWJ over the three forms C/P/C are recorded for each stem.

Apart from *aw-as(e)-* (item 1), there is no stem for which the *-ase-* variant is recorded as predating the *-as-* variant; for the six cases in which the *-ase-* variant has no lexical entry (items 2 and 5–9), we may assume that the failure of the NKD to recognize the stem in *-ase-* effectively eliminates the possibility that that stem is older than its counterpart in *-as-*. The data of Table 1, then, are consistent with the claim that, with a small number of exceptions, lexical *-ase-* arises only as a variant of preexisting *-as-*. It should be noted, however, that the figures of that table do not distinguish lexical from syntactic causatives except in the case of *niow-as(e)-*, where the search results were examined individually and only those representing the lexicalized meaning 'hint at' were tabulated. In Section 4.4.5, in contrast, we will be concerned precisely with the boundary between lexical and syntactic expressions — more specifically, with the question of just what part of an apparent VP idiom is recorded in the lexicon. As background for the argumentation of Section 4.4.5, Section 4.4.4 introduces the phenomenon of possessor-raising causatives.

Table 1. Dates and frequencies of stems in -*as*- ~ -*ase*-

Intr. stem + gloss	Stem in -*as*-	Date	Frequency	Stem in -*ase*-	Date	Frequency
1 aw- 'meet'	aw-as-	1696	176 (1%)	aw-ase-	8th c.	14768 (99%)
2 kagayak- 'gleam'	kagayak-as-	974	51 (12%)	[kagayak-ase-]	–	392 (88%)
3 niow- 'smell (i)'	niow-as-	1001	17 (14%)	niow-ase-	1799	104 (86%)
4 uk- 'surface'	uk-as-	1069	118 (35%)	uk-ase-	1904	217 (65%)
5 sum- 'be clear'	sum-as-	1220	241 (74%)	[sum-ase-]	–	86 (26%)
6 her- 'decrease'	her-as-	17th c.	1803 (99.6%)	[her-ase-]	–	7 (0.4%)[*]
7 kusar- 'rot'	kusar-as-	1615	0 (0%)	[kusar-ase-]	–	41 (100%)
8 hikar- 'shine'	hikar-as-	1681	13 (4%)	[hikar-ase-]	–	280 (96%)
9 hasir- 'run'	hasir-as-	1820	28 (3%)	[hasir-ase-]	–	1018 (97%)
10 kik- 'have effect'	kik-as-	1906	78 (36%)	kik-ase-	1949	139 (64%)

[*] Out of 64 occurrences of *herase*-, 57 were judged to instantiate Potential *her-as-e-* 'can reduce (t)' rather than causative *her-ase*-. The possibility that the Table 1 statistics for other stems of the form X-*ase*- include small numbers of Potentials X-*as-e*- cannot be excluded, although in many cases the low frequency of X-*as*- can be assumed to render that possibility negligible.

4.4.4   Possessor-raising causatives[10]

In a typical causative sentence, there is a clear distinction between causing and caused events, and the causative subject, ordinarily an agent, represents an entity that plays no role in the caused event. In certain cases where Japanese -*(s)ase*- takes an unaccusative clause as its complement, however, the causative subject represents the possessor of the theme argument of the unaccusative clause, and the distinction between causing and caused events is subtle or nonexistent. In illustration, consider the relationship between sentences (13a) and (13b).

(13) a. Tubaki   no   kaori   ga   tadayot-te i-ta.
          camellia GEN fragrance NOM waft-CNJ be-PF
      b. Tubaki   ga   kaori   o   tadayow-ase-te i-ta.
          camellia NOM fragrance ACC waft-CAUS-CNJ be-PF
          'The fragrance of camellias hung in the air.'

In (13a), unaccusative *tadayow*- 'drift, float, waft' takes a theme argument *tubaki no kaori* 'the fragrance of camellias' that receives nominative case; the possessor *tubaki* 'camellias' is assigned genitive case DP-internally. In (13b), where *tadayow*-

---

10. For discussion of Japanese causative sentences (and transitives more generally) in the context of possessor raising, see Hasegawa 2007. For a possessor-raising analysis of one class of Japanese adversity passives, see Kubo 1992: 287–288.

is suffixed with causative *-ase-*, on the other hand, *tubaki* is the nominative subject, and its possessum *kaori* 'fragrance' receives the accusative case that *-ase-* assigns. (14) is a parallel pair of examples.

(14) a. Sakura no ki no hana ga   migoto-ni   sai-te   i-ta.
          cherry GEN tree GEN flower NOM splendid-ADV bloom-CNJ be-PF
      b. Sakura no ki ga migoto-ni hana o   sak-ase-te   i-ta.
          cherry GEN tree NOM splendid-ADV flower ACC bloom-CAUS-CNJ be-PF
          'The cherry tree was blooming splendidly.'

Examples (15) and (16) (adapted from a blog entry and a newspaper article, respectively), where only the causative version is shown, are cases in which causativization in a subordinate clause allows the matrix subject to control the null subject of that clause.

(15) [Gyo-kyoo   no kei-tora]$_i$ ga   [Ø$_i$ hata o   nabik-ase-Ø],   toozyoo
      fishing-co-op GEN light-truck NOM   flag ACC flutter-CAUS-ADV appearance
      si-ta.
      do-PF
      'The light truck of the fishing co-op, its flag fluttering, made its appearance.'
      (lit. 'made its flag flutter and ....')

(16) [Sentoo no   naginata-boko]$_i$ ga   [Ø$_i$ syarin o   kisim-ase-Ø],
      lead   GEN halberd-float   NOM   wheel ACC creak-CAUS-ADV
      sizyou-karasuma o   syuppatu si-ta.
      (placename)   ACC departure do-PF
      'The lead float, its wheels creaking, departed Shijo-karasuma.' (lit. 'made its
      wheels creak and ....')

(13b), (14b), and (15)–(16) exemplify external possession (Payne and Barshi 1999, Deal 2017), the appearance of a possessor outside the DP that contains the possessum. Cases of external possession can be classified according to whether the possessor bears a thematic role, such as affectee, that cannot be attributed to its initial position. If it does bear such a role, there are two thematic positions associated with the possessor, and the relationship between them is analogous to control. If, on the other hand, the possessor displays no additional thematic role as a consequence of its external status, the relationship between its surface position and its initial position is analogous to raising. In the case of (13b), (14b), and (15)–(16), there appears to be no thematic role that the possessor has acquired by virtue of becoming a causative subject, suggesting a raising analysis. In particular, the possessor in those examples is arguably not a cause, the expected thematic role for an inanimate causative subject. To see this, note first that a causative sentence with an inanimate subject and an unaccusative complement clause normally has an unaccusative paraphrase in which the causative subject appears as the complement of *ni yotte* 'as a result of', as illustrated in (17).[11]

(17) a. Hanako no ayamati ga   Taroo o   sin-ase-ta.
        Hanako GEN mistake NOM Taroo ACC die-CAUS-PF
        'Hanako's mistake caused Taro to die.'

     b. Hanako no ayamati ni yotte   Taroo ga   sin-da.
        Hanako GEN mistake as a result of Taroo NOM die-PF
        'Taro died as a result of Hanako's mistake.'

For sentences like (17a), the ability of the causative subject to appear as the complement of *ni yotte* in an unaccusative paraphrase suggests that, in the causative sentence, that subject bears the thematic role "cause". Conversely, unacceptability of a *ni yotte* paraphrase would suggest that the causative subject in question does not bear that thematic role. It is notable, then, that for examples like (13)–(16), the *ni yotte* paraphrases are degraded or frankly unacceptable (for simplicity, I mark both the Japanese sentences and their English translations with the asterisk):

(18) a. Sakura no ki ga   hana o   sak-ase-te   i-ta.   (cf. (14b))
        cherry GEN tree NOM flower ACC bloom-CAUS-CNJ be-PF
        The cherry tree was blooming (lit. 'making its flowers bloom').

     b. *Sakura no ki ni yotte   hana ga   sai-te   i-ta.
        cherry GEN tree as a result of flower NOM bloom-CNJ be-PF.
        *'The flowers were blooming as a result of the cherry tree.'

(19) a. Densya ga   syarin o kisim-ase-te   i-ta.   (cf. (16))
        train   NOM wheel ACC screech-CAUS-CNJ be-PF
        The train's wheels were screeching. (lit. 'The train was making its wheels screech.')

     b. *Densya ni yotte   syarin ga kisin-de   i-ta.
        train   as a result of wheel NOM screech-CNJ be-PF
        *'The wheels were screeching as a result of the train.'

If the possessor subjects of examples like (18a) and (19a) bear no thematic role other than that associated with their initial position, it follows that either the *-(s)ase-* of such examples introduces no specifier position or else the specifier position it introduces is athematic, with the possessor subjects of those examples

---

11. Pylkkänen (2008: 91–92) claims that DP *ni yotte* indicates the presence of an implicit argument, either a causer or a causing event, and is consequently inadmissible in unaccusative clauses, which have neither. In fact, unaccusatives (*sin-* 'die', *oti-* 'fall', *kusar-* 'rot', etc.) occur freely with *ni yotte* phrases, as internet searches quickly show. On the assumption that unaccusatives do indeed have no implicit cause or causer argument, then, it follows that DP *ni yotte* in unaccusatives does not illuminate argument structure, but is purely adverbial.

moving through the athematic Spec(CausP) on their way to Spec(TP) (cf. Hasegawa 2007: 73). For concreteness, I will assume the latter option, and, without exploring the motivation for the movement in question, I will refer to such examples below as "possessor-raising causatives" and to the variant of the causative suffix that appears in them as "possessor-raising *-(s)ase-*".[12] I will further assume that possessor-raising *-(s)ase-* introduces no causing event and is a semantically null, purely formal element, as the passive suffix is typically understood to be (Parsons 1990: 91); as a result, pairs like the (a) and (b) sentences of (13) and (14) are paraphrases of each other. As a semantically transparent formal element, possessor-raising *-(s)ase-* is clearly a variant of syntactic *-(s)ase-*.

There are strict constraints on the distribution of possessor-raising *-(s)ase-*. First, as noted above, its complement must be unaccusative; in a transitive clause (unergatives included), the agent in Spec(vP) will block raising of a possessor under minimality. Thus, for example, *hannin ga [keisatu no me] o sorasita* 'the criminal diverted the eyes of the police' does not vary in the same meaning with *keisatu ga hannin ni [Ø me] o sorasaseta*. Second, the possessum must ordinarily be inalienably possessed, although considerations of space preclude an exploration of that restriction here. In the examples above, which have inanimate possessors, the inalienability condition is satisfied either by the possessum's being a physical subpart of the possessor ((15) and (16)) or by its being an emanation or outgrowth of the possessor ((13) and (14); on the inalienability of the latter type of possessum, see Lichtenberk et al. 2011: 663).[13] As the last examples of this section, let us examine two cases of possessor raising in which the possessor is human and the possessum a body part. Both examples illustrate the fact that possessor-raising *-(s)ase-* may select an unaccusative idiom even when a transitive version of the idiom exists, thus evading the blocking effect we observed in Section 4.3 for **hakusya o kak-ar-ase-*, taken there to be blocked by *hakusya o kak-e-* 'spur on, accelerate (t)'.

Consider first the idioms *mune ga itam-* (lit. 'one's breast hurts') and *mune o itam-e-* (lit. 'hurt one's breast') 'be grieved, worried'. Because of the appearance of the transitive stem *itam-e-* in the latter, blocking would predict that *mune o itam-ase-*, the causative of intransitive *mune ga itam-*, should be impossible, and in fact

---

12. Given its athematic subject position, possessor-raising *-(s)ase-* constitutes a prima facie violation of Burzio's generalization, since it clearly assigns accusative case. For an account of transitivity and little v that abandons Burzio's generalization entirely, see Hasegawa 2007.

13. The failure of *tiimu no kiai ga haitte iru* 'the team is in fighting spirit' (noted by a reviewer for de Chene 2022b) to alternate with **tiimu ga kiai o hairasete iru* can plausibly be attributed to the inalienability condition: *kiai* 'determination, enthusiasm, fighting spirit' represents not an inalienable property, but a transient emotional state.

Miyagawa (1989:127) marks it as ungrammatical. But *mune o itam-ase-* appears with some frequency online, and there are two occurrences of it in the BCCWJ over the forms C/P/C, one reproduced in (20) below.

(20) Kono ko   ga   ore e   no hatu-koi de   mune o   itam-ase-te
      this child NOM 1.SG toward GEN first-love with breast ACC ache-CAUS-CNJ
      i-ru.
      be-CNC
      'This kid is experiencing the pains of first love for me.'

Regarding (20), it is clear first of all that the possessor *kono ko* 'this child' acquires no new thematic role, neither agent nor (inadvertent) cause, as a result of becoming the causative subject. (20) thus qualifies as an example of possessor raising as characterized above. It also satisfies the conditions on possessor-raising *-(s)ase-* just noted: *mune ga itam-* is unaccusative, and there is a relation of inalienable possession between *kono ko* and the theme argument *mune* 'breast'. (21) is a similar example, also from the BCCWJ, that involves the causative of the idiom *hara ga her-* 'get hungry'; as noted in Section 4.3, this fails to be blocked by transitive *hara o her-as-* 'wait for a meal, get hungry'.

(21) Ie   de hara   o   her-ase-ta   neko ga   gyaagyaa sawai-de
      house at stomach ACC decrease-CAUS-PF cat NOM loudly   make.noise-CNJ
      (i-)ru.
      (be-)CNC
      'There is a hungry cat squalling at home.'

It is natural to speculate that the ability of (20) and (21) to evade the expected blocking effect is tied to their status as possessor-raising causatives. The relationship between the two phenomena is not one-to-one, however. To begin with, *hara o her-ase-* occurs not only in the meaning 'get hungry', as in (21), but in the meaning 'avoid eating' (e.g. in order to be hungry later), where the subject is clearly agentive. The latter use has in common with the former that the causative subject is in a relationship of inalienable possession with the theme, but this condition is also satisfied in **hone o ore-sase-* (Miyagawa 1989:127) without resulting in evasion of the blocking effect (cf. *hone ga ore-* 'require great effort' (lit. 'bones break'), *hone o or-* 'exert great effort' (lit. 'break bones')). The strongest statement consistent with the data we have seen, then, is that a relationship of inalienable possession between the causative subject and the theme is a necessary condition for an idiomatic intransitive + causative combination to coexist with a transitive version of the same idiom.

Idioms with possessor-raising *-(s)ase-* like those of (20) and (21) make it clear that the *-ase-* of a transitive idiom may represent syntactic *-(s)ase-*. We will see further examples confirming this fact in Section 4.4.5. In closing this section, it should be emphasized that possessor-raising -(s)ase- by no means exhausts the phenomenon of external possession in Japanese. In particular, many ordinary transitive sentences display external possession, sometimes outside the relatively strict conditions that we have seen to govern the distribution of possessor-raising -(s)ase-. Thus, in *Taro ga tokoya de kami o kitta* 'Taro had his hair cut (lit. 'cut his hair') at the barber's' ((3d), Hasegawa 2007: 67), external possession is observed in spite of the fact that there is no corresponding unaccusative clause and the encoded event is agentive. A thorough investigation of external possession in Japanese would take us well beyond the scope of the present chapter.

4.4.5   -(a)se- and -(s)ase- in VP idioms

There is one transitive idiom cited in Miyagawa 1989: 124–126 whose verb does not appear in Table 1, *hana o sak-ase-*, literally 'make flowers bloom'. The reason the verb of that idiom is absent from the table is that dictionaries of the contemporary language decline to accord entries to either *sak-ase-* or *sak-as-*. If we follow the intuitions of Japanese lexicographers, then, there are no lexicalized stems of that form. If so, what is the structure of *hana o sak-ase-*, and how is it generated?

Transitive *hana o sak-ase-* has an intransitive counterpart *hana ga sak-*, literally 'flowers bloom'. Dictionaries list two meanings for *hana ga sak-*, 'become animated, lively' (*nigiyaka ni naru*) and 'flourish' (*sakaeru*). Correspondingly, the two meanings listed for *hana o sak-ase-* are 'make animated, lively' (*nigiyaka ni suru*) and 'cause to flourish' (*sakaeru yoo ni suru*). The dictionary definitions, then, are consistent with the possibility that transitive *hana o sak-ase-* is simply the compositionally interpreted syntactic causative of intransitive *hana ga sak-*. If so, the idiom recorded in the lexicon will be roughly [[hana $_{DP}$] sak $_{VP}$] 'become animated; flourish'. When this unaccusative VP is selected in the syntax by causative -(s)ase-, the latter will supply a causative meaning and license an agentive argument and accusative case. Nothing more will need to be said about the form or meaning of *hana o sak-ase-*.

It should be emphasized in this connection that the idiomatic meaning of *hana o sak-ase-* does not in and of itself establish that *sak-ase-* is a lexical causative, although this is one reading of Miyagawa's (1989: 123–126) treatment of such idioms. More generally, VP idioms in (presumably) any language undergo inflection without entailing that the inflectional elements in question are part of the idiom's lexical form. If *-ase-* can be analyzed as inflectional in *hana o sak-ase-*, then, that suffix is external to the lexicalized idiom, just as is, for example, the past tense marker of *kicked the bucket*. While it might appear that analyzing the *-ase-* of *hana o sak-ase-* as syntactic would make it difficult to account for the variant *hana o sak-as-*, which occurs at least four times in the BCCWJ, the fact, already noted, that syntactic *-(s)ase-* varies under certain conditions with *-(s)as-* means that there will be no barrier to treating the relatively infrequent *hana o sak-as-* as involving the syntactic causative suffix as well. Section 4.5 will have more to say about syntactic *-(s)as-*.

It is clear that instances of *hana o sak-ase-* do not belong to the class of possessor-raising causatives identified in Section 4.4.4; notably, there is no relationship of inalienable possession between the causative subject and any argument of the unaccusative clause. It is the unmarked variant of syntactic *-(s)ase-*, then, that occurs in such sentences. It is nevertheless the case that *hana o sak-ase-* examples share with possessor-raising causatives a property that sets them apart from more typical causatives in which the causative subject represents an entity that is external to the caused event, namely that the set of participants in the situations represented by the causative and corresponding intransitive sentences coincide. This is illustrated by the examples of (22).

(22) a.   Doosookai de omoide-banasi ni   hana   ga   sai-ta.
          reunion   at memory-story LOC flower NOM bloom-PF
          'There was much lively reminiscing at the reunion.'

     b.   Doosookai no   sankasya   ga   omoide-banasi ni   hana   o
          reunion   GEN participant NOM memory-story LOC flower ACC
          sak-ase-ta.
          bloom-CAUS-PF
          'The participants in the reunion engaged in much lively reminiscing.'

The subject of (22b), *doosookai no sankasya* 'the participants in the reunion', is absent from (22a), but the referents of that noun phrase are present in the situation that (22a) represents.

A still closer approach to a possessor-raising causative is provided by an example like *me o hikar-ase-* 'keep a close watch' (lit. 'make eyes shine'), illustrated along with its virtually synonymous intransitive counterpart *me ga hikar-* (lit. 'eyes shine') in (23) (either expression may also take a DP in *ni* representing the object of surveillance).

(23) a.   Keisatu no   me ga   hikat-te   i-ru.
          police   GEN eye NOM shine-CNJ be-CNC

     b.   Keisatu ga   me o   hikar-ase-te   i-ru.
          police   NOM eye ACC shine-CAUS-CNJ be-CNC
          'The police are keeping a close watch.'

In (23b), as opposed to (22b), the causative subject is in fact coreferential with the possessor of the theme. (23b) is nevertheless not a possessor-raising causative, because its causative subject is agentive, as attested by the naturalness of, for example, *me o hikaraseru koto ni sita* 'decided to keep a close watch'. Rather, (23b) illustrates what might be called a "possessor-control" causative, with the causative subject binding a zero pronominal in the possessor position of an inalienably possessed noun. I will assume that such cases involve the general, unmarked variant of syntactic *-(s)ase-*; for (23), the lexical form of the idiom will be [[DP me ~DP~] hikar ~VP~] 'DP keeps a close watch'.

It must be noted, however, that the conclusion that the *-ase-* of *me o hikar-ase-* is syntactic is at odds with Kuroda's (1993:31) claim that the applicability of syntactic causativization to *me o hikar-ase-* entails, under the ban on double *-(s)ase-* noted above, that that expression involves lexical *-ase-*. Regarding this question, I would like to suggest that in a narrow range of circumstances, double syntactic causatives may in fact be systematically allowed.

Consider the verbs *karam-* 'twine/wrap around (i), come into relation with' and *karam-e-* 'twine/wrap around (t), bring into relation with' (cf. also *karam-ar-* 'twine/wrap around (i), get tangled'). It might be expected that transitive *karam-e-* would block use of causative *karam-ase-* in the expression of manipulative causation, but this expectation is not borne out. In the meaning 'entwine the fingers (individually or mutually)', for example, both *yubi o karam-e-* and *yubi o karam-ase-* occur freely; the frequencies of those expressions in the BCCWJ over the forms C/P/C are 6 for the former and 4 for the latter. Given that *karam-ase-* can be assumed, on the basis of the isoradical transitive *karam-e-*, to be a syntactic causative, a strict interpretation of the ban on double *-(s)ase-* would predict the ungrammaticality of *karam-ase-sase-* 'cause to entwine'. It is not difficult, however, to find cases that counterexemplify this prediction, as in (24)–(25), adapted from a blog and an online novel, respectively.

(24) Kagi ni   asi o   karam-ase-sase-ta.
      key   LOC leg ACC wrap.around-CAUS-CAUS-PF
      'I got it to wrap its legs around a key.' [it = stag beetle]

(25) Kubi ni   ude o   karam-ase-sase-ta.
      neck LOC arm ACC wrap.around-CAUS-CAUS-PF
      'He had her wrap her arms around his neck.'

While space limitations preclude in-depth exploration of the issue here, it would appear that the syntactic causative of an unaccusative clause whose theme argument is inalienably possessed by the causative subject may undergo causativization in spite of the fact that the result is a sequence of two syntactic *-(s)ase-*. Thus, in another of Kuroda's (1993:9, 32) examples, *hatarak-* 'work' (like English *work*) is unergative in the meaning 'perform labor', but unaccusative in the meaning 'function, be activated'; as a result, **X ni heitai-tati o hatarak-as-ase-* 'make X make the soldiers work' (with the short form -(s)as- of -(s)ase- before another auxiliary) is degraded, but X *ni atama o hatarak-as-ase-* 'make X use her head (i.e. mental powers)' (lit. 'make her head work'), with unaccusative *hatarak-* and an inalienably possessed theme, is fine. Parallel is the example [*seito-tati ni*] *soozoo-ryoku o hatarak-ase-sase-ta* '(I) made [the students] use their imagination' (lit. 'imaginative power'), from a report on elementary school teaching methods (Fujii 2019:16). If these examples with *karam-* and *hatarak-* are indicative of a general exemption from the double -(s)ase- ban for unaccusatives with inalienably possessed themes, that exemption will apply to *me ga hikar-* 'eyes shine', and causativization of *me o hikar-ase-* will not speak against the hypothesis that the -ase- in question represents syntactic -(s)ase-.[14]

I have suggested that, among the VP idioms offered by Miyagawa (1989:125–126) as illustrating lexical -(s)ase-, there are some whose -ase- is in fact external to the relevant idiom, representing inflectional material composed with the idiom in the syntax. These VPs do involve -(s)ase-, then, but that suffix is syntactic rather than lexical. In (22b) and (23b), the complement of syntactic -(s)ase- is unaccusative, but there are also parallel cases in which -(s)ase- selects a transitive idiom. Thus, because *saihu o ak-e-* (lit. 'open one's wallet') can mean 'pay, pick up the tab', *saihu o ak-e-sase-* has the meaning 'make (someone) pay' (Miyagawa 2012:201). -sase- here is clearly a syntactic element, because its complement is a full transitive vP. Thus, even if, counterfactually, the semantics of *saihu o ak-e-sase-* were noncompositional, that fact would be evidence not for lexical -(s)ase-, but for the lexicalization as a unit of a CausP headed by syntactic -(s)ase-. This is the analysis that Miyagawa (2012:200) proposes for *tabe-sase-*, the causative of *tabe-* 'eat', in the meaning 'support financially' (Miyagawa's gloss is 'take care of'). In fact, since *tabe-* has the secondary meaning 'make a living' (*seikei o tateru, seikatu suru*), it seems clear that the meaning 'support financially' (*seikatu saseru*) for *tabe-sase-* is compositional rather than idiomatic, so that the -sase- of that expression is syntactic, just like the -sase- of *saihu o ak-e-sase-*. Miyagawa's proposal, however, raises the question of whether idioms that incorporate syntactic -(s)ase- do exist.

Lexicalization of inflectional material is well attested in Japanese, as noted in Section 3.7. In particular, Adverbial forms of verbs are often lexicalized as nouns (*odori* 'dance'; cf. *odor-* 'to dance'); less frequently, Conjunctive forms are lexicalized as adverbials (*sitagatte* 'consequently'; cf. *sitagaw-* 'obey'). Lexicalization of combinations involving stem-forming suffixes, although rarer, occurs as well. Potential -e- appears in *hanas-e-* 'easy to talk to; flexible, accommodating' (lit. 'can talk to'), and passive -(r)are- in *nom-are-* 'be overwhelmed' (lit. be drunk'), *osow-*

---

14. I leave for future research the project of providing a unified account for the role of inalienability in governing (a) possessor raising and (b) the scope of the double -(s)ase- constraint.

are- 'be tormented by a frightening dream' (lit. 'be attacked'), and *ate-rare-* 'be made to feel uncomfortable, especially by displays of intimacy on the part of others' (lit. 'be hit'). Lexicalized *-(s)ase-*, finally, occurs in *kane o tukam-ase-/nigir-ase-* 'bribe' (lit. 'cause to grasp money') and *ame o syabur-ase-/name-sase-* 'yield something to an adversary in order to gain an advantage later' (lit. 'allow to suck candy'). It must be emphasized, however, that inflectional suffixes do not become derivational or lexical as the result of lexicalization of forms that include them, as illustrated by the lexicalization in unpredictable meanings of the English plural forms *guts* and *balls* that was referred to in Section 3.7. Lexicalization of forms including syntactic *-(s)ase-*, then, while attested, is not evidence for *-(s)ase-* as a lexical suffix.

Above, we have observed that many instances of *-ase-* in idioms appear to represent syntactic *-(s)ase-* combined with an independently occurring idiom. This will not be a plausible analysis, however, if there is no idiom that coincides with the complement of *-(s)ase-*, as is the case with *mimi o sum-ase-* 'listen attentively' (lit. 'clear the ears'; see Table 1, item 5). In such an example, the transitive stem in *-ase-* will be part of the lexical representation of the idiom, here [[mimi $_{DP}$] [[sum] ase $_V$] $_{VP}$], and *-ase-* will be a lexical suffix. Given the generalization that, with limited exceptions, lexical *-ase-* arises as a replacement for earlier *-as-* (Sections 4.4.2 and 4.4.3), it will not be surprising in such a case to find evidence for that diachronic development. In the case of *mimi o sum-as(e)-*, the replacement of *-as-* by *-ase-* is still very much in progress; the BCCWJ shows 132 occurrences of *mimi o sum-as-* (64%) over the forms C/P/C versus 74 of *mimi o sum-ase-* (36%). That this variation is salient for speakers is shown by online discussion concerning whether, in addition to conservative (and uncontroversially acceptable) *mimi o sum-as-*, the innovative form *mimi o sum-ase-* is "correct" or not (see references in note 18 below).

In the present section, examining representative phrases of the form [DP o V-ase-] and [DP o V-sase-] taken by Miyagawa (1989, 2012) and Harley (2008) as evidence for lexical *-(s)ase-* on the basis of apparent idiomatic uses, we have seen that there are some, exemplified by *me o hikar-ase-* 'keep a close watch' and *saihu o ak-e-sase-* 'make (someone) pay', in which the causative suffix represents syntactic *-(s)ase-* and is external to the lexicalized idiom. In others, exemplified by *mimi o sum-ase-* 'listen attentively', *-ase-* is lexical, but cannot be *-(s)ase-* even on Miyagawa and Harley's account because of the prior existence of lexical *-as-*. We also observed that full CausP constituents headed by syntactic *-(s)ase-* may undergo lexicalization (*kane o nigir-ase-* 'bribe'). In the end, however, we have found no evidence that lexical *-(s)ase-* exists, consistent with the conclusion of Section 4.2.2 that lexical *-sase-* is unattested and lexical *-ase-* is *-(a)se-*. There is one important question raised by our discussion that remains unanswered, namely that of the

motivation for the diachronic tendency to replace stems in -as- with stems in -ase-
that was documented in Section 4.4.3, and I turn to that issue in Section 4.5.

4.5   Toward an understanding of the replacement of -as- by -ase-

In taking up the question of the motivation for the replacement of -as- by -ase-
over time, I will propose that variation between lexical -as- and lexical -ase- can
be understood only in the context of variation between -(s)as- and -(s)ase- for the
syntactic causative suffix, and will start with a consideration of the latter.

Variation between -(s)as- and -(s)ase- has both a geographical and a temporal
dimension. Geographically, -(s)as- is to a first approximation limited to Western
Japan apart from Kyushu.[15] As a response to the survey item *kak-ase-ru* 'make
write' (map 119) in the GAJ, *kak-as-u* is common in the Kansai and Chugoku
regions and in Shikoku, and occurs in Ishikawa, Toyama, and western Niigata
Prefectures along the Japan Sea coast, but with the exception of three survey
points (one each in Aichi, Shizuoka, and Saitama Prefectures) that report both
kak-ase-ru and *kak-as-u*, is absent from Aichi, Gifu, and Fukui Prefectures in
central Japan and, apart from the Japan Sea coast areas just noted, everywhere
north and east of there. It should be noted, however, that before passive -(r)are-,
causative -(s)as- appears with considerable frequency both in Kyushu and in Eastern Japan, giving *kak-as-are-ru* in place of *kak-ase-rare-ru* for 'be made to write'
(GAJ map 125).

Historically, causative -(s)as- appears only marginally before the year 1600,
as evidenced by its absence up to that date from the period-specific conjugation
tables of works like Yamaguchi and Akimoto 2001.[16] During the Edo period
(1603–1868), however, -(s)as- emerged as a major competitor to -(s)ase-, and it

---

15. In the following discussion, I exclude from consideration Hokkaido, settled heavily by
Japanese speakers only in the late 19th century.

16. The statement that "Historically, the *sas* form was the original causative morpheme which
gave rise to the *sase* form around the 12–15th centuries" (Shibatani 1973:346 (note 21), quoted in
Miyagawa 1984 [2012]:292 (note 2 to Chapter 7)), is at variance with the facts (see note 8 above);
it seems to be based on a misunderstanding of a passage on page 89 of Miyaji 1969. The crucial point is that for classical (Heian period) Japanese, the verbal citation form, the Conclusive,
typically underdetermines the stem, and a specification of conjugation type is required in order
to resolve the indeterminacy. The classical causative suffix had the citation forms -su-Ø (for C-
stems) and -sasu-Ø (for V-stems), but inflected according to the *shimo nidan* ('lower bigrade')
conjugation, so that the causative stem, coinciding with the Adverbial, was -se-/-sase-. In each
case, the C-stem alternant is analyzed as added to a stem augmented with *a*; a segmentation
that instead assigns that *a* to the suffix yields -ase-/-sase-, just as in the contemporary language.

maintained that status not only through the era in which the Japanese of Kyoto and Osaka (*Kamigata-go*) was the unchallenged prestige and literary dialect, but after 1750, when the dialect of Edo (modern Tokyo) began to increase in status. The contemporary common or standard language, however, has adopted the eastern variant on this point as on a number of other details of verbal and adjectival morphology (see Frellesvig 2010:399): *kak-as-u* 'cause to write' appears only twice in the BCCWJ, as opposed to 102 times for *kak-ase-ru*. Reflecting this, *-(s)as-* is absent from conjugation tables for the modern language (Yamaguchi and Akimoto 2001:908 (contrast p.906)), although it remains in speaker consciousness as an informal or regional variant.

Consider now the morphological relationship between the syntactic causative *niow-ase-* 'cause to smell' and the lexicalized verb *niow-as-* 'hint at' as the use of syntactic *-(s)as-* began to spread in the 17th century. With the establishment of variation between *niow-ase-* and *niow-as-* for 'cause to smell', it would not be surprising if that variation was extended to *niow-as-* 'hint at'. From the point of view of eastern dialect speakers in particular, the innovative variant *niow-as-* 'cause to smell' will have been perceived as a western regionalism, and if that perception were extended to *niow-as-* 'hint at', the creation of a variant *niow-ase-* would follow. It is thus probably not coincidental that the first citation (1799) of *niow-ase-* 'hint at' in the NKD is from a work by an Edo author (Rakutei Bashō, *Kuruwa Setsuyō*).[17]

For the contemporary language, similarly, the idea that ongoing extension of *-ase-* at the expense of *-as-* in cases like *mimi o sum-as(e)-* 'listen attentively' is motivated by the desire to avoid forms that could be perceived as dialectal and thus nonstandard has been proposed in anonymous online commentary.[18] That this tendency operates in particular with respect to forms in Perfect *-ta* or Conjunctive *-te*, suffixes that historically were added to the Adverbial in *-i*, is suggested by the comments of Hasegawa (2007:69 (note 3)), who reports that a form like *kusar-as-i-ta* 'caused to rot' as a variant of *kusar-ase-ta* may have a substandard or over-colloquial flavor that does not extend to the corresponding Conclusive in *-(r)u*. That the extension of *-ase-* is driven by avoidance of *s*-stem forms with *t*-initial suffixes is borne out by the statistics of the BCCWJ in a number of cases where change is ongoing and both conservative and innovative forms are common. Thus for *mimi o sumas(e)-*, the conservative *s*-stem variant predominates heavily in the

---

17. Conversely, the first citation (1696) of innovative *aw-as-* 'join' (see Table 1), competing with the *aw-ase-* that dates back to the 8th century, is from Western Japan (Tominaga Heibee, *Kumanosan Kaichō*).

18. https://detail.chiebukuro.yahoo.co.jp/qa/question_detail/q1343185618 (see also https://oshiete.goo.ne.jp/qa/8070018.html).

Conclusive (50 *sumasu*, 11 *sumaseru*), but is favored by a much smaller margin in *t*-suffixed forms (83 *sumasita/te*, 63 *sumaseta/te*). For the combination *kosi o uk-as(e)-* 'raise one's lower back, begin to stand up; do restlessly' (see Miyagawa 1989: 126), similarly, the variant in *-as-* predominates narrowly in the Conclusive (10 *ukasu*, 8 *ukaseru*), but is outnumbered nearly two-to-one by *-ase-* in *t*-suffixed forms (33 *ukasita/te*, 64 *ukaseta/te*).

If the replacement of *-as-* by *-ase-* is indeed motivated by avoidance of forms that could seem dialectal or substandard, we might expect that replacement to operate most reliably in cases where the corresponding intransitive is suffixless,[19] as it is for example in *mimi o sum-as(e)-* (cf. *sum-* 'be clear'), since in that case the stem in *-as-* will coincide with a western intransitive + causative combination. In the majority of examples, this is in fact the case, but replacement of *okur-as-* 'delay' by *okur-ase-* in the presence of intransitive *okur-e-* 'be late', discussed above, and ongoing replacement of *kir-as-* 'run out of (a product)' by *kir-ase-* in the presence of *kir-e-* '(a product) runs out' (both cited by Kuroda (1993: 19) as illustrating lexical *-ase-*) show that this restriction is not absolute. In the case of *okur-as(e)-*, as was noted, replacement of *-as-* by *-ase-* is essentially complete. In the case of *kir-as(e)-*, in contrast, conservative *kir-as-* remains dominant, with 137 occurrences in the BCCWJ over the forms C/P/C (58%) versus 100 for *kir-ase-* (42%).

In fact, examples involving the suffix *-(a)kas-* show that the tendency in question is not limited to *-as-*. Consider the case of *ne-kas(e)-* 'put to sleep' (cf. intransitive *ne-* 'sleep'). The NKD shows that while *ne-kas-* is attested from the middle of the 18th century, *ne-kase-* appears only at the end of the 19th.[20] In the BCCWJ, however, *ne-kase-* is far more frequent, with 369 occurrences over the forms C/P/C (83%) as against 78 for *ne-kas-* (17%). In another stem involving *-(a)kas-*, *amay-akas-* 'indulge, spoil' (cf. intransitive *amay-e-* 'presume upon'), the BCCWJ indicates that replacement with *amay-akase-* is still in an incipient stage, with 146 instances of the conservative form (98%) and only 3 of the innovative form (2%). Internet searches, however, suggest that *amay-akase-* is already quite common.

The picture that emerges from the above observations is that of a very general tendency to replace transitive stems of the form Xas- with stems of the form Xase-, driven at least in part by speakers' desire to avoid forms that might be perceived as nonstandard. Like many other morphological changes, this tendency appears

---

19. Harley (2008: 49 (note 22)) claims that "lexical *sase*" is in fact restricted to such cases.

20. The putative NKD example of *ne-kase-* from 1750–76 appears to be misclassified. The form is *nekaseba* 'if (one) lays (it) down', arguably to be analyzed as an *s*-stem Provisional *ne-kas-eba*. The alternative analysis *ne-kase-ba*, with *-ba* added to the *Mizenkei* of *ne-kase-*, is rendered unlikely by the fact that Conditional *Mizenkei* + *ba* had for the most part gone out of use by 1600 (Sakakura 1975: 273).

to be checked by high token frequency, as illustrated by the resistance to change of *her-as-* 'decrease (t)', whose token frequency as recorded in Table 1 is more than ten times greater than that of any of the other verbs surveyed apart from *sum-as-* 'clear (t)'. While there is a need for further work documenting this tendency in detail and exploring its motivation more systematically, it seems undeniable that it has exerted a considerable influence on the evolution of Japanese transitive stem formation and will continue to do so for the foreseeable future.

4.6   Conclusion

Let us review the main results of this chapter. In Section 4.2, we saw that, as predicted by the *a*-Deletion rule (1), the postvocalic alternant of lexical *-ase-* is not *-sase-*, but *-se-*. For *-sase-*, in contrast, there is no evidence that it ever occurs as a lexical suffix. In order to interpret lexical *-ase-* as an instantiation of *-(s)ase-*, then, it would be necessary to ignore both the rule-governed complementary distribution of *-ase-* and *-se-* and the fact that lexical *-sase-* is unattested. There are thus two distinct causative suffixes, lexical *-(a)se-* and syntactic *-(s)ase-*. Nor can the distinct alternations shown by those suffixes be attributed to the rules of different strata of the phonology, as I suggested would be possible for lexical *-(a)re-* and passive *-(r)are-*. Both the hypothesis that *-(s)ase-* is the unique causative suffix and the hypothesis that, while *-(a)se-* and *-(s)ase-* both exist, systematic differences in phonological strata allow them to be identified with each other, then, can be taken to be disconfirmed.

It is nevertheless the case that a wide variety of examples have been identified in the literature (Miyagawa 1989, Harley 2008) as "lexical *-(s)ase-*". Section 4.4 examined representative examples, concluding that while some are lexical *-(a)se-*, others are syntactic *-(s)ase-*. The failure to find any evidence for lexical *-(s)ase-* supports the conclusion that there is no Japanese causative suffix that spans the syntactic/lexical boundary. As a result, causatives are consistent with the position of Chapter 3 that, while Japanese inflectional morphology is syntactic, the derivational morphology of transitive and intransitive stems is not.

It is worth considering briefly why our conclusions about Japanese causatives differ from those of Miyagawa and Harley cited above. I would identify the root of those differences with two assumptions that those authors make but that we have not. The first is that any occurrence of causative or transitivizing *-ase-* represents the suffix *-(s)ase-*. We have seen that, because there is also a derivational suffix *-(a)se-*, this assumption is unwarranted. The assumption that all *-ase-* are *-(s)ase-* leads to the misidentification as lexical *-(s)ase-* of items that are in fact lexical *-(a)se-*, as in the case of *aw-ase-* 'join' (Miyagawa 2012: 198–199) or *niow-*

ase- 'hint at'. The second assumption made by Miyagawa and Harley that we have found unwarranted is that any occurrence of *-ase-* that is "associated with noncompositional meaning" (Miyagawa 2012:206) is lexical — that is, (in principle) root-selecting.[21] We have seen a number of exceptions to this principle, for example *hana o sak-ase-* 'make animated', where I claimed that *-ase-* is syntactic and that the lexicalized idiom is simply [[hana $_{DP}$] sak $_{VP}$]. The assumption that "associated" noncompositional meaning unfailingly diagnoses lexical status for a causative suffix, then, leads to the misidentification as lexical *-(s)ase-* of items that are in fact syntactic *-(s)ase-*.

There is one final issue that should be touched upon in closing the chapter. As just noted, in making the case in Section 4.2.2 that derivational *-(a)se-* and inflectional *-(s)ase-* cannot be collapsed as high (vP-selecting) and low (√P-selecting) variants of a single morphosyntactic element, it was pointed out for the sake of contrast that, given a particular choice of stem-level and word-level phonological rules, a high/low attachment analysis would in fact be possible for derivational *-(a)re-* and inflectional *-(r)are-*. The fact that the grammatical framework argued for here, according to which derivational suffixes belong to lexical entries, precludes such a high/low attachment analysis raises the question of what alternative account is possible for the apparent coincidence in form displayed by the latter two suffixes, and for the partial similarity of *-(a)se-* and *-(s)ase-* as well. I will claim that the appropriate explanation is diachronic in nature.

It is well established that a derivational affix, as a result of grammaticization of its meaning and expansion of its range of application, may develop into an unambiguously inflectional element. This is, for example, the history of the Latin perfect passive participle formant *-tu-*, which descends from a Proto-Indo-European suffix *-tó-* that derived adjective stems from roots in the zero grade (see e.g. Sihler 1995:621ff.). The same kind of development must have been behind the emergence of the consonant-stem forms *-are-* and *-ase-* of the "new" Japanese passive and causative suffixes, which replaced earlier *-aye-* and *-asime-*, respectively: only sparsely attested in the Old Japanese of the eighth century, the innovative suffixes are firmly established when the language reemerges in the tenth century after a period of more than a hundred years in which it was heavily overshadowed as a written medium by Classical Chinese (see Frellesvig 2010:178–179). More mysterious is the origin of the vowel-stem alternants of those suffixes, *-rare-* and *-sase-*, first attested around the beginning of the tenth century (see the relevant entries of the NKD and Frellesvig 2010:237). These morphs appear to reflect copying of

---

21. In explicating the relevant phrase structure, Miyagawa (2012:204–205) writes "VP" rather than "√P", but the heads of his VPs are roots, as in his example *ag-*, a root that underlies intransitive *ag-ar-* 'rise' and transitive *ag-e-* 'raise'.

the suffix-internal consonant into the suffix-initial position, but any details of their development that might have been illuminated by documentary evidence have been rendered irretrievable as a result of the ninth-century gap in attestation of the language.[22]

The possibility of a high/low attachment analysis for derivational *-(a)re-* and passive *-(r)are-* depends on one further condition as well, namely the treatment of suffix-initial *r* as epenthetic and thus as absent from phonological representation. As we will see in Chapter 8, however, there is no evidence for an epenthesis analysis of suffix-initial *r* before the first half of the 18th century and, the question of documentary evidence aside, reason to believe that that analysis would have been impossible before around 1600. In sum, then, the possibility of analyzing *are* as an element that can attach at two different syntactic levels depends on a sequence of developments that begins in the ninth century and does not conclude until roughly the 17th. The first of those developments reflects a general tendency, often observed in the process of creolization, to grammaticize elements that are less than fully grammatical. The last of them, however, must be accounted for fortuitous: if no epenthesis analysis had been adopted, or if some consonant other than *r* had been analyzed by speakers as epenthetic, the state of affairs that could be taken to suggest a high/low attachment analysis for *-(a)re-* and *-(r)are-* would not have arisen. In sum, it appears that the similarities between transitivity suffixes and causative and passive morphology in Japanese that have attracted the attention of many students of the language are the result of a contingent sequence of historical events. More generally, I would submit that when tantalizing formal parallels between derivational and inflectional morphology are observed, the null hypothesis is that they are to be understood in diachronic rather than synchronic terms.

4.7   Interim summary

The arguments of Chapters 1 and 2 show that inflectional affixes, as the realization of syntactic elements, must have listed representations. The evidence of Chapters 3 and 4, on the other hand, is difficult to explain unless roots and derivational affixes do not: if roots and derivational affixes had listed representations, we would expect them to act as syntactic atoms just as (stems and) inflectional affixes do, so that, contrary to the claims of Chapter 3, inflectable stems could be

---

22. A copying operation with the requisite properties can be observed in English child language substitutions like *Renee* → *Nini* and *Jackie* → *Cockie*, where outputs conform to a template C_iVC_ii exemplified also by *Daddy* and *Mommy*.

syntactically derived. Taken together, then, the data of Chapters 1 through 4 argue for a clear boundary between the listed and the generated that coincides with the boundary between derivation and inflection, and for a syntax-morphology interface that represents a well-defined compromise between that postulated by inferential theories of inflection, which deny listed representations to inflectional affixes, and that postulated by DM, which grants listed representations to derivational affixes. Beginning in Chapter 5, we will see that parallel conclusions follow from examination of the phenomenon of morphophonological reanalysis. Before entering into our consideration of that topic, however, it will be useful to draw out an implication of the conception of inflectional affixes that we are assuming.

In Section 1.5, we adopted the DM principle of late insertion as it applies to inflectional material, so that inflectional affixes are morphosyntactic feature complexes in the lexicon and in the syntax and receive phonological realization only at spellout. This means that affixes as morphosyntactic feature complexes and affixes as phonological strings are drawn from distinct lists (see e.g. Harley and Noyer 1999:3). Chapters 1 through 4 have dealt with inflectional affixes as morphosyntactic objects, examining their relative order and their semantic interpretation. In dealing with inflectional affixes as morphophonological objects in Chapters 5 through 8, in contrast, we will necessarily be treating items that play no role in the narrow syntactic computation. Our claims about morphosyntactic affixes in Chapters 1 through 4, however, generate a prediction about what we should find in the realm of morphophonology. Since a listed morphosyntactic affix must eventually be phonologically realized, and since a listed morphophonological affix must realize some morphosyntactic feature complex, a general restriction on one of the two sets should be mirrored by a parallel restriction on the other. Given our argument that, in the domain of Japanese verbal morphology, the set of listed morphosyntactic suffixes is limited to inflectional types, then, we expect the same to be true of the set of listed morphophonological suffixes. This prediction is borne out: as argued below, inflectional affixes are subject to reanalysis of their phonological form and must thus have listed phonological representations, while there is no reason to believe that the same is true of derivational affixes. While the syntactic data of Chapters 1 through 4 and the phonological data of Chapters 5 through 8 might at first glance appear to constitute mutually unrelated types of evidence, then, the bipartite concept of inflectional affixes entailed by late insertion suggests that those two types of data, and the conclusions they support, might better be seen as two sides of the same coin.

CHAPTER 5

The suffixal alternations
of Japanese verbal inflection

5.1 Introduction: Levels of adequacy in phonology

Since the introduction of the concepts of descriptive and explanatory adequacy in Chomsky 1964b (see also Chomsky 1964a), the terms "description" and "explanation" have defined the twin projects of generative linguistic inquiry, the goal of description being the characterization of the steady-state endpoint of the language acquisition process and that of explanation being the characterization of the starting point of that process, the initial state or innate endowment. These two goals apply to all areas of linguistic competence and are independent of whether the transition from the initial state to the steady state is taken to be mediated by an evaluation procedure (Chomsky 1957: 51), by parameter setting (Chomsky 1981: 4), by constraint (re)ranking (McCarthy 2002: 208), or by some other mechanism.

In the area of morphophonology, the existence of multiple observationally adequate analyses for many data sets made it evident quite early that descriptive adequacy could not be attained merely on the basis of analyzing patterns of distribution and alternation. At the same time, the existence of cases in which speakers seemed to have arrived at analyses strikingly different from those predicted by the standard assumptions of phonologists (see e.g. Hale 1973: 414–421) made it clear that explanatory adequacy could not be attained merely by adopting a priori a particular definition of simplicity — for example, the feature-counting evaluation metric of Chomsky and Halle 1968, taken to apply to the lexicon (see pp. 381–382) as well as to rule schemata. Two representative quotations illustrating these realizations, the first focusing on the problem of description, the second on the problem of explanation, are given below.

> Generative grammarians have also claimed that a description of the phonological structure of a language is simultaneously a characterization of the linguistic knowledge of native speakers of the language. .... But in order for this implication to be valid, we must be able to corroborate it by corpus-external evidence ....
>
> (Kenstowicz and Kisseberth 1979: 153)

[S]howing that introducing the alternation condition can lead to more complex analyses cannot by itself refute the alternation condition, since the point at issue is precisely whether simplicity is the correct evaluation measure. .... To avoid begging the question in investigations of this problem we must look for *external evidence* as to the correctness or incorrectness of specific analyses which are required or forbidden by the constraints at issue.

(Kiparsky 1971 [1982]: 59–60 (italics in original))

Both of the above quotations imply a research program, set forth explicitly in Kenstowicz and Kisseberth 1977:3 (and anticipated in slightly different terms in Andersen 1969: 829), that would seek to determine the relevant explanatory principles through examination of a critical mass of cases for which the descriptively adequate analysis is known from external evidence. The principles thus discovered could then be used to predict the descriptively adequate analysis in cases for which no such evidence is available. In Chapters 5 through 8, I will pursue this project through a detailed investigation of ongoing and completed change in the verbal morphophonology of Japanese and the Ryukyuan languages, bringing data from Portuguese, Korean, and Modern Greek to bear on the question of explanatory principles in Chapter 7. We will find that morphophonological change clearly bears out the conclusion of Chapters 1 through 4 that the morphological units that have listed representations are stems and inflectional affixes.

5.2   Background: A typology of alternations

Alternation is the phenomenon of grammatically (as opposed to sociolinguistically) conditioned variation in minimal meaningful units — that is, morphemes. Variation in morpheme shape, however, apart from suppletion, results from rules or constraints that target submorphemic units, segments or feature bundles. A typical instance of alternation, correspondingly, may be conceptualized not only as affecting a morpheme, but as affecting a segment or a feature bundle as well: the alternation that German /ra:d/ 'wheel' undergoes as a result of syllable-final devoicing (alternatively, fortition) may be expressed as [ra:d] ~ [ra:t], as [d] ~ [t], or as [+voice] ~ [–voice]. In this section, I will offer a typology of alternations that will allow us to place the case studies we will examine below in a larger context. I take as a point of reference the hypothesis that speakers analyze alternations by postulating underlying representations and phonological rules that derive surface forms (Halle 1962) and focus on the questions of how those URs and rules are chosen and what units they involve.

Consider first automatic alternations, those that are responses to exceptionless phonotactic constraints, concentrating in particular on neutralizing alternations, as opposed to cases of complementary distribution. Given the principle that the underlying value of an alternating feature [F] in any morpheme is that which occurs in environments where the value of [F] is unconstrained and [+F] and [−F] (or the presence versus absence of [F]) thus contrast, neutralizations that are automatic responses to exceptionless constraints raise no substantive questions of UR or rule choice. For example, consider Russian *pirók* 'pie (nom.sg.)', *pirag-á* 'id. (gen.sg.)', where the stem-final obstruent alternates in the feature [voice] and the preceding vowel alternates in the feature [round]. In obstruents, [voice] is unconstrained intervocalically in Russian but must be [−voice] word-finally; in low back vowels, [round] is unconstrained under stress but must be [−round] when stressless. The voicing value of the stem-final obstruent is thus [+voice], that being the value that occurs intervocalically; the rounding value of the preceding vowel is [+round], that being the value that occurs under stress. As a result, the morpheme-level UR of 'pie' is /pirog/, a representation which happens to diverge from each of its occurring allomorphs (see Kenstowicz and Kisseberth 1977:32–33, 1979:203–204). Assuming that cases of complementary distribution are also to be analyzed in terms of URs and rules, they will require one or more additional principles of UR choice, but there is no reason to believe that they differ significantly from neutralizations in other respects.

The situation is more various for nonautomatic or morphophonological alternations. Observe first that, over time, nonautomatic alternations may remain stable, undergo leveling, or undergo extension; we will see examples of all three of these scenarios below. It is unquestionable that the status of a given alternation in this regard may be ambiguous, as when an alternation is extended in some instances but leveled in others (see e.g. Penny 2002:183 on the alternation of *e* and *o* with *ie* and *ue* under stress in Spanish verb stems). It is thus necessary to consider the tripartite division in question to be a specification of ideal types. With that qualification, however, I will take the diachronic profile of a nonautomatic alternation as diagnostic of how it has been analyzed by speakers, as detailed below. That diachronic profile, then, will serve as one type of external evidence for what analysis has been adopted.

Consider first an alternation that is unambiguously undergoing extension, coming over time to apply to a wider range of forms than was earlier the case. It seems clear that such an alternation must be due to a rule exceptions to which are gradually being eliminated. This scenario can therefore be understood straightforwardly in terms of the hypothesis, introduced above, that speakers analyze alternations by postulating URs and phonological rules. For example, in the case from the history of Portuguese that we will consider in more detail in Chapter 7, a vocalic alternation between [+low] under stress and [−low] when stressless in the prefinal syllable of verb stems has been extended from stems in which the alternation is due to sound change to stems which originally displayed nonalternating [–low] vowels. This development can be explained if the value of [low] in stressless contexts (always [–low]) was taken as underlying and a rule was postulated making [–high] vowels in the prefinal syllable of verb stems [+low] under stress. The relevant vowels of nonalternating stems will have been marked originally as exceptions to the lowering rule, and over time, the exception feature will have been lost from lexical representations, resulting in generalization of that rule.

As this example illustrates, regardless of the unit in terms of which the alternants are stated, the postulation of URs for a nonautomatic alternation partitions the set of alternants into basic and nonbasic subsets, and the postulation of a rule partitions the nonbasic alternants further into regular and irregular subsets. In the Portuguese case, irregularity consists simply in failing to undergo the postulated rule and is thus naturally captured by an exception feature. In other cases, irregularity consists in being marked to undergo a competing rule. This is the case, for example, in the Modern Greek example considered in Chapter 7, where truncation and epenthesis compete as hiatus resolution strategies at noun stem boundary. This second type of irregularity is naturally captured by a feature that triggers a "minor" rule, one that is undergone only by items specifically marked to do so (see Lightner 1968). Finally, the irregularity induced by the analysis of a nonautomatic alternation in terms of URs and a rule may be morpheme-specific and thus not subject to capture by either an exception feature or a rule feature. This is the case in the Japanese and Ryukyuan example of ongoing and completed regularization that constitutes the central data of Chapters 5 through 8. Irregularity that is morpheme-specific will be reflected in partially or totally (weakly or strongly) suppletive lexical representations for individual morphemes; we have already seen an example of what this will look like in the Japanese case in the representation <s>ase</V__>, equivalent to "*sase* after a vowel, *ase* otherwise", that was proposed in Chapter 4 for the productive Causative suffix.

In our discussion of the analysis of nonautomatic alternations, we have to this point assumed that irregularity will tend over time to be lost from lexical representations without providing a precise characterization of what it means to be irregular. A first approximation to a definition of irregularity is provided by Kenstowicz and Kisseberth (1977: 61), who suggest that there is a "tendency for arbitrary nonphonetic properties to be lost in linguistic change." Both the exception feature we claimed to be involved in the Portuguese change sketched above and the rule feature that we claimed to be involved in the Modern Greek case qualify uncontroversially as arbitrary nonphonetic properties. But it seems clear that the phonological information in a suppletive nonbasic allomorph — for example, the bracketed material in the representation proposed above for the Japanese

Causative suffix — is equally subject to loss over time. I will therefore assume that any lexical information in excess of a single phonological matrix, whether it be diacritic or phonological in content, counts as irregularity in the relevant sense.

The assumption that irregularity will tend to be lost from lexical representations over time receives a psychological interpretation in terms of the research tradition (Marcus et al. 1992: vi, 15–18; Albright 2002: 10–12) that takes failure to retrieve irregular forms from memory as the central element in an account of the phenomenon of (over)regularization, whether in child language or in diachronic change. The basic intuition involved is that "morphological production involves competition between the retrieval of memorized forms and the creation of new ones by rule … if existing ones are not learned, remembered, or accessed fast enough" (Garrett 2008: 128). This formulation characterizes perfectly a situation in which, as claimed above for an alternation that is undergoing extension, irregular forms coexist with a rule that is capable of generating innovative substitutes for them when they are not successfully retrieved.

When the diachronic profile of a nonautomatic alternation involves leveling rather than extension, however, it seems clear that speakers have not in fact taken the alternation as rule-governed. In such a case, there will be a distinction between basic or default alternants, which will constitute the target of leveling, and nonbasic or marked alternants that are in the process of being eliminated. There will be no contrast, however, between regular and irregular alternants within the nonbasic set: all nonbasic alternants will involve either a rule feature or partial or total suppletion and will thus be irregular in the sense indicated above. As in the case of extension, leveling may occur at the level of the feature or segment as well as at the level of the morph. This is illustrated by the history of Old English *cēos-an*/*cor-en* 'choose/chosen' (see e.g. Fertig 2016: 440), where each of the three stem segments underwent a distinct alternation in OE: while the two consonantal alternations were subsequently leveled, the ablaut alternation of the vowel has remained unchanged.

Consider finally the case of a nonautomatic alternation that is stable over a considerable period of time. The logic of our treatment of extension and leveling entails that an alternation that displays neither must have been analyzed without any contrast between default and marked alternants. This is because such a contrast is predicted to result in extension if a rule for the alternation has also been postulated and in leveling otherwise. Setting aside cases involving unique URs, analyses lacking a contrast between default and marked alternants will be characterized by lexical representations that code all alternants in parallel fashion, thus providing no basis for eliminating any alternant in favor of any other. More specifically, such a "symmetrical" analysis will either list each alternant with the environment in which it occurs or list all alternants without specification of environment and treat the choice between them as the outcome of general principles; we will see analyses of both these subtypes in Section 5.4.

Above, we have reasoned from the diachronic profile of a nonautomatic alternation to the essential properties of its analysis by speakers. The flowchart (1) below, conversely, represents diachronic profile as a function of two binary analytic choices, whether or not defaults are posited and, if so, whether or not a productive rule is posited as well.

(1)

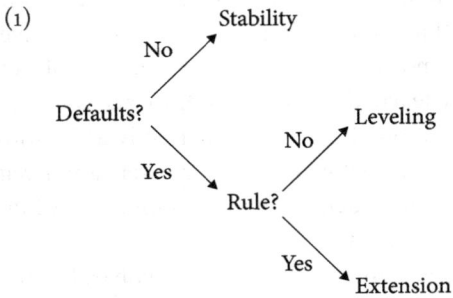

Below, we will be concerned almost exclusively with nonautomatic alternations for which both defaults and rules have been postulated and which therefore have undergone or are undergoing extension.

The remainder of this chapter is structured as follows. Section 5.3 introduces the inflectional suffix alternations of the Japanese verb, and Section 5.4 examines four observationally adequate analyses of those alternations, computing for each the predictions (if any) it makes regarding potential change. Section 5.5 then compares those predictions with the facts of change in progress, concluding that, as already suggested in Chapter 4, an analysis that takes consonant-stem suffix alternants as underlying and derives regular vowel-stem forms by intervocalic epenthesis of r at verb stem boundary is the descriptively adequate one. Section 5.6 looks at the properties of that analysis in more detail, and Section 5.7 examines alternative explanations that have been proposed in the literature for the ongoing changes that are taken here as evidence for it. Section 5.8 summarizes the chapter's conclusions.

5.3   Japanese verbal suffix alternations

As already touched on in Section 4.2.1, the inflectional suffixes of the Japanese verb can be divided into two sets depending on the alternations they display and on whether or not they induce alternations in the stems they attach to. The members of the larger set of suffixes alternate between a vowel-initial form after consonant-final stems and a consonant-initial form (or zero) after vowel-final stems; in combination with such suffixes, stems (apart from *se-/si-/su-/s-* 'do' (and compounds thereof) and *ko-/ki-/ku-* 'come') are nonalternating. The members of the smaller set of suffixes begin with *t ~ d* after all stems and are nonalternating apart from the voicing alternation of their initial consonant, but they trigger the complex set of stem alternations known as *onbin*, referred to in Section 2.3.6.1. Here we will be concerned only with the former set of suffixes, which will be seen to constitute a well-defined morphophonological subsystem. As an introduction to those suffixes and their alternations, Table 1, using stems *mat-* 'wait' and *mi-* 'see', displays two representative examples, the Conclusive in *-(r)u* and the Negative (Western Japanese variant) in *-(a)n*.

Table 1. Sample suffix alternations

Category	C-Stem	V-stem
Conclusive	mat-<u>u</u>	mi-<u>ru</u>
Negative	mat-<u>an</u>	mi-<u>n</u>

Concerning the underlying or lexical representations of the suffixes of Table 1, there are at least the following possibilities: (a) C-stem alternants (*-u, -an*) are basic; (b) V-stem alternants (*-ru, -n*) are basic; (c) longer alternants (*-ru, -an*) are basic; (d) there are no unique basic forms; all alternants are lexically listed. Because the segment-zero alternations are not fully predictable given the shorter alternants, choice (c) is the one that maximizes phonological predictability, as we will see in more detail below.

    For Tokyo and many other locations, the full set of suffixes that show V-initial forms after C-stems and C-initial forms after V-stems consists of the nine items of Table 2. The Passive, Causative, and Potential suffixes of that table create verb stems; the Eastern Japanese variant *-(a)na-* of the Negative suffix creates adjective stems. A number of suffixes are like the Negative in displaying regional variation; there are also many locations that lack certain of the suffixes of Table 2 or display additional suffixes with parallel alternations.

    The inflectional category labels of Table 2 follow for the most part the terminology introduced in Chapter 2 for Dunan and employed also in Chapter 4. This entails certain divergences from the terminology of works like Bloch 1946, McCawley 1968, and Martin 1975. First, as in Table 1, I retain the label "Conclusive", applying it to the citation form in *-(r)u*; for Japanese, in which the Conclusive : Adnominal contrast, previously observed in vowel-stem conjugation, was lost by about the 14th century, that label can be understood as an abbreviation of "Imperfect Conclusive/Adnominal". Similarly, and in accordance with the mean-

Table 2. Full set of alternating suffixes (Tokyo and other locations)

	Category	C-stem	V-stem	Alternation
1	Conclusive	mat-u	mi-ru	Ø ~ r
2	Provisional	mat-eba	mi-reba	Ø ~ r
3	Passive	mat-are-	mi-rare-	Ø ~ r
4	Volitional	mat-oo	mi-yoo	Ø ~ y
5	Causative	mat-ase-	mi-sase-	Ø ~ s
6	Adverbial	mat-i	mi-Ø	i ~ Ø
7	Negative	mat-an(a-)	mi-n(a-)	a ~ Ø
8	Imperative	mat-e	mi-ro	e ~ ro
9	Potential	mat-e-	(mi-rare-)	(e ~ rare)

ing of Japanese terminological equivalents, I have preferred "Volitional" (*isikei*) to "Hortative" and "Adverbial" (*ren'yookei*) to "Infinitive". The label "Provisional", however, has been used for the form in -*(r)eba* (in the native grammatical tradition, the *Izenkei* 'Realis form' + *ba*), leaving "Conditional" (*zyookenkei*) free for application in Chapter 6 to the form in -*(a)ba* (*Mizenkei* 'Irrealis form' + *ba*). *t*-initial suffixes will play only a minor role in our discussion, but I will adopt "Perfect" (short for "Perfect Conclusive/Adnominal") and "Conjunctive" as labels for the inflected forms in -*ta* and -*te*, respectively.

As indicated in the rightmost column of Table 2, suffixes 1–3 show the *r*-zero alternation that we saw in Table 1, suffixes 4–5 show alternations of other consonants with zero, suffixes 6–7 show vowel-zero alternations (including the *a*-zero alternation seen in Table 1), and suffix 8 shows an apparently suppletive alternation. The alternation of suffix 9 is distinct from the other alternations, I will claim, in resulting from syncretism: in conservative dialects, the Potential suffix has only the C-stem allomorph -*e*-, and the corresponding V-stem form -*rare*- results from the fact that -*are*- is the default realization of a morphosyntactic feature that is shared by the categories Passive and Potential, as we will see in more detail below. Published analyses of the alternations of the suffixes of Table 2 illustrate all four of the proposals for lexical representations that were noted above for the two suffixes of Table 1: C-stem alternants, V-stem alternants, and longer alternants as lexical or underlying representations, and symmetrical listing of all alternants. Even before considering the question of an associated phonological rule, then, it is clear that this is a system of alternations with multiple observationally adequate analyses. Section 5.4 examines four such analyses, based respectively on the four possible choices for lexical representations just identified.

5.4   Four observationally adequate analyses and their predictions

An analysis taking the alternating suffixes of Table 2 to have URs that coincide with their C-stem alternants is proposed by de Chene (1985, 1987, 2016). As noted in Chapter 4, the hypothesis of C-stem suffixes as underlying is paired in that analysis with a rule inserting r intervocalically at verb stem boundary.[1] Call this combination "Analysis A":

(2)   Analysis A
    a.   URs: C-stem suffixes
    b.   Rule: $\emptyset \rightarrow r / V_{Vb}]$ ___ [V (= (3), Chapter 4)

Given that (2b) inserts r intermorphemically, if the first three V-stem forms of Table 2 reflect the operation of that rule, they will be segmented *mi-r-u, mi-r-eba, mi-r-are-*. Under Analysis A, then, the V-stem suffix alternants in question will coincide with the corresponding C-stem alternants, and the suffixes will, strictly speaking, be nonalternating. Setting aside the syncretic alternation of the Potential, the table's remaining V-stem suffix alternants, however, will be irregular, and the lexical representations of the suffixes in question will be weakly suppletive, as we will see in detail below.

An analysis taking the alternating suffixes of Table 2 to have URs that coincide with their V-stem alternants is proposed by McCawley (1968: 93ff.). McCawley (1968: 95) pairs the hypothesis of V-stem suffixes as underlying with a rule that deletes *r, s,* and *y* after a consonant at verb stem boundary.[2] Call this combination "Analysis B":

---

1. It has been proposed (Labrune 2014) that all occurrences of Japanese r are ultimately epenthetic, arising from insertion intervocalically in Proto-Japanese. Two problems this thesis must address are (a) as a sound change, an "excrescent" segment is plausible only insofar as it can be explained as an articulatory consequence (as in *nr > ndr*) or an auditory interpretation (as in *ia > ija*) of the transition between adjacent segments; (b) many Japanese r are widely taken (Martin 1966, Whitman 1985, Whitman 2012) to be cognate with Korean *l*, with even scholars who are skeptical of a genetic relationship between the two languages admitting "reliable" cognate candidates showing this correspondence (Vovin 2010: 238).

2. While it is sometimes suggested (Hasegawa 1999: 63, Miyagawa 1999: 236) that deletion of the second of two successive consonants represents a general principle of Japanese phonology, the usual treatment of clusters is in fact assimilation of the first C to the second: /kar + ta/ 'clip' + Perfect → [katta], /kaw + ta/ 'buy' + Perfect → [katta]; /but- + sak-/ 'beat' + 'tear' → [bussak-] 'tear violently', /hik- + sage-/ 'draw' + 'hang' → [hissage-] 'carry'; /it + kai/ 'one' + 'time' → [ikkai], /it + sai/ 'one' + 'year (of age)' → [issai], /it + pai/ 'one' + 'glass' → [ippai].

(3)   Analysis B
　　　a.   URs: V-stem suffixes
　　　b.   Rule: C [+cont] → Ø / C $_{\text{Vb}}$] [___

The condition [+continuant] on the consonant undergoing deletion in rule (3b) reflects the fact that, unlike *r, s,* and *y, t* does not delete after a stem-final consonant, as illustrated by the examples /kar + ta/, /kaw + ta/ → [katta] of note 2. Under Analysis B, the first five C-stem suffix alternants of Table 2 will be regular, correctly predicted by the application of (3b) to word-level URs. Again setting aside the Potential, the remaining C-stem alternants will be irregular. It should be noted that if *t*-initial suffixes are analyzed as added not to stems but to Adverbial forms, recapitulating their historical development, the restriction to [+continuant] consonants in (3b) will be unnecessary, since clusters with second member *t* will result from a rule of syncope that can be ordered after that rule, counterfeeding it (for a recent defense of this analysis, see Oshima 2014).

An analysis taking the alternating suffixes of Table 2 to have URs that coincide in each case with the longer of their two alternants is proposed by Kuroda (1960) and Chew (1973), paired with a rule that deletes both the second of two consonants and the second of two vowels at verb stem boundary. Using the feature [syll(abic)] to distinguish consonants and vowels, as in rule (5) of Chapter 2, call this combination "Analysis C":

(4)   Analysis C
　　　a.   URs: longer suffixes
　　　b.   Rule: [αsyll] → Ø / [αsyll] $_{\text{Vb}}$] [___

If *t*-initial suffixes are not to be treated as exceptions to (4b), they will have to be added to Adverbial forms, in line with the possibility just suggested with respect to Analysis B. Under Analysis C, the first seven of the shorter suffix alternants of Table 2 will be regular, and only that of the Imperative will be irregular.

Finally, analyses according to which both C-stem and V-stem suffix alternants are lexically listed are proposed by Bloch (1946 [1970]: 24), who specifies environments for both classes of alternants, and by Ito and Mester (2004), who propose that alternant choice is determined by ranked constraints, rendering environmental specification unnecessary. Under an analysis of this type, there are no rules and no defaults, so that the question of irregularity does not arise.

We observed in Section 5.2 that the postulation of URs for a nonautomatic alternation partitions the set of alternants into underlying or basic and nonbasic subsets, and that the postulation of a rule partitions the nonbasic alternants further into regular and irregular subsets. Table 3 summarizes the tripartition of alternants into underlying, regular derived, and irregular induced by Analyses

A, B, and C for the first eight categories of Table 2, with underlying alternants unmarked in each case, regular derived alternants (including the r + C-stem suffix combinations of Analysis A) underlined, and irregular alternants shaded.

Table 3. Underlying, regular derived (__), and irregular ( ) alternants according to Analyses A, B, and C

		Analysis A		Analysis B		Analysis C	
		C-stem	V-stem	C-stem	V-stem	C-stem	V-stem
1	Conclusive	mat-u	mi-r-u	mat-u	mi-ru	mat-u	mi-ru
2	Provisional	mat-eba	mi-r-eba	mat-eba	mi-reba	mat-eba	mi-reba
3	Passive	mat-are-	mi-r-are-	mat-are-	mi-rare-	mat-are-	mi-rare-
4	Volitional	mat-oo	mi-yoo	mat-oo	mi-yoo	mat-oo	mi-yoo
5	Causative	mat-ase-	mi-sase-	mat-ase-	mi-sase-	mat-ase-	mi-sase-
6	Adverbial	mat-i	mi-Ø	mat-i	mi-Ø	mat-i	mi-Ø
7	Negative	mat-an(a-)	mi-n(a-)	mat-an(a-)	mi-n(a-)	mat-an(a-)	mi-n(a-)
8	Imperative	mat-e	mi-ro	mat-e	mi-ro	mat-e	mi-ro

It is immediately clear from Table 3 that Analysis C is the most successful of the three analyses in terms of maximizing phonological predictability of suffix alternants, given that it treats seven of eight suffix alternations as regular. Analysis B, with five alternations treated as regular, is the next most successful analysis in this regard, and Analysis A, with only three alternations treated as regular, is the least successful.

The fact that an analysis of a nonautomatic alternation in the form of URs and a rule induces a tripartition of alternants like those displayed in Table 3 means that any such analysis makes predictions about the future diachronic profile of the alternation. First, because there is no way for either URs or regular derived alternants to exhibit "competition between the retrieval of memorized forms and the creation of new ones by rule" (Garrett 2008: 128), such an analysis predicts that those two sets of alternants should, other things being equal, remain stable. Second, because it is to be expected that irregularity will be eliminated over time, such an analysis predicts a tendency for irregular alternants to be replaced by innovative substitutes derived from the postulated URs by the postulated rule. Given the data of Table 3, it is straightforward to calculate the predictions for change made by Analyses A, B, and C: Analysis A predicts that each of the five shaded V-stem suffix alternants listed under Analysis A in Table 3 should be replaced by the corresponding C-stem suffix preceded by epenthetic r, Analysis B predicts that each of the three shaded C-stem suffix alternants listed under Analysis B in that table

should be replaced by the corresponding V-stem suffix minus its initial consonant, and Analysis C predicts that the single shaded shorter suffix alternant listed
under Analysis C in the table, similarly, should be replaced by the corresponding
longer suffix alternant minus its initial consonant. These predictions are displayed
in Table 4 (the form given for the Negative suffix under Analysis B in that table
assumes that *n*, unlike *t*, is subject to deletion).

Table 4. Predicted innovative forms in case of regularization

		Analysis A	Analysis B	Analysis C
4	Volitional	mi-r-oo		
5	Causative	mi-r-ase-		
6	Adverbial	mi-r-i	mat-	
7	Negative	mi-r-an(a-)	mat-(a-)	
8	Imperative	mi-r-e	mat-o	mat-o

Because epenthetic *r* is intermorphemic according to rule (2b), the changes predicted by Analysis A may be thought of, at the level of the morph, as straightforward leveling.

The three analyses each make one further prediction concerning what should
be expected if Potential *-e-* is generalized to V-stems — that is, if the lexical condition that restricts that suffix to C-stems is lost. For Analysis A, that prediction is
that the addition of *-e-* to V-stems should trigger *r*-Epenthesis, resulting in *-r-e-*.
Analysis B, in contrast, includes no principle that would alter a sequence of vowels at verb stem boundary and thus predicts that in case of generalization, Potential *-e-* should appear unaltered after vowels as it does after consonants. Analysis
C, finally, involves a rule deleting the second of two vowels at verb stem boundary
and thus predicts that the V-stem Potential suffix alternant should be zero.[3]

We are now ready to confront the predictions of our three analyses with the
facts of change in progress. Before doing so, however, we should raise the question
of the predictions made by the fourth type of observationally adequate analysis of
the alternations of Table 2 identified above, that in which all alternants are lexically

---

3. Given that the observed innovative V-stem Potential suffix alternant is *-re-*, in accordance
with the predictions of Analysis A, the logic of Analyses B and C will dictate taking that form
as underlying, with the result that the *-e-* ~ *-re-* alternation will be regular under both analyses.
The incorrect predictions cited, however, underline the fact that Analyses B and C have no way
of explaining why *-re-* should be the innovative form. In arising first as a C-stem suffix and only
later being generalized to V-stems, Potential *-e-* follows the same diachronic trajectory as Passive *-(r)are-* and Causative *-(s)ase-*, whose historical development was treated in Section 4.6.

listed in full and no rules or defaults are postulated. In presenting a typology of alternations in Section 5.2, we suggested that such "symmetrical" analyses predict stability for a nonautomatic alternation, given that they fail to provide any basis on which one alternant could be preferred to another. In view of the alternative possibility that such analyses make no diachronic predictions at all, the prediction of stability is not a logical necessity. In either case, however, it seems clear that there are no particular diachronic developments predicted by symmetrical analyses, in the Japanese case or in general.

5.5   Change in progress: The spread of *r*-Epenthesis

With the publication of the six-volume, 350-map *Grammar atlas of Japanese dialects* (GAJ = Kokuritsu Kokugo Kenkyujo 1989–2006), referred to above in Sections 2.3.5 and 4.5, data concerning verbal inflection has become available for 807 locations in Japan, 41 from the Ryukyu dialect area and 766 from the Japanese dialect area proper (see also the grammatical sections of Onishi 2016a, based on a later survey). In the present chapter, I concentrate on Japanese proper, proceeding to a consideration of Ryukyuan varieties in Chapter 6. Under the idealizing assumption that they have developed independently of each other, a set of related dialects like that recorded in the GAJ constitutes a kind of linguistic laboratory or natural experiment. More specifically, the GAJ in principle gives us 766 trials of an experiment in morphological and morphophonological development dating from the period of Proto-Japanese unity to the time of the survey, although, as we will see in Chapter 8, there is evidence that the innovations with which we will be concerned date from no earlier than the year 1600. The idealization of independent development, of course, is likely to be imperfectly realized when particular innovative forms appear in geographically contiguous areas, making contact a possible factor in their spread.

Data for the GAJ was gathered in interviews between local consultants (men most of whom were born before 1925 and were thus in their middle fifties and above at the time of the survey in 1979–1982) and survey workers, typically dialect specialists at local universities; each survey item asked consultants to provide a local equivalent for an expression presented in standard Japanese. The GAJ is thus fundamentally based on self-reporting and shares the potential drawbacks of that methodology (see Labov 2001: 194ff. and references cited there), although the interview format did allow survey workers to suggest forms not volunteered by consultants. In many cases, furthermore, the GAJ does not add significantly to what was already known from the descriptive dialect literature about the occurrence of particular forms or constructions in particular locations (see Tojo et al.

1961, Iitoyo et al. 1982–1986, and references cited therein). Its great virtues, in addition to the visual convenience of its maps, are that it is an exhaustive, uniform nationwide survey and that its results are quantifiable.

The verdict of the GAJ is unambiguous. First, the prediction of Analysis A that stability should be observed for (a) C-stem alternants and (b) the three V-stem alternants that coincide with their respective C-stem alternants but are preceded by epenthetic r is confirmed, if in some cases indirectly. For certain of those alternants, the GAJ shows that, while they exhibit a degree of variation, typically as the result of regional phonological developments, there is no evidence that the inherited form is irregular and in the process of being replaced by a regularized substitute. For others, such as C-stem Adverbial -*i* and Imperative -*e*, the fact that the suffix alternants in question are known to be essentially invariant throughout Japanese (and, modulo phonological change, in Ryukyuan languages as well) is reflected in the lack of survey questions devoted to the relevant forms.

Second, and more strikingly, the GAJ data confirm the prediction of Analysis A that the remaining five V-stem alternants should be unstable and in particular that, as indicated in Table 4, they should be subject to replacement by the corresponding C-stem alternants, with hiatus at stem boundary then triggering r-Epenthesis. Table 5 shows data from representative GAJ survey items on the frequency of those five r-plus-C-stem-suffix combinations (below, "r-suffixes") and the parallel V-stem Potential suffix -*r-e-* that we noted is predicted by Analysis A in case of loss of the condition restricting Potential -*e-* to C-stems.

Table 5. Frequency of innovative r-suffixes for representative GAJ survey items[*]

Survey item	Stem	Volume (Map)	Innovative form	Innovative locations	Reference set	Innovative percentage
4 ne-yoo	ne- 'sleep'	3 (108)	ne-r-oo etc.	141	505	28%
5 ko-sase-ru	ko- 'come'	3 (120)	ko-r-ase-ru etc.	267	747	36%
6 mi wa sinai	mi- 'see'	4 (161)	mi-r-y-aa-sen etc.	109	504	22%
7 mi-na-i	mi- 'see'	2 (74)	mi-r-an (mi-y-an)	122 (21)	738	17% (3%)
8 mi-ro	mi- 'see'	2 (86)	mi-r-e	174	747	23%
9 kiru koto ga dekiru	ki- 'wear'	4 (176)	ki-r-e-ru	283	608	47%

[*] Apart from irregular *se-/si-/su-/s-* 'do' and *ko-/ki-/ku-* 'come' and verbs that vary by region between C-stem and V-stem inflection, the V-stem survey items, by category, are (4) *ne-, oki-, ake-* 'arise', *ake-* 'open (t)'; (5) *ake-*; (6) *mi-*; (7) *mi-, ne-, oki-, ake-*; (8) *mi-, oki-, ake-*; (9) *oki-, ki-* (4 items).

In the table, inflectional category is indicated by the number in the leftmost column; the parenthesized items in the category 7 row refer to occurrences of *miyan* (19 from the Kii peninsula and 2 from southern Kyushu) that represent a regular phonological development of *miran*, as we will see in more detail below.[4] The percentages in the last column of the table, which give a rough idea of the strength of each innovative *r*-suffix, are the ratios of the figures in the two previous columns, where the reference set is the set of locations deemed potentially capable of showing that suffix. The reference set was calculated, for each survey item in question, by subtracting from 766 (a) the number of nonresponding locations for the item in question and (b) either the number of locations that systematically lack the relevant basic alternant (i.e. the corresponding C-stem suffix alternant) or, when that figure was unavailable due to a lack of relevant survey items, the number of locations whose responses to the survey item in question involved a construction or form distinct from that of the standard Japanese model.[5]

The figures of Table 5 are useful as a means of comparing the relative strength of the six innovative *r*-suffixes because in computing them, two factors that would otherwise have skewed the results were controlled for. The first of these, as already indicated, was variation by category in the number of locations that could in principle have displayed the relevant innovative suffix. The second is variation by category in the number of relevant GAJ survey items: for the Adverbial, whose many uses were not systematically investigated, there are only three relevant items (maps 21 and 161–162), while for the Potential, there are seven (maps 175–179 and 184–185). More revealing than the figures of Table 5 with regard to the overall strength of the evidence for Analysis A, however, is the percentage of the 766 GAJ locations that display one or more of the six innovative *r*-suffixes, showing that Analysis A is in force at that location. Table 6 shows the number of locations and percentage of the whole represented thereby for the six innovative *r*-suffixes individually and for the disjunctions of suffixes 4–8 and 4–9. Even excluding Potential *-r-e-* (Category 9), the most common member of the set, over 60% of all locations display at least one innovative suffix, while, when the Potential is included, the percentage rises to over 80%. The significantly higher frequency of Potential *-r-e-* compared to the other innovative *r*-suffixes can plausibly be attributed to the dis-

---

4. The innovative Negative suffix occurs only in the Western Japanese form *-ran;* this is perhaps because speakers with irregular eastern *-na-* identify it with the homophonous negative existential adjective, an identification that would be rendered impossible by innovative **-rana-*.

5. By category number, the two figures in question are as follows (NR = nonresponding, BL = base lacking, DC = distinct construction): (4) NR 1, BL 260 (map 109); (5) NR 19, BL 0; (6) NR 55, DC 207; (7) NR 1, BL 27 (map 80); (8) NR 8, DC 11; (9) NR 9, BL 150 (maps 173–174, 181–183) (one location in both sets).

tinct mechanism of change we have postulated for the Potential — specifically, loss of a contextual restriction as opposed to loss of irregular allomorphy (i.e. excess diacritic or phonological information).

Table 6. Frequency of innovative *r*-suffixes over all GAJ survey items

	Suffix	Number	Percent
4	Vol -*r-oo*	159	20.8
5	Cau -*r-ase-*	273	35.6
6	Adv -*r-i*	129	16.8
7	Neg -*r-an*	142	18.5
8	Imp -*r-e*	205	26.8
9	Pot -*r-e-*	419	54.7
	Any of 4–8	472	61.6
	Any of 4–9	620	80.9

The evidence supporting Analysis A, then, is extremely widespread. Further, there are a number of reasons why even the figures of Table 6 understate the extent of that evidence. One reason, already referred to, is the fact that the Adverbial form was not a focus of investigation for the GAJ; that form occurs in the survey items that do contain it more or less by accident. Systematic investigation would almost certainly have revealed many more instances of innovative Adverbial -*r-i* than are recorded in Table 6, as can be inferred from examples of that suffix that show up in the GAJ data for survey items other than the three on which the Table 6 figure was based.

For example, Tokyo Japanese displays a number of weak imperative constructions that involve the Adverbial (see Martin 1975: 964–965), and it is clear that the same is true of many regional varieties. Only in a few areas, however, is such a construction salient enough as a substitute for the Imperative to emerge as a response to an Imperative survey question; when it does, we sometimes see innovative Adverbial -*r-i*, as in forms like *okirin* (~ *okin*) "get up!" from location 656816 on the Atsumi Peninsula in Aichi Prefecture (for discussion of this construction, (*o*)+Adverbial+*n*(*sai*), in the region in question, see Yoshikawa 1972: 152–154). Location 636625 in Yamaguchi Prefecture shows parallel forms. The Adverbial-based potential expressions of Kyushu also reveal innovative Adverbial -*r-i* in a number of cases; sample forms, based on *ki-* 'wear, put on' are *kiri-kiru* (~ *ki-kiru*) (738398, Kumamoto Prefecture) and *kiri-ga-naru* (839421, Kagoshima Prefecture) 'can put on' (map 175). None of these occurrences of -*r-i* are reflected in Table 6.

It is safe to say that comprehensive data on Adverbial-based constructions would raise the Table 6 figure for that suffix considerably.

A second reason that the figures of Table 6 understate the extent of the evidence for Analysis A is that there are areas in which, to a first approximation, intervocalic *r* is subject to deletion, so that when irregular V-stem suffixes are eliminated, the expected *r*-initial substitutes show up without their *r*. In particular, there are 22 locations, for the most part overlapping with the 21 recorded in Table 5 as displaying *miyan*, that show generalization to V-stems of C-stem Negative *-an* in accordance with the predictions of Analysis A, but no evidence of *r*-Epenthesis for that suffix, which appears as *-yan*.[6] The fact that *-r-an* occurs in neighboring areas and that 20 of the 22 locations show evidence for a process converting intervocalic *r* to zero or *y* in the form of *r*-less variants of Passive/Potential *-r-are-* and/or Provisional *-r-eba* makes it plausible that, as suggested above, *-yan* represents a regular phonological development of *-ran*. Two interpretations of this development seem possible: *r* may either change directly to *y* or delete completely, with *y* then representing phonologization of the transition between the front stem vowel and the vowel of the suffix.[7] Since none of the 22 locations in question shows any innovative *r*-suffix from categories 4–8 (although twelve of them have Potential *-r-e-*), admitting them as evidence for Analysis A would raise the Table 6 figures not only for the Negative but also for Categories 4–8 by slightly under three percentage points.

A third and final reason that not all of the evidence for Analysis A appears in Table 6 is that the set of innovative *r*-suffixes observed across the range of Japanese dialects is by no means limited to the six that we have examined. Let us look briefly at several additional examples of *r*-suffixes whose historical origin and development are relatively clear.

Among the many honorific auxiliary verbs (morphologically speaking, inflectional stem-forming suffixes) displayed by the 17th-century Japanese of the Kyoto/Osaka area (*Kamigata-go*) is one that takes the form *-assyar-* ~ *-asyar-* after C-stems and *-sassyar-* ~ *-sasyar-* after V-stems (Matsumura 1971:972, Yamaguchi and Akimoto 2001:904). This suffix thus in principle shows the same *s*-zero alter-

---

6. Two points showing *miyan* do not belong to this set of 22 because they have *-ran* for a V-stem other than *mi-* (*okiran* at 750472, *neran* at 833350); three points of the 22 do not show *miyan*, their *-yan* being restricted to V-stems other than *mi-* (*neyan* at 750046 and 750391, *neyan* and *akeyan* at 658735). The 19 points that the two sets share are 654612, 655476, 655506, 656387, 656423, 656514, 656673, 657332, 657379, 657543, 657685, 658088, 658438, 659044, 659147, 659501, 750408, 751369, 924994.

7. The former interpretation is suggested by the change *ru > i* (*arusi > aisi* 'exists and' (Mie Prefecture, Umegaki 1962:114), *kuruma > kuima* 'vehicle' (Kagoshima Prefecture, Kyushu Hogen Gakkai 1991:236), where *r* appears to be the source of palatality in the output vowel.

nation as the Causative suffix, and is in fact composed historically of Causative -(s)ase- plus the old Conclusive form -raru of the Passive suffix (Matsumura 1971: 264) reanalyzed as -rar-u, with the subsequent development -(s)aserar- > -(s)asear- > -(s)asyaar- > -(s)assyar- ~ -(s)asyar-. In several areas, however, as shown by the data for GAJ map 291, the V-stem alternant -sassyar- has been or is being replaced by -r-assyar-, parallel to the replacement of Causative -sase- with -r-ase-.[8] Similarly, the honorific auxiliary -(s)ahar- of the Shonai region of Yamagata Prefecture, identified with -(s)asyar- by the NKD, displays variation between conservative V-stem -sahar- and innovative V-stem -r-ahar- (Kokuritsu Kokugo Kenkyujo 1953: 226).

An example where the original alternation is of the form V ~ Ø rather than C ~ Ø is provided by the Volitional suffix -(a)zu of Nagano, Yamanashi, and Shizuoka Prefectures (GAJ maps 106–111), which goes back to Muromachi period -(a)uzu and Kamakura period -(a)muzu (Matsumura 1971: 968, 962); the historical development will have been *kak-amuzu > kakaůzu > kakauzu > kakaazu > kakazu* "let's write" and *oki-muzu > okiůzu > okiuzu > okiizu > okizu* "let's get up". Variation between conservative V-stem -zu and innovative V-stem -r-azu is displayed by all five of the candidate stems (maps 106–108, 110–111) at GAJ location 567318, which otherwise lacks innovative r-suffixes, and parallel innovations, with variant forms of the suffix, are observed at 660401 (C-stem -ada, V-stem -da ~ -r-ada), 661368 (C-stem -aza, V-stem -za ~ -r-aza), and 662454 and 663432 (C-stem -asu, V-stem -su ~ -r-asu).

In our final example, the "spontaneous activity" suffix -(r)asar-, best known as characteristic of Hokkaido and northern Tohoku (and observable over much of that range as a Potential suffix expressing an inherent property in GAJ map 181), the replacement of an a ~ Ø alternation with r ~ Ø has evidently gone to completion in many locations; Sasaki and Yamazaki (2006), for example, cite no V-stem form other than -r-asar-.[9] Examples in the dialect section of the entry for the auxiliary *saru* in the NKD, however, provide evidence that -(r-)asar- descends from a suffix of the form -(a)sar- that is attested in multiple meanings starting in the 16th century. As in our other examples, in other words, the conservative V-stem alternant (here, -sar-) was irregular; its loss resulted in the basic alternant (-asar-)

---

8. Points 469792, 562484, 563227; 653922, 654853, 655824, 662070; 722975, 732095, 737096.

9. Sasaki (2018, 2019: 212–213) points out, however, that a V-stem alternant -sasar- has begun to appear in recent years. Given that he also reports recent influence from Tokyo Japanese on the form of the Causative suffix, with earlier V-stem -r-ase- now facing competition from -sase-, this development would appear to be explicable as the result of proportional influence of the Causative on the Spontaneous according to the formula -rase- : -sase- :: -rasar- : X (X = -sasar-).

being added to V-stems as well as C-stems, triggering *r*-Epenthesis and thus the emergence of an innovative *r*-suffix -*r-asar*-.

It is clear, then, that evidence for Analysis A is not only extremely widespread, but is open-ended, in that it is not limited to the six innovative *r*-suffixes of Tables 5 and 6. In contrast, there is evidence disconfirming each of the predictions of Analyses B and C. First of all, Analyses B and C predict, contrary to fact, that the V-stem suffix alternants of categories 4–8 should be stable, since under those analyses, the V-stem suffix alternants in question either coincide with URs or are regularly derived. Regarding innovative forms, perhaps the clearest prediction of Analyses B and C, common to the two analyses, is for C-stem Imperatives in -*o*. As noted above, the GAJ has no C-stem Imperative survey items, reflecting a paucity of interesting variation for this category nationwide, but unpublished results of the preparatory survey for the GAJ do show a handful of apparent C-stem Imperatives in -*o* from the vicinity of Kanazawa city, Ishikawa Prefecture. Such forms, however, recorded in the dialectological literature with -*oo* as well as -*o* (Iwai 1959:100ff., Iwai 1961:100), are in origin imperative uses of Volitionals.[10] There is thus no reason to doubt the stability of C-stem Imperative -*e*, counterexemplifying again the predictions of Analyses B and C. In sum, those two analyses may be taken to be disconfirmed by the available data, implying that Analysis A is the unique descriptively adequate analysis of the system of alternations in question. In the next section, we will examine Analysis A in more detail, looking first at the lexical representations that analysis postulates for the nine suffixes of Table 2 and then at morphological restrictions on the environment of the *r*-Epenthesis rule it postulates.

5.6   Analysis A: A closer look

Section 2.3.5 introduced the realization rules that are responsible for the insertion of phonological material into syntactic terminals at spellout. We saw that, under the Subset Principle, all the features specified in the rule must be present in the terminal that is the target of insertion, with a rule matching in more features taking precedence over a rule matching in fewer features. The latter condition resolves competition among rules that differ in the number of matching feature specifications, but a third condition is needed to resolve competition among rules that match in the same number of feature specifications but differ in the complexity of their environments, namely that a rule with a more complex environment takes precedence. As noted by Halle and Marantz (1993:120, 123), both the second

---

10. Thanks to Takuichiro Onishi (p.c.) for clarification on this point.

and the third conditions may be viewed as subcases of the principle, first articulated by Pāṇini, that rules apply in order of decreasing complexity.

For the most part, the question of the morphosyntactic features that are realized by the inflectional suffixes of Table 2 is orthogonal to the morphophonological issues we are concerned with here. An exception, however, arises from the syncretism that I claimed obtains between the Passive and the Potential in the V-stem paradigm, for which we now need a concrete account. Syntactically, the Passive and the Potential are both unaccusative constructions: they fail to introduce an external argument, with the result that it is the theme argument that moves to the surface subject position and receives nominative case (although in contemporary Japanese a transitive casemarking pattern is also an option for the Potential). The two constructions were marked by the same suffix -(r)are- for all verbs from roughly the 9th through the 15th centuries (see e.g. Yamaguchi and Akimoto 2001: 842–843, 846–847); this situation was disturbed starting in the late 15th century by the gradual emergence of a dedicated Potential suffix -e- for C-stems, which took until about 1800 to become fully general (Aoki 2010: 3–39).

I will assume, then, that the Passive and Potential share a morphosyntactic feature specification [+UA] (for "unaccusative") and are differentiated in that the Potential is [+UA +Pot] while the Passive is [+UA −Pot]. As shown in (5) below, -are- will be the default realization of the feature specification [+UA], preempted by -e- only when [+UA] is accompanied by [+Pot] and the environment of insertion is postconsonantal.

(5)   a.   [+UA +Pot] $\leftrightarrow$ e / C __
      b.   [+UA] $\leftrightarrow$ are

We may note that an alternative account under which the Potential alternation -e- ~ -rare- is due (like, for example, the Imperative alternation -e- ~ -ro) to lexically listed allomorphy would require claiming that there are two semantically parallel suffixes that coincidentally have the same postvocalic form -rare-.

For the remaining suffixes of Table 2, I will for convenience assume a one-to-one correspondence between morphosyntactic features and inflectional categories. Concerning the phonological form of the suffixes, URs must of course be listed. Irregular alternants — more precisely, the excess phonological or diacritic information that their generation requires — must be listed as well. I will assume that while a UR is listed without any environmental restriction, the information necessary for the generation of an irregular alternant is accompanied by a specification of environment. As a result, under the principle that a rule with a more complex environment takes precedence over one with a less complex environment, insertion of an irregular alternant will preempt insertion of the corresponding UR. I will also assume that regular derived alternants are not in general lexically listed without taking this assumption to preclude the possibility that speakers may at times record those alternants in memory. (6) below, incorporating (5), shows lexical representations under Analysis A for the nine suffixes of Table 2 (with the Negative suffix in its Eastern Japanese form).

(6) 1 [+Cnc] ↔ u   4 [+Vol] ↔ <y>oo</V__>   7 [+Neg] ↔ >a<na</V__>

2 [+Prv] ↔ eba   5 [+Cau] ↔ <s>ase</V__>   8 [+Imp] ↔ $\left\{\begin{matrix} \text{ro / V} \\ \text{e} \end{matrix}\right.$ ${}^{\text{V}}$__$\Big\}$

3 [+UA] ↔ are   6 [+Adv] ↔ $\left\{\begin{matrix} \emptyset\text{/ V} \\ \text{i} \end{matrix}\right.$ ${}^{}$__$\Big\}$ 9 [+UA +Pot] ↔ e / C __

The representations for categories 4 and 5 employ angled brackets, whereby the disjunction of XYZ and Y is represented as <X>Y<Z>. This allows us to write the material shared by the two alternants of the suffix, *oo* in the Volitional and *ase* in the Causative, only once, capturing the fact that the recurrence of that material is not coincidental. The possibility of using angled brackets for this purpose in those two categories, however, depends on the longer alternant occurring in the more complex environment; when the reverse is true, as in category 7, that convention is inapplicable. In order to allow in the latter case as well a representation of the suffix in which the material shared by the two alternants appears only once, I use a "reverse angled bracket" notation >X< Y <Z> (Y nonnull) as an abbreviation for the disjunction of YZ and XY.

Having examined the lexical representations associated with Analysis A, let us now turn our attention to the rule it postulates, repeated as (7).

(7) Ø → r / V $_{\text{Vb}}$] __ [V

It is not difficult to show that without further qualification, rule (7) is too general. Below, I refine our understanding of the conditions under which it applies by presenting five pairs whose first member illustrates the operation of *r*-Epenthesis and whose second is a minimally different formation in which *r*-Epenthesis fails to apply and hiatus either remains unresolved or is resolved through coalescence and monophthongization.

The first minimal pair contrasts innovative Potential *mi-r-e-* 'can see', where *r*-Epenthesis applies at the boundary between the stem *mi-* 'see' and the Potential suffix *-e-*, with the stem *mi-e-* 'be visible', where hiatus remains unresolved at the boundary between *mi-* and the derivational suffix *-e-* (cf. note 1, Chapter 4). In the examples below, a single underline marks a sequence of vowels that undergoes *r*-Epenthesis, and a double underline marks an apparently parallel sequence that does not.

(8) a. mi̱-e̱- [mire-] 'can see'
     b. mi̱-e̱- [mie-] 'be visible'

(8a), as an inflectional formation, will be syntactically derived, while (8b) will
be lexically listed. In accordance with the principle that the internal structure of
one level is invisible at later levels ("bracket erasure"; see e.g. Kaisse and Shaw
1985:11), I will assume that no indication of stem-internal structure accompanies
the entry of a stem's phonological representation into the derivation. If so, the
stem (8b) will be effectively monomorphemic when *r*-Epenthesis applies, and the
structural description of that rule will not be satisfied.

The second minimal pair contrasts Potential *mi-r-e-* (= (8a)) and Potential *i-
e-* 'can say', both inflectional.

(9) a. mi̱-e̱- [mire-] 'can see'
     b. i̱-e̱- [ie-]   'can say'

The stem of 'say' is /iw-/, as shown by its shape before *a*-initial suffixes (Passive *iw-
are-*, Causative *iw-ase-*, Negative *iw-ana-*). *w* eventually deletes before any vowel
other than *a*, but must clearly still be in place when *r*-Epenthesis applies. I will
assume a word-level and a phrase-level stratum within the postsyntactic (post-
spellout) phonology, with *r*-Epenthesis belonging to the former and *w*-Deletion
to the latter. *w*-Deletion is essentially exceptionless, and may thus be considered
an automatic repair triggered by violation of the constraint $*w$ [V −low].[11]

The third minimal pair contrasts *mi-r-are-* 'be seen' and *mi-oe-* (where *oe-* is
/ow-e-/) 'finish looking', both syntactically derived (for the syntactic status of the
latter, see Kageyama 1999:301–303 and references cited there).

(10) a. mi̱-are- [mirare-] 'be seen'
      b. mi̱-o̱e- [mioe-] 'finish looking'

Passive *-are-* and *oe-* 'finish' differ morphologically in that the former is an affix
and the latter a stem, so that while (10a) is an example of affixation, (10b) is an
example of compounding. Correspondingly, I will take pairs like (10) to show that
the rightward element in the environment of *r*-Epenthesis must be grammatical
rather than lexical. Abbreviating the positive value of the feature [Grammatical]
as "Af" (for *affix*), the *r*-Epenthesis rule (7) may thus be rewritten as (11).

(11) $\emptyset \rightarrow r$ / V$_{Vb}$] __ [$_{Af}$ V

---

11. Vance (2008:90–92), however, discusses possible cases of (a) counterfeeding and (b) violation in loanwords.

In conjunction with the minimal pair of (8), the upshot of (10) is that *r*-Epenthesis applies only in inflectional formations: it is excluded from derivation (and from lexical compounds) by its postsyntactic status in conjunction with the convention of bracket erasure, and it is excluded from syntactic compounds by the requirement that the rightward element of its environment be affixal.

The last two minimal pairs involve dialect forms with irregular V-stem suffix alternants that are vowel-initial, but fail to trigger *r*-Epenthesis. The first of these pairs contrasts the innovative and conservative Imperative forms of *mi-* 'see, look' recorded at GAJ locations 641131, 642049, and 642157 in the Izumo region of Shimane Prefecture (the diaeresis is the IPA centralization diacritic).

(12) a. mï-e [mïre] 'look!' (innovative)

      b. mï-ï [mïï] 'look!' (conservative)

The second contrasts the innovative and conservative Volitional forms of *oki-* 'get up' recorded at GAJ locations 728951 (Nagasaki Prefecture) and 734265 (Fukuoka Prefecture).

(13) a. oki-oo [okiroo] 'let's get up' (innovative)

      b. oki-u [okyuu] 'let's get up' (conservative)

(12b) and (13b) illustrate the fact that V-stem Imperative -*i* and V-stem Volitional -*u* are both widely attested in Western Japan and Kyushu (see GAJ maps 85–87 and 106–108, respectively). Forms with those suffix alternants appear to satisfy the input conditions of *r*-Epenthesis, but they do not undergo it. They do, however, undergo a different hiatus resolution process, namely the coalescence of two adjacent syllables into one. This can be inferred from the monophthongization apparent in (13b) and from the fact that monophthongized Imperative forms such as *akee/akii < ake-i* 'open it!' (GAJ map 87) are widely attested as well; these monophthongizations may be assumed to occur only syllable-internally. It should be noted that parallel monophthongizations are triggered by the homophonous adjectival suffixes Conclusive -*i* and Polite Adverbial -*u*, as illustrated by examples like (14) and (15) (the monophthongizations of (14) are dependent on speech level and region; for evidence that the vowel sequences in question belong to the same syllable even when monophthongization does not occur, see Vance 1987:74).

(14) a. taka-i [takee] 'expensive'

      b. hido-i [hidee] 'outrageous'

(15) a. arigata-u [arigatoo] 'grateful(ly)'

      b. yorosi-u [yorosyuu] 'good, well'

In fact, both V-stem Imperative *-i* and V-stem Volitional *-u* appear marginally in Tokyo Japanese, the first in *ko-i*, the Imperative of 'come', the second in *-masyoo* < *-mase-u*, the Volitional of the Polite auxiliary. Here as well, syllable coalescence may be assumed to have operated; while *ko-i* 'come!' resists monophthongization in Tokyo, it is *koo* over wide areas of Eastern Japan and *kee* or *kii* in parts of Western Japan and much of Kyushu (GAJ map 90), and we have already seen that parallel vowel sequences in adjective inflection are tautosyllabic even in the absence of monophthongization. It seems natural to assume, then, that Imperative *-i* and Volitional *-u* are marked to trigger a minor rule of syllable coalescence, which creates a bimoraic nucleus from a sequence of vowels in hiatus, and that that rule is ordered before *r*-Epenthesis, bleeding it.

There is reason to believe, however, that an account based on syllable coalescence does not capture the actual reason that V-stem Imperative *-i* and V-stem Volitional *-u* fail to trigger *r*-Epenthesis. Note to begin with that, because the vowels of sequences like *i* + *a/o* and *e* + *a/o* remain in hiatus (see Vance 2008: §§3.3, 6.7), such an account predicts that if there were, for example, an irregular V-stem suffix alternant of the form *-a*, *r*-Epenthesis should apply before it. This is not obviously the case, however. For the same reason, a syllable coalescence account would license treating the *r* of V-stem Imperative *-ro* as epenthetic, but it is not clear that it is appropriate to do so.

An alternative intuition about why V-stem Imperative *-i* and Volitional *-u* do not trigger *r*-Epenthesis is that the input conditions of the rule require a default suffix alternant in its rightward environment. In effect, this intuition would say, *r*-Epenthesis is a mechanism for allowing default suffix alternants to be used after vowel-stems as well as after consonant-stems, and thus applies only before a default form. In support of this idea, observe first that *r*-Epenthesis is naturally seen as a generalization of the *r*-zero alternation of the first three suffixes of Table 2, represented below as (16).

(16) a. Conclusive   -u   ~ -ru
      b. Provisional   -eba   ~ -reba
      c. Passive   -are- ~ -rare-

As we will see in more detail in Chapter 8, while the *r*-zero alternation of (16a) and (16b) goes back to the 8th century, and that of (16c) goes back to the 10th, the innovative *r*-epenthetic forms of the remaining categories are not attested until the modern period.

Suppose now, counterfactually, that the original alternations of the three categories of (16) had been either those indicated as A or those indicated as B in (17), where the V-stem alternants of the A set result from the V-stem alternants of (16) by permutation of their first vowels, and the V-stem alternants of the B set result from those of the A set by permutation of the alternants themselves.

(17) Hypothetical alternations in the three categories of (16)

		A		B	
a.	Conclusive	-u	~ -ra	-u	~ -rere
b.	Provisional	-eba	~ -ruba	-eba	~ -ra
c.	Passive	-are-	~ -rere-	-are-	~ -ruba-

In either of those cases, it seems fair to say, there would have been no motivation for analyzing the initial *r* of the V-stem suffixes as epenthetic, and thus no reason to expect extension of initial *r* to other categories. The innovative generalization governing *r*-Epenthesis, in other words, is not just that V-stem suffix alternants are *r*-initial, a condition that is satisfied by the V-stem alternants of A and B in (17) as well as by those of (16). Rather, the generalization is that regular V-stem suffixes are identical with default forms (= C-stem suffixes) apart from epenthetic *r*.

If this intuition is correct, the rightward environment "[$_{Af}$ V" given for *r*-Epenthesis in (11) above is still too general and needs to be revised so as to make the rule sensitive to whether the affix in question is a default form or not. Concerning the formal mechanism by which this is to be accomplished, we may first of all eliminate the possibility that what is involved is a lexical diacritic, whether on default or nondefault forms: our interpretation of lexical diacritics entails that they are subject to loss over time, and a diacritic on default forms would in addition be inconsistent with their unmarked nature, making *r*-Epenthesis into a minor rule. The option of allowing *r*-Epenthesis to examine lexical entries to determine whether particular suffix alternants are defaults or not is also unattractive, given that it would introduce globality into the phonological computation. A third approach that amends slightly the process of exponence (vocabulary insertion) that we have assumed will avoid both of these problems.

The rules of exponence that introduce phonological material into syntactic terminal elements may of course be guided by listed environments; this is the case, for example, in the representations given in (6) above for suffixes 4 through 9. It is generally assumed, however, that the environment has no direct reflex in the phonological exponent. I will modify this assumption by the introduction of a mechanism that will allow phonological computation to distinguish between contextually restricted exponents and context-free default forms when it is necessary to do so. Specifically, let us assume that a phonetically uninterpretable element "e" is added to the phonological feature matrix of an exponent that is inserted in response to a listed environment; like a diacritic feature specification, the element e will be deleted before the derivation reaches the interface with the sensorimotor or articulatory-perceptual (Chomsky 1995: 131, 168) system. In the Japanese case, if the formulation of *r*-Epenthesis in (11) is then supplemented with the condition "the affix of the rightward environment does not contain e", the restriction of that rule to default forms will be captured. This account, then, constitutes a viable and arguably more insightful alternative to the syllable coalescence account of the failure of *r*-Epenthesis to apply in the Imperative and Volitional forms of (12b) and (13b).

It should be noted that the element e will be crucial in blocking the application of *r*-Epenthesis only when the relevant suffix is vowel-initial and the relevant stem is vowel-final, as is the case in (12b) and (13b). Consider in this context the nine categories of (6). For categories 1 through 8, V-stem suffixes, the suffix alternants with listed environments, are consonant-initial (or zero); for category 9, the single alternant has a listed environment, but that environment requires the stem to be consonant-final. In all of those cases, then, the segmental environment will preclude the application of *r*-Epenthesis even apart from the presence of e.

In this section, after introducing the lexical representations associated with Analysis A, we have investigated the environment in which the *r*-Epenthesis rule of that analysis applies. We have seen that the element following the insertion site must be inflectional — that is, that it can be neither a stem nor a derivational suffix. Above, I proposed that a specification identifying it as [+Grammatical] precludes its being a stem and that erasure of stem-internal structure on entry into the derivation precludes its being a derivational suffix. Finally, I have argued that *r*-Epenthesis requires the triggering suffix to occur in its underlying or default form and have proposed a mechanism to ensure that outcome. It is important to note that none of these restrictions is peculiar to *r*-Epenthesis and Analysis A. In particular, because hiatus either survives intact in the environments where *r*-Epenthesis fails to apply or (in the case of Imperative -*i* and Volitional -*u*) is resolved by syllable coalescence, the rule of Analysis C, which deletes the second of two vowels across verb stem boundary, would have to be restricted in exactly the same way.[12]

5.7 Alternative accounts of innovative *r*-epenthetic forms

Innovative forms like *mire* 'look!' and *miroo* 'let's look', taken in Section 5.5 as confirmation of the predictions of Analysis A, have been interpreted in other ways

---

12. Fukushima's (2004: 195 (note 4)) criticism of the *r*-Epenthesis rule of de Chene 1987 for incorporating the restrictions in question is thus misguided: the restrictions on where hiatus is (dis)allowed are a fact of the data rather than of any particular analysis thereof.

by scholars working in the Japanese linguistic and dialectological tradition. In this section I examine those alternative interpretations and argue that the account based on Analysis A provides a better understanding of the innovations in question. I will consider first accounts that attribute the relevant innovative forms to the influence of *r*-stem conjugation and then accounts that seek to explain innovative forms as direct transformations of the conservative forms they replace.

5.7.1 The putative influence of *r*-stem inflection

On the view developed above, when a vowel-final verb stem such as *mi-* 'look' comes to display innovative forms like Imperative *mire*, Volitional *miroo*, Negative *miran*, Adverbial *miri*, and Causative *mirase-*, those forms are to be understood as the result of regularization pursuant to the adoption of Analysis A as a synchronic account of suffix alternations. Concretely, as we have seen, regularization takes the form of elimination of irregular vowel-stem suffix alternants in favor of default suffixes, with the resulting juxtaposition of vowel-final stems and vowel-initial suffixes triggering the application of *r*-Epenthesis. The Japanese dialectological tradition, in contrast, has tended to view such innovative forms in isolation from questions of synchronic analysis and to associate their *r* with the stem-final *r* of verbs like *kir-* 'cut', *ter-* 'shine', *nar-* 'become', *tor-* 'take', and *sur-* 'rub'. Often this association is simply presupposed, typically by use of the common label *itidan katuyoo no ra-gyoo godanka* 'the assimilation of vowel-stem to *r*-stem conjugation' or variants thereof. Sometimes the influence of *r*-stem conjugation in the genesis of the innovative forms is directly asserted; a recent example is Onishi 2016c: 152. And in the most explicit formulations of the "*r*-stem influence" hypothesis, four-term proportions are appealed to in order to account for the innovative forms; a typical example (Matsumaru 2006: 40) is the proportion *kiru*: *kire* = *miru*: X (X = *mire*) as motivation for the innovative Imperative *mire* 'look!'. Here, I will take such proportions as representative of the *r*-stem-based interpretation of the innovative forms in question.

In arguing that the Analysis A account of those innovative forms is to be preferred to the *r*-stem-based account, the central fact I will appeal to is that the innovations in question progress suffix by suffix (alternatively, inflectional category by inflectional category) in each dialect, as opposed to (among other possibilities) progressing stem by stem (lexeme by lexeme), progressing in random order across the set of all inflected forms, or occurring simultaneously. Thus, the city of Tsuruoka in Yamagata Prefecture (Kokuritsu Kokugo Kenkyujo 1953: 191–193) shows innovative forms for three of the five categories identified above (the Imperative, Volitional, and Causative), the city of Toyohashi in Aichi Prefecture is recorded (Yoshikawa 1972: 152–155) as showing innovative forms for four categories (all but the Causative), and in general, each innovative dialect is characterized by its inventory of innovative categories — under Analysis A, the inventory of categories for which irregular vowel-stem suffix alternants have been eliminated, leaving the default form as the sole lexical representation.

To say that the replacements in question do not progress stem by stem does not mean that, for a given category, all vowel-final stems come to show innovative or regularized forms at the same time. For example, stems whose final vowel displays the "bigrade" alternation of front vowel with *u* do not in general regularize until that alternation has been leveled ("bigrade blocking", discussed in Chapter 8).[13] What it does mean is that it is unnecessary to refer to individual stems or lexemes in specifying the course of regularization in a given dialect or in comparing two dialects regarding the extent to which they show regularization. In contrast, reference to individual suffixes or categories is inescapable in such contexts, as the above examples illustrate. Under the Analysis A interpretation of the innovative forms, the suffix-by-suffix progression of the changes follows immediately from the fact that that analysis locates irregularity in suffix alternants. Under the interpretation of those forms according to which they result from "analogy" (Matsumaru 2006: 40, Onishi 2016c: 152) to *r*-stem forms via proportions such as *kiru : kire = miru : X* (X = *mire*), in contrast, there is no way, I claim, to capture the fact that the changes progress suffix by suffix.

To see this, observe that when the forms of the above proportion are segmented into stems and suffixes, we obtain *kir-u : kir-e = mi-ru : X* (X = *mi-re*). In the segmented proportion, however, the stem-final *r* of *kir-* no longer plays any role; the same relationships are captured by a proportion *kak-u : kak-e = mi-ru : X* (X = *mi-re*) (*kak-* 'write') or, indeed, by a proportion *-u : -e = -ru : X* (X = *-re*). In order to attribute motivation for the changes to *r*-stem inflection, in other words, the proportional account must assume unsegmented forms. It must assume, that is, that in generating the innovative items, speakers analogize inflected words to one another without regard to the segmentation of those words into stems and suffixes. On this hypothesis, however, there is no way to distinguish between changes that occur suffix by suffix and changes that occur stem by stem or in random order.

Another property of the set of innovative *r*-epenthetic forms that is naturally accommodated only under the Analysis A interpretation is the extreme rarity,

---

13. The phenomenon of bigrade blocking means that the bigrade alternation is a confound on any attempt to establish a direct correlation between stem length and susceptibility to regularization under Analysis A. In particular, when polysyllabic stems display the bigrade alternation but monosyllabic stems do not, as is the case in parts of eastern Kyushu (see e.g. Itoi 1961: 260–261), restriction of regularization to monosyllables follows from bigrade blocking and requires no additional constraint referring to stem length.

across Japanese dialects, of the obstruent-final V-stem allomorphs that are predicted by proportions like *kiru*: *kitta* = *miru*: X (X = *mitta*), where *-ta* is the
suffix of the Perfect; it is worth noting that the forms in question make no
appearance in the GAJ because the observed variation was not considered significant enough to warrant a survey question. In the dialectological literature, the
failure of these forms to be more widely attested is considered mysterious (see
Kobayashi 2004: 593–594). But on the interpretation offered here, under which
innovative *r*-suffixes are due to *r*-Epenthesis, there is no mystery: the environment of that rule requires two vowels in hiatus, so that no prediction is generated for forms with consonant-initial suffixes like *-ta*.

Obstruent-final allomorphs of historical V-stems are in fact observed in certain Kyushu dialects, notably those of Kagoshima and Kumamoto Prefectures.
In Kagoshima, historical *i*-stems and monosyllabic *e*-stems inflect exactly like
r-stems, and so have obstruent-final allomorphs before Perfect *-ta* (Goto
1961: 279); in Kumamoto, obstruent-final allomorphs are observed for historical
i-stems and monosyllabic *e*-stems even though Adverbial *-r-i* is lacking and the
remaining categories show variation between innovative and conservative forms
(Akiyama 1961: 224–225, Kyushu Hogen Gakkai 1991: 240, 231). The natural inference is that, due to the accumulation of innovative *r*-suffixes in the V-stem paradigm, speakers of those dialects have reanalyzed epenthetic *r* as part of the stem
or are in the process of doing so (de Chene 1985: 180, de Chene 1987: 166, Konishi
2011: 49, de Chene 2016: 57). The adoption of the obstruent-final stem allomorph
characteristic of *r*-stem inflection is then a consequence of that reanalysis.

As the evidence we have seen above shows, the descriptive label "assimilation
of vowel-stem to *r*-stem conjugation" is a misnomer when applied to the gradual
spread of default suffixes augmented by epenthetic *r*, motivated as those changes
are by a pattern of suffix alternation (i.e. that of (16)) that has no intrinsic connection to *r*-stems. At the natural endpoint of the relevant sequence of changes, however, the distinct mechanism of reanalysis of epenthetic *r* as stem-final produces
a result to which the label in question, somewhat ironically, applies after all (see
Konishi 2011: 58 (note 2)).

5.7.2   Category-specific accounts of innovative *r*-suffixes

Forms with innovative *r*-suffixes have also been interpreted in the literature as
direct transformations of the conservative forms they replace, much as if one
were to seek to explain the 17th-century replacement of *raught* /rɔːt/ by *reached*
/riːtʃt/ as the past tense of English *reach* by postulating a change process /ɔː/ >
/iːtʃ/. Such an account is particularly well known for innovative V-stem Potential
-re-, a suffix that has attracted more attention than the other innovative *r*-suffixes

because it is characteristic of Tokyo Japanese (in this section, I write epenthetic *r* as part of the various innovative suffix alternants). Since the 1990s, the ongoing replacement of Potential *-rare-* by *-re-*, interpretable given *r*-Epenthesis simply as the generalization of Potential *-e-* from C-stems to V-stems, has become known as *ra-nuki* ("*ra*-removal"),[14] a label embodying the claim that *-re-* results from deletion of *ra* in the potential use of *-rare-* (leaving the passive and other uses untouched); this claim has been taken up by, among others, Ito and Mester (2004) and Fukushima (2004).

Category-specific accounts for innovative *r*-suffixes, however, are not limited to the *ra*-deletion analysis of Potential *-re-*. In fact, they have been proposed for all such suffixes with the possible exception of Adverbial *-ri* (see e.g. Kobayashi 2004:582–595). The left-hand side of Table 7 below summarizes such accounts by juxtaposing conservative and innovative V-stem suffix alternants and displaying the morpheme-specific changes necessary to account for the innovative forms on the hypothesis that they arise from transformation of the conservative ones. For comparison, the right-hand side of the table juxtaposes C-stem suffixes and innovative V-stem suffixes, showing that the latter can be produced from the former in each case by insertion of *r*.

Table 7. Comparison of transformative and substitutive accounts of innovative *r*-suffixes

		V-stem (old)	V-stem (new)	Change	C-stem	V-stem (new)	Change
4	Volitional	-yoo	-roo	y → r	-oo	-roo	Ø → r
5	Causative	-sase-	-rase-	s → r	-ase-	-rase-	Ø → r
6	Adverbial	-Ø	-ri	Ø → ri	-i	-ri	Ø → r
7	Negative	-n	-ran	Ø → ra	-an	-ran	Ø → r
8	Imperative	-ro	-re	o → e	-e	-re	Ø → r
9	Potential	-rare-	-re-	ra → Ø	-e-	-re-	Ø → r

The left-hand side of the table makes it abundantly clear that there is no generalization to be obtained by direct comparison of conservative and innovative forms. This is underlined by a comparison of the rules for the Negative and the Potential, which are inverses of each other, the first inserting the syllable *ra* and the second deleting it. It is nevertheless not difficult to come up with post facto motivations for such rules, as the following two quotations involving precisely those two apparent changes illustrate.

---

14. The word is absent from the first edition of *Daijirin* (Matsumura 1988) and the fourth edition of *Kojien* (Shinmura 1991), two standard dictionaries, but present in the second edition of the former (Matsumura 1995) and the fifth edition of the latter (Shinmura 1998). Its origin, then, can be dated quite precisely.

[B]ecause N has a weak degree of independence as a sound, [speakers] have perhaps attempted to stabilize the form by inserting *ra* ....

(Kobayashi 2004: 591 (my translation))

[D]eletion of a syllable ... reduces articulatory effort, and ... sets apart the potentials, ... relieving ... -*rare*- of the ... burden of covering five separate constructions.

(Fukushima 2004: 188)

The ease with which such "functional" accounts can be formulated means that
they must be treated with extreme caution.

The problems faced by transformative accounts of innovative *r*-suffixes, however, are not limited to the arbitrary and unsystematic nature of the changes they
postulate. Because transformative accounts take innovative *r*-suffixes to be based
on their conservative counterparts, while the substitutive account takes them to
be based on consonant-stem suffixes, and because those two types of "bases" have
distinct geographical distributions for some categories, the two accounts make different predictions for those categories concerning the range over which innovative forms should be observed. A clear example is provided by Imperatives. With
minor exceptions, C-stem Imperative -*e* occurs throughout Japan, while over the
same geographical range, the three conservative V-stem Imperative suffixes -*i*, -*yo*,
and -*ro* exhibit (for *i*-stems) a roughly concentric distribution, with -*i* occupying
western Honshu and most of Shikoku, -*yo* observed in narrow bands on either side
of the -*i* region, and -*ro* confined to Northwestern Kyushu and Eastern Japan (see
GAJ map 86; for *e*-stems, Imperative -*i* originated earlier and has spread further).
-*ro*, then, occurs in only a proper subset of the localities that have -*e*. As a result,
any account of innovative Imperative -*re* that relates it directly to -*ro* (Kobayashi
2004: 588, Lawrence 2004: 25–26, Martin 1975: 960) predicts that -*re* should be
confined to the -*ro* region, while a substitutive account of -*re* as based on C-stem -*e*
predicts that -*re* should, other things being equal, be observed nationwide.

On this point it is the prediction of the substitutive analysis that is borne out:
innovative Imperative -*re* commonly occurs in areas where the conservative suffix it replaces is not -*ro*, but -*yo* or -*i*. This is true, to begin with, over an extensive portion of central and southern Kyushu totaling 40 GAJ survey points, all
of which report at least one occurrence of -*re*, no occurrence of -*ro*, and at least
one occurrence of a non-*ro* conservative V-stem Imperative suffix.[15] The same
conditions are satisfied by one or more locations in (a) the Izumo region of Shimane Prefecture, (b) the Hata region of Kochi Prefecture, (c) the Tajima region of

---

15. The survey points are: mainland Kagoshima except for 836382 (21 locations); 739405,
830466, 831372, 831452, 832440, 833436, 834556, 835428 (Miyazaki); 736312, 737331, 737399,
737412, 738221 (Kumamoto); 822996, 824818, 839421, 924994 (offshore Kagoshima); 733434,
736769 (Oita). Of these points, 833350 (mainland Kagoshima) and 924994 show the development of intervocalic *r* to *y* or zero.

Hyogo Prefecture, (d) the island of Awajishima in Hyogo Prefecture, (e) the environs of Hashimoto city in Wakayama Prefecture, (f) the Yoshino region of Nara Prefecture, (g) the environs of Mikawa Bay in Aichi Prefecture, and (h) the Eastern Mino region of Gifu Prefecture.[16] The descriptive dialect literature confirms the presence of innovative Imperative -*re* in all these areas and in some cases indicates its presence in additional locations lacking -*ro*, such as Oita city in eastern Kyushu (see Itoi 1983: 257). As already illustrated in (12) above, many of the locations in question show variation between Imperatives in -*re* and Imperatives in -*yo* or -*i* for one or more stems, so that it is possible to observe in progress the replacement of the latter with the former, unmediated by any occurrence of -*ro*.

The same argument can be made with respect to the Volitional, whose C-stem suffix alternant -*oo* has a distribution that includes both areas with conservative V-stem -*yoo* and areas with conservative V-stem -*u*. A transformative account of innovative V-stem -*roo* that relates it to conservative -*yoo*, as in Table 7, will thus predict that it should be observed only in the area with -*yoo*, while a substitutive account of -*roo* as based on C-stem -*oo* will predict that it should be observed throughout the area with -*oo* regardless of the conservative V-stem alternant. Again it is the prediction of the substitutive account that is confirmed: in particular, the greater part of Kyushu shows -*u* to the exclusion of -*yoo* as a conservative alternant, but nevertheless displays innovative -*roo*. (13) above has already illustrated variation between -*u* and -*roo* for two locations where -*yoo* is absent.

It is clear, then, that in some cases, category-specific "transformational" accounts of innovative *r*-suffixes face empirical problems in addition to the conceptual problems identified above in connection with Table 7.[17] Like the interpretation of innovative *r*-suffixes attributing them to influence from *r*-stem conjugation that was discussed in Section 5.7.1, then, an interpretation that attributes those suffixes to category-specific change processes appears to pose no serious challenge to the analysis developed in Sections 5.4 through 5.6, an analysis according to which inno-

---

16. Survey points (a) 641131, 642049, 642157; (b) 746200, 747138; (c) 641910, 642809; (d) 647995; (e) 657294; (f) 659300, 659398, 659420; (g) 654733, 654853, 655765, 655824, 655955, 656816; (h) 651909. 645839, midway between the (c) and (d) areas, and 652852, midway between the (g) and (h) areas, also satisfy the conditions in question.

17. There is also one case in which the substitutive account might appear to face an empirical challenge: the data for seven GAJ survey points counterexemplify that account's prediction that innovative V-stem Potential -*re*- should not appear in the absence of C-stem -*e*-. In all seven cases, however, either the descriptive dialect literature or the GAJ results for neighboring locations suggest that -*e*- can in fact be assumed to be present in the area in question. For 733397, 733671, 736525 (Oita) and 734265 (southern Fukuoka), see Tsuda 2000. For 723882 (Nagasaki), see the immediately adjacent 723767 and 723898. For 373577 (Iwate), see Komatsushiro 1961: 192. 172535, finally, the only Hokkaido location not to report -*e*-, apparently fails to do so because all C-stem Potential responses employ a construction that echoes the survey question.

vative *r*-suffixes result from the application of *r*-Epenthesis pursuant to simplification of lexical entries by loss of irregular V-stem suffix alternants.

5.8   Conclusion

Chapter 5 opened by distinguishing between observational and descriptive adequacy in morphophonology and suggesting that, in our present state of knowledge, corpus-external evidence will typically be necessary to identify the descriptively adequate analysis of a given morphophonological data set. In the course of the chapter, I appealed to diachronic change in progress as the external evidence that allows us to identify the descriptively adequate analysis of the suffixal alternations of the Japanese verb, in particular those alternations that are sensitive to whether the stem ends in a vowel or in a consonant. As argued beginning in Section 5.5, that analysis is the one defined by postulation of consonant-stem suffix alternants as underlying and derivation of regular vowel-stem alternants by intervocalic epenthesis of *r* (above, "Analysis A").

In conclusion, it is important to note that while the scope of Analysis A extends to all inflectional elements, stem-forming suffixes like the Passive, Causative, and Potential in addition to inflectional endings, it clearly does not extend to derivational elements. This is illustrated by the near-minimal contrast between the (western) Negative suffix -*(a)n* and the verb-stem-deriving suffix -*(a)m*- that we observed in Chapter 3: while the former is subject to Analysis A's *r*-Epenthesis rule, yielding an innovative form -*r-an* that surfaces when irregular V-stem -*n* is eliminated, the latter remains completely unaffected by the adoption of Analysis A. This difference between inflection and derivation is readily explained if inflectional affixes have listed representations that are subject to reanalysis, while derivational affixes do not. In Chapter 7, we will see further that stems, like inflectional affixes, are subject to morphophonological reanalysis; in contrast, roots, like derivational affixes, are apparently not. It will turn out, then, that the scope of morphophonological reanalysis corresponds precisely to the set of elements that in Chapters 1 through 4 were argued to be subject to syntactic combination, namely stems and inflectional affixes.

We have not yet reached the end, however, of the story of Analysis A as the descriptively adequate analysis of Japanese inflectional suffix alternations. This is because elimination of irregularity under that analysis and consequent expansion of the scope of the *r*-Epenthesis rule has progressed further in most Ryukyuan languages than it has in any dialects of Japanese other than those of southern Kyushu. We turn in Chapter 6 to evidence for the adoption of Analysis A in Ryukyuan languages.

Analysis A in Ryukyuan

6.1 Introduction

As we saw in Chapter 5, the process of regularization under Analysis A remains incomplete in almost all Japanese dialects. Moreover, there are many dialects in which the majority of irregular vowel-stem suffix alternants are stable, so that evidence for the adoption of Analysis A is sparse. With one major exception, regularization under Analysis A is much more uniformly advanced in Ryukyuan languages, and there are a number of Ryukyuan dialects in which regularization has gone to completion, with irregular forms remaining, if at all, in a small set of very common verbs. This is true in particular for the Shuri dialect of Okinawan, the best documented of all Ryukyuan varieties. In considering evidence for the adoption of Analysis A in Ryukyuan languages, Chapter 6 concentrates to begin with on Shuri. Section 6.2 first summarizes the basic facts of the Shuri system of verbal inflection from a synchronic standpoint. Section 6.3 then discusses the evolution of that system and the evidence that Analysis A was adopted by speakers in the prehistory of Shuri. Section 6.4 considers alternate interpretations of regularization under Analysis A in Shuri that are based on points of overlap, arising from phonological change, among the paradigms of the relevant stem-types. Section 6.5 widens the scope of the inquiry to consider evidence for the adoption of Analysis A first in other Northern Ryukyuan (Amami and Okinawan) dialects and then in Sakishima (Miyako, Yaeyama, and Dunan/Yonaguni) dialects. In conclusion, Section 6.6, in the context of the endangered status of many minority dialects, raises the question of the role of children in driving regularization under Analysis A.

6.2 Synchrony: The essentials of Shuri verb inflection

In introducing the inflectional system of the Shuri verb, I will concentrate on questions of morphological segmentation and the degree to which the alternations of stems and suffixes are predictable in terms of general principles. I rely for the basic facts of the system on Hattori 1955, Uemura 1963, and Tsuhako 1997, and on the invaluable *Okinawa-go jiten* (Kokuritsu Kokugo Kenkyujo 1963; below, DOL); readers are referred to those sources for details not provided here.

All Shuri verb stems end in a consonant; the Shuri cognates of Japanese vowel-final verb stems uniformly end in *r* (see e.g. Tsuhako 1997: 382–383).[1] As in Japanese, there are nine stem-final consonants. Shuri verb stems ending in the consonants *k, g, s, t, n, b, m* correspond to Japanese verb stems ending in the same consonants. *d*-stems are the result of reduction processes operating on stems ending in B*Ur*-, where B is *b* or *m* and U is *u* or *i*: in that sequence, BU becomes mora nasal, after which *r* becomes *d*. Shuri *r*-stems, finally, correspond not only to Japanese *r*-stems (other than those that became *d*-stems) and to Japanese vowel-stems, but to Japanese *w*-stems as well.

The verbal inflectional suffixes of Shuri can be divided into three groups depending on their effect, if any, on a stem-final consonant. What I will call Class I or "neutral" suffixes do not affect a stem-final consonant, allowing it to appear in its basic form; below, I will on occasion refer to the stem of Class I forms as the "basic stem". A number of these suffixes are illustrated in Table 1 for stems *kak-* 'write', *tur-* 'take', and *kees-* 'return' (J *kak-, tor-, kaes-*); for the Causative forms, I follow Toyama 2013a, 2013b, 2015.

Table 1. Shuri Class I (neutral) suffixes

	/kak-/	/tur-/	/kees-/
Negative	kak-an	tur-an	kees-an
Volitional	kak-a	tur-a	kees-a
Conditional	kak-aa	tur-aa	kees-aa
Prohibitive	kak-una	tun-na	kees-una
Provisional	kak-ee	tur-ee	kees-ee
Imperative	kak-i	tur-i	kees-i
Passive	kak-arir-	tur-arir-	kees-arir-
Causative 1	kak-as-	tur-as-	*
Causative 2	kak-asimir-	tur-asimir-	kees-imir-

The affinity of the Shuri verbal paradigm with that of Japanese is clear from the forms of Table 1; among the notable differences are the raising of mid vowels and the reanalysis of vowel-stems as *r*-stems that are apparent in the Shuri forms

1. Some analyses, however, treat (some or all) Shuri *r*-stems as vowel-final, necessitating *r*-initial basic forms for a large number of suffixes and a rule deleting *r* after a stem-final consonant (Ashworth 1973, Arakaki 2003, Miyara 2015). In fact, apart from a slightly wider range of contexts in which stem-final *r* deletes, there would seem to be no more grounds for taking *r*-stems to be vowel-final than for so analyzing stems ending in any other consonant.

(in addition to *tur-* 'take', see Imperative *-i* (J *-e*), Passive *-arir-* (J *-are-*), Causative 2 *-asimir-* (J *-asime-*)). Conditional *-aa* varies with *-awa* and corresponds to (premodern) J *-aba;* Provisional *-ee* alternates with *-iwa* in *-iwa-du* (*-du* Focus) and corresponds to J *-eba* (Uemura 1963: 69). Apart from the reduction of *ru* to mora nasal before *n* in the Prohibitive of 'take' (cf. Section 2.3.6.3), the stems of Table 1 are nonalternating in the forms given. With the same exception, the first seven suffixes are nonalternating as well. Both Causative suffixes, however, show unexpected behavior in the paradigm of *s*-stems: the Causative 2 stem is shorter than expected, and the Causative 1 stem is lacking entirely. When we note that on the basis of the other two stem types the expected forms for *kees-* 'return' would be **kees-asimir-* and **kees-as-*, it becomes clear that there is a unified explanation for the two cases: a word-level rule of haplology deletes the first of two *s*-initial syllables, resulting in *keesimir-* and *kees-*. The *s* of the former, while originating in the suffix, is interpreted as stem-final, giving the form of the table; the latter is unusable as a Causative because it coincides segmentally with the lexical stem.[2]

The members of a second set of suffixes, Adverbial *-i*, Conclusive *-ju-n*, and Adnominal *-ju-ru*, share the property of palatalizing a stem-final consonant, with each of *t d k g* being replaced by the corresponding palato-alveolar (written *c z*), *r* deleting, and *m* becoming *n* before *j* but not before *i*. Because these palatalizations display no lexical conditioning, I will assume that palatalized stem alternants are derived by rule rather than lexically listed, although I will not formulate the necessary rules here. Of these three Class II or "palatalizing" suffixes, *-i* corresponds transparently to Japanese Adverbial *-i*, while *-ju-n* and *-ju-ru* represent grammaticization of a construction, originally expressing progressive aspect, that consisted of the Adverbial plus an inflected form of the auxiliary *or-* < **wor-* 'be'. Table 2 below shows Adverbial, Conclusive, and Adnominal forms for the three verbs of Table 1 plus *kuug-* 'row' (J *kog-*), *tat-* 'stand' (J *tat-*), *nind-* 'sleep' (J *nemur-*), *sin-* 'die' (J *sin-*), *tub-* 'fly' (J *tob-*), and *jum-* 'read' (J *yom-*), thus illustrating all nine Shuri stem-final consonants.[3]

---

2. The literature reveals a degree of confusion regarding the distribution and analysis of the Causative stems. DOL (entries *-simi=juN* and *=sjuN*) claims complementary distribution of the two suffixes, with *-asimir-* limited to *s*-stems (as well as failing to note the haplology involved in *s*-stem forms). Toyama (2013a: 107, 2015: 86) avoids recognizing haplology by attaching *-asimir-* to roots rather than stems for transitives like *wak-as-* 'boil', a procedure that has no syntactic or morphological basis and which will not in any case work for *s*-stems that contain no suffix (e.g. *kurus-* 'kill'). Miyara (2015: 397–398), finally, treats Causative 1 *-as-* (his *-ras-*) as an "inducivizing" morpheme and takes the form of the Causative 2 suffix, as might be suggested by its *s*-stem alternant, to be *-imi-* (i.e. *-imir-*). *-asimir-* is then interpreted as a suffix sequence showing that causativization generally (i.e. for all but *s*-stems) presupposes "inducivization".

Table 2. Shuri Class II (palatalizing) suffixes

	/tur-/	/jum-/	/tub-/	/sin-/	/nind-/
Adverbial	tu-i	jum-i	tub-i	sin-i	ninz-i
Conclusive	tu-ju-n	jun-u-n	tub-u-n	sin-u-n	ninz-u-n
Adnominal	tu-ju-ru	jun-u-ru	tub-u-ru	sin-u-ru	ninz-u-ru

	/tat-/	/kees-/	/kuug-/	/kak-/
Adverbial	tac-i	kees-i	kuuz-i	kac-i
Conclusive	tac-u-n	kees-u-n	kuuz-u-n	kac-u-n
Adnominal	tac-u-ru	kees-u-ru	kuuz-u-ru	kac-u-ru

The members of our third and final set of suffixes are the Shuri counterparts of the *t*-initial Japanese suffixes that condition the stem alternations known as *onbin*; in Shuri, *onbin* involves the truncation of all stem-final consonants except *t* and certain instances of *r*. As in Japanese, suffix-initial *t* alternates, in Shuri along two dimensions, voicing and place of articulation (dental versus palato-alveolar). For *d*-stems and *r*-stems, these suffix alternations are in part lexically determined, so that, for marked cases, the lexicon must record the suffix alternant that a given stem takes. For all other stems, however, the two alternations are predictable: suffix-initial *t* voices after the voiced stem finals *b*, *m*, *n*, *g* and becomes palato-alveolar (below, "palatalizes") after the coronal and dorsal stem finals *s*, *t*, *n*, *k*, *g* (*r* and *d* < *r* trigger neither alternation). Table 3 shows Perfect Adverbial, Conclusive, and Adnominal forms for the nine verbs of Table 2 (the Perfect Adverbial is the form identified as the Conjunctive in Dunan and Japanese).[4]

As with the forms of Table 2, I will assume that the stem and suffix alternants illustrated in Table 3 are derived by rule rather than lexically listed. For *d*-stems and *r*-stems, however, there are, in addition to the unmarked types shown in Table 3, cases in which the suffix-initial *t* of Class III forms palatalizes to *c* and,

---

3. With respect to Conclusive/Adnominal forms for which variation is reported in the literature (*keesun ~ keesjun, tujun ~ tuin, junun ~ jumun*), Table 2 reflects the recorded pronunciations of the Okinawa Center of Language Study's Shuri-Naha dialect phonetic database, which is unfortunately no longer online.

4. Uemura (1963: 58) and Tsuhako (1997: 383), among many others, follow Hattori (1955: 332) in assigning to stems what we (and e.g. Ashworth 1973: 73–80) are taking as suffix-initial *t*. That treatment, however, precludes an explanation of why the consonant in question is always a coronal stop (plain or affricated) and exchanges the two alternations we have just seen (one a simple assimilation of voicing) for a set of seven or more arbitrary alternations of stem finals (e.g. *b ~ d* for *b*-stems and *t ~ tc* for *t*-stems).

Table 3. Shuri Class III (truncating) suffixes

	/tur-/	/jum-/	/tub-/	/sin-/	/nind-/
Perfect Adv	tu-ti	ju-di	tu-di	si-zi	nin-ti
Perfect Con	tu-ta-n	ju-da-n	tu-da-n	si-za-n	nin-ta-n
Perfect Adn	tu-ta-ru	ju-da-ru	tu-da-ru	si-za-ru	nin-ta-ru

	/tat-/	/kees-/	/kuug-/	/kak-/
Perfect Adv	tat-ci	kee-ci	kuu-zi	ka-ci
Perfect Con	tat-ca-n	kee-ca-n	kuu-za-n	ka-ca-n
Perfect Adn	tat-ca-ru	kee-ca-ru	kuu-za-ru	ka-ca-ru

for *r*-stems, cases in which stem-final *r* assimilates to the suffixal consonant rather than deleting.[5] The two *d*-stems that palatalize suffix-initial *t* (*kund-* 'tie up' (J *kubir-*), Perfect *kun-can; nnd-* 'look' (J *mi-*), Perfect *nn-can*), first of all, will have to be marked in the lexicon to do so.

Historically, palatalization in *kuncan* and *nncan* can be attributed to the high front vowel *i* in the last syllable of the original stem. Similarly, monosyllabic Shuri *ir*-stems that correspond either to Japanese *ir*-stems or to Japanese *i*-stems show palatalization of suffix-initial *t*. Further, those corresponding to Japanese *ir*-stems, as well as several that correspond to Japanese *i*-stems, also show assimilation of stem-final *r* to the suffixal consonant in place of truncation. Both types of irregularity will have to be marked in the lexicon; typical cases, with Perfect Conclusive forms indicated, are *ir-, i-can* 'sit' (J *i-* (animate existential)), *cir-, ci-can* 'wear' (J *ki-*); *ʔir-, ʔic-can* 'enter; be necessary' (J *ir-*), *cir-, cic-can* 'cut' (J *kir-*), *ɸir-, ɸic-can* 'dry (i)' (J *hi-*). With the exception of the four stems specified in note 5, however, all remaining *r*-stems — polysyllabic *r*-stems, monosyllabic *ur-* and *ar*-stems, and monosyllabic *ir*-stems corresponding to Japanese *er*-stems, *e*-stems, and T*ur*-stems (T a coronal obstruent) — all show the unmarked *onbin* pattern illustrated in Table 3 by *tur-*.

5. There are also three disyllabic stems of the shape (C)V*rir-* in whose *onbin* forms expected (C)V*ri-t-* has developed to (C)V*t-t-*. Assuming lexical listing of the *onbin* stem alongside the basic (Table 1) stem, these are /ʔirir-, ʔit-/ 'insert' (J *ire-*), / ɸirir-, ɸit-/ 'pick up' (J *hirow-*), and the Passive auxiliary /-arir-, -at-/ (J *-are-*). The (situational) Potential auxiliary, which has a basic stem /-ar-/, is homophonous with the Passive in the forms of Tables 2 and 3, and will thus require a lexical entry /-ar-, -arir-, -at-/.

6.3   Diachrony: The history of Shuri *r*-stem inflection

6.3.1   The antiquity of the C-stem versus V-stem distinction

Because the Shuri cognates of Japanese vowel-stem verbs are *r*-stems, it is not obvious on inspection that Shuri or similar dialects have ever had vowel-stem inflection. In this section, we will see that comparative, internal, and philological evidence converge in showing that the dialect does indeed descend from an ancestor with the same contrast between vowel-stem and consonant-stem inflection that characterizes Japanese. Section 6.3.2, referring to the written records of the 16th through 18th centuries, then shows how that contrast was lost. Section 6.3.3, finally, traces the history of *w*-stems, which will be seen to have passed through a V-stem stage on the way to being reanalyzed as *r*-stems.

Perhaps the clearest evidence that Shuri and Ryukyuan languages in general descend from an ancestor with the same C-stem versus V-stem distinction as Japanese is that one of them, the language of the Miyako Islands, preserves that distinction intact, showing none of the innovations that, in other Ryukyuan and Japanese varieties, lead in the direction of a merger of V-stem and *r*-stem inflection; our discussion of Dunan in Chapter 2 has already made reference to the conservatism of Miyako in this respect. Crucially, individual verbs agree (modulo sound change and with isolated exceptions) in their stem-final segment between Miyako and Japanese, and individual C-stem and V-stem suffix alternants agree in shape as well, once relatively recent changes are factored out. Both in stems and in suffixes, then, Miyako and Japanese display a degree of correspondence with regard to the C-stem/V-stem distinction that would be difficult or impossible to explain as the result of parallel innovation. Table 4 (cf. Table 5, Chapter 2) displays partial paradigms for *kak-* 'write' and *oki-/uki-* 'arise' for Tokyo and Hirara (formerly Hirara city, now part of Miyakojima city), the administrative center of the Miyako Islands, with Hirara data from Karimata 1997a, 1999, supplemented by Nakamoto 1990 and Uchima 1984a, 1984b. The symbol *ï* represents a high vowel that corresponds for the most part to both Japanese *i* and Japanese *u* after coronal obstruents (Uchima 1984a: 261, 263) and *r* (see below) and to Japanese *i* elsewhere and has various realizations in Miyako dialects; in Hirara its degree of occlusion is sufficient to produce frication, and, typically transcribed /ʑ/, it is often a syllabic *s* or *z* (Karimata 1997a: 390).[6]

---

6. The stem vowel of Hirara *uki-* 'arise' can be assumed to reflect Proto-Ryukyuan **e* rather than **i* (see Pellard 2016: 110–111 and references cited there), thus explaining its failure to shift to *ï*.

Table 4. C-stem and V-stem inflection in Hirara and Tokyo

	'write'		'arise'	
	Hirara	Tokyo	Hirara	Tokyo
Negative	kak-an	kak-ana-	uki-n	oki-na-
Volitional	kak-a	kak-oo	uki-Ø	oki-yoo
Adverbial	kak-ï	kak-i	uki-Ø	oki-Ø
Conclusive	kak-ï	kak-u	uki-ï	oki-ru
Provisional	kak-iba	kak-eba	uki-riba	oki-reba
Imperative	kak-i	kak-e	uki-ru	oki-ro
Passive	kak-ai-	kak-are-	uki-rai-	oki-rare-
Causative 1	kak-as-	kak-ase-	*	oki-sase-
Causative 2	kak-asïmi-	kak-asime-	uki-sïmi-	oki-sime-

Looking at the forms of Table 4 line by line, it is clear first that while Tokyo shows the "adjectivalization" of the Negative suffix that has been characteristic of Eastern Japanese since some time before 1600 (Rodriguez 1604–1608 [1955]: 612), the two dialects display the same *a*-zero alternation for this suffix that goes back to the earliest Japanese. In the Volitional, Hirara *kaka* (like the corresponding Shuri form) and Tokyo *kakoo* represent alternative monophthongizations (see GAJ map 109) of *kakau* < *kak-amu*; while Hirara *uki* follows from *okiu* < *oki-mu* by the same processes that give *kaka* (i.e. progressive spreading followed by shortening), Tokyo *okiyoo* displays analogical reshaping of the expected *okyuu*, a change that will be considered in detail in Chapter 8. Where the two dialects differ in the first two lines of the table, then, it is Hirara that is the more conservative.

The Hirara Adverbial and Conclusive (i.e. Conclusive/Adnominal) forms require some comment.[7] First, the failure to distinguish those two forms is a general feature of Hirara consonant-stem inflection, and the same is true, with minor exceptions, throughout Miyako. For stems ending in *t, s, r,* and *m*, this merger is explicable as the outcome of regular sound change (Karimata 1999: 36). For stems ending in *k, g, b,* and **p* (synchronically, an empty consonant, on which see Section 6.3.3 below), on the other hand, it must be attributed to leveling, which in Hirara and most other dialects favors the Adverbial for the first three of those stem-types and the Conclusive for the last.[8]

---

7. I set aside here alternative Conclusives in **-mu*, attested throughout the Ryukyus (see Nakamoto 1990: 462).

In contrast to consonant-stem inflection, the inflection of vowel-stems distinguishes the Adverbial and the Conclusive, with the first, as in Tokyo, identical with the stem and the second displaying a suffix *-ï*. The latter suffix is in fact a regular phonological development of the *-ru* of the Tokyo form. To see this, first note that in monomorphemic forms, both *ri* and *ru* yield *ï* in Hirara (examples from Uemura 1997:324, Karimata 1999:36, Pellard 2009:318): *jaï* 'spear', *tuï* 'bird', *uï* 'melon', *ii* 'west' (J *yari, tori, uri, iri*); *saï* 'monkey (calendrical sign)', *juï* 'night', *kuïma* 'wheel' (in *kuïma-bo*: 'flail'), *pïsï* 'noon' (with *r* > *s*) (J *saru, yoru, kuruma, hiru*). The hypothesis that V-stem Conclusive *-ï* derives from *-ru* is therefore entirely consistent with known phonological developments. Further, that that suffix descends from a form with a coronal consonant is indicated by dialects where *ri* and *ru* develop not to *ï*, but to *l*, and which thus show forms like *pïdal* 'left' corresponding to J *hidari* and *alk-* 'walk' corresponding to J *aruk-* (see Pellard 2009:292, 318): in those dialects, the V-stem Conclusive suffix is *-l*, a form related to the presumed antecedent shape *-ru* by deletion of the vowel rather than the consonant.[9] In sum, for vowel-stems, the Hirara and Tokyo Conclusive forms correspond precisely.

In the remainder of the table as well, the correspondence between Hirara and Tokyo forms is straightforward, given centralization of *i* and raising of *e* and *o*. This statement requires qualification, however, for the Passive and Causative 1 suffixes: Hirara Passive *-(r)ai-* is cognate not with *-(r)are-*, for which we would expect **-(r)ari-*, but (cf. Thorpe 1983:189–190) with the suffix *-aye-* that in Old Japanese competed with *-are-* and was eventually supplanted by it (see Frellesvig 2010:63); Hirara Causative 1 *-as-*, while cognate with Japanese *-(s)ase-*, displays the consonant-final form in which that suffix always appears in Ryukyuan (see GAJ maps 118–120) and lacks a V-stem alternant. It should also be noted that the V-stem (Conclusive and) Provisional forms of both dialects reflect leveling of the bigrade stem alternation *i/e ~ u* noted in Section 5.7.1. The detailed agreement between the C-stem and V-stem paradigms of Hirara (and Miyako generally) and those of Tokyo (and Japanese generally) shows that the distinction between consonant-stem and vowel-stem inflection must be attributed to Proto-Japonic,

---

8. Dialects show a good deal of variation along these parameters; for example, Irabu (Hirayama et al. 1967:150–151) has *k/g*-stem forms that represent leveling in favor of the Conclusive and **p*-stem forms that have resisted leveling and maintain the Adverbial/Conclusive distinction.

9. For Nagahama on Irabujima, see Nakamoto 1990:561; for Nakasuji on Taramajima, see Hirayama et al. 1967:158–159 and Uchima 1984a:282; for Taramajima without further specification, see Nakamoto 1990:562.

the common ancestor of all Ryukyuan and Japanese varieties.[10] It follows from this, of course, that the Shuri failure to distinguish the two classes is secondary.[11]

We have seen that there is comparative evidence that Shuri must descend from an ancestor with a C-stem versus V-stem distinction. There is in fact a small amount of evidence for this proposition internal to Shuri itself, in the paradigm of 'come' (Japanese *ko-/ki-/ku-*), whose basic stem is /kuu-/. The Negative of 'come', to begin with, is *kuun*, a form which, uniquely among Shuri verbal Negatives (apart from the negative existential *neen*, treated in Section 6.4), shows the irregular V-stem allomorph *-n* of the Negative suffix that we saw in the Hirara data of Table 4; with Shuri *kuu-n* should be compared the innovative form *kuu-r-an* that is reported for Nagahama in Yomitan Village, 20 kilometers to the north (GAJ map 83; see also Nakamoto 1990: 577–579). Similarly (Hattori 1955: 338, Uemura 1963: 66), Volitional *kuu* preserves irregular V-stem -Ø (cf. C-stem *-a*), and Conditional *kuuwa* preserves irregular V-stem *-wa* (cf. C-stem *-awa ~ -aa*). In addition to comparative evidence, then, we have a degree of internal evidence that Shuri must have inherited a distinction between C-stem and V-stem inflection.

The third type of evidence that Shuri descends from an ancestor with a C-stem versus V-stem distinction is philological, deriving from the records of Classical Ryukyuan (see Takahashi 1997a: 422–423) and in particular the *Omoro Soshi* (/soosi/, historical kana spelling *sausi*), a collection of 1248 poems (excluding duplicates) in 22 volumes compiled at the Shuri royal court between 1531 and 1623 and whose texts are said to date back as far as the 12th or 13th century. Some of the *Omoro* poems have Amami origins (Takahashi 1997a: 422), but most can be taken to represent a language ancestral to the modern Shuri dialect (for an introduction to the *Omoro Soshi* in English, see Serafim and Shinzato 2021).

The language of the *Omoro Soshi* differs from contemporary Shuri in a number of respects. With regard to the contrast between mid and high vowels, while the merger of /o/ with /u/ is well underway, /e/ remains distinct from /i/ except in syllables with zero onset. Intervocalic *r* has not yet been lost before *i*. In verbal inflection, the inherited Conclusive/Adnominal form survives, and the Adverbial +

---

10. This conclusion calls into question the claim that the origins of V-stem inflection are so recent that "any reconstruction of pJ verb inflection must be based exclusively on the primary verb classes, and should not take account of the forms of the bigrade verbs." (Frellesvig 2008: 190)

11. It has been claimed (Hirayama et al. 1967: 135, 139) that the major verbal forms of Miyako incorporate **wor-* 'be', as we have seen to be the case for the Conclusive and Adnominal in Shuri. While there are certain dialectal forms that can be seen as supporting that interpretation, for dialects like Hirara, where the relationship of the verbal paradigm with that of Japanese appears transparent, the hypothesis in question is superfluous and will require numerous phonological reductions that have no independent motivation.

wor- construction that subsequently, in supplanting it, restored the Conclusive: Adnominal contrast is attested only in its original progressive meaning. Leveling of the bigrade stem-vowel alternation *i/e ~ u* has gone to completion (on all these points, see Takahashi 1991a, 1991b, 1997a). For our purposes, however, the most important fact about the language of the *Omoro Soshi* is that in it, the introduction of the innovative *r*-suffixes predicted by Analysis A, while unmistakably in progress, remains incomplete. That this process has begun is shown most clearly by the fact that innovative Imperative *-r-e* has been generalized to all vowel-final stems apart from 'come' (the Imperative of 'do' is unattested); that it remains incomplete is shown most clearly by the fact that conservative Adverbial *-Ø* is almost universally retained, with only a small number of monosyllabic V-stems showing innovative *-r-i* (see Takahashi 1991a: 332, 342, 344). We thus have, in addition to external and internal linguistic evidence, evidence from the documentary record that Shuri's failure to distinguish vowel-stem and consonant-stem (in particular, *r*-stem) inflection is historically secondary.

6.3.2   Loss of the C-stem versus V-stem distinction

Having established that contemporary Shuri descends from an ancestor with a distinction between C-stem and V-stem inflection, I will examine in this section the process by which that distinction was lost — specifically, the process by which V-stems became *r*-stems. I will pursue the hypothesis that the crucial factor in the assimilation of V-stem to *r*-stem inflection was speakers' adoption of Analysis A, as introduced in Chapter 5, for suffixes that alternate depending on the consonant/vowel polarity of the stem-final segment. As indicated there, adoption of Analysis A is confirmed by the appearance of the regularized forms that analysis predicts — specifically, innovative V-stem suffix alternants that, apart from epenthetic *r*, coincide with the corresponding C-stem alternants. We have already seen that, in the language of the *Omoro Soshi*, the V-stem Imperative suffix (irregular verbs apart) is uniformly *-r-e*, in accordance with the predictions of Analysis A. It is thus clear that that analysis was already in force at the stage of pre-Shuri recorded in the *Omoro Soshi* and therefore that its adoption predates the earliest written records. As for the irregular V-stem suffix alternant that *-r-e* replaced, while that alternant is not attested in the *Omoro Soshi* (or anywhere in Northern Ryukyuan), Miyako *-ru* < *-ro* combined with the retention of *-ro* in northwestern and central Kyushu (see GAJ maps 85–88, 91) makes *-ro* the most likely possibility.[12]

---

12. A small number of Okinawan GAJ survey points (122148, 125104, 127026) report V-stem Imperative suffix alternants of the form *r* + back vowel, but in all cases these are regular under Analysis A, the back vowel element being the corresponding C-stem alternant.

Among the Shuri suffixes introduced in Section 6.2, those that can be assumed to have originally had irregular V-stem alternants, apart from the Imperative and the Adverbial, are the Negative, the Volitional, the Conditional, and the two Causative suffixes. In all five cases, these are suffixes that, under the traditional Japanese analysis of verbal inflection, are added to the *Mizenkei*, which for consonant-stems consists of the stem augmented by *-a-*. Equivalently, if the suffixes in question are interpreted as being added to stems, they will show an *a*-zero alternation, with *a* appearing in C-stem alternants and Ø in V-stem alternants. Specifically, the forms that these suffixes take or would be expected to take in the language of the *Omoro Soshi* are Negative *-(a)n*, Volitional *-(a)n ~ -(a)*, Conditional *-(a)ba*, Causative 1 *-(a)s-*, and Causative 2 *-(a)sime-*. Attestation of V-stem forms for these suffixes is sparse in the Omoro poems; in particular, V-stem Causatives are apparently not attested at all (see Takahashi 1991b: 217–219, 1991a: 344–458). But to the extent that relevant V-stem forms do appear, they present a mixture of conservative and innovative shapes. Thus, the Conditional appears as *-ba* in *osi-age-ba* (Omoro 3.12) and *osi-tate-ba* (Omoro 1.17 etc.), but as *-r-aba* in *osi-uke-r-aba* (Omoro 13.3). Against this pattern of variation, it is noteworthy that attested examples of *Mizenkei* suffixes on monosyllabic V-stems (*mi-* 'see', *e-* 'obtain') are all of the form *-r-aX* (see Takahashi 1991a: 333–334, 344), suggesting that, corresponding with what we observed above for the Adverbial, shorter V-stems underwent regularization before longer V-stems did.

In the *Omoro Soshi*, then, the regularization predicted by Analysis A is complete in the Imperative, in progress in *Mizenkei* categories, and barely underway in the Adverbial. Crucial information about the stage that regularization had reached by the 18th century is provided by the texts of the *Kumiodori* (genre dating from 1719) and *Ryuka* (major collections published 1795–1802). The language of the *Kumiodori* and *Ryuka*, along with that of the *Omoro Soshi* and other early sources, is recorded in the *Okinawa kogo daijiten* (Hokama et al. 2011; below, HDO) and forms the basis for the conjugation tables of that dictionary. Those tables reveal that in the 18th century, regularization of V-stem suffixes, while still only incipient in the Adverbial, had gone to completion in *Mizenkei* categories, leaving Adverbial *-Ø* as the only irregular V-stem suffix that had not yet been replaced by the corresponding C-stem suffix preceded by *r*.

Let us now consider the role, in the process of assimilation of V-stem to *r*-stem inflection, of the Shuri suffixes that do not alternate according to the C/V polarity of the stem-final segment. For these suffixes, the Perfects in *-ta-/-ti* (Table 3) and the innovative Conclusive and Adnominal in *-ju-* (Table 2), the question of regularization under Analysis A does not arise, given that the domain of that analysis is limited to suffixes that do distinguish C-stem and V-stem alternants. Nor, since the suffixes in question begin with consonants, will they provide occasion for the application of *r*-Epenthesis, which requires a sequence of vowels in hiatus at stem boundary. Forms with *t*-initial and *j*-initial suffixes, however, will have posed no barrier to the ultimate merger of V-stem with *r*-stem inflection because of phonological changes that eliminated stem-final *r* before *t* and *j* while leaving suffixal *t* unvoiced and unpalatalized. In the relevant categories, in other words, deletion of stem-final *r* before *t* and *j*, by creating a vowel-final stem allomorph, had the effect of neutralizing the distinction between *r*-stem and V-stem inflection in favor of the latter. In *onbin* (Class III) forms, where stem-final *r* occurred before *t*, loss of *r* is complete in the *Omoro Soshi*, and thus dates from a time before the earliest records (Takahashi 1991a: 330). In the innovative Conclusive and Adnominal in -*ju*-, loss of stem-final *r* occurred by the 18th century, more or less simultaneously, it appears, with grammaticization of those forms. This is shown by the conjugation tables of the HDO, in which the innovative Conclusive and Adnominal for *r*-stems display no trace of *r*, as in the Conclusive *na-ju-n* and Adnominal *na-ju-ru* of *nar*- 'become'.

By about 1800, then, irregular Adverbial -Ø was the only remaining obstacle to the merger of V-stem with *r*-stem inflection. Analysis A, as we have seen, predicts -*r-i* as a regular replacement for -Ø, but by 1800, intervocalic *r* was beginning to be subject to loss before *i*. This is shown, again, by the conjugation tables of the HDO, where the Adverbial of *nar*- varies between *nar-i* and *na-i*. As a result, what we observe in the modern Shuri Adverbial is the result of loss of the irregular suffix alternant -Ø in favor of default -*i* without any evidence of *r*-Epenthesis, given the constraint *ri that was in effect at the time. Thus, the Shuri Adverbial of *ʔukir*- 'receive' (J *uke*-) or *ʔukir*- 'arise' (J *oki*-) is *ʔuki-i* (Hattori 1955: 333, Uemura 1963: 59, Tsuhako 1997: 383).

It might seem reasonable to assume that as long as even one suffix remained unregularized, historical vowel-stems continued to be vowel-final, and the *r* of innovative *r* + C-stem suffix combinations remained epenthetic. In Section 5.7.1, however, we saw evidence from Kumamoto Japanese that the reanalysis of epenthetic *r* as stem-final may begin before regularization is complete in all categories, and in particular before the elimination of irregular Adverbial -Ø in favor of -*r-i*. In Shuri, similarly, it is likely that the process of reanalysis of vowel-stems as *r*-stems took place gradually over a considerable period. Even after the completion of that process, however, the *r*-Epenthesis rule of Analysis A has remained active, as shown most clearly by ongoing regularization in the paradigm of polysyllabic *aw*-stems, discussed immediately below in Section 6.3.3. The period of activity of *r*-Epenthesis in Shuri, then, extends from prehistoric times up through the present.

6.3.3   Tertiary r-stems

In Section 6.3.2, I sketched the process that created what may be called the secondary r-stems of Shuri from vowel-stems. We saw that, while merger of V-stem and r-stem conjugation in the three Perfect forms and in the innovative Conclusive and Adnominal was the result of loss of r before t and j, assimilation of V-stem to r-stem inflection in Class I categories and the Adverbial resulted from accumulation in the V-stem paradigm, over a period of centuries, of innovative r-suffixes resulting from regularization under Analysis A, followed by reanalysis of originally epenthetic r as stem-final. In this section, I will extend the account of Section 6.3.2 to what I will call tertiary r-stems, the set of Shuri r-stems that correspond to Japanese w-stems. It is important to be aware from the outset, however, of the differences as well as the similarities between the two cases.

As in the case of V-stems, merger of w-stem with r-stem inflection in *onbin* forms and the Conclusive and Adnominal can be attributed to phonological change: like r, w has zero reflex before t and j (see HDO: 775), and before t this is already true in large part in the language of the *Omoro Soshi* (see Takahashi 1991a: 192–195). In contrast to the case of V-stems, however, no elimination of irregular suffix alternants needs to be postulated in connection with the shift of w-stems to r-stem inflection, given that w-stems had always taken C-stem suffixes. In extending the account of Section 6.3.2 to w-stems, then, the focus will be on whether or not the innovative stem-final r of historical w-stem forms can be attributed to r-Epenthesis, formalized as (11) in Chapter 5. Consequently, in order to answer that question affirmatively, I will need to argue that w-stems went through a vowel-final stage on their way to r-stem inflection. Let us begin with some historical background.

Stem-final w is the reflex of Proto-Japonic *p, a consonant that when intervocalic merged with *w in both Japanese and Ryukyuan, with w then deleting before any vowel but a. This sequence of changes was complete in Japanese by about 1100 (Frellesvig 2010: 207), and seems to have been complete in the language of the *Omoro Soshi* as well (Takahashi 1991b: 5).[13] With respect to the distribution of w, then, the historical stage preserved in the *Omoro Soshi* corresponds to that of contemporary Japanese: w occurs only before a and is thus found in the paradigm of w-stem verbs only before suffixes that begin with that vowel, for example Negative -an, Volitional -a, and Conditional -aba.

In the following centuries, however, w weakened and deleted before a as well when a back vowel preceded. The development awa > aa, to begin with, is attested

---

13. There are exceptions in contemporary Shuri, however: the prefix *opo- 'great' (J oo-) is ʔuhu-, and *sipo 'salt' (J sio) appears as sipu- in sipukarasan 'salty' (Uemura 1997: 336).

to by *kana* spellings involving the length symbol (dash) in texts such as those collected in Hokama and Tamaki 1980, whose oldest sources (see Hokama and Tamaki 1980:637–639) date from the early 18th century: *aa* < *awa* 'foam', *kaara* < *kawa-ra* 'river' (see the relevant entries of the HDO). That *w* was lost in the sequence *uwa* < *uwa/owa* as well can be inferred from the Shuri reflexes of words like **kupa* 'mulberry' (J *kuwa*) and **kupa* 'hoe' (J *kuwa*): parallel to the development of *kwii* 'voice' (J *koe*) from *kui* < *koe* < *kowe*, **kupa* develops to *kuwa* > *kua* > *kwaa*. In both cases, that is, after intervocalic *w* disappears, the second of two adjacent vowels spreads leftwards into the first, which desyllabifies. The sequence *iwa*, finally, is stable, as illustrated by Shuri *ʔiwa* 'rock, crag', *niwa* 'garden' (J *iwa*, *niwa*).[14] Both the development of *awa* to *aa* or (in the Amami dialect area) *oo* and the preservation of *iwa* are characteristic of the Ryukyus as a whole.[15]

Turning now to the historical development of *w*-stem inflection, we may note first that there is a consensus that the language of the *Omoro* poems shows as yet no evidence of the eventual shift of *w*-stems to the *r*-stem paradigm (Hokama 1960:108, Takahashi 1991a:192, Takahashi 1991b:8, 423). While the conjugation table on page 775 of the HDO would suggest that the same is true for the *Ryuka* and *Kumiodori* texts of the 18th century, examination of the entries for individual *w*-stems in that dictionary reveals that a high proportion of them are beginning to display sporadic cases of *r*-stem forms, at roughly the same time, it would seem, as *w* began to be lost before *a*. Let us now survey the situation in contemporary Shuri, classifying inherited (i.e. pre-Shuri) *w*-stems by syllable count and the vowel preceding *w*. Inherited polysyllabic *ow*-stems and *uw*-stems, first of all, are uniformly *ur*-stems in Shuri: *jatur-* 'employ' (J *yatow-*), *sukur-* 'rescue' (J *sukuw-*). Polysyllabic *aw*-stems are en route to becoming *ar*-stems, but this process remains incomplete, as we will see in more detail immediately below. Monosyllabic *ow*-stems and *uw*-stems have become Shuri *uur*-stems, and monosyllabic *aw*-stems have become *oor*-stems: *suur-* 'accompany' (J *sow-*), *suur-* 'suck' (J *suw-*), *koor-* 'buy' (J *kaw-*). Of the two stems in which stem-final *w* was preceded by a front vowel, finally, *wew-* 'become intoxicated' (J *yow-*) is *wiir-*, and *iw-* 'say', while a (short vowel) *r*-stem in most of southern Okinawa (Hirayama et al. 1966:272, 274), has the basic stem *ʔj-* in Shuri.[16]

---

14. All three developments admit sporadic exceptions in Shuri: *ʔawa* 'millet'; *ʔuwar-* 'finish'; *ʔj-an* 'doesn't say' < *i(j)-an* < *iw-an*.

15. Examples for *awa* are provided by Hirayama et al. (1966:67, 89, 105, 117) for Northern Ryukyuan, by Karimata (2005:79) for Hirara, and by Karimata (1997b:405) for Ishigaki; for *iwa*, see Kokuritsu Kokugo Kenkyujo 1966–1974 map 193 (*niwa* 'garden'). Kikaijima is exceptional in retaining *awa* in two of three locations surveyed by Hirayama et al. (1966:89) and in having *aa* in the third.

I noted above that in order to extend to *w*-stems the Analysis A account of the V-stem-to-*r*-stem shift, it will be necessary to argue that *w*-stems went through a vowel-final stage. The monomorphemic forms such as *aa* < *awa* 'foam' showing that *w* following a back vowel was lost in pre-Shuri before *a* just as it had been lost earlier before all other vowels provides reason to suspect such a vowel-final stage, assuming of course that the introduction of *r*-stem forms in the *w*-stem paradigm did not precede the loss of *w* before *a*. More concrete evidence, however, is provided by the survival of the hypothesized vowel-final stems to this day for one subclass of Shuri inherited *w*-stems, namely polysyllabic *aw*-stems. In the DOL, stems descending from monosyllabic *w*-stems and polysyllabic *ow-/uw*-stems have listings that are completely parallel to those of primary and secondary *r*-stems. In particular, the Negatives of those stems, representing Class I forms, have the shape X*ran*: *tuuran* 'doesn't question' (J *tow-*), *jaturan* 'doesn't employ' (J *yatow-*) (compare *turan* 'doesn't take' (J *tor-*), *ciran* 'doesn't wear' (J *ki-*)). The Negatives of polysyllabic *aw*-stems, however, are in most cases listed without *r*, implying a stem that ends in *a*: *waraan* 'doesn't laugh' (J *waraw-*), *naraan* 'doesn't study' (J *naraw-*). Crucially, it is clear at the same time that these vowel-final shapes do not represent the endpoint of the historical development of their respective stems: the accompanying grammatical sketch (Uemura 1963: 60; see also Tsuhako 1997: 383) makes it clear that Negatives of the shape X*aran* (and parallel forms for other Class I suffixes) are also possible, and the Negatives of some stems (*jasina(r)an* 'doesn't care for, bring up' (J *yasinaw-*), *sitaga(r)an* 'doesn't obey' (J *sitagaw-*)) are listed with both alternants. That this variation represents ongoing replacement of X*aan* by X*aran* is confirmed not only by the fact that original monosyllabic *w*-stems and polysyllabic *ow-/uw*-stems have all developed into *r*-stems in Shuri, but by the fact that polysyllabic *aw*-stems, too, have become *r*-stems in the neighboring Naha dialect (see Uchima and Nohara 2006).

In conjunction with the data from monomorphemic forms, then, the *a*-final forms of inherited polysyllabic *aw*-stems constitute reason to conclude that inherited *w*-stems of all types must have gone through a V-final stage on their way to *r*-stem inflection in Shuri.[17] The postulated V-final stage raises certain questions, however. First, if the stem of *waraan* is really vowel-final, it is unclear why hiatus

---

16. The long vowels of monosyllabic stems appear to be the result of influence from *onbin* forms, as suggested by (a) the fact that vowel length in the *onbin* stem ("*u-onbin*"), but not yet in the basic stem, is a distinctive characteristic of monosyllabic as opposed to polysyllabic *w*-stems already in the *Omoro Soshi* (Takahashi 1991b: 192–195) and (b) the fact that *iw-* 'say', the only monosyllabic *w*-stem, then and now, without length in the *onbin* stem is also the only one that ends up without a long vowel in the basic stem.

17. For the two front-vowel *w*-stems, a tendency for stem-final *w* to be lost before *a* is apparent as early as the *Omoro Soshi* (Takahashi 1991a: 193–194).

at stem boundary is not resolved by application of *r*-Epenthesis, given our conclusion above that Analysis A has been in force since prehistoric times. We should note in this connection that *waraan* is the form reported for five of six southern (main island) Okinawan locations surveyed by Hirayama et al. (1966: 272), suggesting that it is a stable realization of the stem-suffix combination in question and not simply a short-lived transitional stage between *warawan* and *wararan*. A second question that arises in principle is why a vowel-final stem *wara-* should take consonant-stem suffixes in the first place, although this issue is rendered largely moot by the fact that by the time stem-final *w* was lost before *a*, irregular vowel-stem suffixes other than Adverbial -Ø had already been eliminated. Let us look more closely at the nature of the stem-final element in *waraan*.

It is well known that all articulatory correlates of a consonant may be lost without affecting that consonant's place in syllable structure, as evidenced by phenomena like rule application and allomorph selection. Thus, in French, deleted [h] ("*h* aspiré"), typically in loanwords, blocks the rules of elision and liaison, and in Turkish, deleted [ɣ] (orthographic ğ "yumuşak ge") conditions the selection of consonant-stem noun suffixes. Clements and Keyser (1983; see 96–113 for French and 67–73 for Turkish) argue at length that such cases are appropriately treated by postulating representations in which the "deleted" consonant is an abstract consonantal syllable-structure position that is associated with no articulatory content, what we may call an "empty consonant".

Correspondingly, I suggest that when *w* was lost before *a* in pre-Shuri and there was no longer any evidence for postulating final *w* in stems like 'laugh', those stems were first reanalyzed as ending in an empty consonant, which we may represent as "C". In the case of 'laugh', this will mean a representation /waraC-/, and the failure of *r*-Epenthesis to apply to a form like Negative /waraC-an/ will be the result of the fact that the intervocalic environment of that rule is not satisfied. Eventually, however, /waraC-/ will have faced competition from the vowel-final representation /wara-/, reflecting the fact that the stem ended phonetically in a vowel. To the extent that the vowel-final representation of the stem is adopted, the Negative will be /wara-an/, a representation which will undergo *r*-Epenthesis to give *wara-r-an*.

Contemporary variation between conservative *waraan* and innovative *wararan*, then, along with parallel forms for other Class I suffixes, reflects ongoing reanalysis of the stem from a representation ending in an empty consonant to one ending in a vowel. Monosyllabic *w*-stems (apart from *iw-* 'say') and polysyllables of the shape X*ow-*/X*uw-* will have followed this reanalysis through to completion, coming to show the results of *r*-Epenthesis before all Class I suffixes. As a result, epenthetic *r* will have been reanalyzed as part of the stem, resulting in the merger of *w*-stem with *r*-stem inflection; since, as noted above, *w* had already disappeared before *t* and *j*, no barrier to this merger will have been posed by *onbin* forms or innovative Conclusives and Adnominals, where stem-final *r* had also gone to zero. Summarizing the developments we have seen in this section, then, a stem like that corresponding to Japanese *yatow-* 'employ' will have passed through four stages in pre-Shuri with regard to its stem-final segment: /jatuw-/, /jatuC-/, /jatu-/, and /jatur-/. It is only for polysyllabic stems of the shape X*aw*- that this sequence of developments remains incomplete.

6.4   Points of contact among *r*-stems, V-stems, and *w*-stems

Above, we began with the question of whether or not Ryukyuan languages, and in particular Shuri Okinawan, display evidence that speakers have adopted Analysis A for verbal inflectional suffixes that alternate depending on the C/V polarity of the stem-final segment. On the basis of what we saw in Sections 6.2 and 6.3, we can say that Shuri does indeed display evidence of the adoption of Analysis A, and in a particularly decisive form. First of all, with respect to primary vowel-stems, Shuri illustrates the logical endpoint of the changes entailed by that analysis, namely the total assimilation of vowel-stem inflection to the inflectional pattern of *r*-stems. Second, because of the creation of secondary vowel stems from historical *w*-stems and the ongoing nature of the assimilation of those vowel-stems to *r*-stem inflection, it displays evidence at the same time for intervocalic *r*-Epenthesis at verb stem boundary as a living generalization that is still being extended.

As with the parallel changes in dialects of Japanese proper that were discussed in Chapter 5, the changes that we have explained as regularization under Analysis A in the history of Shuri have been interpreted in other ways by scholars working in the native Japanese linguistic tradition. Section 5.7 discussed interpretations of this sort that appeal to the putative influence of *r*-stem inflection and interpretations that treat innovative forms as direct transforms of the conservative forms they replace; the arguments that were made there concerning those modes of interpretation apply equally to developments in Shuri and other Ryukyuan varieties. There are also, however, accounts of the Shuri developments reviewed above that appeal to the points of contact among *r*-stem, V-stem, and *w*-stem conjugation that result from the loss of *r* and *w* before *t*-initial and *j*-initial suffixes. In this section, I will argue that those accounts are both conceptually and empirically inadequate.

The pre-Shuri loss of stem-final *r* and *w* before *t* and *j* that we observed in Sections 6.3.2 and 6.3.3 had the result that V-stems, *r*-stems, and *w*-stems all came to have *onbin* forms of the shape XV-tY and innovative Conclusives and Adnominals of the shape XV-jY. The relatively recent loss of intervocalic *r* before *i* created an overlap between *r*-stems and *w*-stems in the Adverbial as well. These points of contact among the paradigms of the three stem-types form the basis for a number of attempts in the literature to explain in proportional terms the assimilation of V-stems and *w*-stems to the *r*-stem paradigm in Shuri and other Ryukyuan dialects. Thus Hattori (1955: 333) suggests regarding Class I forms and the Adverbial of stems corresponding to Japanese *ki-* 'wear', *kaw-* 'buy', and *uke-* 'receive' that "these are evidently items due to analogy from the *onbin* stem" (here and below, my translation); this idea is echoed for *w*-stems (but apparently not for V-stems) by Uemura (1963: 60). While neither Hattori nor Uemura offer any elaboration, it seems clear that they are envisioning proportions such as *tutan*: *turan* = *ʔukitan*: X (X = *ʔukiran*) or *tutan*: *turan* = *kootan*: X (X = *kooran*), where *tur-*, *ʔukir-*, and *koor-* correspond to Japanese *tor-* 'take', *uke-* 'receive' (and *oki-* 'arise') and *kaw-* 'buy', respectively.

In parallel fashion, Uchima (1984b: 247–248; see also Uchima 1982 and works cited there) suggests regarding the assimilation of *w*-stems to *r*-stem conjugation that "If analogy did operate, it was presumably Adverbial forms that constituted its pivot." This proposal thus envisions proportions such as *tui*: *turan* = *umui*: X (X = *umuran*), where *umu(w)-* corresponds to Japanese *omow-* 'think'. The innovative Conclusive would support a parallel proportion *tujun*: *turan* = *umujun*: X, and since stem-final *i* < *i e* did not desyllabify in the Conclusive and Adnominal (*ʔukijuru* < *ʔukiuru* < *uke+oru*), there are also potential proportions of the same type for V-stems, for example *tujun*: *turan* = *ʔukijun*: X. It should be kept in mind that such proportions may be rendered inapplicable by phonological change; thus, for example, monophthongization of the word-final V*i* sequences of *w*-stem Adverbials (*wara-i* > *waree* 'laugh', *umu-i* > *umii* 'think'), optional in Shuri (Uemura 1961: 65, Tsuhako 1997: 383), will compromise the Adverbial as a point of contact between *r*-stem and *w*-stem inflection. Setting this issue aside, however, let us ask whether the Shuri assimilation of V-stems and *w*-stems to *r*-stem inflection in Class I forms and the Adverbial, explained above as the result of regularization pursuant to the adoption of Analysis A, should in fact be understood in terms of proportions of the type just illustrated. In considering this question, I will concentrate to begin with on V-stems.

In principle, a proportional account of a given change should argue that there is a basic/derived relationship between the first and second terms of the relevant proportions (in the terms of Kuryłowicz 1945–49, a relationship between *formes de fondation* and *formes fondées*). It should also specify a reason for the observed direction of influence — in the present case, from *r*-stems on the one hand to V-stems and *w*-stems on the other — that is, the grounds for the relation between the first and third terms of the proportions. Proportions based on *onbin* forms as pivot, for example, can be seen as presupposing that those forms constitute a derivational base for the rest of the verbal paradigm, so that the plausibility of the proportions depends on the plausibility of that derivational proposal. Even if we set aside such questions, however, there are compelling reasons to believe that the assimilation of V-stem to *r*-stem inflection in Shuri is not due to proportional relationships of the type just reviewed. The first argument to that effect derives from the parallelism between Shuri and Japanese developments.

We saw in Section 5.7.1 that the diachronic process that ends with the assimilation of V-stems to the *r*-stem paradigm proceeds category by category in Japanese as it did in pre-Shuri — specifically, by the accumulation in the V-stem paradigm of C-stem suffixes preceded by epenthetic *r*. In fact, there is reason to believe that the course of change in Japanese and in pre-Shuri is parallel at a finer level as well. We observed above that in the history of Shuri, Imperatives regularized before *Mizenkei* categories, with Adverbials regularizing last. Precisely the same hierarchy of susceptibility to regularization, however, is found by Jinnouchi (1989:336) to characterize Fukuoka Japanese. To the extent that the Shuri and Japanese developments display a common course in addition to their common endpoint, the invited conclusion is that the same grammatical mechanism is at work in both cases. The points of contact between the *r*-stem and V-stem paradigms that we have seen in Shuri, however, do not obtain in Japanese, where *r*-stems show obstruent-final allomorphs before *t*-initial suffixes and Adverbial + *or*- constructions have not been grammaticized as inflected forms. Adopting for Shuri a proportional account based on either *t*-suffixed forms or *j*-suffixed forms as pivot will thus mean claiming that closely parallel developments in Ryukyuan and Japanese are due to totally unrelated mechanisms.

In addition to this conceptual argument against the proportional approach, there is an empirical one, namely that proportional accounts will not cover the full range of explicanda with regard to the spread of *r*-stem inflection in Shuri and in Ryukyuan more generally. This is because there are cases in which the introduction of innovative *r*-suffixes proceeds in the absence of the cross-paradigmatic points of contact that the proportions require. This phenomenon is illustrated in Shuri by the negative existential verb *neen* 'doesn't exist', which consists historically of *nee-* < *nai* (itself meaning 'doesn't exist') plus the conservative V-stem Negative suffix alternant *-n* (for commentary, see HDO: 786–787). Shuri *neen* has the paradigm of a verbal negative (see Uemura 1961:64–65, 75–77), so that *nee-n* (like e.g. *kak-an* 'doesn't write') serves not only as the (Imperfect) Conclusive and Adnominal, but also as the Adverbial, and *nee-n-ta-n* (like *kak-an-ta-n* 'didn't write') serves as the Perfect Conclusive and Adnominal. *neen* varies with *neeran* in the Conclusive and Adnominal, however, and *neentan* with *neerantan* (see Tsuhako 1997:380). While there is a possibility that this variation is stable as opposed to representing ongoing replacement, it seems clear that *neen* is the older of the two forms and that *neeran* is a later innovation (Nishioka 1993:28, Iha 1933 [1975]:544–545).

Innovative *neeran* is naturally explained as the result of regularization under Analysis A, specifically as elimination of the irregular suffix alternant -*n* and the application of *r*-Epenthesis to the representation /nee-an/ (compare the variation between Shuri *kuu-n* and Yomitan *kuu-r-an* for the Negative of 'come', noted above in Section 6.3.1). There is no explanation for that form under a proportional account of the extension of *r*-stem inflection in Shuri, however, because the required points of contact with the *r*-stem paradigm either fail to exist or generate counterfactual predictions. In particular, the Adverbial *tui*, Conclusive *tujun*, and Adnominal *tujuru* of *tur-* 'take' bear no similarity to *neen*, and while Perfect Conclusive *tutan* and *neentan* both end in -*tan*, a proportion *tutan* : *turan* = *neentan* : X would predict the unattested *neenran.[18]

Outside Shuri, a more general example illustrating that the introduction of innovative *r*-suffixes in the paradigm of vowel-final stems in Ryukyuan is not dependent on any preexisting surface similarity with *r*-stem inflection is provided by the development of the paradigm of *si̇-* < *se-* 'do' in Amami Oshima and, with the exception of Tokunoshima, the Amami dialect area generally (see Hirayama et al. 1966:201–256 and Nakamoto 1990:669–688); for concreteness, I cite forms from Naze on Amami Oshima (Hirayama et al. 1966:201–203). While Negative *si̇ran*, Volitional *si̇ro*, and Imperative *si̇ri̇* are easily explained as the result of regularization under Analysis A, the Imperfect Adverbial and Conclusive (J *si, si̇+ori*) are *si* and *sjun/sjuri*, and the Perfect Adverbial and Conclusive (J *si-te, si-ta*) are *si* and *san*, with no trace of suffix-initial *t*. Proportions based on the Adverbial (*turi* : *turan* = *si* : X) or Conclusive (*turjun* : *turan* = *sjun* : X) will thus predict Negative *san* (the attested form in Tokunoshima and in Okinawan), and proportions based on *onbin* forms (*tuti̇* : *turan* = *si* : X) will have no determinate outcome at all. It seems evident, then, that a proportional approach to the assimilation of vowel-stem to *r*-stem conjugation in Ryukyuan will be incapable of dealing with the full range of data that must be accounted for.

For *w*-stems, the evidence against a proportional account of the shift to *r*-stem conjugation is necessarily sparser: since *w*-stem conjugation is generally stable in Japanese,[19] there is no argument from the desirability of a unified treatment of

---

18. Accounts of *neeran* that treat it as deriving from *nai-ar-anu* (Nishioka 1993:28) or *nahe-ar-anu* (Tsuhako 1997:381), where -*ar*- is the inanimate existential verb, are ad hoc in that there appear to be no other likely exemplars of such a construction. Notably, while affirmative adjectival forms involve -*ar*- throughout the Ryukyus (Uemura 1997:348–349), adjectival negatives are not formed with -*ar-anu* anywhere in the region (GAJ map 137), and the same appears to have been true of pre-Shuri.

Ryukyuan and Japanese developments; and since, minor exceptions aside, there are no irregular *w*-stems in Ryukyuan, there is no opportunity to show that the relevant changes take place even in the absence of paradigmatic points of contact. There is, however, a generalization about the course of the transition from *w*-stem to *r*-stem inflection that is expected under an account according to which innovative instances of *r* originate in intervocalic epenthesis but not under a proportional account. This is that, as we have already argued for Shuri, *w*-stems go through an intermediate vowel-final stage on their way to *r*-stem inflection. In closing this section, let us look at data from the Amami dialect area in which the shape of innovative forms provides support for the hypothesis that *w*-stems shift to *r*-stem inflection only subsequent to loss of stem-final *w*.[20]

As noted above, monomorphemic *awa* in Amami dialects other than those of Kikaijima develops not to the *aa* observed in Okinawan, but to *oo*, presumably through the stages *awa > owa > oa > oo*. Before stem-final *w*, however, the shift of *a* to *o* is inhibited not only in the three Kikaijima locations surveyed by Hirayama et al. (1966), but in nine of the ten Amami Oshima locations as well. In those twelve locations there is no introduction of *r*: 'doesn't laugh' is *warawan* in nine of them and minor developments thereof in the remaining three. In Koniya, the administrative center of Setouchi-cho in southern Amami Oshima, in contrast, and in all nine Tokunoshima, Okinoerabujima, and Yoronto locations, the stem vowel has shifted to *o*, so that the expected form, reported for Isen-cho in southern Tokunoshima, is *warowan*. But in Koniya and the remaining eight southern locations, we find not *warowan*, but *waroran* or variants or developments thereof (Okinoerabu *waroram(u)*, Yoron *waronnu < *waroranu*).

The fact that, in Amami dialects, stem-final *r* in place of historical *w* is observed only in the presence of preceding *o* has no explanation under a proportional account of the shift of *w*-stems to *r*-stem inflection like those considered above: there is no reason under such an account that *warawan* should not be replaced directly by *wararan*.[21] Under an account that attributes the introduction of *r* to the operation of *r*-Epenthesis, on the other hand, the restriction is easily explained: in order for *r*-Epenthesis to apply, *w* must be lost, and in order for *w* to

---

19. An exception is the transfer of *w*-stems to the *r*-stem paradigm reported for Aomori Prefecture (Konoshima 1961: 144).

20. Merger of *w*-stem with *r*-stem conjugation quite clearly occurs only in Northern Ryukyuan; the two paradigms remain distinct in Sakishima languages, as shown by the twenty dialectal conjugation tables of Hirayama et al. (1967: 131–191).

21. While most locations that fail to show the *w*-stem to *r*-stem shift also retain *r* before *i* and *j*, so that the preexisting point of contact between the two paradigms is limited to *onbin* forms, Koniya (Hirayama et al. 1966: 221–224) shows that retention of *r* is consistent with the shift in question.

be lost, the preceding *a* must shift to *o*. On this interpretation, *waroran* will reflect the development /waraw-an/ > /warow-an/ > /waro-an/ and the application of *r*-Epenthesis to the last of those representations. The distribution of the *w*-stem to *r*-stem shift in the Amami dialect area thus appears to support the account of that shift proposed in Section 6.3.3 above.

6.5   Beyond Shuri

To this point, we have dealt with Ryukyuan varieties other than Shuri primarily to advance our account of Shuri verbal stem types and their historical development. In particular, we have not asked concerning non-Shuri varieties whether they, like Shuri, show evidence that their speakers have adopted Analysis A. In this section, I will make a brief survey of Ryukyuan dialects in this regard.

In having completely eliminated vowel-stem inflection, Shuri is typical of many Okinawan dialects: explicit statements to the effect that there is no contrast between C-stem and V-stem inflection are available, in addition to Shuri, for Ojima on the southeast coast (Hirayama et al. 1966: 269), Ishikawa in the south-central part of the island (Hirayama et al. 1966: 263), and Nakijin on the Motobu Peninsula in the northwest (Shimabukuro 1997: 365). More generally, throughout Northern Ryukyuan, distinctive V-stem inflection survives, if at all, only under very strict conditions, namely in Adverbial forms of polysyllabic stems and sometimes in the Adverbial-based Conclusive and Adnominal as well. Thus in Hentona (Kunigami Village) in northeastern Okinawa, for which Hirayama et al. (1966: 256) note the existence of a stem-type contrast that corresponds to C-stem versus V-stem inflection, monosyllabic historical V-stems have fully assimilated to *r*-stem inflection, and polysyllabic historical V-stems take *r*-suffixes (Negative *-ran*, Volitional *-ra*, etc.) in Class I forms. It is only in Class II forms of polysyllables, then, that *r*-stem and V-stem inflection visibly diverge. For example, whereas the primary *r*-stem *tur-* 'take' (J *tor-*) and the secondary *r*-stem *kʔir-* 'wear' (J *ki-*) have the Adverbials *tui* (< *tur-i*) and *kʔii* and the corresponding Conclusives *tuin* and *kʔiin*, the V-stem *agi-* 'raise' (J *age-*) has the Adverbial *agi-*, preserving irregular V-stem -Ø, and the Conclusive *agin* (not **agiin*).

While the conjugation tables of Hirayama et al. (1966: 201–275) and the map of Nakamoto (1990: 542) present slightly different geographical distributions for retention of Adverbial -Ø in the paradigm of polysyllabic V-stems, it is clear that the Amami dialect area is more conservative in this regard than Okinawan. That all Northern Ryukyuan dialects show unambiguous evidence for the adoption of Analysis A, however, can be seen in the distribution of innovative *r*-suffixes for the Negative, Volitional, and Imperative of V-stems (Nakamoto 1990: 540, 541, 544).

This picture changes sharply, however, when we cross the border between Northern and Southern (Sakishima) Ryukyuan into Miyako. We have already seen in Table 4 above that Hirara Miyako shows inherited irregular V-stem suffix alternants or phonological developments thereof in the Negative, Volitional, Adverbial, Imperative, and Causative 2. That the same is true of Miyako dialects in general is shown by the maps of Nakamoto (1990: 540–544): conservative suffixes are reported for 20 of 20 locations for the Negative,[22] 23 of 23 for the Volitional, 18 of 19 for the Adverbial, and 19 of 19 for the Imperative (see also Hirayama et al. 1967: 131–162).[23]

The conservatism of Miyako, however, is not shared by Yaeyama dialects or by Dunan/Yonaguni, all of which show evidence for the adoption of Analysis A in the form of innovative V-stem suffix alternants that, apart from epenthetic *r*, coincide with the corresponding C-stem alternants. Innovative V-stem Imperative -*r-i*, to begin with, is characteristic of the entire area (Nakamoto 1990: 544), and most dialects show additional innovative *r*-suffixes as well. Thus Ishigaki has Causative 1 -*r-as*- and Causative 2 -*r-asïmi*- (Karimata 1997b: 408) and displays variation between conservative -*n* and innovative -*r-un* (cf. C-stem -*un*) for the Conclusive and between conservative -Ø and innovative -*r-u* (cf. C-stem -*u*) for the Adnominal (Miyara 1995: 50–51); Hirayama et al. (1967: 165) report variation between conservative and innovative forms for the Negative and Volitional as well. Dunan, similarly, as we saw in Chapter 2, preserves only a single conservative V-stem suffix, Causative 2 -*mir*- < -*simir*-.

The absence of evidence for Analysis A in Miyako, in conjunction with the family tree of Japonic displayed as (2) in Chapter 2 and repeated below as (1), entails that the adoption of Analysis A in Japanese, Northern Ryukyuan (Amami and Okinawan), and Macro-Yaeyama (Yaeyama and Dunan), boxed in (1), must have been independent events.

(1)

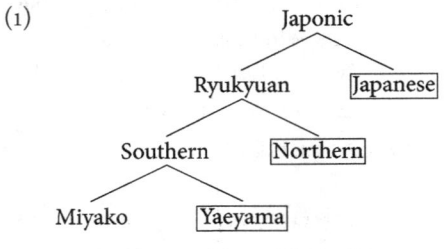

---

22. Uchima (1984b: 478), however, reports *Mizenkei* -*ra*- alongside -Ø for stems such as *uti*- 'drop (i)' (J *oti*-) in Nishizato, adjacent to Hirara.

23. The Miyako forms reported (Nakamoto 1990: 514ff., 531) for 'wear' (J *ki*-) appear to reflect a phonologically regular shift of *r* to *s* in Conclusive **kiru* (cf. Hirara *pïsï* 'noon' < **piru* (J *hiru*)) followed by reanalysis of the stem as *s*-final.

This is because if that analysis had been adopted at the Japonic, Ryukyuan, or Southern (Sakishima) levels, evidence for it would be observed in Miyako, contrary to fact. The separate adoption of Analysis A in three branches of Japonic constitutes compelling evidence that it represents a natural analytic response to the relevant set of alternations. The basis for the naturalness of Analysis A and the reason that, nevertheless, it was not adopted in Miyako are questions that will be pursued in Chapter 7.

6.6   Epilogue

Throughout Japonic, the most striking examples of regularization under Analysis A tend to come from relatively isolated areas where the natural course of language change has plausibly been less subject to the retarding influence of normative pressure than in the cultural capitals of western and eastern Japan. Today, however, many of the regional varieties that exhibit the strongest tendencies toward regularization are endangered (regarding Ryukyuan languages in particular, see Heinrich et al. 2015:1). It is thus natural to ask whether there are sources of evidence other than ongoing change that might bear on the question of how speakers analyze the suffix alternations in question.

In this connection, I would like to suggest that the role of children in advancing the elimination of irregularity is an area that might benefit from more attention than it has hitherto received. There is anecdotal evidence suggesting that this role is probably significant. Thus, for example, Nakajima (1972:111–112) notes for the town of Inami, adjacent to Kakogawa city in Hyogo Prefecture, that innovative Negative -r-an, Volitional -r-oo, and Imperative -r-e are attested, but that Adverbial -r-i is not. He adds, however, that -r-i occurs in the speech of children. Similarly, the consultant for GAJ point 660034 in Nagano Prefecture reports that he used innovative mi-r-an 'doesn't look' as a child, but reverted to conservative mi-n as an adult. Insofar as the tendency to replace irregular V-stem suffixes with default forms augmented by r-Epenthesis is rooted in child language acquisition, it probably has a secure future even if some of the dialects, Ryukyuan and Japanese, that presently exemplify it most abundantly do not.

CHAPTER 7

Explaining the choice of Analysis A

7.1 Introduction

The evidence of Chapters 5 and 6 leaves little doubt that Analysis A is the descriptively adequate analysis of the suffixes to which it applies, the Japanese verbal inflectional suffixes that alternate according to the C/V polarity of the stem-final segment. As became clear in Section 5.4, however, given a verbal paradigm like that of Tokyo Japanese, where the formula "V-stem suffix = r + C-stem suffix" is valid only for the three categories Conclusive, Provisional, and Passive, Analysis A is less accurate at predicting the full set of relevant suffix shapes than are the alternative observationally adequate Analyses B and C. This fact raises the question of how speakers' choice of Analysis A can be understood — the question, that is, of what explanatory principles underlie that choice — and it is that question that is the theme of Chapter 7. After a short introduction to the concept of explanatory adequacy and how I take that concept to apply to morphophonology in Section 7.2, I narrow down the space of possibilities for an account of the choice of Analysis A in Section 7.3 by identifying a number of proposals concerning morphophonological analysis that are counterexemplified by that choice or by the relevant alternations themselves. In Section 7.4, I introduce case studies from Portuguese and Korean showing that speakers may select underlying representations for morphophonological alternations from environments of neutralization, thereby creating a great deal of lexical irregularity. Those case studies are shown to support a model of analysis choice in which, while both the choice of URs and the choice of a rule are based on considerations of type frequency, the two are chosen separately and in that order, and candidate analyses are not subject to evaluation as unified wholes. Section 7.5 shows that this model accounts correctly for the choice of Analysis A, but at the same time raises doubts about the relevance of type frequency to the competition, as rule candidates, between epenthesis of r and truncation of the suffix-initial vowel. In validation of those doubts, Section 7.6 introduces a case study from Modern Greek in which consonant epenthesis is the default method of hiatus resolution at stem boundary in spite of a considerable type frequency deficit with respect to the alternative of stem vowel truncation. It then proposes that the priority of epenthesis in the Modern Greek case follows from a principle rewarding minimization of the phonological distance between underlying and surface form at the level of the morpheme. Section 7.7, correspondingly, concludes that a full understanding of the choice of Analysis A must incorporate both type frequency and phonological distance considerations. Section 7.8, finally, situating Japanese *r*-Epenthesis in the context of other attested stem-boundary consonant epenthesis rules, argues that *r*-Epenthesis cannot be attributed to syllable-structure constraints and identifies outstanding issues concerning the origin and properties of such rules.

7.2   Explanatory adequacy in morphophonology

While observational and descriptive adequacy are concepts that apply to language-specific grammar, explanatory adequacy, the third level of adequacy proposed by Chomsky (1964a, 1964b), applies to grammatical theory, or universal grammar: explanatory adequacy "is achieved when ... linguistic theory provides a general basis for selecting" (Chomsky 1964a: 63) a descriptively adequate grammar from the set of observationally adequate alternatives. In terms of language acquisition, while descriptive adequacy is the appropriate goal for an account of the stable endpoint of the acquisition process, explanatory adequacy is the appropriate goal for an account of the initial state of the language faculty, the starting point of acquisition.

In principle, then, explanatory adequacy is the status attained by a theory of universal grammar when that theory permits the choice of the descriptively adequate grammar of any speaker's internalized language given the primary data that serves as input to the acquisition process. In practice, however, it is often convenient to speak of explanatory adequacy in less global, more local terms. Rizzi (2016: 100), for example, writes, "A particular descriptively adequate analysis meets explanatory adequacy when UG provides general principled reasons for choosing it over imaginable alternatives." Similarly, I will say below that explanatory adequacy is obtained with respect to a particular descriptively adequate analysis if there are plausible explanatory principles that account for the choice of that analysis from the set of observationally adequate alternatives.

Until around 1980, generative linguistic theory was taken to include (a) a set of constraints limiting the class of possible grammars and (b) an evaluation procedure that would choose the more highly valued of two alternative candidate grammars presented to it along with a corpus of primary linguistic data ((14) (iii) and (v), Chomsky 1965: 31). Correspondingly, explanatory adequacy would be attained if the combination of (a) and (b) resulted in the selection of the descriptively adequate grammar for any choice of primary linguistic data. In the Principles and Parameters framework (Chomsky 1981), on the other hand, linguistic theory takes the form of a set of inviolable principles and a set of parametric options. Explanatory adequacy is then attained if, for any choice of primary linguistic data, the descriptively adequate grammar results from setting of the parameters in question in response to that data. Research in the Minimalist Program (Chomsky 1995 and subsequent work) falls within the Principles and Parameters approach, with the principles typically identified with an invariant computational system and parametric variation confined to lexical items (Chomsky 1995:170).

The history of generative grammar thus makes available two basic models for the attainment of explanatory adequacy, one involving constraints on grammars and an evaluation metric, the other involving universal principles and the setting of parameters. In addressing questions of explanation in morphophonology, it is the former model, I will claim, that is the more readily applicable and thus the more fruitful. Correspondingly, Chapter 7 will consider multiple principles of the form "Given two observationally adequate analyses of a given data set, prefer the analysis that maximizes property P", and Chapter 8 will propose a principle that restricts the class of possible morphophonological analyses. It is in this way, then, that I will suggest it is possible to approach the problem of explanatory adequacy in morphophonology.

7.3   Hypotheses inconsistent with the choice of Analysis A

In reviewing hypotheses about morphophonological analysis that have been proposed in the literature but are counterexemplified by adoption of Analysis A, I begin with one that involves the nature of morphophonological rules. Hypotheses 2 and 3 concern criteria for the choice of underlying representations, and hypotheses 4 and 5 each postulate a metric that applies to a morphophonological analysis as a whole.[1]

> Hypothesis 1: Faced with a mutually competing set of alternations resulting from a particular choice of URs, speakers postulate a corresponding set of stochastic rules each of which applies with a likelihood proportional to the prevalence in the lexicon of the corresponding alternation.

---

1. The discussion below refers throughout to criteria that are hypothesized to govern speakers' choice of morphophonological analyses. It should be clear, however, that talk of speakers "choosing" an analysis is metaphorical and that speakers do not literally weigh candidate analyses against each other. Rather, they are endowed with principles that enable them to home in on particular analyses, given particular input data, and it is those principles that one is attempting to model in proposing criteria of evaluation or conditions restricting the range of possible analyses.

In decision-theoretic terms, Hypothesis 1 represents a "probability matching" theory of morphophonology; the "probability maximization" alternative is that the alternation with the highest lexical frequency becomes the default or regular alternation and that other alternations, being irregular in the sense of requiring extra lexical specification, are subject to elimination over time in favor of the default. Concrete proposals incorporating a probability matching approach to morphophonology typically include a mechanism guaranteeing that the stochastic rules in question come into play only with respect to novel items; for the existing vocabulary, lexical knowledge is held to take precedence (Albright et al. 2000: 6; Zuraw 2000: xiv, 9; Becker 2009: viii, 23). Nevertheless, ongoing change in the existing lexicon has also been analyzed in probability matching terms (Jun 2010, on which see Section 7.4.2 below), and it is worth asking what the implications of that approach would be for the Japanese case.

Given the choice of C-stem alternants as basic for the eight categories of Table 3 in Chapter 5, an alternation of zero with r applies in three categories (Conclusive, Provisional, and Passive), an alternation of a vowel with zero in two (Adverbial and Negative), and alternations of zero with y and s in one each (Volitional and Causative, respectively). As a result, a probability matching theory of morphophonology suggests that to the extent that innovative forms are observed, those displaying vowel deletion should occur two thirds as often as those displaying epenthesis of r, and those displaying epenthesis of y and s should occur one third as often. It also predicts that the V-stem forms of the first three categories, those displaying epenthesis of r, should show variation just as do the V-stem forms of the remaining five categories. In fact, while innovative forms showing epenthetic r are extremely numerous, as we have seen, I am not aware of any case in which any of the other three alternations has been extended. Further, the r-zero alternation of the first three categories, modulo unrelated changes, is stable. It thus seems clear that Hypothesis 1 makes incorrect predictions about the Japanese case.

> Hypothesis 2: Speakers obey surface phonotactic constraints in choosing basic or underlying representations.

Hypothesis 2 has been widely cited and discussed since it was proposed as a tendency by Hale (1973: 419–420) in a discussion of Maori verbal inflection. In Japanese, consonant-final verb stems would be inadmissible as surface forms, and their postulation thus violates Hypothesis 2. Considerations parallel to Hypothesis 2 have been appealed to in the literature in raising doubts about the existence of C-final stems in Japanese, Vance (1987: 197–199) referring specifically to Hale's discussion, Nasukawa (2010) appealing more generally to a monostratal model of phonology. Our discussion of Japanese verbal inflection and the changes it is undergoing, however, has depended at every point on postulating consonant-final stems; Analysis A, in particular, in taking C-stem suffixes as basic, presupposes the existence of such stems. Speakers' choice of Analysis A thus clearly counterexemplifies Hypothesis 2. I suggest that that hypothesis is too strong; the relevant generalization, which will cover cases of the Maori type but correctly refrain from making predictions about the Japanese case, refers to the concept of isolation form, an inflected form that coincides with the stem on which it is based. That generalization is that, at least when the existence of an isolation form holds across an entire lexical category, isolation forms tend to be taken as basic (broadly parallel proposals go back at least as far as Vennemann 1974:364). The discussion of Korean in Section 7.4 below will appeal to the concept of isolation form; Hale's Maori data will be cited as a case of stem-boundary epenthesis in Section 7.8.

> Hypothesis 3: Speakers choose URs for (nonautomatic) inflectional alternations on semantic criteria, taking alternants with more general or inclusive semantics as basic vis-a-vis alternants whose semantics is more highly specified.

Hypothesis 3 is arguably the import of Kuryłowicz's (1945–49) well-known second law, which mandates basic status for alternants or categories that occur in environments where a semantic contrast is neutralized (e.g. for masculines vis-a-vis feminines if the former category has a gender-neutral use), given that occurrence in an environment of neutralization is prima facie evidence of inclusive semantics. It is also a major tenet of Natural Generative Phonology (Vennemann 1972:240, Hooper 1979:114ff.), and has more recently been defended by Garrett (2008:139–142). There are in general no semantic distinctions, however, among morpheme alternants whose distribution is determined by purely phonological factors, as is typically the case for suffix alternations. For a semantic account of the Japanese alternations analyzed in Chapters 5 and 6 to be possible, for example, there would have to be some semantic feature common to all of the thousands of C-stem verbs and none of the thousands of V-stems. Such cases show, then, that there can be no general semantic theory of UR choice.

> Hypothesis 4: Speakers choose an analysis so as to maximize the number of nonbasic morpheme alternants that are predictable.

The goal of maximizing the predictability of nonbasic alternants is a plausible one, since in so doing, speakers are minimizing the amount of lexical irregularity involved in the analysis. It is also consistent with the feature-counting evaluation metric of classical generative phonology (referred to in Section 5.1), since minimizing the number of feature specifications that must be used in recording irregular allomorphs will in general minimize the total number of feature specifications required for lexical representations. As observed at the outset of this chapter, however, we have already seen the metric of Hypothesis 4 to be counterexemplified by the choice of Analysis A, given that that analysis treats as irregular five out of eight nonbasic suffix alternants (Table 3, Chapter 5), as opposed to the three of Analysis B and the one of Analysis C.

> Hypothesis 5: Speakers choose an analysis so as to maximize the number of inflected forms that are predictable.

An alternative to the hypothesis that speakers attempt to maximize the predictability of nonbasic allomorphs is suggested by the work of Albright (2002: ix), who proposes a model of paradigm acquisition incorporating the principle that base forms are chosen so as to "permit[Ø] accurate productive generation of as many forms of as many words as possible." While the hypothesis that speakers attempt to maximize the predictability of inflected forms across the entire lexicon has considerable conceptual plausibility, it, too, is counterexemplified by speakers' choice of Analysis A. This is because, when inflectional stem-forming suffixes are taken into account, the great majority of inflected verb forms, those based on lexical C-stems as well as those based on lexical V-stems, are V-stem forms — that is, have V-stem endings. As a result, Analyses B and C, under which basic forms of suffixes coincide in most or all cases with V-stem alternants, will do better at predicting inflected forms than will Analysis A.

In verifying this claim, I will assume, as just indicated, that the paradigm of a given lexical stem includes not only forms consisting of the lexical stem plus an ending (i.e. word-forming suffix), but also forms in which one or more inflectional stem-forming suffixes are added to the stem before an ending is. In the same way that the paradigm of the Latin verb stem *laudā-* 'praise' includes not just the (2nd person singular) present (active indicative) form *laudā-s*, with a single inflectional suffix, but also the corresponding imperfect *laudā-bā-s*, with two, and the pluperfect *laudā-v-erā-s*, with three, then, the paradigm of a Japanese verb like C-stem *mat-* 'wait' will include not only the Provisional *mat-eba*, but also the Passive Provisional *mat-are-reba*, the Causative Provisional *mat-ase-reba*, and the Causative-Passive Provisional *mat-ase-rare-reba* ~ *mat-as-are-reba*. Because the relationship of C-stem Potential *-e-* to conservative V-stem Passive-Potential *-rare-* raises issues that are irrelevant to the predictability calculation below, I leave Potentials out of that calculation. Inflected forms of Negatives, which are morphological adjectives in eastern dialects and, with minor exceptions, are distinct from verbal forms in all dialects, have also been disregarded. For present purposes, then, the paradigm of *mat-* will consist of the forms of Table 1.

Table 1. Paradigm of *mat-* 'wait'

Category	Lexical	Passive	Causative	Caus-Pass
Conclusive	mat-u	mat-are-ru	mat-ase-ru	mat-ase-rare-ru
Provisional	mat-eba	mat-are-reba	mat-ase-reba	mat-ase-rare-reba
Volitional	mat-oo	mat-are-yoo	mat-ase-yoo	mat-ase-rare-yoo
Adverbial	mat-i	mat-are-Ø	mat-ase-Ø	mat-ase-rare-Ø
Negative	mat-ana-	mat-are-na-	mat-ase-na-	mat-ase-rare-na-
Imperative	mat-e	mat-are-ro	mat-ase-ro	mat-ase-rare-ro

As may easily be verified, 18 of the 24 forms of Table 1 (all except those of the left-most column) are V-stem forms. For a V-stem like *mi-* 'see', all 24 of the paradigm's forms will be V-stem forms.

Evaluating Analyses A, B, and C with respect to Hypothesis 5 will require knowing what percentage of verbal forms is predictable under each of those analyses. I will assume that a suffix alternant is predictable under a given analysis if it is either basic or regularly derived (i.e. if it is not irregular) under that analysis and that an inflected form is predictable under a given analysis if and only if all of its suffixes are. For example, under Analysis A, *mat-oo* 'let's wait' is predictable, since *-oo* is basic (and thus predictable) under that analysis, but *mi-yoo* 'let's look' is not, since *-yoo* is irregular. Under Analysis B, both forms are predictable, because *-yoo* is basic under that analysis and *-oo* is regularly derived.

In order to calculate what percentage of the full set of verbal forms is predictable under a given analysis, we need to know (a) what percentage of the forms of a sample C-stem and a sample V-stem are predictable under that analysis and (b) what percentage of the verbal lexicon is constituted by C-stems and V-stems, respectively. With regard to the latter question, it is often observed that C-stems are roughly twice as common as V-stems in the lexicon of Japanese, and have been throughout the recorded history of the language (see for example Suzuki 1977: 202–210 and Keino 1972: 7–8). de Chene (2016: 66–67), using electronic versions of three medium-sized Japanese dictionaries, calculates the percentage of C-stems among regular verbs in the contemporary language as 66.8%, a figure that the inclusion of irregular verbs (in particular, lexicalized verbs consisting of a Sino-Japanese morpheme plus *se-/si-/su-/s-* 'do') reduces to 66%.[2]

---

2. The relative lexical frequency of the eleven occurring stem-final segments is approximately as follows: e (29.6%), i (3.0%), r (22.1%), s (17.4%), k (8.4%), m (8.2%), w (6.6%), t (2.2%), g (1.6%), b (0.8%), n (0.02%). These figures are based on searches of Nishio et al. 2000 and exclude irregular verbs.

Consider now the question of predictability of inflected forms under Analysis A, referring to the paradigm of *mat-* in Table 1. Under Analysis A, all six of the inflected forms of the lexical stem *mat-* will be predictable, but only two each of the forms of *mat-are-*, *mat-ase-*, and *mat-ase-rare-*, namely the Conclusive in *-ru* and the Provisional in *-reba*. Thus for a C-stem verb, 12 of 24 forms will be predictable, or 50%. Similarly, just two of the forms (Conclusive and Provisional) of the lexical V-stem *mi-* and the corresponding Passive stem *mi-rare-* will be predictable, and none of the forms of *mi-sase-* or *mi-sase-rare-*, given that all such forms will include one or more suffix alternants that are irregular under Analysis A. For a V-stem, then, only 4 of 24 forms (16.7%) will be predictable. In sum, Analysis A predicts 50% of the forms of 66% of all lexical verb stems, and 16.7% of the forms of the remaining 34%. Since $(.50 \times .66) + (.167 \times .34) = .387$, this means that it predicts roughly 39% of all verbal inflected forms.

Now consider Analysis B. Under that analysis, three of the six inflected forms of *mat-* will be predictable, namely the Conclusive in *-u*, the Provisional in *-eba*, and the Volitional in *-oo*, as will all six inflected forms of *mat-are-*, *mat-ase-*, and *mat-ase-rare-*. For a C-stem verb, then, 21 of 24 forms will be predictable, or 87.5%. Further, all 24 inflected forms of a V-stem verb like *mi-* will be predictable. In sum, Analysis B predicts 87.5% of the forms of 66% of all verbs, and 100% of the forms of the remaining 34%. Since $(.875 \times .66) + (1 \times .34) = .918$, this means that it predicts roughly 92% of all verbal inflected forms, well over twice the percentage predicted by Analysis A. Analysis C, finally, will predict everything except Imperative *mat-e*. It will predict, that is, 95.8% (23 of 24) of C-stem forms and 100% of V-stem forms — in sum, since $(.958 \times .66) + (1 \times .34) = .972$, roughly 97% of all verbal forms. Just as with the hypothesis that speakers aim to maximize the predictability of nonbasic morpheme alternants, then, the hypothesis that speakers aim to maximize the predictability of inflected forms results in Analysis A, the descriptively adequate analysis, being judged least highly valued of the three observationally adequate analyses we have considered.

7.4   Neutralizing choices of underlying representations

7.4.1   Two case studies

Hypotheses 4 and 5 of Section 7.3 both posit that speakers choose a morphophonological analysis so as to maximize predictability, either of nonbasic morpheme alternants or of inflected forms. Even apart from the case of Analysis A in Japanese, however, it is not difficult to show that speakers' analytic choices do not always maximize the degree to which alternants or inflected forms are predictable in terms of general principles. This is because there are cases in which speakers can be shown to have selected underlying representations for an alternation from an environment in which contrasts among alternants are neutralized, thereby creating a large body of lexical items for which the alternation is lexically conditioned. In this section, I will present two examples of such a neutralizing choice of URs as background to a first account for the adoption of Analysis A in Japanese. The first example involves the Portuguese developments already referred to in Section 5.2 in connection with the typology of alternations proposed there.

The Western Romance seven-vowel system *i e ɛ a ɔ o u* (*e* < Latin *ĭ/ē*, *ɛ* < *ĕ*; *o* < *ŭ/ō*, *ɔ* < *ŏ*) was subject to an automatic neutralization rule reducing unstressed *ɛ ɔ* to *e o*. In verbal conjugation, stress fell on the last vowel of the root in some forms and on the thematic vowel or a following suffix in others; these two sets of forms are known as "rhizotonic" (root-stressed) and "arhizotonic", respectively. As a result, root vowels *ɛ *ɔ (as in the reflexes of L *nĕg-ā-* 'deny' and *rŏg-ā-* 'ask') alternated between ɛ ɔ in rhizotonic and e o in arhizotonic forms, while root vowels *e *o (as in the reflexes of L *pĭsc-ā-* 'fish', and *pŭt-ā-* 'prune') were nonalternating in the relevant respect.

In Portuguese, as illustrated in Table 2, the alternation between stressed ɛ ɔ and unstressed e o was extended to originally nonalternating stems (see Williams 1938: 206ff.).

Table 2. Extension of lowering in Portuguese verb stems

Gloss	Arhizotonic	Original rhizotonic	Original alternation	Portuguese rhizotonic	Portuguese alternation
'to deny'	neg-a-	nɛg-a-	e ~ ɛ	nɛg-a-	e ~ ɛ
'to ask'	rog-a-	rɔg-a-	o ~ ɔ	rɔg-a-	o ~ ɔ
'to fish'	pesk-a-	pesk-a-	——	pɛsk-a-	e ~ ɛ
'to prune'	pod-a-	pod-a-	——	pɔd-a-	o ~ ɔ

As indicated in Section 5.2, the extension of the alternation between ɛ ɔ and e o can be seen as the result of two analytic decisions. First, in a neutralizing choice of URs, unstressed alternants were taken as underlying, creating an arbitrary lexical distinction between stems whose root vowel e o alternated with ɛ ɔ under stress and stems whose root vowel e o was nonalternating.[3] In this situation, the

---

3. While reanalysis of verb stems left isoradical noun and adjective stems unaffected (/pɔrte/ 'transportation, cargo' as against reanalyzed /portar/ 'carry' (L *pŏrtāre*)), this can be difficult to show in many cases because of sound changes that raised stressed ɛ ɔ, notably before syllables in *o* (see Williams 1938: §§34, 37).

alternating pattern was taken as regular, resulting in a rule of Lowering under stress in verb stems (cf. Harris 1974:75) that represents inversion (Vennemann 1972) of the automatic rule merging unstressed ε $\mathfrak{\jmath}$ with e o. I write Lowering as in (1), where "Vb", as before, stands for "verb stem", and the final V thereof is the thematic vowel, -a- in the above examples.

(1) $$\begin{bmatrix} V \\ -\text{high} \\ +\text{stress} \end{bmatrix} \rightarrow [+\text{low}] \; / \; \underline{\hspace{1em}} C_0 \, V_{vb}]$$

Nonalternating stems were originally lexical exceptions to Lowering; as the exception feature was lost from their lexical entries, they came to undergo the rule, so that today, the only mid vowels that meet the input conditions of (1) but fail to undergo it are those that are exempt for phonological reasons such as nasalization, hiatus with a suffixal vowel, or adjacency to a palatal consonant (Hensey 1972:290–291, Azevedo 2005:74). It should be added that while in a-stem (1st conjugation) verbs like those illustrated in Table 2, all nine rhizotonic forms, the singular imperative and forms 1236 (i.e. the three singular forms and the third person plural) of the present indicative and subjunctive, show the effects of Lowering, in e- and i-stem (2nd and 3rd conjugation) verbs, only the singular imperative and forms 236 of the present indicative do, the remaining rhizotonic forms showing a stressed vowel that agrees in height with the (deleted) thematic vowel (see e.g. Harris 1974:62, Mateus and d'Andrade 2000:82).

Our second example of a neutralizing choice of URs is drawn from Korean, where obstruents undergo automatic neutralization of laryngeal (C: C^h: C$^?$) and manner (t: s: c) contrasts syllable-finally ("Coda Neutralization"). As a result, the fifteen obstruents p p^h $p^?$ t t^h $t^?$ s $s^?$ c c^h $c^?$ k k^h $k^?$ h that contrast in syllable onsets are reduced in codas to the three possibilities p t k. An obstruent other than p t k that occurs as the final segment of a verb or noun stem appears unchanged before vowel-initial suffixes and clitics as a result of resyllabification, but alternates with its neutralized counterpart before consonants. Cluster-reduction processes, which sometimes feed Coda Neutralization, mean that there are alternations of clusters with p t k as well. In verbal inflection, all these alternations are stable, showing no tendency to be leveled or extended. In noun stems, however, they are undergoing a mixture of leveling and extension, as illustrated in Table 3 (see Ito 2010, Jun 2010, and references cited there). Specifically, while stems ending in s (os- 'clothing') are stable, stems ending in coronal obstruents other than s, such as juc^h-, the name of a traditional stick game (glossed 'yut'), display a tendency for their alternation to be replaced by the $t \sim s$ alternation. Stems ending in marked labial or velar obstruents or in clusters, on the other hand, display a tendency for their alternations to be leveled in favor of the neutralized syllable-final form, as shown by the last three examples of the table.

Table 3. Leveling and extension in Korean noun stems

Gloss	Syllable-final	Conservative resyllabified	Conservative alternation	Innovative resyllabified	Innovative alternation
'clothing'	ot.	o.s	t. ~ .s	o.s	t. ~ .s
'yut'	jut.	ju.c^h	t. ~ .c^h	ju.s	t. ~ .s
'knee'	murip.	muri.p^h	p. ~ .p^h	muri.p	———
'kitchen'	puək.	puə.k^h	k. ~ .k^h	puə.k	———
'price'	kap.	kap.s	p. ~ p.s	ka.p	———

As in the Portuguese case, these developments can be seen as the result of two analytic decisions. First, in a neutralizing choice of URs, syllable-final alternants have been taken as underlying, resulting in arbitrary lexical distinctions among multiple types of underlying *p t k* depending on the alternant that is observed prevocalically. In this situation, the *t ~ s* alternation has been taken as regular for coronal stem-finals, resulting in a rule taking *t* to *s* when it is both syllable-initial and final in a noun stem ("Assibilation", shown as (2)); as in the Portuguese case, the innovative rule is the result of inversion, here of (one case of) the Coda Neutralization rule. This analysis of ongoing changes in Korean noun inflection, it should be noted, goes back at least to Ko 1989 (Ito 2010: 365–366).

(2)   t → [+cont] / . __ $_N$]

Nonalternating *t*-stems were originally lexical exceptions to Assibilation but have been almost completely regularized (Ito 2010: 363). For labial and velar stem-finals, the null alternation (nonalternating pattern) has been taken as regular, with the result that other alternations are subject to leveling. For all three points of articulation, stem alternants that end in clusters or marked obstruents other than *s*, as illustrated in Table 3 by *juc^h, murip^h, puək^h,* and *kaps*, are lexically listed along with the corresponding default forms (*jut, murip, puək, kap*), but with a condition restricting them to the prevocalic environment (in all cases, the two alternants are in fact collapsible with angled brackets). As the environmentally restricted irregular alternants are lost, the corresponding nouns assume regular behavior, stem-final *p* and *k* ceasing to alternate and stem-final *t* coming to alternate prevocalically with *s* (although there are also competing subtendencies among the coronals, as shown diachronically by (8), Ito 2010: 363 and discussed in detail in Jun 2010). The Korean situation, combining leveling and extension, is thus an ideal illustration of the typology of morphophonological alternations proposed in Section 5.2, according to which two binary analytic decisions, whether defaults are posited and, if so, whether a productive rule is posited as well, generate three diachronic profiles, namely stability, leveling, and extension.

Adapting terms used by Pinker (2002:287) to label two opposing visions of society and human nature identified by Sowell (1987), we might say that proposals that speakers are guided by predictability in choosing morphophonological analyses represent a "utopian" vision of morphophonology, one according to which speakers constitute rational actors in pursuit of well-defined goals. The phenomenon of neutralizing choices of underlying representations, on the other hand, suggests instead a "tragic" vision of morphophonology in which speakers are at times driven, in defiance of considerations of predictability, to decisions about UR choice that will saddle their descendants for many generations to come with considerable lexical irregularity. In more neutral terms, the Portuguese and Korean cases illustrate a mode of evaluation in which, rather than selecting a morphophonological analysis as a unitary whole ("unitary evaluation"), speakers choose URs with no attention to the question of a possible rule and proceed to the latter question only subsequent to the establishment of URs ("sequential evaluation"). We will return to the issue of sequential evaluation below.

7.4.2   An alternative interpretation

Before moving on, however, it is important to examine an alternative interpretation that might be placed on the diachronic developments involved in the Portuguese and Korean cases. This is that, rather than taking neutralized alternants as underlying and postulating an innovative inverted rule, speakers have relexified stems that show innovative forms in the environment of contrast in such a way that the original neutralization rule will account for the innovative alternation. In Portuguese, this would mean that speakers have relexified originally non-alternating stems like *pesk-a-* 'to fish' and *pod-a-* 'to prune' as *pɛsk-a-* and *pɔd-a-*. In Korean, taking the examples of Table 3 as representative, it would mean that speakers are in the process of relexifying *jucʰ-*, *muripʰ-*, *puəkʰ-*, and *kaps-*, respectively, as *jus-*, *murip-*, *puək-*, and *kap-*. I will call this alternative the "(pure) relexification" account of the changes in question, as opposed to the "(reanalysis and) regularization" account proposed in Section 7.4.1.

When there is evidence for productive application of an innovative rule, relexification accounts are often criticized for failing to capture or reflect this productivity. Thus, with regard to English "intrusive *r*", Bermúdez-Otero (2011:2036–2037) writes, "restructuring scenarios in which /ə/ is replaced by /əɹ/ in underlying representations ... fail to account for the regular and productive nature of *r*-intrusion", and with regard to Uyghur *y*-zero and *r*-zero alternations, Vaux (2008: 46–47) notes that "to say that all long-vowel roots have been historically reanalyzed as ending in *y* or *r* ... relegates to the domain of arbitrary lexical content something that otherwise receives a simple phonological explanation." This argument is applicable to the Korean case, where recent loanwords display productive extension of the *t* ~ *s* alternation to innovative stem-final *t*. Thus, for example, /lopot/ 'robot' has the accusative [robosil] from /lopot-il/, the dative [robose] from /lopot-e/, and so on for all vowel-initial clitics. On the regularization account of the Korean changes, this follows from rule (2). On the relexification account, it will have to be the result of a constraint limiting underlying stem-final coronals to *s*, so that *robot*, when borrowed, is automatically lexified as /lopos/.

Another consideration that appears to favor regularization over relexification accounts of morphophonological change is that the former come equipped with an explicit understanding, in both grammatical and psychological terms, of the long period of variation or competition between conservative and innovative forms that typically characterizes such change and of the diachronic directionality displayed by that variation. As discussed in Section 5.2, the basic principle is that irregularity, characterized as diacritic or phonological information in excess of a single phonological matrix, tends to be lost from lexical representations, a phenomenon whose psychological interpretation is failure to retrieve irregular forms from memory. Relexification accounts, in contrast, would appear to have no ready grammatical or psychological interpretation for the competition between conservative and innovative UR candidates that they would need to postulate and for the endpoint of that competition in the triumph of the innovative forms.

In particular cases, however, perhaps the most decisive difference between regularization and relexification accounts will be whether or not the analytic decisions involved in each can be motivated in terms of explanatory principles of some plausibility and generality. Consider first in this regard the Portuguese case. The regularization account postulates that, in the prefinal syllable of a verb stem, the value of [low] in stressless contexts was taken as underlying. At the level of the stem rather than the feature, this means that URs coincide with the stem alternants of arhizotonic forms (below, "arhizotonic stem alternants"). Can the choice of arhizotonic alternants as underlying be motivated?

Taking a conservative variety of the language as representative, a Portuguese verb has approximately 60 inflected forms, six person-number combinations each for nine subparadigms plus two imperative and four nonfinite forms. As we have seen, precisely nine of those 60 forms are rhizotonic. Arhizotonic forms thus constitute 85% of the verbal paradigm, and rhizotonic forms 15%. It seems plausible that it is this frequency difference, explicated in Section 7.5 below as a subcase of type frequency, that accounts for the underlying or default status of arhizotonic forms. In contrast to the regularization account of the Portuguese changes, the relexification account postulates that formerly nonalternating mid-vowel stems were relexified with low vowels. This relexification might be attributed to an innovative constraint on URs to the effect that [−high] vowels in the prefinal syllable of a verb stem must be [+low].[4] It is unclear, however, how the introduction of such a constraint on URs could be motivated. It thus appears that the regularization account, but not the relexification account, provides an understanding of the choice of underlying representations in the Portuguese case that can be grounded in independently motivated principles.

There is a further aspect of the Portuguese reanalysis that is unexpected on a relexification account. This is that Lowering, written in (1) to require a mid vowel as input, also applies in a small set of stems whose final root vowel is high, notably *frig-i-* 'fry', *fug-i-* 'flee', *sub-i-* 'climb', and *sum-i-* 'vanish'. Given (1), such stems can be accommodated by adding a diacritic to their lexical entries and revising the rule to refer to that diacritic, as in Harris 1974. But it cannot be the case that these stems have been relexified with low vowels, because that would predict a mid vowel rather than the observed high vowel in arhizotonic forms.[5]

Our account of the Portuguese data has not dealt with the basis for the second analytic decision of the reanalysis, the choice of the alternating rather than the nonalternating pattern as regular. In fact, the basis for that decision is less than completely clear, given that a preliminary survey of Portuguese verb stems suggests no decisive frequency differential between inherited verbs with $^*\varepsilon$ $^*\upsilon$ in the last syllable of the root and inherited verbs with $^*e$ $^*o$ in that position. Moving now to the Korean case, we will find, in contrast, that a principled explanation is available for both the choice of URs and the choice of a rule. Combined with the ongoing nature of the relevant changes and the relatively detailed data that is available on them, this will mean that a judgment in favor of a regularization account as against a relexification account can be reached in the Korean case with an even greater degree of assurance than it was in the Portuguese.

In asking whether the analytic decisions involved in the reanalysis and regularization account of the Korean changes summarized in Table 3 can be motivated in terms of plausible explanatory principles, let us first consider the choice of URs. Above, I equated the environments of the syllable-final and resyllabified alternants of that table with preconsonantal and prevocalic position, respectively.

---

4. Isoradical noun and adjective stems would be unaffected: while *escovar* 'to brush' (L *scōpāre* 'to sweep') and *beber* 'to drink' (L *bĭbĕre*) would be relexified with low vowels, *escôva* 'brush' (L *scōpa* 'broom') and *bêbedo* 'drunken' (L *bĭbĭtus*) would retain mid vowels.

5. While pretonic mid vowels tend to raise, the pretonic mid: high contrast is maintained in careful pronunciation (Azevedo 2005: 40).

Syllable-final alternants, however, appear word-finally as well as preconsonantally as the result of the deletion of clitics, particularly those marking structural case. The occurrence of syllable-final alternants word-finally gives those alternants the status of isolation forms and provides a plausible motivation for their choice as underlying, in line with the discussion of Hypothesis 2 in Section 7.3. Like the rule inversion analysis itself, the claim that syllable-final morpheme alternants are basic in Korean nominal inflection because of the salience or independence resulting from their status as isolation forms goes back to Ko 1989 (Ito 2010: 365).

As noted above, taking syllable-final alternants of Korean noun stems as underlying represents a neutralizing choice of URs, resulting in multiple types of stem-final *p t k* that must be distinguished lexically according to the segment with which they alternate prevocalically. At the same time, we saw, there is one alternation at each point of articulation that is being extended at the expense of the others and can thus be presumed to be regular, the *t ~ s* alternation for coronals and the null alternation for labials and velars. If we now ask on what basis that choice has been made, it seems clear that the answer is lexical frequency (see Jun 2010 and references cited there). (3) below shows the pairing of preconsonantal and prevocalic alternants for noun stem finals along with the lexical frequency of each prevocalic alternant and the percentage of the stems at the relevant point of articulation constituted thereby. The data of (3) was obtained by applying the concordance program Geuljabi II to the .txt files of Kim and Kang 2000; for similar statistics (excluding nouns ending in clusters), see Albright 2008: 171 and Jun 2010: 149.[6]

(3)

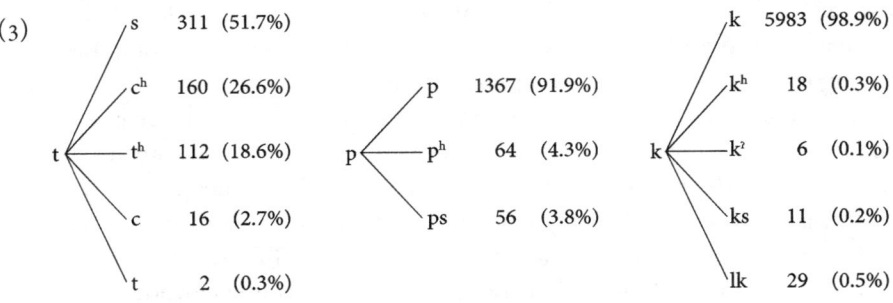

As the figures of (3) show, at each point of articulation, it is the alternation with the highest lexical frequency that is being extended. As we will see in Section 7.5, this makes the choice of regular alternation amenable to explanation in terms of a generalized concept of type frequency. In sum, under the regularization account,

---

6. Kim and Kang 2000 is based on data from the then-extant Sejong Corpus; for current Korean corpora, see https://kli.korean.go.kr/corpus/main/requestMain.do?lang=en.

the Korean changes summarized in Table 3 are naturally seen as the result of two well-motivated analytic decisions, a neutralizing choice of URs based on the tendency to take isolation forms as underlying and a deneutralizing (Nevins and Vaux 2007:38) choice of regular alternation based on type frequency.

Let us now turn to the question of what the prospects are for a principled explanation of the ongoing changes in Korean noun inflection under a relexification account of those changes. Such an account might posit an innovative constraint on URs restricting obstruent finals in noun stems to *p s k*, a constraint that might in turn be seen as motivated by the lexical statistics of (3).[7] But the stability of alternations due to Cluster Reduction and Coda Neutralization in verbal inflection, combined with lexical statistics for verb stem finals that are similar to those observed in nouns, shows immediately that lexical imbalances like those of (3) are, in and of themselves, insufficient to produce instability. (4) displays lexical counts and percentages for verb stem finals parallel to those given for nouns in (3).

(4)

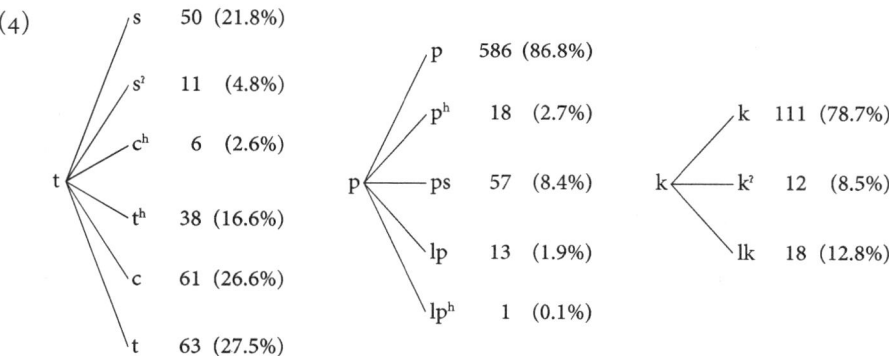

Apart from the fact that there is no clear winner among the coronals, the lexical statistics of (4) are broadly parallel to those of (3). But in contrast to those of (3), the lexical statistics of (4) are phonologically inert, associated with no instability or variation in the corresponding alternations. This contrast would appear to be inexplicable on a relexification account of the ongoing changes in noun inflection. It is readily understandable, however, in the context of the reanalysis and regularization account proposed above. For verbal inflection, the stability of alternations due to Cluster Reduction and Coda Neutralization argues that the analysis of them that is in force involves no irregularity. This, in turn, is possible only if the URs of verb stems coincide with their contrastive prevocalic alternants. The neu-

---

7. Thus, Nevins and Vaux (2007:47) say of the coronal obstruents in particular that "learners are using lexical statistics in constructing URs."

tralizing choice of URs postulated by the regularization account for noun stems, in contrast, puts the members of the three sets of alternations in (3) in direct competition with each other for the role of regular alternation at that point of articulation, and it is only at this point that lexical statistics come into play.

There are yet other possible interpretations of the Korean changes. One (Ricardo Bermúdez-Otero, p.c.) is that they represent the lexical diffusion of the rule of Coda Neutralization in the domain of the noun stem, where lexical diffusion of rule R proceeds through loss from lexical entries of marked feature specifications and their replacement by unmarked specifications supplied by R (Kiparsky 2003: 320). This interpretation runs afoul of the fact that irregular alternations of coronal obstruents are replaced by the $t \sim s$ alternation rather than by the null alternation, as the lexical diffusion hypothesis would predict (see de Chene 2014: 4). Another interpretation is that the Korean alternations are governed by a set of stochastic rules whose strength is proportional to the prevalence in the lexicon of the corresponding alternation (Jun 2010), following the "probability matching" theory of morphophonology examined under Hypothesis 1 in Section 7.3. This possibility runs afoul of the fact that, like historical p-stems and k-stems, historical s-stems are essentially invariant in contemporary Korean (see de Chene 2014: 10–11), contrary to the predictions of the probability matching theory but as expected if, as assumed here, the lexical entries of such stems contain no irregularity — no phonological or diacritic information, that is, in excess of a single phonological matrix. Finally, there is the possibility that the Korean changes reflect changes in the ranking of violable constraints under the assumptions of Optimality Theory. Space considerations preclude a detailed investigation of that possibility here, but the highly complex account of the Korean facts in Davis and Kang 2006 provides a graphic illustration of the degree to which a framework that recognizes neither defaults nor rules will struggle to come to terms with data that represent the gradual elimination of exceptions to an innovative generalization.

In sum, we have seen in this section that speakers sometimes make neutralizing choices of underlying representations and that, when they do, they sometimes deal with the resulting indeterminacy by postulating deneutralizing rules that invert an earlier derivational relationship (Vennemann 1972). Among the implications of those facts are that the notions of default and rule are essential to the description of the full range of phonological phenomena displayed by the world's languages and that, in spite of the explanatory power of the concept of the phonological life cycle (Bermúdez-Otero 2007: 503–504, Bermúdez-Otero and Trousdale 2012: 692ff., Kiparsky 2015: 577–578, among others), not all phonological rules originate in sound change and subsequent domain narrowing (Bermúdez-Otero 2011: 2024–2025, Bermúdez-Otero 2015: 382) operating thereon.

The question we now need to ask is whether this sequence of neutralizing choice of URs followed by deneutralizing choice of rule provides an appropriate model for understanding the adoption of Analysis A in Japanese and in Ryukyuan languages.

7.5   Type frequency, token frequency, and Analysis A

Neutralizing choices of underlying representations disconfirm the hypothesis that speakers invariably seek to maximize the degree to which a morphophonological analysis as a whole predicts elements like morpheme alternants or inflected forms. But they are perfectly consistent with the idea that there are frequency-based principles that govern UR choice and rule choice individually. In this section, I will argue that the two components of Analysis A, the choice of C-stem alternants as underlying and the *r*-Epenthesis rule, follow from a generalized version of type frequency that applies to both the choice of URs and the choice of regular alternations.

Narrowly defined, type frequency applies to linguistic units such as the segment or the word and is equivalent to frequency across the lexicon; token frequency, in contrast, refers to frequency in a text or corpus. Bybee (2001: 10, 119) broadens the notion of type frequency by defining it as the lexical frequency of a "pattern", where the latter concept is general enough to cover items as diverse as phonotactic configurations (e.g. initial three-member consonant clusters), rhythmic configurations (e.g. antepenultimate stress), and affixes. In asking what factors determine whether speakers will generalize a pattern, Bybee (1995 [2007]: 173–175; 2001: 118–121) emphasizes that when type frequency and token frequency diverge, it is patterns with high type frequency, and not those with high token frequency, that tend to be generalized.

For present purposes, we need a concept of type frequency that, as a first condition, allows us to compare the relative strength of the allomorphs of an alternating morpheme (understood here and below to mean "unit with a lexical entry"), either a stem or an affix, considered as candidates for that morpheme's UR. To that end, we may take an inflected form to be composed of a stem inserted from the lexicon and a morphosyntactic feature complex developed by the syntax. The type frequency of a stem alternant can then be defined as the percentage of eligible morphosyntactic feature complexes with which it combines, and the type frequency of an affix alternant can be defined as the percentage of eligible stems with which it combines. For example, we observed in Section 7.4.2 that in a Portuguese verb paradigm, rhizotonic and arhizotonic forms are distributed in the ratio 9 (15%) to 51 (85%). For any verb stem, then, the type frequency of its rhizotonic alternant will be 15%, and that of its arhizotonic alternant 85%. Similarly, we saw in Section 7.3 that 66% of the Japanese verbal lexicon consists of consonant-stems, and 34% consists of vowel-stems. For any verbal inflectional suffix, then, the type frequency of its C-stem alternant will be 66%, and that of its V-stem alternant 34%.

In this context, the fact that the regular alternation at each point of articulation in the Korean case appears to have been chosen on the basis of lexical frequency suggests that, at a suitable level of abstraction, there is a single frequency-based principle that determines not only what alternants are basic, but also what alternations are regular. In either case, this principle will choose from a well-defined candidate set the member that has the widest distribution with respect to a specified set of co-occurring elements. In the case of UR choice, the candidate set will be the set of all alternants of a given stem or affix; in the case of rule choice, it will be the maximal set of alternations (rule candidates) sharing a given input configuration or structural description — for example, the set composed of the three alternations with input p ($p \sim p$, $p \sim p^h$, $p \sim ps$) in (3) above. Calling this principle "Generalized Type Frequency", I state it as in (5).

(5)   **Generalized Type Frequency (GTF)**
Given the maximal set of alternants of a morpheme, considered as candidates for the underlying form of that morpheme, or the maximal set of alternations sharing an input configuration, considered as candidates for the regular alternation with that input configuration, define the type frequency of each candidate as the percentage of eligible co-occurring elements with which it occurs. The successful candidate is then the one with the highest type frequency.

The set of eligible co-occurring elements will vary depending on whether the object of evaluation is a UR candidate or a rule candidate and on whether the relevant alternation involves stems or affixes. Incorporating proposals already made above, (6) specifies the four sets in question.

(6)   Eligible co-occurring elements for UR candidates (alternants) and rule candidates (alternations)
a.   for an affix alternant, the set of lexical stems with which the affix occurs
b.   for a stem alternant, the set of morphosyntactic feature complexes with which the stem occurs
c.   for an affix alternation, the set of affixes to which the alternation could in principle apply
d.   for a stem alternation, the set of stems to which the alternation could in principle apply

In establishing evaluation measures for UR candidates and rule candidates separately, GTF assumes the notion of sequential evaluation, whereby speakers choose

URs first and only then proceed to the question of a possible rule. In particular, the fact that competing rule candidates must share an input configuration means that rule candidates are evaluated only in the context of a particular choice of URs.

GTF can be seen to divide into four subcases depending on the set of co-occurring elements. The choice of URs in the Portuguese case is the result of subcase (6b), and the choice of regular alternations in the Korean case is the result of subcase (6d). Returning now to the question of how to explain the choice of Analysis A in Japanese, it is not difficult to see that that choice follows from the remaining two subcases of GTF, (6a) and (6c). We have already noted that for each Japanese verbal inflectional suffix, the type frequency of its C-stem alternant will be 66% and that of its V-stem alternant 34%. According to GTF subcase (6a), this means that the C-stem alternant will be underlying in each case. Assuming that result, the set of candidates for a regular alternation, given the input configuration of hiatus at verb stem boundary, consists of epenthesis of r (3 cases out of 8 eligible suffixes, type frequency 37.5%), epenthesis of y (1 case, type frequency 12.5%), epenthesis of s (1 case, type frequency 12.5%), and deletion of the second vowel (2 cases, type frequency 25%). GTF subcase (6c), then, predicts correctly that the regular alternation should be epenthesis of r.

It appears, then, that we have an answer to the question of why Analysis A has been favored over other observationally adequate accounts of the Japanese alternations, and in that sense an approach to explanatory adequacy for that analysis. At the same time, however, there are reasons to find the type frequency account of the origins of the r-Epenthesis rule less than fully satisfying. The first is that there is reason to believe that, along with type frequency, token frequency can be a crucial factor in increasing the salience of an alternation and thus the likelihood that speakers will take that alternation as the basis for a rule. The evidence for the relevance of token frequency in the case at hand comes from the failure of Miyako dialects to adopt Analysis A, documented in Section 6.5.

In Section 5.6, discussing the failure of irregular vowel-initial V-stem suffixes like Imperative -*i* and Volitional -*u* to trigger r-Epenthesis, we observed that that rule is naturally seen as a generalization of the inherited r-zero alternation of the three suffixes Conclusive -*(r)u*, Provisional -*(r)eba*, and Passive -*(r)are-*. In Section 6.3.1, we saw that Hirara Miyako Provisional -*(r)iba* and Passive -*(r)ai-* display this r-zero alternation as well. Miyako, that is, shows the r-zero alternation that underlies the r-Epenthesis rule in two of the three categories that originally displayed it. Crucially, however, it lacks the r-zero alternation in the Conclusive because of the reduction of *ru* (and *ri*) either to *ï* or to *l*, in addition to phonological and analogical developments that merged Conclusives and Adverbials in the C-stem paradigm.

Searches of the BCCWJ show that that corpus contains 4,424,682 verbal Conclusive/Adnominal forms, 152,104 Provisional forms, and 784,935 occurrences of the Passive suffix. Out of a total of 5,361,721 tokens of suffixes that display an inherited r-zero alternation, that is, 4,424,682, or 82.5%, are Conclusive/Adnominal forms. If we assume that the high token frequency of the Conclusive/Adnominal plays an essential role in making the r-zero alternation salient enough to be taken by speakers as the basis for a rule, we will have a natural explanation for Miyako's failure to adopt r-Epenthesis, namely the changes that effaced the r-zero alternation in that category. Conversely, in the absence of any competing explanation for Miyako's failure to generalize the r-zero alternation that it displays in the Provisional and the Passive, that failure suggests the importance of token frequency in motivating the emergence of a rule of r-Epenthesis.

A second reason to question the type frequency account of the origins of r-Epenthesis involves the competition between epenthesis of r and the alternative rule candidate of deletion of the second of two vowels at verb stem boundary. To begin with, the type frequency differential between epenthesis of r and vowel deletion is small. More crucially, however, the type frequency explanation takes no account of the fact that, given C-stem Conclusive -u, Adverbial -i, and Imperative -e, a rule deleting the suffixal vowel at verb stem boundary would create zero V-stem suffix alternants for all three categories, neutralizing the distinction between those categories for V-stems. This observation might suggest an account based on a constraint along the lines of Realize Morpheme, which "requires every underlying morpheme to receive some phonological exponence" (Kurisu 2001: 37). The case study from Modern Greek that I introduce in Section 7.6, however, suggests that there is a principle favoring epenthesis over truncation as a means of hiatus resolution at stem boundary in a wider range of cases than would be covered by such a constraint, and it is that principle that I will take to apply to the competition between epenthesis and truncation in Japanese.

7.6   Truncation and ð-Epenthesis in Modern Greek nominal inflection

7.6.1   Hiatus at noun stem boundary

As is well known (Casali 1997, 1998), hiatus, the juxtaposition of heterosyllabic vowels (V_1V_2), is disfavored in many languages. At the same time, creation of hiatus by the addition of vowel-initial suffixes to vowel-final stems is extremely common. As a result, many languages display strategies for resolving hiatus at stem boundary, among them truncation of V_1 or V_2, coalescence of V_1 and V_2, and epenthesis of a consonant between V_1 and V_2. In Modern Greek (MG), two distinct hiatus-resolution strategies, truncation of V_1 and epenthesis of *ð*, compete with each other in the inflection of nonneuter nouns.[8] These two strategies are illustrated in (7) and (8), respectively, where the suffixes *-s* and *-es* realize nom.sg.m. and nom./acc.pl.m./f. for the relevant declension classes. When not otherwise indicated, lexical information is from the online version of the Triandafyllidis Dictionary, Institute of Modern Greek Studies 1998 (below, DSMG).

(7) a. nikití-s   'victor'
    b. nikit-és   'id. (pl.)'

(8) a. ganomatí-s   'tinker'
    b. ganomatí-ð-es 'id. (pl.)'

In Sections 7.6.2 and 7.6.3, I argue that, of these two hiatus resolution strategies, *ð*-Epenthesis constitutes the default option, in particular for masculine nouns. On that proposal, while *ð*-Epenthesis will be subject to no lexical restriction, Truncation will be limited to stems marked, either individually or as the result of redundancy rules of more or less generality, to undergo it. The default status of *ð*-Epenthesis, however, is in apparent tension with the fact that truncating masculines far outnumber epenthesizing masculines in the MG lexicon. In Section 7.6.4, I propose an explanation for the fact that *ð*-Epenthesis is the default hiatus resolution strategy in spite of this type frequency deficit.

It should be noted that while the inflectional patterns in (7) and (8) have been presented here as involving phonological processes of truncation and epenthesis, and thus as embodying alternative repair mechanisms for the disfavored configuration of hiatus at stem boundary, this is by no means a consensus view in descriptions of MG noun morphology. The truncating pattern in (7) can be described, for example, by treating what I have assumed to be a stem-final vowel as a separate morpheme (a "theme vowel") and stipulating that that morpheme is present in singular forms, but not in plurals (Mackridge 1985: 135–136). Some authors, on the other hand (see Ralli 2000: 205 (note 8), 222), take both the truncating and the epenthesizing patterns to involve listed stem allomorphy. Below, the postulation of phonological processes, particularly epenthesis of *ð*, will be seen to be justified by the understanding of ongoing change that it allows.

---

8. While both masculines and feminines show a contrast between truncating and epenthesizing stems, epenthesizing masculines far outnumber epenthesizing feminines, and I concentrate here on the inflection of the former.

7.6.2 ð-Epenthesis as a default: Standard Modern Greek

There are at least two kinds of consequences we might expect if ð-Epenthesis is the default strategy for the treatment of hiatus in masculine nouns. The first is that that rule should apply without exception in the inflection of masculine stems for which it is implausible that memorized lexical information exists. Such stems might include, for example, proper names, loanwords, acronyms, and ono-matopoeia (Marcus et al. 1995). In the case of MG masculines, at least personal names and loanwords support an argument on this basis for the default status of ð-Epenthesis.

Many MG masculine given names are indeclinable; many others, including most that end in -os, decline in the singular only. Those that do have plural forms, however, most of them common names ending in -is, are almost invariably epenthesizing (truncating Ilías, pl. Ilíes is an exception). Two examples, the first from Sotiropoulos 1972: 66 (note 26), are given in (9)–(10) (/ɣj/ is [j]).

(9)   a.   ɣjáni-s   'John'
      b.   ɣjáni-ð-es 'id. (pl.)'

(10) a.   θomá-s   'Thomas'
      b.   θomá-ð-es 'id. (pl.)'

Family names in -is are epenthesizing as well (Thumb 1910 [1912]: 51), as illus-trated in (11) (Sotiropoulos 1972: 66 (note 26)).

(11) a.   Ipsilándi-s   'Ypsilanti'
      b.   Ipsilándi-ð-es 'id. (pl.)'

Turning now to borrowings, masculine loanwords whose stems end in vowels other than o are almost invariably epenthesizing, as illustrated in (12)–(14) (an exception is levéndis, pl. levéndes 'fine young man', an apparently early loan from Turkish (Horrocks 1997: 321)).

(12) a.   ananá-s   'pineapple' (French, originally from Tupi)
      b.   ananá-ð-es 'id. (pl.)'

(13) a.   valé-s   'valet'   (French)
      b.   valé-ð-es 'id. (pl.)'

(14) a.   manávi-s   'grocer'   (Turkish)
      b.   manávi-ð-es 'id. (pl.)'

Regarding neologisms more generally, the stock of epenthesizing masculines is increased by productive derivation with suffixes of the form -á- whose outputs are typically (a) nouns of occupation or (b) augmentatives/pejoratives (see e.g. Householder et al. 1964: 46). In (15) below (Vazou and Xydopoulos 2007: 236), the derivational base, retained here in its orthographic form, is an acronym, pronounced /oik/, designating the Underwater Demolition Squad (Omáda Ypo-bruxíon Katastrofón) of the Greek Navy.

(15) a. OYK-á-s   'member of the OYK'
      b. OYK-á-ð-es 'id. (pl.)'

The second prediction that follows from the hypothesized default status of ð-Epenthesis is that diachronically, we should expect to see the range of that rule expand at the expense of the range of truncation. This is because the rule feature that triggers the (minor) rule of truncation is an example of the sort of irregularity or excess information that tends over time to be lost from lexical entries, as first set out in Section 5.2. That this prediction is borne out is shown most clearly in Standard MG by those nouns that are historically truncating, but which are now optionally epenthesizing, indicating ongoing change in favor of epenthesis:[9]

(16) a. patéra-s   'father'
      b. patér-es   'id. (pl.)' (conservative)
      c. paterá-ð-es 'id. (pl.)' (innovative)

(17) a. pramateftí-s   'peddler'
      b. pramateft-és   'id. (pl.)' (conservative)
      c. pramateftá-ð-es 'id. (pl.)' (innovative)[10]

Similarly, historically nonepenthesizing *vasiléa-* 'king' has largely been replaced by epenthesizing *vasiljá-*, and, of the conservative names of the months of the year, all nonepenthesizing, eleven have epenthesizing colloquial variants (e.g. *Márti-* for *Mártio-* 'March').

---

9. Internet searches suggest that the conservative form is largely restricted to metaphorical uses ('fathers of the church/nation') in (16) and vastly less frequent than the innovative form in (17), so that the change to epenthesizing status is substantially complete in these examples.

10. The pattern of (17), with the agentive suffix *-ti-* alternating in epenthetic plurals with *-ta-* (obligatorily under stress and optionally otherwise), is ascribed to only five nouns in the DSMG, but said to be characteristic of a considerably larger group in descriptions from the early and middle 20th century (Thumb 1910 [1912]: 52, Householder et al. 1964: 49); as Horrocks (1997: 219) notes, the epenthetic forms were by and large not taken into the contemporary standard or common language, which coalesced after the end of military rule in 1974.

7.6.3 ð-Epenthesis as a default: Anatolian dialects

We have seen that there is evidence from Standard MG suggesting that epenthesis of ð is the default stem boundary hiatus resolution strategy in masculine nouns, including cases in which the range of epenthesis is being expanded at the expense of truncation. In regional dialects, where the pace of language change is less constrained by literacy, standardization, and prescriptivism (cf. Section 6.6), we find in some cases a more dramatic expansion of the range of ð-Epenthesis. In illustration, we will look briefly at two Asia Minor dialects of Greek, now moribund, that are discussed by Melissaropoulou (2013). The first is the dialect of Livisi in Lycia (southwest Anatolia), for which Melissaropoulou's data comes from Andriotis 1961: 23.

In order to understand the Livisi developments, it is necessary to look at the paradigms of the two main types of MG masculine nouns, the o-stems with nominative plurals in -i < -oi (Ralli's (2000) Class 1) and the stems, epenthesizing and truncating, which end in other vowels and have nominative/accusative plurals in -es (Class 2). Table 4 shows the paradigms in Standard MG of epenthesizing ("E") psarás 'fisherman', truncating ("T") náftis 'sailor', and o-stem ðrómos 'road'. I assume that o-stems are truncating, but that there is a redundancy rule to that effect, so that they do not have to be so marked individually.

Table 4. Inflection of Standard MG masculine nouns

		Class 2 (E)	Class 2 (T)	Class 1
Sg	Nom	psará-s	náfti-s	ðrómo-s
	Gen	psará	náfti	ðróm-u
	Acc	psará	náfti	ðrómo
	Voc	psará	náfti	ðróm-e
Pl	Nom	psará-ð-es	náft-es	ðróm-i
	Gen	psará-ð-on	naft-ón	ðróm-on
	Acc	psará-ð-es	náft-es	ðróm-us

With Table 4 as background, Table 5 shows the Livisi paradigms of three Class 2 nouns, psarás 'fisherman', náftis 'sailor', and kritís 'judge', following Melissaropoulou 2013: 138 (full paradigms for Class 1 nouns are not given). Livisi shows raising of unstressed mid vowels, so that gen.pl. -on appears as -un, and it preserves earlier acc.sg. -n.

Table 5. Inflection of Class 2 nouns in Livisi

Sg	Nom	psará-s	náfti-s	krití-s
	Gen	psará	náfti	krití
	Acc	psará-n	náfti-n	krití-n
	Voc	psará	náfti	krití
Pl	Nom	psará-ð-i	náfti-ð-i	kritá-ð-i
	Gen	psará-ð-un	náfti-ð-un	kritá-ð-un
	Acc	psará-ð-us	náfti-ð-us	kritá-ð-us

There are two notable developments apparent in the paradigms of Table 5 with respect to those of Table 4. The first is that the plurals of all three nouns in Table 5 display Class 1 endings; expected nom./acc.pl. *-is < -es is not observed. The second is that *náftis* and *kritís*, truncating in Standard MG, have become epenthesizing in Livisi (*kritís* displays as well the alternation between *i* and *a* that we saw in (17) above). These developments suggest that, across the entire set of masculine nouns, Class 1 endings are unmarked with respect to those of Class 2, and that across the set of Class 2 nouns (at least), epenthesis is the default hiatus resolution strategy.

Melissaropoulou (2013:137) in fact notes about Livisi that even some *o*-stems display epenthesizing forms, although this development appears to be sporadic. In the dialect of Silli, which was spoken in south-central Anatolia near the city of Ikonion (today's Konya), however, all (Karatsareas 2011:49) or nearly all (Dawkins 1916:47) masculines, *o*-stems included, undergo epenthesis in plural forms. With intervocalic (and initial) *ð* having become *r*, typical *o*-stem examples are *ártupu-s* 'human being' (Standard MG *ánθropo-s*), nom.pl. *ártupu-r-i* (Dawkins 1916:47), with the plural stem identical to the singular stem, and *xristjanó-s* 'Christian', nom.pl. *xristjáni-r-i* (Melissaropoulou 2013:138), with the plural form built on an innovative stem alternant that incorporates the original ending (cf. Standard MG *xristjan-í*).

It thus seems clear that developments in nonstandard dialects support the claim that epenthesis of *ð* is the default stem boundary hiatus resolution strategy in MG masculine nouns. In conclusion, it should be noted that, while the epenthetic forms we have seen above are all plurals, the occurrence of epenthetic gen.sg. forms in *-ju* for *o*-stem nouns in multiple Cappadocian dialects (Dawkins 1916:105, 107, 109, etc.) argues that epenthesis applies before any vocalic ending regardless of number. That epenthesis of *ð* is not limited to plurals is shown as well by the fact that it applies in Standard MG before a small number of derivational suffixes, as in *kafe-ð-áki* 'coffee (dim.)' (see Sotiropoulos 1972: 48 for more examples).

7.6.4   Explaining the default status of *ð*-Epenthesis

The Generalized Type Frequency principle of Section 7.5 was claimed to account for the choice of stem URs in the Portuguese case and affix URs in the Japanese case, as well as for rule choice in both the Japanese and Korean cases. The default status of Greek *ð*-Epenthesis, however, cannot be explained on the basis of type frequency, since epenthesizing stems are a clear minority among Standard MG masculine nouns. Concretely, of the 2,985 Class 2 masculines in the DSMG, 2,187 (73%) are truncating, and only 798 (27%) epenthesizing.[11] When Class 1 masculines, analyzed above as truncating, are included in the calculation, the percentage of epenthesizing masculines drops to under 13%. The Greek case, then, suggests that speakers will choose epenthesis over deletion as the rule-governed, default means of hiatus resolution at stem boundary even in the face of a considerable type frequency deficit.

In seeking to explain this preference, I will appeal to two leading ideas. The first, already implied by the discussion of Section 2.3.2 concerning rules and morphomes and illustrated by the single-feature changes of Portuguese Lowering and Korean Assibilation ((1) and (2) above), is that, in choosing among candidate analyses for a given set of morphophonological alternations, speakers value a close relation between input and output representations. In line with that generalization, I propose that there is a principle of evaluation that rewards minimal input-output divergence in a candidate analysis. There are two possible formulations of such a principle, one on which it evaluates full candidate analyses against one another, and one on which it assumes a choice of URs and evaluates only rule candidates. I adopt the latter, narrower formulation here, stating it as in (18).

(18)   **Minimal Divergence Principle (MDP)**
       Given two rule candidates for a given input configuration, prefer the candidate that occasions the lesser divergence between input and output.

The second leading idea I will appeal to in explaining the choice of epenthesis over truncation as the default hiatus resolution strategy in the Modern Greek case is that epenthesis, by allowing all underlying segments of both stem and suffix to appear in the surface form, represents a less severe distortion of the input representation than does truncation. Given that both truncation and epenthesis involve an input-output divergence of precisely one segment, it might appear that they

---

11. Five stems that show both options were excluded from the calculation.

should be equivalent in their effect on the input-output relationship. Suppose we assume, however, that stem-boundary epenthetic consonants are inserted inter-morphemically, thus belonging to the morphological word without belonging to any of its constituent morphs. In that case, it will be possible to see stem-boundary epenthesis as involving less input-output divergence than truncation — in fact, as involving in principle a completely faithful or transparent input-output relation, one that involves zero divergence between the two representations at the level of the morph. Correspondingly, if Modern Greek ð-Epenthesis is stated as in (19) ([+m] = masculine), the choice of that rule over a competitor that truncates the stem vowel of a masculine noun before a vowel-initial ending will be accounted for under (18).[12]

(19) $\emptyset \rightarrow ð \,/\, V_{N[+m]}] \underline{\quad} [V$

As indicated above, the lexically unrestricted rule (19) will coexist with a trunca-tion rule that is limited to stems marked to undergo it.

Given the MDP, then, we can account for the priority of epenthesis over trun-cation in Modern Greek, but only under the additional condition that epenthe-sis be intermorphemic. In the absence of the MDP, on the other hand, we could not exclude the possibility that epenthetic ð in Modern Greek is inserted into stems, in line with the morphemic affiliation that is often assumed for it (e.g. Triandaphyllidis 1949 [2004]: 120, Ralli 2000: 222) or, for that matter, into suffixes. In this case, then, a descriptive indeterminacy is resolved by an explanatory prin-ciple — that is, a general condition on speakers' choice of analyses. In the same way, if we wish to account for the choice of epenthesis of r over deletion of the suffixal vowel in Japanese under the MDP, it will follow that epenthetic r must be intermorphemic, as we have assumed since Chapter 4.

7.7   The choice of Analysis A: Summary and conclusion

The MDP account of the outcome of competition between epenthesis of r and deletion of the suffixal vowel as rule candidates can be adopted without otherwise altering the explanation for the choice of Analysis A that was proposed in Section 7.5: analyses taking V-stem or longer suffix alternants as underlying will be excluded by Generalized Type Frequency for URs, and only the four rule can-didates with C-stem suffixes as URs will be entertained. Of those, epenthesis of s

---

12. McCarthy and Prince (1993: 120) claim, similarly, that "epenthetic elements have no mor-phological affiliation", but they do not conclude that such elements have no effect on the input-output relation.

and *y* will be eliminated by GTF, and deletion of the suffixal vowel, in addition to losing to epenthesis of *r* on type frequency, will be eliminated by the MDP.

As noted above, however, it is also possible to interpret the MDP as a principle of unitary analysis, one that evaluates full candidate analyses against one another, necessarily on the basis of the rules they posit. On this interpretation, all epenthesis analyses, regardless of the URs they assume, will be consistent with the MDP, and all deletion analyses, including Analyses B and C, will be excluded. For example, analyses taking V-stem alternants as underlying and postulating epenthesis of *a* (as in the Negative) or *i* (as in the Adverbial) will be among the analyses consistent with the MDP. Like analyses taking C-stem alternants as underlying and postulating epenthesis of *s* or *y*, those analyses will be excluded by a criterion of type frequency, given that they apply in a single category each.

The Generalized Type Frequency account of the choice of Analysis A in Section 7.5, however, embodies the claim that the fundamental flaw in Analyses B and C is not that they postulate deletion rules, but that they fail to reflect the default nature of consonant-stem inflection. The asymmetry between C-stem and V-stem inflection is confirmed by the fact that the major changes that have affected the Japanese verb during the historical period, the neutralization of the Conclusive: Adnominal contrast in the 13th and 14th centuries (Frellesvig 2010: 329) and the subsequent leveling of the stem vowel alternation *i/e* ~ *u*, treated in detail in Chapter 8, both assimilated V-stem to C-stem inflection by eliminating features of the former that had no counterpart in the latter. I will assume that the GTF account is correct in taking the postulation of C-stem suffixes as underlying to be an essential element of the explanation of why Analysis A was adopted, and will thus not embrace a unitary analysis interpretation of the MDP.

In the end, then, the understanding of the adoption of Analysis A to which we are led incorporates a number of distinct elements, including cases (6a) and (6c) of Generalized Type Frequency, the Minimal Divergence Principle (18), and the idea that, in addition to type frequency, token frequency may increase the salience of an alternation. It is to be hoped that future research will further elucidate the extent to which each of these factors is operative in the process of morphophonological analysis.

7.8   *r*-Epenthesis as an exemplar of the stem-boundary epenthesis rule

Above, I have approached the question of the choice of Analysis A by comparing it with other possible analyses of the system of alternations at issue. Another approach to that question would attempt to motivate Analysis A, and its *r*-Epenthesis rule in particular, by reference to putatively universal constraints that are satisfied by the output of that rule. For example, de Lacy (2006: 81–82), citing Mester and Ito 1989 and (a 1998 working papers version of) Lombardi 2002 (both of which refer to de Chene 1985), includes Japanese *r*-Epenthesis on a list of cases for which "Epenthesis is … forced by some general prosodic requirement", and continues, "The most common motivation for epenthesis is the demand for syllables to have onsets." A weaker version of this constraint, taking account of the frequency of vowel-initial words in many languages, would require onsets only for word-internal syllables, thus penalizing hiatus in the domain of the word.

In the case of Japanese, however, the prevalence of unresolved word-internal hiatus makes it difficult to argue that *r*-Epenthesis is motivated by any general prohibition of that phenomenon. Root-internally, there are many instances of hiatus resulting historically from deletion of earlier *p* and *w* before nonlow vowels.[13] At derivational suffix boundary, in addition to the cases of suffixation of *-e-* to vowel-final roots (*mi-e-* 'be visible', *ko-e-* 'cross, exceed') that we saw in note 1 of Chapter 4, there are numerous cases of hiatus resulting from automatic deletion of root-final *w* before nonlow vowels (*ow-ar-* 'end (i)', *o-e-* 'id. (t)') and of root-final *y* before front vowels (*hay-as-* 'grow (t)', *ha-e-* 'id. (i)'). Hiatus is unrestricted at all types of compound boundary, as illustrated for verb-verb compounds in Section 5.6. Finally, as seen in the same section, automatic deletion of stem-final *w* before nonlow vowels counterfeeds *r*-Epenthesis, reintroducing hiatus at verb stem boundary, so that the *w*-stem *kaw-* 'buy', for example, has the partial paradigm Adverbial *ka-i*, Imperative *ka-e*, Negative *kaw-ana-*, Volitional *ka-oo*, Conclusive *ka-u*. In sum, Japanese shows that a language may have a robust, if morphologically restricted, intervocalic epenthesis rule in the absence of any general tendency to proscribe hiatus.

Approaches that attempt to treat epenthesis as a response to syllable-structure constraints also typically attempt to treat the choice of epenthetic consonant as in principle predictable, in particular in terms of segmental markedness constraints (McCarthy and Prince 1993: 117, de Lacy 2006: 79). In addressing this question, it is crucial to distinguish, following Blevins (2008), between epentheses that are "natural" in the sense of directly "reflecting the phonologization of … sound change" (Blevins 2008: 81) and epentheses that are "unnatural" in the sense that their history involves reanalysis, typically rule telescoping or rule inversion. Blevins suggests that natural epentheses are for the most part limited to insertion of the glides *j w* intervocalically and the laryngeals *h ʔ* at prosodic boundaries. Unnatural epentheses, on the other hand, are essen-

---

13. Representative examples, some already seen in Section 2.3.4, are *ie < ipe* 'house', *sio < sipo* 'salt', *ue < upe* 'top, above', *uo < uwo* 'fish', *koi < kopi* 'love', *koe < kowe* 'voice', *ai < awi* 'indigo', *mae < mape* 'front', *sao < sawo* 'pole'.

tially unconstrained regarding the choice of epenthetic segment. This follows if, as Blevins (2008: 97) suggests, "any consonant which can be lost through natural phonetic processes in the syllable coda can give rise to regular epenthetic alternations" as a result of rule inversion, a point that is also emphasized by Vaux (2001).

It nevertheless seems fair to say that there is a widespread impression that, among morphologically conditioned epenthetic consonants, coronals occur with greater than chance frequency.[14] Both Japanese *r*-Epenthesis and Modern Greek ð-Epenthesis illustrate this tendency; several other relatively well-established examples are given in (20).[15]

(20) a. Maori *whaka-hopu-t-ia* 'be caused to catch', replacing *whaka-hopuk-ia*
             (Hale 1973: 414, 417)
       b. French *taba-t-ière* 'snuffbox', replacing *tabaqu-ière*   (Nyrop 1908: 56)
       c. Sanskrit *mádhu-n-as* 'honey (abl./gen.sg.), replacing *mádhv-as*
             (Whitney 1889: 120–121)
       d. Ancient Greek *onóma-t-os* 'name (gen.sg.)', replacing **onómn-os*
             (Sihler 1995: 296–297)
       e. Proto-Algonquian **ne-t-ehkw-ema* 'my louse'   (cf. Bloomfield 1946: 95)
       f. Axininca Campa *i-n-koma-t-i* 'he will paddle' (*n* = nasal archiphoneme)
             (Payne 1981: 108)

The eight cases of epenthetic coronals we have seen, six of them in (20), differ a great deal with regard to how well the diachronic background of their respective epenthesis rules is understood. In cases where multiple coda consonants are lost more or less simultaneously and relevant information is available, the choice of a default epenthetic consonant may be predictable in terms of frequency considerations. Thus, as Blevins (2008: 97) notes, the choice of *t* as epenthetic in the Maori case of (20a) correlates with type frequency (although she points out at the same time that there are Maori dialects in which *h* or *ŋ* is the default epenthetic consonant, perhaps as a result of token frequency). The choice of *t* in (20b) seems likely to be based on type frequency as well. In (20c), there is no competition among multiple candidates for the status of default epenthetic consonant, but innovative

---

14. Claims to this effect (de Lacy 2006: 80–81, Hall 2011: 275–278) typically do not distinguish between epentheses with and without morphological conditioning, but Lombardi (2002) notes repeatedly that (p. 239) "coronals are epenthetic only in morphologically restricted cases."

15. In this context, it is also important to mention the claim (Morley 2018: 685) that "there is little evidence that phonological (vs. phonetic) epenthesis is an accessible analysis to a learner engaged in morphological learning," illustrating as it does the need to check conclusions reached through phonological experimentation against the attested facts of phonological grammars.

forms can be attributed to generalization of a rule that has its origin in the para-digm of those neuter *n*-stems (e.g. *bráhma(n)*- 'prayer') that display an apparent full grade of the *n*-suffix throughout their paradigm (de Chene 1983: 689–690).

In contrast to (20a)–(20c), where the origin of the epenthetic consonant is relatively well understood, the source of the epenthetic *t* of (20d) is a notorious unresolved problem in the history of Greek (Beekes 1995: 187, Sihler 1995: 297), with clear models for the *t*-zero alternation essentially limited to *méli* ~ *mélit*- 'honey'. The Modern Greek *ð*-zero alternation may be similar in having a limited number of models. This is because, in a development evidence for which goes back to the late 5th century (Holton et al. 2019: 302), the singular paradigm of original consonant-stem nouns was remodeled by taking the accusative form as the stem. This resulted in shifts such as (in transliteration) *phylak-s/phylak-a* 'guard' > *phylaka-s/phylaka-Ø* and *mykē-s/mykēt-a* 'fungus' > *mykēta-s/mykēta-Ø*, thus incorporating the original stem-final consonant into a vowel-final stem and, in the case of a dental stem final, eliminating its C-zero alternation. If this development was largely complete before *ð*-Epenthesis arose, models for that rule will have been limited to the handful of original *d*-stems in which the nomi-native allomorph was generalized instead, such as *phyg-ad-* 'fugitive' and *mig-ad-* 'mixed-blood individual', and in which the development *phyga-s/phygad-a* > *phyga-s/phyga-Ø* will have set up an alternation of zero in the singular with *ð* before the vowel-initial endings of the plural. If *ð*-Epenthesis arose before the elimination of consonant-stem inflection, on the other hand, there will have been many more models for it, given the relative productivity of the suffixes *-ad-* and *-id-* in the earlier language (Buck 1933: 340).

The origin of the Algonquian *t*-zero alternation of (20e) is opaque because of its time depth; in fact, Goddard (2013: 64–65 and references cited there) points out that Algonquian *t*-Epenthesis has counterparts in Wiyot and Yurok, implying that it is of Proto-Algic age. The origin of Axininca Campa *t*-Epenthesis is poten-tially illuminable through comparative work, but I am not in a position to com-ment further on that possibility. Japanese *r*-Epenthesis, finally, is another case in which the origin of the relevant alternation may well be unknowable in full detail, in spite of a number of attempts in the literature to identify it.[16]

In this section, we have seen that Japanese *r*-Epenthesis is not plausibly attrib-utable to constraints on syllable structure and that it is an exemplar of an estab-lished morphophonological rule type, epenthesis of a consonant at inflectional boundary. An account of the apparent naturalness of this rule type is provided by the MDP, (18) above, in conjunction with the hypothesis that stem-boundary

---

16. Relevant proposals include those of Unger 1977: 70, Whitman 1985: 49, Unger 2000: 669, and Whitman 2016: 33–36; for critical discussion, see de Chene to appear § 4.

epenthetic consonants are inserted intermorphemically. A number of questions concerning inflectional boundary consonant epenthesis, however, invite further investigation, notably that of how robust a preexisting alternation needs to be in order to trigger the induction of an epenthesis rule, the question of whether the apparent bias in favor of coronals among morphologically conditioned epenthetic consonants is genuine, and the question of the degree to which, if it does prove to be genuine, it can be accounted for by considerations of frequency.

CHAPTER 8

The timing of the adoption of Analysis A

8.1 Introduction

Chapter 7 dealt with the question of what principles dictate the choice of Analysis A from among the available alternatives. A complementary problem is posed by the fact, noted in Section 5.6, that while the *r*-zero alternation of Conclusive *-(r)u* (originally the Adnominal) and Provisional *-(r)eba* (originally Realis *-(r)e + ba*) goes back at least to the 8th century, and the *r*-zero alternation of Passive *-(r)are-* dates to the 10th, there is no evidence for the innovative *r*-suffixes of other categories before the modern period. Fragmentary attestation of those suffixes begins only in the 18th century, and they are not securely recorded until Kokugo Chosa Iinkai 1906, the first systematic survey of Japanese dialects.[1] Additionally, the failure of Rodriguez (1604–1608 [1955]: 607–613) to mention suffixes like Imperative *-r-e* and Negative *-r-an* in his section on nonstandard dialects appears to establish 1600 as a terminus post quem for innovative *r*-suffixes, given that he records in some detail the morphological idiosyncrasies of the Western Kyushu Japanese of the time.

The *r*-zero alternation of *-(r)u*, *-(r)eba*, and *-(r)are-*, then, seems to have remained stable, but inert, from roughly the 10th century to the 18th. Ideally, we would like to be able to account for this long period of inertness and explain why it ended. Fortunately, it turns out that modern Kyushu dialects retain evidence suggesting why the reanalysis that led to the extension of the *r*-zero alternation, the adoption of Analysis A, would have been impossible before the 17th century.

8.2 The bigrade alternation

In contemporary Tokyo Japanese and the majority of other dialects, regular vowel-final verb stems are nonalternating. Over the larger part of the recorded history of the language, however, the stem vowel (*i* or *e*) of most vowel-stems alternated with *u* in the Adnominal > Conclusive and the Realis > Provisional, as well

---

1. Hikosaka 1999 provides a detailed review of the first attestations of Imperative *-r-e*, Volitional *-r-oo*, and Negative *-r-an*, both in Kokugo Chosa Iinkai 1906 and in earlier sources back to the first half of the 18th century.

as in the zero-suffixed Conclusive form that was displaced by the Adnominal in the 13th and 14th centuries. This is illustrated in Table 1, which shows partial paradigms of *oki-* 'arise', *uke-* 'receive', *se-/si-* 'do', and *ko-/ki-* 'come' as of the year 1600 (here and below, I elide *u*-final alternants in citing verb stems).

Table 1. Vowel-stem inflection in 1600

	'arise'	'receive'	'do'	'come'
Negative	oki-nu	uke-nu	se-nu	ko-nu
Adverbial	oki-Ø	uke-Ø	si-Ø	ki-Ø
Conclusive	oku-ru	uku-ru	su-ru	ku-ru
Provisional	oku-reba	uku-reba	su-reba	ku-reba

Because the *i/e* ~ *u* alternation has the orthographic consequence that stem alternants are written with syllabary characters from two different rows or "grades" of the standard five-by-ten syllabary table, verbs showing that alternation (apart from the irregulars 'do' and 'come') are characterized in the traditional Japanese analysis of verbal conjugation as following the bigrade (*nidan*) paradigm, as opposed to the unigrade (*itidan*) paradigm of nonalternating verbs. Below, I will adopt this terminology for stems like *oki-* and *uke-* and, as in Section 5.7.1, refer to the stem alternation *i/e* ~ *u* as the "bigrade alternation".

The diachronic course of the leveling of the bigrade alternation in favor of the front vowel *i/e* has been governed by two main factors, stem length (monosyllabic versus polysyllabic) and the identity of the stem vowel (*i* versus *e*), with the first member of the opposition being relatively favorable to leveling in each case and the second relatively unfavorable. Of the dozen or so monosyllabic *i*-stems of Old Japanese, first of all, some were already nonalternating, some displayed variation between leveled and unleveled forms, and some, while alternating at that stage, underwent leveling in the course of the following centuries (see Frellesvig 2010: 106 and the entries of Omodaka et al. 1967). By around the year 1200, then, there were no monosyllabic bigrade *i*-stems left, a generalization which holds as well of all modern dialects. For monosyllabic *e*-stems, leveling of the bigrade alternation began by the 14th century (Yamaguchi & Akimoto 2001: 336) with the verb *he-* 'pass through', and the remaining handful of monosyllabic *e*-stems (*e-* 'obtain', *de-* 'emerge', *ne-* 'sleep', *ke-* 'kick' (*ker-* in most modern dialects)) had become nonalternating in the prestige dialects of central Japan by the 17th century (Yamaguchi & Akimoto 2001: 892). Today, the bigrade alternation survives in monosyllabic *e*-stems only in northwestern Kyushu and at a handful of isolated points to the south (GAJ map 66).

Leveling of the bigrade alternation in polysyllabic stems had begun in central dialects by the 17th century (Yamaguchi & Akimoto 2001: 892), but it began even earlier in eastern dialects (Kokugo Gakkai 1980: 76, 856) and was noted as a characteristic of eastern speech at the turn of the 17th century by Rodriguez (1604–1608 [1955]: 29). In contemporary dialects, the bigrade alternation of historical polysyllabic *i*-stems survives in eastern Kyushu and to some extent in the north and west of the island and at several locations in Wakayama Prefecture in the southern Kii peninsula (GAJ map 61). More than half of the Kyushu locations that preserve *okuru* as the Conclusive of historical *oki-* 'arise', however, have reanalyzed the stem as *oke-* under the pressure of the far more numerous *e*-stems (see GAJ map 72). For polysyllabic *e*-stems, finally, the great majority of Kyushu dialects (as well as two Wakayama locations) preserve the bigrade alternation, although leveling is underway in some of them.

We have seen that the bigrade alternation that originally characterized virtually all Japanese vowel-stems survives in Kyushu, in particular for polysyllabic *e*-stems. Crucially, the innovative *r*-suffixes of Table 5, Chapter 5 are also widely attested in Kyushu, but (almost) exclusively in the unigrade paradigm. The bigrade alternation, that is, appears to block the introduction of innovative *r*-suffixes. At the same time, leveling of the bigrade alternation appears to trigger the introduction of innovative *r*-suffixes (as noted by Onishi 2016b: 150), so that those suffixes appear in the paradigms of all and only verbs that have undergone leveling. This complementary distribution between innovative *r*-suffixes and the bigrade alternation is illustrated in Table 2, where innovative *r*-suffixes are underlined, with forms from Takachiho in northwestern Miyazaki Prefecture (Itoi 1961: 261).

Table 2. Unigrade and bigrade inflection in Takachiho

	'arise'	'raise'
Conclusive	oki-r-u	agu-ru
Provisional	oki-r-eba	agu-reba
Imperative	oki-r-e	agii < age-i
Volitional	oki-r-oo	agyuu < age-u
Negative	oki-r-an	age-n

At a first level of abstraction, the failure of innovative *r*-suffixes to appear in the bigrade paradigm of Table 2 suggests an answer to the puzzle of why the *r*-zero alternation of *-(r)u*, *-(r)eba*, and *-(r)are-* remained analytically inert for at least eight centuries: as long as the bigrade alternation remained unleveled, the reanalysis of suffix-initial *r* as epenthetic appears to have been impossible. In the next two sections, I will examine in more detail this "bigrade blocking hypothesis", the hypothesis that the bigrade alternation blocks the adoption of Analysis A. Section 8.3 will show that suffix-specific reanalysis can mimic the results of regularization under Analysis A, creating forms that look like counterexamples to the bigrade blocking hypothesis but that can be explained in ways that are consistent with it. Section 8.4 will then investigate in detail the degree to which the predictions of the bigrade blocking hypothesis are confirmed in modern Japanese dialects.

8.3   A class of apparent exceptions to the bigrade blocking hypothesis

We have taken the appearance of innovative *r*-suffixes like Imperative *-r-e*, Volitional *-r-oo*, and Negative *-r-an* as a sign that Analysis A has been adopted in a given dialect or location. Suppose, however, that there was a dialect displaying, for one or more stem types, a single apparent innovative *r*-suffix, and that there was an explanation for that suffix not involving Analysis A. We might then be justified in hesitating to conclude from the appearance of that suffix alone that Analysis A has been adopted for the relevant stem types in that dialect.

Consider in this context the dialect of the Goto Islands of Nagasaki Prefecture, for which the GAJ supplies data from three locations and Hirayama and Oshima (1969) provide more detailed data from five. Throughout the area, the bigrade alternation has been leveled for *i*-stems like *oki-* 'arise' and in the Provisional of *e*-stems like *uke-* 'receive' and the irregular *se-/si-* 'do'. As a result, the Conclusive and Provisional of those three verbs are phonetic developments of *okiru/okireba, ukuru/ukereba*, and *suru/sereba*, with surface forms reflecting the deletion of final high vowels and reduction, typically to glottal stop, of the resulting word-final consonants. The Imperative, Volitional, and Negative of *oki-* have innovative *r*-suffixes in all locations and thus coincide with the Takachiho forms of Table 2, although variation with conservative forms is reported in some cases. What is unexpected is that the Imperative suffix *-re* appears not only with *i*-stems like *oki-*, but with *se-/si-* 'do' and *e*-stems like *uke-*, leaving irregular *ko-/ki-* 'come', whose Imperative is *ko-i*, as the only vowel-stem verb at any of the locations in question without an Imperative in *-re*.

Because *uke-* and *se-/si-* retain the bigrade alternation in the Conclusive, their Imperatives in *-re*, if due to regularization under Analysis A, would represent a violation of the bigrade blocking hypothesis. It is noteworthy, however, that because of the leveling of that alternation in the Provisional of those verbs (*ukureba > ukereba; sureba > sereba*), the innovative Imperatives in *-re* coincide in all cases with the corresponding Provisional form minus -*ba*. Further, they duplicate in this respect a relationship that holds for consonant-stem verbs (Imperative *kak-e*, Provisional *kak-eba*). This coincidence raises the possibility that innovative *e*-stem Imperatives in -*re* (including *sere* 'do!') are backformed from the Provisional on the model of consonant-stem forms, an analysis that may be expressed proportionally as *kakeba: kake :: ukereba: (ukere)*. Semantically, this analysis would have a natural basis in the widespread tendency in Japanese dialects and in Japonic languages more generally (see note 6, Chapter 2) for the Provisional to be used as a suggestion and thus, by extension, as a weak imperative, as in Tokyo *soo sureba (doo desu ka)*? '(How about) if (you) did that?' It should also be noted that the conservative Imperatives replaced by *ukere* and *sere* will, judging by the surrounding area, have been *ukero* and *sero*, forms with the same stem alternant and a minimally different suffix.

What provides the most decisive evidence for this account of Goto *e*-stem Imperatives in -*re*, however, is the Provisional of *ko-/ki-* 'come'. While the expected form *kureba* is recorded by Hirayama and Oshima (1969: 81) for Fukue, the largest population center in the area, the four remaining locations treated in that work plus all three GAJ points (including Fukue) report *koiba* or phonological developments thereof (*koeba, keeba, keba*). The form *koiba*, inexplicable on phonological grounds, can only be accounted for as a replacement for *kureba* formed from the irregular Imperative *koi* of *ko-/ki-* plus -*ba*. The analysis that treats the Provisional as [Imperative + *ba*], suggested in the last paragraph, thus appears to be at work here, albeit with a contrary direction of derivation (*kake: kakeba :: koi: (koiba)*).[2] Tiersma (1978, 1982) has interpreted bidirectional derivational relationships in inflectional morphology as the result of "local markedness", under which plural forms, for example, will tend to be treated as derivationally basic vis-a-vis singulars for nouns denoting objects that typically occur in pairs. In the present case, both the irregularity and the high token frequency of *koi* 'come!' are naturally seen as motivating its use as a derivational base (on these two factors, see Bybee 1985: 57–58): as noted above, *koi* is the only Goto Imperative with the suffix -*i* (as is true for many other dialects as well); and in the BCCWJ, the ratio of Imperative to Conclusive forms for 'come' (6.0%) is more than twice as high as the same ratio over all verbs (2.6%).

---

2. Evidence for this analysis can be cited from Eastern Japan as well; five GAJ survey points in Yamanashi Prefecture report *okiroba* (in three cases alongside *okirjaa < okireba*) for the Provisional of *oki-* 'arise' (cf. Imperative *okiro*), and two neighboring points in Ibaraki and Chiba Prefectures report *ogiroba* or *oyiroba* (GAJ map 126). On the latter area, see also Sasaki 2019: 215–216.

If the account of Goto *e*-stem Imperatives in *-re* offered above is correct, that case illustrates that suffix-specific developments can mimic the outcome of regularization under Analysis A, resulting in forms that appear to violate the bigrade blocking hypothesis but in fact can be explained in a manner consistent with it. I return to the question of counterexamples to bigrade blocking at the end of the next section.

8.4   The extent of conformity with the bigrade blocking hypothesis

In evaluating the degree to which modern dialects conform to the bigrade blocking hypothesis, I will use primarily the data of the GAJ, supplemented where appropriate by that of Kyushu Hogen Gakkai 1991. I will organize the discussion around the two oppositions that were identified above as governing the history of bigrade leveling, stem length and identity of the stem vowel. For each verb class or stem type as defined by those oppositions, there is a representative stem whose forms were surveyed by the GAJ. For each of those stems, I will first inventory the set of locations that report only unleveled forms for the stem's Conclusive or, depending on the availability of data, for either the Conclusive or Provisional (below, the "target set"); these are the locations which I will judge to have preserved the bigrade alternation and to which I will therefore take the bigrade blocking hypothesis to apply. Next I will examine the inflectional categories surveyed in the GAJ that could in principle show innovative *r*-suffixes and, over the locations of the target set, compute the percentage that, in accordance with the bigrade blocking hypothesis, fail to do so. This percentage will be the measure of conformity with the bigrade blocking hypothesis for the stem type in question.

I begin with polysyllabic *e*-stems, which, as noted above, preserve the bigrade alternation over a wider area than any of the other stem types. Of the 121 Kyushu locations surveyed by the GAJ, 85 have exclusively *akuru* or phonetic developments thereof (notably *akut*) for the Conclusive of the representative polysyllabic *e*-stem, *ake-* 'open (t)' (map 64). These 85 points thus constitute the target set for this verb class. GAJ survey items for *ake-* include the Imperative, Volitional, Negative, and Causative, all of which could in principle show innovative *r*-suffixes. There are thus in the data of the GAJ 340 potential violations of the bigrade blocking hypothesis for the representative polysyllabic *e*-stem. I will consider these innovative *r*-suffixes one by one.

In Kyushu as a whole, twelve locations report *akere* as at least one option for the Imperative of *ake-* (map 87). Four of these are outside the target set, however, and three others are the Goto Islands locations for which I argued above that Imperative *-re* is the result of a suffix-specific reanalysis. Of the remaining five locations, this latter interpretation seems plausible for at least one, where the Provisional of *ko-/ki-* 'come' is *koeba*.[3] If so, unexplained occurrences of Imperative *-re* in the target set are limited to the remaining four locations. There is also one unexplained occurrence in the target set of Volitional *-roo* (map 107) and two unexplained occurrences of Causative *-rase-* (map 118). Out of the 340 potential violations of the bigrade blocking hypothesis for *ake-*, then, there are only seven actual violations, so that the percentage of compliance with that hypothesis is 333 out of 340, or 97.9%.

Turning now to historical polysyllabic *i*-stems (reanalyzed as *e*-stems in a number of locations, as noted above), the GAJ provides data for the stem *oki-* 'arise' on both of the forms that historically show the alternant *oku-*, the Conclusive and the Provisional. There are 31 GAJ locations that report only *okuru* or phonetic developments thereof for the Conclusive (map 61), and 27 locations that report (among forms with the suffix *-reba*) only *okureba* or phonetic developments thereof for the Provisional (map 126). 23 locations belong to both of these sets, so that there are 35 locations in the target set, the set of locations that display only unleveled forms for one or both of the Conclusive and Provisional. The forms of *oki-* surveyed in the GAJ that could in principle show innovative *r*-suffixes are the Imperative, Volitional, and Negative, so that there are 105 potential violations of the bigrade blocking hypothesis for that stem.

The GAJ reports two occurrences of Imperative *okire* and one occurrence of Negative *okiran* from target set locations in northwestern Kyushu. It also records two target set locations in northwestern Miyazaki Prefecture that show innovative *r*-suffixes for all three of the relevant categories. The data of both Kyushu Hogen Gakkai 1991:154 and Onishi 2016b:151, on the other hand, place those latter two points within the area that shows leveled *okiru* for the Conclusive; since both report *okiryaa* < *okireba* for the Provisional, this would remove them as counterexamples to the bigrade blocking hypothesis.[4] On the basis of the GAJ data, then, there would be nine violations of that hypothesis out of a possible 105, for a compliance rate of 91.4%. Relying instead on the testimony of Kyushu Hogen Gakkai 1991 and Onishi 2016b regarding the distribution of *okiru*, the target set is

---

3. This is survey point 737096 (Minamikushiyama, Nagasaki Prefecture). While the GAJ reports the corresponding Imperative as *koyoo* (the Standard Japanese Volitional form), Kyushu Hogen Gakkai 1991:156–157 records *koi* for a nearby town (Kuchinotsu) and the entire surrounding area.

4. The GAJ survey points are 737497 (Gokase) and 739405 (Shiiba). It is worth noting that Onishi (2006:89), working with the GAJ data, attributes the apparent presence of Negative *okiran* beside Conclusive *okuru* in this area to influence from the adjacent dialect rather than to grammatical reanalysis.

reduced from 35 to 33 locations, and there are only three violations out of a possible 99, for a compliance rate of 97.0%.

For the monosyllabic *e*-stem *ne-* 'sleep', the GAJ data suggest a sharply lower rate of compliance with the bigrade blocking hypothesis. There are 21 locations that report only *nuru* or phonetic developments thereof (*nut, nuʔ, nui*) for the Conclusive of that stem, and two inflected forms that could in principle show innovative *r*-suffixes, the Negative and the Volitional. Of the resulting 42 potential bigrade blocking violations, 16 are in fact realized; both Negative *neran* and Volitional *neroo* are relatively common at the locations of the target set. The bigrade blocking compliance rate is therefore 26 out of 42, or 61.9%.

Finally, consider the irregular stems *se-/si-* 'do' and *ko-/ki-* 'come', which retain the bigrade alternation over most of the country in the Conclusive and, to a somewhat lesser extent, in the Provisional as well. That there is a tendency for the bigrade blocking hypothesis to be observed with these two verbs, first of all, can be illustrated with the Negative. For *se-/si-*, innovative Negative *seran* is attested in the GAJ (map 84) only at one point in the Goto Islands and at four points in the Mikawa Bay region of Aichi Prefecture, always in variation with conservative *sen*. At the Goto Islands location, while the Provisional is leveled *sereba*, the Conclusive is reported as *sui* (< *sur* < *suru*), so that Negative *seran* represents a violation of the bigrade blocking hypothesis. In the Mikawa Bay region, however, the stem is nonalternating *se-* over a relatively wide area, showing Conclusive *seru* (GAJ map 70), Provisional *sereba* or reduced *se(r)yaa* (map 131), and Adverbial *seri* (Yoshikawa 1972:152). No bigrade blocking violation thus results. Innovative Negative *koran* 'doesn't come' is even more limited in distribution than *seran*, being attested, in variation with conservative *kon*, only at three points in the Izumo region of Shimane Prefecture (GAJ map 83). At those three points, while the stem has not become totally nonalternating, the fact that the bigrade stem alternant *ku-* is in the process of being eliminated is shown by the innovative Provisional forms *korya(a)/kora*.

At the same time, however, it is clear that certain innovative *r*-suffixes, notably the stem-forming suffixes Causative *-rase-* (~ *-ras-*) (map 120) and, to a lesser extent, Potential *-re-* (map 178), show far too wide a distribution with *ko-/ki-* to allow dismissal of the innovative forms as isolated exceptions. One possible factor in this relatively wide distribution of Causative *ko-rase-* and Potential *ko-re-* is geographical diffusion of forms that, given the irregularity of *ko-/ki-*, are likely to have been lexicalized. Such diffusion has a clear precedent in Imperative *ko-i* 'come!' (map 90), which, uniquely among vowel-stem Imperatives in *-i* (contrast map 87) has, with its phonetic derivatives, a distribution that includes all of Kyushu (see also Kyushu Hogen Gakkai 1991:156–157) and much of Eastern Japan. While geographical diffusion may have played a part in the spread of *ko-rase-* and *ko-re-*, however, the near universality of unleveled Conclusive *kuru* shows that the origin of those innovative forms cannot be attributed to regularization under Analysis A if the bigrade blocking hypothesis is to be maintained. Rather, it would seem, they must be explained by appealing to surface analogy with forms that do owe their innovative *r*-suffixes to Analysis A. Crucially, given the extremely high rates of compliance with bigrade blocking for polysyllabic stems, this kind of surface analogy would need to be postulated only for the four monosyllabic *e*-stems and the two irregulars — that is, for precisely the set of monosyllabic alternating vowel-final stems.

In this section, I have evaluated the degree to which modern Japanese dialects conform to the bigrade blocking hypothesis. I have shown that for polysyllabic stems, both *e*-stems and *i*-stems, the rate of compliance approaches 100%, but that it is significantly lower for the small number of monosyllabic stems, both regular *e*-stems and irregular 'do' and 'come'. While I have suggested that this difference can be accounted for in terms of the sensitivity of monosyllables to surface analogical influences, the issue deserves further investigation. There can be little doubt, however, that the phenomenon of bigrade blocking, as epitomized by dialects that have multiple innovative *r*-suffixes, but only for nonalternating stems (Table 2 above), represents a linguistically significant generalization. In the remainder of the chapter, I turn to the question of how to account for that generalization. Section 8.5 explores the possibility that bigrade blocking results from the structure assigned to alternating stems, in the end concluding that that approach does not lead to a cogent explanation of the phenomenon. Sections 8.6 and 8.7 then pursue a completely different approach to bigrade blocking, one that links the susceptibility of an alternation to leveling to the phonological distance between alternants.

8.5   Representational approaches to bigrade blocking

r-Epenthesis ((11), Section 5.6) is written to apply at stem boundary. As a result, one straightforward reaction to the phenomenon of bigrade blocking would be to conclude that in dialects that preserve the bigrade alternation, the stems of the relevant verbs cannot be analyzed as ending in the alternating vowel. This is because if they did, Analysis A would treat them no differently from stems ending in non-alternating vowels, and one would expect them to come to display the innovative *r*-suffixes that are the hallmark of regularization under that analysis. As an alternative to analyzing the stem of a bigrade verb as ending in the alternating vowel, the stem might be taken to be the string ending in the preceding consonant. Under this proposal, the Takachiho Conclusives and Negatives of Table 2, for example, would have the structures [oki]r[u], [oki]r[an] and [ag][uru], [ag][en].

While the proposal to treat bigrade verbs as consonant-stems might seem to be validated by the fact that the consonant-final sequence in question is precisely what all inflected forms of a bigrade stem have in common, that proposal has immediate negative consequences. One is that if bigrades are C-stems, they will have to carry a lexical mark to distinguish them from regular or unmarked C-stems, which, as noted in Section 7.3, constitute approximately two thirds of the verbal lexicon. This in turn predicts that if and when bigrades regularize, they should become regular C-stems. But this never occurs; bigrades always regularize as nonalternating V-stems. A second problem is that if what has been treated above as the alternating stem vowel $i/e \sim u$ is instead the first segment of a variety of suffixes, the two presumed alternants will never belong to the same morpheme. There will thus be no way to express the elimination of the bigrade alternation as leveling and, more generally, no way to motivate it.

A somewhat more sophisticated variant of the C-stem approach to bigrades would treat the alternating vowel as a suffix, roughly analogous to the Indo-European thematic vowel. Abbreviating *stem* and *theme* as "St" and "Th", respectively, the structure of the Takachiho Conclusives and Negatives cited above could then be [oki $_{St}$]r[u], [oki $_{St}$]r[an] and [[ag $_{St}$][u] $_{Th}$][ru], [[ag $_{St}$][e] $_{Th}$][n], with *r*-Epenthesis written so as to apply at a stem boundary that is not contained within a theme. This treatment of bigrade forms would avoid the negative consequences of the bigrades-as-C-stems proposal that were noted in the last paragraph: bigrade stems would be distinguished from regular C-stems in the lexicon by the presence of the thematic vowel rather than by a diacritic, and, given the treatment of the alternating vowel as a separate morpheme, elimination of the bigrade alternation would be a straightforward example of leveling.

The thematic vowel proposal, however, has a more subtle problem. Observe first that a hypothetical restriction on *r*-Epenthesis to the effect that the vowel-final verb stem involved must be nonalternating would constitute a global condition on the rule, since verification of nonalternating status would require reference to multiple forms. Note now that the thematic vowel will have to be absorbed into the verb stem when its alternation is leveled, so that the forms of newly nonalternating stems become subject to *r*-Epenthesis. This latter point, however, underlines the fact that the thematic vowel proposal — treating what appears to be a stem-final vowel as a separate morpheme when and only when it alternates — is little more than a way to make the existence of the alternation structurally visible, thus allowing reference to it without postulating a frankly global condition on the relevant rule.

It thus appears that a representational approach to bigrade blocking is unlikely to provide a convincing explanation of the phenomenon. Alternatively, it might appear possible to recharacterize Analysis A in such a way that incompatibility with the bigrade alternation would follow, for example by specifying that that analysis requires alternations absent from C-stem inflection to be absent from V-stem inflection as well. Narrowing the characterization of Analysis A in some such way, however, would in effect write bigrade blocking into the definition of that analysis, and would thus remain an arbitrary stipulation.

8.6   Phonological distance and susceptibility to leveling: Three examples

There is reason to believe that phonological distance between alternants is one of the many factors that determine whether or not leveling takes place in any given case. I will motivate this idea with three brief examples from European languages in Section 8.6 before proceeding in Section 8.7 to Japanese cases, bigrade blocking among them, in which phonological distance appears to be implicated in the diachronic order in which alternations are leveled within the inflected word. Throughout, I abstract away from the question of the relative contributions of articulatory and perceptual factors to the relevant measure of phonological distance, assuming an informal metric whose unit is the phonological feature.

The first example involves the inflection of Old English verbs like *streċċ-an* 'spread out' < PGmc. **strak-jan* and *þeċċ-an* 'cover' < PGmc. **thak-jan*, whose present tense forms reflect (in addition to the fronting of /ɑ/ to /æ/ ("Anglo-Frisian Brightening")) Umlaut (/æ/ > /ɛ/) and the palatalization and gemination of the stem-final velar consonant, all three effects conditioned by the palatal semi-vowel of the ancestral form. In past tense forms (indicative and participle), which lacked this palatal element, none of these changes occurred, and a form like past indicative 1sg./3sg. **strak-te* developed regularly to /stræxte/, with the stem vowel then undergoing Breaking to give /stræɑ̯xte/, written *streahte*. At this stage, then, the stem vowel displayed the alternation /ɛ/ ~ /æɑ̯/, and the stem-final consonant the alternation /ċċ/ ~ /x/ (see Fertig 2016: 440–441).

Consider now the phonological distance between the alternants in the two cases. The nuclei /ɛ/ and /æ/ differ in the feature [low] only. Given the regularity of breaking for /æ/ before [+back] /x/, it is possible that the [+back] offglide of /æɑ̯/ in fact constitutes predictable information, in which case the phonological distance between the alternants /ɛ/ and /æɑ̯/ will reduce to a single feature specification. If the offglide of /æɑ̯/ is distinctive, on the other hand, there will be an additional increment of phonological distance. Since the offglide arguably alters the vowel /æ/ less than would a shift of two features, say to /i/, I will assume that the increment due to the offglide would be the equivalent of one feature specification, for a total of two. The alternants /ċċ/ and /x/, however, in addition to showing a geminate/singleton distinction, differ in their values for [back], [coronal], and [continuant], and are thus separated by the equivalent of roughly four feature specifications.

This phonological distance differential between the vocalic and consonantal alternations is reflected in their subsequent history. In the transition from early to late West Saxon, as noted by Campbell (1961:330) and Fertig (2016:440–441), the stem vowel alternation of the relevant forms was leveled in favor of /ɛ/, so that later texts uniformly show *strehte* in place of *streahte* for the past of *streċċan*. The alternation of the stem-final consonant, in contrast, remains intact. It is clear, then, that the alternation involving less phonological distance was the more susceptible to leveling, and the alternation involving greater phonological distance the more resistant.

In the remaining two examples suggesting the relevance of phonological distance to whether or not leveling is observed, a single segment displays two alternations, with only one of them undergoing leveling. The first of those examples draws on German data cited by Paul (1920:203–205). The stem of a verb like *nehmen* 'take' displays an alternation in the present tense between /nim/ in 2sg. *nimmst* and 3sg. *nimmt* and /nem/ otherwise that goes back to Proto-Germanic (see Ringe 2006:126–128). Open syllable lengthening in the early modern period resulted in a third present tense allomorph /ne:m/ in forms with vocalic endings, specifically 1sg. *nehme* and 1pl./3pl. *nehmen*. Subsequently, /ne:m/ was extended to the 2pl. form in *-t*, as the modern spelling *nehmt* indicates. The alternation *e:/e*, in which the alternants differ only in length, that is, was leveled (as it was throughout the paradigm in verbs like *leben* 'live' that had never had any other alternation), while the alternation *e:/i*, in which the alternants differ both in length and in height, has been retained.

A parallel situation arises in the paradigm of Romanian verbs with *o* in the root-final syllable. Tonic *o* alternates with *oa* (/ǫa/) when followed by a (typically word-final) nonhigh vowel (Lombard 1954:129, Chitoran 2002:201, Alkire and Rosen 2010:255). Atonic *o*, on the other hand, raises to *u*. As a result, the root *port-* in the present indicative of *port-a-* 'carry' (see Alkire and Rosen 2010:269) shows an allomorph *port-* in 1sg. *port* and 2sg. *porți*, an allomorph *pǫart-* in 3sg. and 3pl. *poartă* (*ă* = /ə/), and an allomorph *purt-* in 1pl. *purtăm* and 2pl. *purtați*, where accent falls on the reflex of the stem-forming ("thematic") vowel *-a-*.

In the paradigm of a small number of verbs, the alternation *o/ǫa/u* has been leveled in favor of *u* (Lombard 1954:144, Alkire and Rosen 2010:270), which is the most frequent alternant across the full verbal paradigm because the majority of forms are stressed on the thematic vowel. In several other verbs, however, the unstressed alternant *u* has been replaced by *o*, while the alternant *ǫa* has remained stable. A well-known example of this second development involves *dorm-i-* 'sleep', for which the unstressed root alternant *durm-* is attested in older documents and survives in the dialect of Transylvania (Lombard 1954: 131), but which in the modern standard language has been replaced everywhere in the paradigm by *dorm-*. The set of verbs with the alternation *o/ǫa* for which there is documentary evidence for the stage with atonic *u* either in the historical record or in regional varieties (see Lombard 1954: 131–134) includes *înnod-a-* 'tie', *not-a-* 'note down', *plou-a-* 'rain', *înflor-i-* 'bloom', and *sorb-i-* 'sip'; atonic *u* also survives in the perfect of *coas-e-* 'sew'. Crucially, there appear to be no verbs in which the alternation *o/ǫa* has been leveled while the alternation *o/u* has been maintained. *o* and *u* are separated by a single feature specification, namely that for [high]. *o* and *a*, on the other hand, are separated by two, those for [low] and [round]: since rounding is contrastive for nonlow back vowels in Romanian, the result of making /a/ [–low] will be /ə/ rather than /o/ (see Alkire and Rosen 2010: 254). Assuming that there is an additional phonological distance increment due to the onglide, then, *o* and *ǫa* will be separated by the equivalent of three feature specifications. In sum, it is once again the alternation involving less phonological distance that has proven more susceptible to leveling.

The evidence of this section suggests that, other things being equal, alternations involving only minimal phonological distance between alternants will submit to leveling more readily than alternations involving greater phonological distance. Phonological distance, it goes without saying, may be overridden by other factors as a determinant of leveling. In particular, an alternation that is taken by speakers to express a morphosyntactic distinction, as in the case, referred to above, of English *choose/chosen*, is likely to be retained regardless of phonological distance. Similarly, given the English forms /drink dræŋk drʌŋk/, it can be predicted independently of all phonological considerations that if the distinction between two of them is leveled, it will be the distinction between the second and third, both of which realize the morphosyntactic feature specification [+Past]. Below, however, building on the evidence cited above, I will propose that it is phonological distance that has been the decisive factor in determining the relative chronology of leveling in at least three cases from the history of Japanese, crucially including that involving bigrade blocking.

8.7   The Regularization Priority Principle

8.7.1   Leveling in the Inferential

Consider the sound changes of (1), a set of monophthongizations that occurred in Japanese prior to the year 1600 and whose results are recorded in the grammatical and lexical materials compiled by Portuguese missionaries in the early 17th century.

(1) a.   iu > yuu
     b.   eu > yoo
     c.   ou > oo
     d.   au > ɔɔ

The monophthongizations of (1) display a degree of dialectal variation. Notably, in most of Kyushu, due to the raising of the first element of the diphthong, *eu*, like *iu*, becomes *yuu*, *ou* becomes *uu*, and *au* becomes *oo* (Kamimura 1983:10).

The changes of (1) took place both morpheme-internally (typically in Sino-Japanese morphemes) and in a variety of morphological combinations (see Frellesvig 2010:319). Crucially, they took place across stem boundary in the paradigm of vowel-stem verbs because of the reduction of the Inferential (later Volitional) suffix *-mu* (*-amu* after consonant-stems) to *-u*. Thus, for example, the Inferential of *oki-* 'arise' developed from *oki-u* to *okyuu*, and the Inferential of *ake-* 'open (t)' from *ake-u* to *akyoo*. As a result, both the stem and the Inferential suffix came to alternate for V-stem verbs. This is illustrated in Table 3, where the Adverbial and Negative are used as representative of forms that are based transparently on the vowel-final stem.

Table 3. V-stem Inferentials in 1600

	'arise'	'open'
Adverbial	oki-Ø	ake-Ø
Negative	oki-n	ake-n
...		
Inferential	ok-yuu	ak-yoo

The contemporary Volitional forms *oki-yoo* and *ake-yoo* of Tokyo Japanese and many other dialects are replacements for Inferential *ok-yuu* and *ak-yoo* that result from leveling of the stem and suffix alternations seen in Table 3.

The relative chronology of leveling of the stem and suffix alternations of the Inferential is clear: leveling in suffixes preceded leveling in stems, so that *okyuu* will have passed through the stage *okyoo* before undergoing leveling of the stem alternation and emerging as *okiyoo* (Sakanashi 1982:496, Fukushima 1969). This chronology is confirmed by the relative geographical distribution of the two changes in contemporary dialects, where the locations that have leveled the stem alternation constitute a proper subset of those that have leveled the suffix alternation (GAJ map 106). In addition to locations that show phonologically expected

okyuu, that is, there are locations that preserve (alongside *akyoo < akeu*) the intermediate stage *okyoo*, with the suffix alternation leveled and the stem alternation
intact, but none that show **okiyuu*, with the stem alternation leveled and the suffix alternation intact.[5] The latter form has thus probably never existed. In terms of
blocking, retention of the Inferential suffix alternation has blocked leveling of the
Inferential stem alternation, so that the latter could not begin, I will assume, until
the former was underway as well. These facts are summarized in Table 4, which
shows the attested and unattested reflexes of *oki-u*, the earlier Inferential of *oki-*
'arise', with "+" and "–" indicating whether or not leveling has occurred.

Table 4. Leveling in the Inferential

		Stem alternation	
		–	+
Suffix alternation	–	okyuu	*okiyuu
	+	okyoo	okiyoo

    In the context of the observations of Section 8.6, it is natural to attribute the rel-
ative chronology of leveling in the Inferential to the factor of phonological distance:
while the stem alternations *ok-/oki-* and *ak-/ake-* involve a full segment alternating
with zero, the suffix alternation *-yuu/-yoo* involves the single feature [high]. In conjunction with the earlier examples, then, the Inferential case suggests a principle
to the effect that, within a specified morphological domain, an alternation involving a greater degree of phonological distance cannot be leveled before an alternation involving a lesser degree thereof. The morphological domain within which
pairs of alternations will be subject to this principle must minimally be the size
of a morpheme; I will assume that, for a given pair of alternations, it may extend
across morpheme boundaries to encompass a full inflected word, on condition that
there be inflected forms that, as a result of morpheme concatenation, display values
for both of the alternations in question. Remembering that under the proposals of
Section 5.2, the grammatical trigger of regularization (either leveling or extension)
is the assignment of default structure to lexical entries, the relevant principle can be
stated as a hypothesis about speakers' analytic choices as in (2), where "narrower"
paraphrases "involving lesser phonological distance between alternants".

(2)   **Regularization Priority Principle (RPP)**
       Within the domain of the inflected word, no grammar can assign a default
       value for a given alternation while failing to do so for a narrower alternation.

---

5. *okyuu* is the dominant form in the five-prefecture Chugoku region; *okyoo* occurs primarily
in Shimane and northern Fukuoka Prefectures.

The RPP, and more generally the idea that the attractive force between two objects (and thus their tendency to merge) is stronger the closer together they are, as well as being broadly parallel to the inverse square law for gravity and related phenomena in physics, has linguistic counterparts in concepts like Gradient Attraction (Burzio 2001: 662ff., 2002), which holds that the tendency of two words to influence each other is proportional to the degree of similarity between them.

In the historical development of Inferential forms, *okyuu* and *akyoo* will have been derived from /oki+u/ and /ake+u/, respectively, as long as the monophthongizations *iu* > *yuu* and *eu* > *yoo* remained active phonological rules. When, as in most dialects, the monophthongizations ceased to be active and these derivations became impossible, the alternation between -*yuu* and -*yoo* will have ceased to be predictable, since nothing in stem alternants like *ok*- and *ak*- indicates which of the two Inferential suffix alternants is the appropriate one. It is at this point that leveling will have followed, first for the suffix alternation and then, in a subset of the locations where the suffix alternation had been leveled, for the stem alternation as well. In both cases, the choice of the default or underlying alternant follows from the principle of Generalized Type Frequency, (5) in Section 7.5, which identifies the UR of an alternating morpheme as the alternant that occurs with the largest number of eligible co-occurring elements — for suffix alternants, lexical stems; for stem alternants, morphosyntactic feature complexes or paradigmatic slots. In the case of the suffix alternation, the *e*-final stems with which the alternant -*yoo* occurs are approximately ten times as common as the *i*-final stems that take the alternant -*yuu* (1,261 *e*-stems versus 127 *i*-stems in the CD version of Nishio et al. 2000, consistent with note 2, Chapter 7), and this ratio can be assumed to have held at the relevant historical stage. In the case of the stem alternation, the alternants *ok*- and *ak*- occurred only in the Inferential, and the alternants *oki*- and *ake*- will have occurred in all other forms after leveling of the bigrade alternation and in all other forms except the Conclusive and Provisional before.

It may also be noted that neither leveling of the stem alternation nor leveling of the suffix alternation is explicable in proportional terms, providing evidence that proportional motivation is not required for leveling.[6] Leveling of the stem alternation is not explicable as proportionally motivated because, as a result of the changes of (1), every Japanese vowel-final verb stem will have come to have a consonant-final alternant in the Inferential; this includes *se*-/*si*- 'do', with Inferential *s-yoo* < *se-u*, and *ko*-/*ki*- 'come', with Inferential *k-oo* < *ko-u*. There will thus

---

6. For discussion, see Fertig 2016 and references cited there. Fertig (2016: 423) claims that nonproportional instances of leveling are due to "something akin to the 'interference' mechanisms commonly associated with contamination and folk etymology", but such interference mechanisms appear unpromising as an account of leveling of the Inferential stem and suffix alternations (de Chene 2020b: 199).

have been no proportional model for extension of the vowel-final alternants *ake-*
and *oki-* to the Inferential — no vowel-final stem QV-, that is, capable of supporting a proportion like (with Negative *-n*) QVn : QVyoo :: aken : X (X = akeyoo).
Similarly, because leveling of the suffix alternation *-yoo ~ -yuu* took place before
leveling of the stem alternation, there will have been no proportional model for
the extension of *-yoo* to *i*-stems. This is shown by the proportion (3), which
attempts to motivate that extension.

(3)   aken : akyoo :: okin : X

(3), however, is defective, because the required formal point of contact between
terms one and three fails to exist. More specifically, one would expect the residue
in term one resulting from excluding the string that terms one and two have in
common, namely *en*, to appear in term three, but that expectation is not realized.
Like leveling of the Inferential stem alternation, then, leveling of the Inferential
suffix alternation appears to lack proportional motivation. This result validates the
view, proposed in Section 5.2, that in the general case, leveling is simply regularization — that is, loss of irregularity from lexical entries.

8.7.2   Another case of blocking under the RPP

The relative geographical distribution that we observed for leveling of the Inferential stem and suffix alternations in Section 8.7.1 is paralleled by the relative geographical distribution of leveling of the Inferential stem alternation and leveling
of the bigrade alternation: leveling of the former is observed only in a proper subset of locations that show leveling of the latter. In particular, while there are many
locations, notably the whole of the Chugoku region, that have leveled the bigrade
alternation but retain the Inferential stem alternation, there are none that retain
the bigrade alternation but have leveled the Inferential stem alternation. This situation is summarized in Table 5, parallel to Table 4, which shows attested and
nonattested combinations of Conclusive and Inferential forms for *ake-* 'open (t)'.[7]

Table 5. Leveling of two stem alternations

		Inferential stem alternation	
		−	+
Bigrade alternation	−	akuru / akyoo	* akuru / akeyoo
	+	akeru / akyoo	akeru / akeyoo

7. In the table, the Inferential of *ake-* is written *akyoo* throughout for consistency in spite of the
fact that Kyushu locations have *akyuu* as the phonologically regular form.

The phonological distance differential between the two alternations is clear: the bigrade alternation involves the single feature [back] in the case of *i*-stems and the two features [back] and [high] in the case of *e*-stems, while the Inferential stem alternation, as before, involves the presence or absence of a full segment. Just as retention of the Inferential suffix alternation blocks leveling of the Inferential stem alternation under the RPP, then, retention of the bigrade alternation appears to have the same effect.

Because the range over which the bigrade alternation is retained varies with stem type, it is important to verify the blocking effect of Table 5 for individual stem types. For polysyllabic *e*-stems, the bigrade alternation is maintained in the great majority of Kyushu dialects, as noted above. While leveling of that alternation has begun in some of those dialects, however (GAJ map 64), leveling of the Inferential alternation is not observed: the Volitional of *ake-* 'open (t)' is almost uniformly *akyuu* in Kyushu (GAJ map 107), where, as noted earlier, *yuu* is the phonologically regular Kyushu reflex of earlier *eu*, and no location reports **akeyuu*. For polysyllabic *i*-stems, similarly, the region in eastern Kyushu that retains the bigrade alternation (GAJ maps 61, 126) shows *okyuu* or a direct development thereof for the Volitional of *oki-* 'arise' (GAJ map 106); as noted above, **okiyuu* is not attested. For monosyllabic *e*-stems, the bigrade alternation is preserved for the most part only in northwestern Kyushu (GAJ map 66), and in this area the Volitional of *ne-* 'sleep' is almost uniformly *nyuu* (GAJ map 108). The isolated Wakayama locations that report bigrade forms show ongoing leveling of both the bigrade and the Inferential alternations, so that no counterexample to the RPP arises.

The two irregular verbs *se-/si-* 'do' and *ko-/ki-* 'come' require special consideration in this context, given that in a wide range of dialects, Tokyo Japanese among them, they show leveled Volitionals (*siyoo, koyoo*) while retaining bigrade forms (Conclusive *suru, kuru*; Provisional *sureba, kureba*). I will assume that in such dialects, the bigrade forms were lexicalized as unanalyzable wholes, so that, in spite of apparent segmentability, there were no longer any stem alternants *su-* and *ku-*. If so, no violation of the RPP will have been occasioned by leveling of the Inferential stem alternation for the verbs in question. It should be noted that in Kyushu, where the bigrade alternation remains robust, and in most of Western Japan, the Volitionals of *se-/si-* and *ko-/ki-* are unleveled *syuu/syoo* and *kuu/koo* or developments thereof (GAJ maps 110 and 111).

Consider finally what is known about the relative chronology of leveling of the bigrade and Inferential stem alternations in dialects that underwent both of them, notably the prestige western dialects of the early modern period, referred to as "Kamigata-go" in Sections 4.5 and 5.5. While the two changes overlapped to a large extent, leveling of the bigrade alternation appears to have been well underway by the middle of the 17th century (Sakanashi 1982: 476), with leveling of the Inferential stem alternation becoming pronounced in the second half of the century (Sakanashi 1982: 496). If so, the attested chronology is well within the range of scenarios predicted by the RPP, with leveling of the narrower alternation beginning before leveling of the alternation involving greater phonological distance. It should be noted, however, that fully simultaneous leveling of the two alternations would also be consistent with the RPP as stated.

In Sections 8.7.1 and 8.7.2, we have seen that retention of the Inferential suffix alternation and retention of the bigrade alternation both block leveling of the Inferential stem alternation, as manifested in each case by the relative chronology and relative geographical distribution of leveling for the alternations in question. We may say, then, that both the alternation pair {Inferential suffix, Inferential stem} and the alternation pair {bigrade, Inferential stem} display a blocking effect. Further, we saw that this blocking effect is correctly predicted by the RPP, given that the blocker in each case is the narrower alternation, the one that involves less phonological distance between alternants. For the third pair involving the three alternations we have considered, namely {bigrade, Inferential suffix}, the RPP is inapplicable. This is because there are no forms that display values for both of the alternations in question: forms that display either value for the Inferential suffix alternation, namely V-stem Inferentials, show zero for the stem vowel rather than either of the bigrade alternants *i/e* or *u*. In Section 8.7.3, I turn to the interaction of the three alternations discussed above with the alternations treated by Analysis A, the suffix alternations that are sensitive to the C/V polarity of the stem-final segment. I will consider the pairings of the C/V polarity alternations with the Inferential stem alternation, the Inferential suffix alternation, and the bigrade alternation in that order.

8.7.3   C/V polarity alternations and the RPP

As we first saw in Chapter 5, the verbal suffix alternations that respond to the C/V polarity of the stem-final segment are all segment-zero alternations apart from the suppletive alternation of the Imperative suffix. The Inferential stem alternation is also a segment-zero alternation. Where "C/V polarity" stands for a representative C/V polarity alternation, it would thus appear that there will be no phonological divergence differential for an alternation pair {Inferential stem, C/V polarity} that might serve as the basis for a prediction of blocking under the RPP.

Consider now the alternation pair {Inferential suffix, C/V polarity}. The Inferential suffix alternation, as we have seen, presupposes retention of the Inferential stem alternation. In contrast, the Inferential C/V polarity alternation *y ~ Ø* (*-yoo ~ -oo*) as characterized above assumes a vowel-final stem alternant for *-yoo* and thus presupposes leveling of the Inferential stem alternation. The alternations of the pair {Inferential suffix, C/V polarity}, then, characterize two distinct historical stages, before and after leveling of the Inferential stem alternation, and so do not come into direct competition with each other regarding which should occur first. At the same time, the order Inferential suffix > Inferential stem > Inferential C/V polarity means that leveling of the Inferential suffix alternation must precede leveling of the Inferential *y*-zero alternation. The data of the GAJ is consistent with this chronology: in the area that preserves the Inferential suffix alternation and thus has *okyuu* for the Volitional of *oki-* 'arise' but *akyoo* for the Volitional of *ake-* 'open (t)', the innovative forms *oki-r-oo* and *ake-r-oo* that result from leveling of the *y*-zero alternation are not observed (GAJ maps 106, 107).

We come finally to the alternation pair {bigrade, C/V polarity}. As documented in Section 8.4, with exceptions for monosyllabic stems, retention of the bigrade alternation blocks leveling of C/V polarity alternations. This is illustrated with the stem *ake-* 'open (t)' and the Negative suffix *-(a)n* in Table 6.

Table 6. Leveling of the bigrade and C/V polarity alternations

		C/V polarity alternations	
		–	+
Bigrade alternation	–	akuru / aken	* akuru / akeran
	+	akeru / aken	akeru / akeran

Given the phonological divergence differential between the bigrade alternation and C/V polarity alternations like those of the Negative, this blocking effect follows from the RPP, just as did the blocking effects illustrated in Tables 4 and 5. Historically, as long as the bigrade alternation was given a symmetrical analysis rather than one involving default structure, it will have been impossible to take C-stem suffix alternants as defaults for C/V polarity alternations, thus precluding the adoption of Analysis A. And the fact that the bigrade alternation remained stable, at least in polysyllables, for many centuries indicates that over that period, the analysis in force must indeed have been a symmetrical one, one that did not involve treating the front vowel alternants, the eventual targets of leveling, as defaults. In fact, a simple analysis in terms of morphological categories, under which front vowel alternants occurred in the Adverbial and Imperative and before inflected auxiliaries (including the Negative), while back vowel alternants occurred in the (zero-suffixed) Conclusive, the Adnominal, and the Realis > Provisional will satisfy this condition. It is natural to attribute the longevity of the bigrade alternation, then, to the availability of a plausible analysis of it that did not involve default structure. Once front vowel alternants were taken as defaults and the bigrade alternation began to be leveled, however, there will have been no further obstacle to the adoption of Analysis A.[8]

The history of Japanese verbal morphophonology since the year 1600 is to a large extent defined by leveling of the Inferential suffix alternation, the Inferential stem alternation, the bigrade alternation, and C/V polarity alternations. Above, we investigated the predictions of the RPP for the relative chronology of leveling in all six pairwise combinations of those four (sets of) alternations. While we found the RPP to be inapplicable to three of those combinations, we saw that in the remaining three, as illustrated in Tables 4, 5, and 6 above, the RPP correctly predicts the relative chronology and the relative geographical distribution of leveling. In the end, then, bigrade blocking, the theme of this chapter, turns out to be not an isolated phenomenon, but part of a network of blocking relationships that are regulated by the RPP. It must be emphasized, however, that further research will be necessary to test the cross-linguistic validity of that principle.

Kuryłowicz (1945–49 [1966]: 174) famously claimed that, while linguistic structure lays down the tracks on which analogical change runs, whether and to what extent those tracks are used depends on social rather than strictly linguistic factors. While not challenging Kuryłowicz's view that a fully predictive theory of analogy is likely to remain out of reach, the conclusions of Chapter 8 suggest that the timing of analogical change is in considerable part the consequence of speaker analytic decisions and constraints on the space of analyses that speakers may entertain.

8.8 Looking back at Analysis A

Chapter 8 brings to a close our account of the Japanese verbal suffix alternations, introduced in Chapter 5, that are conditioned by the C/V polarity of the stem-final segment. I have claimed that those alternations are governed by an analysis under which suffix URs coincide with consonant-stem alternants and regular vowel-stem alternants are produced by *r*-Epenthesis. The evidence for this "Analysis A" is constituted by the regularizations it predicts, a set of changes known to Japanese dialectologists as *itidan katuyoo no ra-gyoo godanka* 'the assimilation of vowel-stem to *r*-stem conjugation' and often assumed to be motivated by four-term proportions based on *r*-stem forms. We have seen that, under Analysis A, the motivation for those changes actually has nothing to do with *r*-stem inflection,

---

8. While, as noted above, the relationship between leveling of the bigrade alternation and appearance of the innovative *r*-suffixes that we are taking as evidence of adoption of Analysis A has been characterized in terms of triggering (Onishi 2016b: 150), I will assume that the impression of triggering results from removal of the blocking effect dictated by the RPP in combination with the naturalness of Analysis A.

but resides in the unmarked status of C-stem with respect to V-stem inflection and the preexisting *r*-zero alternation of the Conclusive, Provisional, and Passive suffixes. The case of the C/V polarity alternations and Analysis A thus illustrates the fact that morphophonological change typically represents the gradual elimination of exceptions to an innovative generalization rather than resulting from the extension of proportional relationships among surface forms, a principle eloquently enunciated by Kiparsky (1972: 280) half a century ago.

While Chapter 5 documented the elimination of exceptions to Analysis A in dialects of Japanese proper, Chapter 6 showed that regularization under Analysis A, typically further advanced than in Japanese, is observed as well in all Ryukyuan languages other than Miyako. Chapters 7 and 8 then confronted the more difficult questions posed by Analysis A, first the question of what principles dictate its adoption in favor of alternate observationally adequate analyses of the same data and then the question of why there is a lag of about eight centuries between establishment of an *r*-zero alternation in the Passive, completing the trio of preexisting *r*-zero alternations, and the first evidence for regularization under Analysis A. While our answers to those questions were necessarily provisional, the principles proposed, Generalized Type Frequency and the Minimal Divergence Principle in Chapter 7 and the Regularization Priority Principle in Chapter 8, may be taken as guidelines for further research on morphophonological change.

CHAPTER 9

Conclusion: A sharp boundary

Linguistic phenomena often appear to instantiate continua or to display fuzzy boundaries. The distinction between inflection and derivation in particular has often been characterized as a continuum (Stephany 1982; Bybee 1985: 5, 87; Dressler 1989, among many others), a viewpoint noted already in Section 1.5. In the empirical domain investigated here, that of Japanese verbal morphology, however, we have found a clear-cut boundary between inflection and derivation that shows up on both the syntactic and the phonological sides of the grammar. In Chapters 1 through 4, I argued that while inflectional affixes must be treated as the phonological realization of syntactic terminal elements, derivational affixes cannot be, identifying in support of the latter conclusion four characteristics of verbal derivation that distinguish it sharply from verbal inflection: noncompositional interpretation of suffix sequences, base-specific suffix orders, relative rather than fixed semantics, and diachronic instability of constructional meaning. In Chapters 5 through 8, we saw that stems and inflectional affixes — verbal inflectional suffixes in Japanese, verb stems in Portuguese, noun stems in Korean — are subject to reanalysis of their phonological shape. As reflected in the fact that such reanalyses appear always to be limited to a single lexical category, however, we have seen no reason to believe that systematic morphophonological reanalysis ever applies to roots and derivational affixes. Both the conclusions of Chapters 1 through 4 and the conclusions of Chapters 5 through 8 suggest that stems and inflectional affixes are accessible to speakers in ways that roots and derivational affixes are not. I have proposed that the grammatical correlate of this accessibility is lexical listing, and that both sets of conclusions follow from the hypothesis that only stems and inflectional affixes have listed or lexical representations, as morphosyntactic and as morphophonological objects alike: as morphosyntactic objects, all and only elements with listed representations will be subject to selection from the lexicon as the first step in constructing a syntactic derivation; as morphophonological objects, all and only elements with listed representations will be subject to reanalysis of their phonological shape.

In drawing to a close, it is appropriate to ask how generally the conclusions we have reached primarily on the basis of Japanese verb morphology can be expected to apply to language in general. With regard to morphophonology, the traditional insight that "the domain of analogical leveling is the inflectional paradigm" (Albright 2011: 1975) provides one indication that the generalization that it is precisely stems and inflectional affixes that are subject to morphophonological reanalysis is likely to be close to the mark. With regard to the semantic interaction of affixes as well, there is reason to believe that the "trapped interpretations" that we saw in Chapter 3 to be characteristic of sequences of derivational suffixes in Japanese are a recurrent feature of natural language morphology and provide an important diagnostic for distinguishing lexicalized morphological constructions from those that reflect syntactic operations. I conclude by briefly examining, in illustration of this point, a case of suffix sequences from Modern Greek.

Anagnostopoulou and Samioti (A&S) (2014: 92–98), drawing on earlier literature, provide a revealing typology of Modern Greek participial and adjectival formations in -to-, a suffix dating to Proto-Indo-European that was touched on in Section 4.6. They first note that to-formations that express ability or possibility (e.g. pist-ef-to- 'believable') preserve the verbal properties of their base, as evidenced by their licensing of agent and instrument PPs and agent-oriented adverbs. They next point to two types of to-formations in which preservation of verbal properties is at best marginal, but for which there is evidence of productive generation, compound adjectives of the form aksio-V-to- 'worth V-ing' and formations with privative a- that function as the negation of participles in -meno- (gra-meno- 'written', a-graf-to- 'unwritten'). Here, I will set these three types of to-formations aside, concentrating on the fourth type that A&S identify, "characteristic state" to-formations that A&S classify as participles, but which I will refer to as "to-adjectives".

Some to-adjectives are demonstrably based on a root rather than on a verbal stem, as in θni-to- 'mortal' (cf. peθen- (present) ~ peθan- (aorist) 'die'). In many others, the base is at once a root and a stem, thus posing no obstacle to conceiving of to-adjectives as root-based. In a wide range of cases (see A&S 2014: 97ff.), however, to-adjectives are based on verbal stems that incorporate an overt verbalizing suffix such as -iz- or -ev-, precluding a root-based analysis. Morphologically speaking, this coexistence of stem-based and root-based derivation is unremarkable. But if verbalizing suffixes represent little v, and if little v codes verbal event-type properties, verbalizing morphology in to-adjectives is problematic. This is because to-adjectives, like underived adjectives, represent states and systematically lack the eventive properties associated with verbs, a fact documented in detail in Alexiadou and Anagnostopoulou 2005 and subsequent work. As a result, verbalizing morphology in to-adjectives is seen in the literature to present "certain complications" (Alexiadou and Anagnostopoulou 2005: 9 (note 7)), to constitute "a puzzle" (A&S 2011: 107), or to appear "quite unexpectedly" (A&S 2014: 97). The problem in question is the same as that noted by Harley (2009: 334) for English nominals that are derived from verbs in -ize but that nevertheless lack event structure and argument structure: "v^0 must be absent to account for the absence of verbal extended projection properties, but v^0 must be present to account for the presence of -*ize* within the nominalization." It is also the same problem that we saw in Chapter 3 to be pervasive in sequences of Japanese transitivity suffixes under a DM interpretation thereof, with the properties of inner suffixes "trapped" and failing to surface.

A&S's (2013: 228ff., 2014: 81, 97) solution to the problem of verbalizing suffixes in *to*-adjectives, adumbrated in A&S 2011: 107, is to claim that those suffixes are pure categorizers, with no event-type properties; Anagnostopoulou (2016: 445), similarly, proposes that "verbalizing heads in characteristic state -*tos* participles are semantically empty". As a result, when the suffixes in question occur in verb stems, which do of course have event-type properties, they will have to be accompanied by an "abstract eventive little v" (A&S 2014: 97) — i.e. a second suffix that is a mirror image of the first in being semantically contentful, but phonologically null. We have seen a proposal of this type before, in the hypothetical analysis ((46a), Chapter 3) of Japanese *tunag*- 'tie together' as *tuna-g-Ø*-, where -*g*- and -*Ø*- represent little v and Voice, respectively. There I suggested that the idea of a suffix that supplies the lexical category "verb" but nothing else skirts the realm of paradox because it creates a constituent that is claimed to be verbal, but incorporates no event-type properties and is not subject to verbal inflection (see also note 9, A&S 2013: 232). Modern Greek presents this problem in a more extreme form than it takes in Japanese: given that characteristic state *to*-adjectives may contain any of a variety of verbalizers but never evince verbal properties (A&S 2014: 97), it appears that every verbalizing suffix of the language will need to be analyzed into an overt verbalizer and a null eventivizer. With no concrete evidence for any such sequence, however, it becomes mysterious on what basis children acquiring the language could infer that verbalizers are bipartite in this way.

Panagiotidis et al. (2017) make it clear that individual verbalizing suffixes cannot be associated with particular event-type meanings in Modern Greek, presumably a common state of affairs for verbalizing morphology cross-linguistically. Verbalizing suffixes, then, can be thought of as having multiple event-type allosemes, with alloseme choice determined by the root. If so, verbalizing suffixes in characteristic state *to*-adjectives present a case of trapped interpretations in the sense of Chapter 3, meanings that are attributable to S_1 in $[[R]S_1]$ but are not observed in some further derivative $[[[R]S_1]S_2]$. In such situations, the invited inference is that both S_1 and S_2 are nonsyntactic: a syntactic suffix does not override the meanings of suffixes in its base, nor is the meaning of a syntactic suffix subject to being overridden by higher or more external suffixes. In the case at hand, this will mean that neither verbalizing suffixes such as -*iz*- and -*ev*- nor the -*to*- of characteristic state *to*-adjectives are realizations of syntactic elements and, correspondingly, that both verbs in suffixes like -*iz*- and -*ev*- and characteristic state *to*-adjectives themselves are lexicalized stems rather than syntactic constructions. Given that treatment, it will be possible to write lexical entries and lexical redundancy rules that attribute to the verbalizing suffixes of verb stems the event-type properties they appear to realize, obviating the split of each of those suffixes into an overt categorizer and a null eventivizer. For characteristic state *to*-adjectives derived from such verb stems, on the other hand, redundancy rules can capture the formal relationship between the adjective and its base without attributing to the adjective the base's full set of semantic properties (see Jackendoff 1975: 657–658).

The case of Modern Greek characteristic state *to*-adjectives, then, provides reason to believe that the central conclusion of the present work, that some but not all morphology is syntactic, may prove to be applicable well beyond the domain of Japanese verbal morphology. This affirmation of the weak lexicalist position on the relation of morphology and syntax means that those taking that perspective in their research should pursue their projects with confidence: their basic stance is well supported, and at the same time there remains much work to be done in delimiting the precise boundary between the syntactic and the non-syntactic in morphology.

Abbreviations for works referred to

BCCWJ Balanced Corpus of Contemporary Written Japanese
DOL   Kokuritsu Kokugo Kenkyujo 1963
DSMG   Institute of Modern Greek Studies, Aristotle University of Thessaloniki 1998
GAJ   Kokuritsu Kokugo Kenkyujo 1989–2006
HDO   Hokama et al. (eds.) 2011
NKD   Nihon Kokugo Daijiten Dainihan Henshu Iinkai ... 2000–2002

References

Hyperlinks were current at time of publication.

Adger, David. 2003. *Core syntax. A minimalist approach*. Oxford: Oxford University Press.

Akiyama, Shoji. 1961. Kumamoto. In Misao Tojo, Yoshimoto Endo, Teruo Hirayama, Tadatoshi Okubo, and Takeshi Shibata (eds.), *Kyūshū/Ryūkyū hōgen [Kyushu and Ryukyu dialects]* (*Hōgengaku kōza [Dialectology course]* 4), 208–238. Tokyo: Tokyodo Shuppan.

Albright, Adam. 2002. The identification of bases in morphological paradigms. Doctoral dissertation, University of California, Los Angeles.

Albright, Adam. 2008. Explaining universal tendencies and language particulars in analogical change. In Jeff Good (ed.), *Linguistic universals and language change*, 144–181. Oxford: Oxford University Press.

Albright, Adam. 2011. Paradigms. In Marc van Oostendorp, Colin J. Ewen, Elizabeth Hume, and Keren Rice (eds.), *The Blackwell companion to phonology*, 1972–2001. Oxford: Blackwell.

Albright, Adam, Argelia Andrade, and Bruce Hayes. 2000. Segmental environments of Spanish diphthongization. MS, UCLA. Published in Albright, Adam, and Taehong Cho (eds.). 2001. *UCLA working papers in linguistics 7* (*Papers in phonology 5*), 117–151. Los Angeles: UCLA Department of Linguistics.

Alexiadou, Artemis, and Elena Anagnostopoulou. 2005. On the syntax and morphology of Greek participles. Talk presented at the Workshop on the Morphosyntax of Modern Greek, LSA Institute, Cambridge, MA.

Alkire, Ti, and Carol Rosen. 2010. *Romance languages. A historical introduction*. Cambridge: Cambridge University Press.

Anagnostopoulou, Elena. 2016. Inner and outer morphology in Greek adjectival participles. In Daniel Siddiqi and Heidi Harley (eds.), *Morphological metatheory*, 431–460. Amsterdam: Benjamins.

Anagnostopoulou, Elena, and Yota Samioti. 2011. Idiomatic meaning and the structure of participles. *Selected Papers on Theoretical and Applied Linguistics* (Aristotle University of Thessaloniki) 19: 101–110.

Anagnostopoulou, Elena, and Yota Samioti. 2013. Allosemy, idioms, and their domains: Evidence from adjectival participles. In Raffaella Folli, Christina Sevdali, and Robert Truswell (eds.), *Syntax and its limits*, 218–250. Oxford: Oxford University Press.

Anagnostopoulou, Elena, and Yota Samioti. 2014. Domains within words and their meanings: A case study. In Artemis Alexiadou, Hagit Borer, and Florian Schäfer (eds.), *The syntax of roots and the roots of syntax*, 81–111. Oxford: Oxford University Press.

Andersen, Henning. 1969. A study in diachronic morphophonemics: The Ukrainian prefixes. *Language* 45. 807–830.

Anderson, Stephen R. 1982. Where's morphology? *Linguistic Inquiry* 13. 571–612.

doi Anderson, Stephen R. 1992. *A-morphous morphology*. Cambridge: Cambridge University Press.

doi Anderson, Stephen R. 2005. *Aspects of the theory of clitics*. Oxford: Oxford University Press.

Andriotis, Nikolaos. 1961. *To idíoma tou Livisíou tis Lykías* [*The dialect of Livisi in Lycia*]. Athens: Center of Asia Minor Studies.

Aoki, Hirofumi. 2010. *Gokeisei kara mita Nihongobunpōshi* [*Japanese grammatical history viewed from word-formation*]. Tokyo: Hituzi Syobo.

Arakaki, Tomoko. 2003. A grammatical study of Luchuan — Focusing upon the verb forms in Shuri dialect. In Atsuko Izuyama (ed.), *Studies on Luchuan Grammar*, 163–216. Osaka: Osaka Gakuin Daigaku Joho Gakubu.

Arimoto, Mitsuhiko. 2001a. Ryūkyū Yonaguni Sonai hōgen no dōshi katsuyōkei no goi on'inron [Lexical phonology of the verbal inflected forms of the Ryukyu dialect of Sonai, Yonaguni] (1). *Yasuda Joshi Daigaku Kiyō* [*Bulletin of Yasuda Women's University*] 29. 1–11.

Arimoto, Mitsuhiko. 2001b. Ryūkyū Yonaguni Sonai hōgen no dōshi katsuyōkei no goi on'inron [Lexical phonology of the verbal inflected forms of the Ryukyu dialect of Sonai, Yonaguni] (2). *Kokugo Kokubun Ronshū* (Yasuda Joshi Daigaku) [*Papers on Japanese Language and Literature* (Yasuda Women's University)] 31. 11–19.

Arimoto, Mitsuhiko. 2002a. Ryūkyū Yonaguni Sonai hōgen no dōshi katsuyōkei no goi on'inron [Lexical phonology of the verbal inflected forms of the Ryukyu dialect of Sonai, Yonaguni] (3). *Yasuda Joshi Daigaku Kiyō* [*Bulletin of Yasuda Women's University*] 30. 1–10.

Arimoto, Mitsuhiko. 2002b. Ryūkyū Yonaguni Sonai hōgen no dōshi katsuyōkei no goi on'inron [Lexical phonology of the verbal inflected forms of the Ryukyu dialect of Sonai, Yonaguni] (4). *Kokugo Kokubun Ronshū* (Yasuda Joshi Daigaku) [*Papers on Japanese Language and Literature* (Yasuda Women's University)] 32. 11–15.

Aronoff, Mark. 1976. *Word formation in generative grammar*. Cambridge, MA: MIT Press.

Aronoff, Mark. 1994. *Morphology by itself*. Cambridge, MA: MIT Press.

Ashworth, David. 1973. A generative study of the inflectional morphophonemics of the Shuri dialect of Ryukyuan. Doctoral dissertation, Cornell University.

doi Aso, Reiko. 2015. Hateruma Yaeyama grammar. In Patrick Heinrich, Shinsho Miyara, and Michinori Shimoji (eds.), *Handbook of the Ryukyuan languages*, 423–447. Berlin: De Gruyter.

Audring, Jenny, and Francesca Masini (eds.). 2019. *The Oxford handbook of morphological theory*. Oxford: Oxford University Press.

doi Azevedo, Milton M. 2005. *Portuguese*. Cambridge: Cambridge University Press.

Baker, Mark C. 1988. *Incorporation*. Chicago: University of Chicago Press.

doi Baker, Mark C. 1996. *The polysynthesis parameter*. Oxford: Oxford University Press.

Balanced Corpus of Contemporary Written Japanese: https://clrd.ninjal.ac.jp/bccwj/

doi Bauer, Laurie. 1983. *English word-formation*. Cambridge: Cambridge University Press.

Becker, Michael. 2009. Phonological trends in the lexicon: The role of constraints. Doctoral dissertation, University of Massachusetts, Amherst.

doi Beekes, Robert S. P. 1995. *Comparative Indo-European linguistics. An introduction*. Amsterdam: Benjamins.

doi Bermúdez-Otero, Ricardo. 2007. Diachronic phonology. In Paul de Lacy (ed.), *The Cambridge handbook of phonology*, 497–517. Cambridge: Cambridge University Press.

Bermúdez-Otero, Ricardo. 2011. Cyclicity. In Marc van Oostendorp, Colin J. Ewen, Elizabeth Hume, and Keren Rice (eds.), *The Blackwell companion to phonology*, 2019–2048. Oxford: Blackwell.

Bermúdez-Otero, Ricardo. 2013. The Spanish lexicon stores stems with theme vowels, not roots with inflectional class features. *Probus* 25. 3–103.

Bermúdez-Otero, Ricardo. 2015. Amphichronic explanation and the life cycle of phonological processes. In Patrick Honeybone and Joseph Salmons (eds.), *The Oxford handbook of historical phonology*, 374–399. Oxford: Oxford University Press.

Bermúdez-Otero, Ricardo, and Ana R. Luís. 2016. A view of the morphome debate. In Ricardo Bermúdez-Otero and Ana R. Luís (eds.), *The morphome debate*, 309–340. Oxford: Oxford University Press.

Bermúdez-Otero, Ricardo, and Graeme Trousdale. 2012. Cycles and continua: On unidirectionality and gradualness in language change. In Terttu Nevalainen and Elizabeth Closs Traugott (eds.), *The Oxford handbook of the history of English*, 691–720. Oxford: Oxford University Press.

Blevins, James P. 2016. *Word and paradigm morphology*. Oxford: Oxford University Press.

Blevins, Juliette. 2008. Consonant epenthesis: Natural and unnatural histories. In Jeff Good (ed.), *Linguistic universals and language change*, 79–107. Oxford: Oxford University Press.

Bloch, Bernard. 1946. Studies in colloquial Japanese I. Inflection. *Journal of the American Oriental Society* 66. 97–109. Reprinted in Bloch, Bernard. 1970. *Bernard Bloch on Japanese*, edited with an introduction by Roy Andrew Miller, 1–24. New Haven: Yale University Press.

Bloomfield, Leonard. 1933. *Language*. New York: Holt, Rinehart, and Winston.

Bloomfield, Leonard. 1946. Algonquian. In Harry Hoijer (ed.), *Linguistic structures of native America* (Viking Fund Publications in Anthropology 6), 85–129. New York.

Bonami, Olivier, and Gregory Stump. 2016. Paradigm function morphology. In Andrew Hippisley and Gregory Stump (eds.), *The Cambridge handbook of morphology*, 449–481. Cambridge: Cambridge University Press.

Booij, Geert. 1992. Compounding in Dutch. *Rivista di Linguistica* 4. 37–59.

Booij, Geert. 1993. Against split morphology. In Geert Booij and Jaap van Marle (eds.), *Yearbook of morphology 1993*, 27–49. Dordrecht: Kluwer.

Booij, Geert. 1996. Inherent versus contextual inflection and the split morphology hypothesis. In Geert Booij and Jaap van Marle (eds.), *Yearbook of morphology 1995*, 1–16. Dordrecht: Kluwer.

Bresnan, Joan, Ash Asudeh, Ida Toivonen, and Stephen Wechsler. 2016. *Lexical-functional syntax*, 2nd ed. Oxford: Wiley-Blackwell.

Brown, Dunstan, and Andrew Hippisley. 2012. *Network morphology: A defaults-based theory of word structure*. Cambridge: Cambridge University Press.

Buck, Carl Darling. 1933. *Comparative grammar of Greek and Latin*. Chicago: University of Chicago Press.

Burzio, Luigi. 2001. Zero derivations. *Linguistic Inquiry* 32. 658–677.

Burzio, Luigi. 2002. Surface-to-surface morphology: When your representations turn into constraints. In Paul Boucher (ed.), *Many morphologies*, 142–177. Somerville, MA: Cascadilla Press.

doi Bybee, Joan. 1985. *Morphology*. Amsterdam: Benjamins.

doi Bybee, Joan. 1995. Regular morphology and the lexicon. *Language and Cognitive Processes* 10. 425–455. Reprinted in Bybee, Joan. 2007. *Frequency of use and the organization of language*, 167–193. Oxford: Oxford University Press.

doi Bybee, Joan. 2001. *Phonology and language use*. Cambridge: Cambridge University Press.

Campbell, A. 1961. *Old English grammar*. Oxford: Oxford University Press.

doi Casali, Roderic F. 1997. Vowel elision in hiatus contexts: Which vowel goes? *Language* 73. 493–533.

Casali, Roderic F. 1998. *Resolving hiatus*. New York: Garland.

doi Chen, Victoria, and Bradley McDonnell. 2019. Western Austronesian voice. *Annual Review of Linguistics* 5. 173–195.

doi Chew, John J. 1973. *A transformational analysis of modern colloquial Japanese*. The Hague: Mouton.

doi Chitoran, Ioana. 2002. *The phonology of Romanian. A constraint-based approach*. Berlin: De Gruyter.

Chomsky, Noam. 1955. *The logical structure of linguistic theory*. MS, Harvard University. Partially revised version published as Chomsky, Noam. 1975. *The logical structure of linguistic theory*. New York: Plenum.

doi Chomsky, Noam. 1957. *Syntactic structures*. The Hague: Mouton.

Chomsky, Noam. 1964a. *Current issues in linguistic theory*. The Hague: Mouton. Reprinted in Fodor, Jerry A., and Jerrold J. Katz (eds.). 1964. *The structure of language*, 50–118. Englewood Cliffs, NJ: Prentice-Hall.

Chomsky, Noam. 1964b. The logical basis of linguistic theory. In Horace Lunt (ed.), *Proceedings of the ninth international congress of linguists*, 914–978. The Hague: Mouton.

Chomsky, Noam. 1965. *Aspects of the theory of syntax*. Cambridge, MA: MIT Press.

Chomsky, Noam. 1970. Remarks on nominalization. In Roderick A. Jacobs and Peter S. Rosenbaum (eds.), *Readings in English transformational grammar*, 184–221. Waltham, MA: Ginn.

Chomsky, Noam. 1981. *Lectures on government and binding*. Dordrecht: Foris.

Chomsky, Noam. 1994. Bare phrase structure (MIT Occasional Papers in Linguistics 5). Cambridge, MA: MITWPL. Reprinted in Campos, Héctor, and Paula Kempchinsky (eds.). 1995. *Evolution and revolution in linguistic theory*, 51–109. Washington, DC: Georgetown University Press. Reprinted in Webelhuth, Gert (ed.). 1995. *Government and binding theory and the minimalist program*, 383–439. Oxford: Blackwell.

Chomsky, Noam. 1995. *The minimalist program*. Cambridge, MA: MIT Press.

Chomsky, Noam. 2000. Minimalist inquiries: The framework. In Roger Martin, David Michaels, and Juan Uriagereka (eds.), *Step by step. Essays on minimalist syntax in honor of Howard Lasnik*, 89–155. Cambridge, MA: MIT Press.

doi Chomsky, Noam. 2008. On phases. In Robert Freidin, Carlos P. Otero, and Maria Luisa Zubizarreta (eds.), *Foundational issues in linguistic theory. Essays in honor of Jean-Roger Vergnaud*, 133–166. Cambridge, MA: MIT Press.

Chomsky, Noam, and Morris Halle. 1968. *The sound pattern of English*. New York: Harper and Row.

doi   Chung, Sung-Yeo, and Masayoshi Shibatani. 2018. Causative constructions in Japanese and Korean. In Prashant Pardeshi and Taro Kageyama (eds.), *Handbook of Japanese contrastive linguistics*, 137–172. Berlin: De Gruyter.

doi   Cinque, Guglielmo. 1999. *Adverbs and functional heads. A cross-linguistic perspective*. Oxford: Oxford University Press.

Clements, George N., and Samuel Jay Keyser. 1983. *CV phonology*. Cambridge, MA: MIT Press.

Davis, Stuart, and Hyunsook Kang. 2006. English loanwords and the word-final [t] problem in Korean. *Eohak Yeonku* (Seoul Taehakkyo) [*Language Research* (Seoul National University)] 42. 253–274.

Dawkins, Richard M. 1916. *Modern Greek in Asia Minor*. Cambridge: Cambridge University Press.

doi   Deal, Amy Rose. 2017. External possession and possessor raising. In Martin Everaert and Henk van Riemsdijk (eds.), *The Wiley-Blackwell companion to syntax*, 2nd ed., 1509–1540. Hoboken, NJ: Wiley-Blackwell.

de Chene, Brent. 1983. Morphological *n*-epenthesis in Sanskrit. In Shiro Hattori and Kazuko Inoue (eds.), *Proceedings of the XIIIth international congress of linguists*, 689–692. Tokyo: Comité International Permanent des Linguistes.

doi   de Chene, Brent. 1985. *r*-Epenthesis and the Japanese verb. *Papers in Japanese Linguistics* 10. 172–207.

de Chene, Brent. 1987. Keitai on'inron ni okeru shinriteki jitsuzaisei: Nihongo no dōshi no baai [Psychological reality in morphophonology: The case of the Japanese verb]. In Yukio Otsu (ed.), *Kotoba kara mita kokoro* [*Mind viewed from language*], 145–180. Tokyo: Tokyo Daigaku Shuppankai.

de Chene, Brent. 2014. Probability matching versus probability maximization in morphophonology: The case of Korean noun inflection. *Theoretical and Applied Linguistics at Kobe Shoin* 17. 1–13.

doi   de Chene, Brent. 2016. Description and explanation in morphophonology: The case of Japanese verb inflection. *Journal of East Asian Linguistics* 25. 37–80.

de Chene, Brent. 2017. Root-based syntax and Japanese derivational morphology. In Claire Bowen, Laurence Horn, and Raffaella Zanuttini (eds.), *On looking into words (and beyond)*, 117–135. Berlin: Language Science Press.

de Chene, Brent. 2019. *r*-Epenthesis and Ryukyuan. *Gengo Kenkyu* 155. 101–130.

doi   de Chene, Brent. 2020a. On the (ir)regularity of Dunan verbal morphophonology. *Journal of Japanese Linguistics* 36. 253–289.

doi   de Chene, Brent. 2020b. *r*-Epenthesis and the bigrade alternation: The role of phonological distance in the regularization of Japanese verbal inflection. *Diachronica* 37. 178–214.

doi   de Chene, Brent. 2022a. Sanskrit nominal stem gradation without morphemes. *Word Structure* 15. 28–54.

doi   de Chene, Brent. 2022b. Syntactic and lexical -*ase*- are distinct suffixes. *Journal of Japanese Linguistics* 38. 193–230.

de Chene, Brent. to appear. Stem inalterability in Japonic. *Journal of Japanese Linguistics*.

doi   de Lacy, Paul. 2006. *Markedness*. Cambridge: Cambridge University Press.

Di Sciullo, Anna Maria, and Edwin Williams. 1987. *On the definition of word.* Cambridge, MA: MIT Press.

Dixon, R. M. W., and Alexandra Y. Aikhenvald. 2002. Word: A typological framework. In R. M. W. Dixon and Alexandra Y. Aikhenvald (eds.), *Word. A cross-linguistic typology*, 1–41. Cambridge: Cambridge University Press.

Dressler, Wolfgang U. 1989. Prototypical differences between inflection and derivation. *Zeitschrift für Phonetik, Sprachwissenschaft und Kommunikationsforschung* 42. 3–10.

Embick, David. 2021. The motivation for roots in distributed morphology. *Annual Review of Linguistics* 7. 69–88.

Embick, David, and Alec Marantz. 2008. Architecture and blocking. *Linguistic Inquiry* 39. 1–53.

Fertig, David. 2016. Mechanisms of paradigm leveling and the role of universal preferences in morphophonological change. *Diachronica* 33. 423–460.

Frellesvig, Bjarke. 2008. On reconstruction of proto-Japanese and pre-Old Japanese verb inflection. In Bjarke Frellesvig and John Whitman (eds.), *Proto-Japanese*, 175–192. Amsterdam: Benjamins.

Frellesvig, Bjarke. 2010. *A history of the Japanese language.* Cambridge: Cambridge University Press.

Frellesvig, Bjarke, and John Whitman. 2008. Introduction. In Bjarke Frellesvig and John Whitman (eds.), *Proto-Japanese*, 1–9. Amsterdam: Benjamins.

Fujii, Nozomi. 2019. Kodomo no jikokenkōkanrinōryoku no kōjō o mezashite [Towards an increase in childrens' health self-management abilities]. *Kyōiku Kenkyū Ronbun [Papers in Educational Research]* (Funabashi-shi Sogo Kyoiku Sentaa [Funabashi City Integrated Educational Center]) 54. 14–20.

Fukushima, Kazuhiko. 2004. Conspiracy of form and function for optimization of language change. *Journal of East Asian Linguistics* 13. 181–196.

Fukushima, Kunimichi. 1969. "myū" to "myō" no kōtai [Variation between "myū" and "myō"]. In Masayoshi Oki, Yasuo Kitahara, Hideo Komatsu, Norio Nakada, Kazuo Mabuchi, and Muneaki Morino (eds.), *Saeki Umetomo hakase koki kinen kokugogaku ronshū [Papers in Japanese linguistics offered to Dr. Umetomo Saeki on his 70th birthday]*, 533–551. Tokyo: Hyogensha.

Garrett, Andrew. 2008. Paradigmatic uniformity and markedness. In Jeff Good (ed.), *Linguistic universals and language change*, 125–143. Oxford: Oxford University Press.

Goddard, Ives. 2013. Algonquian linguistic change and reconstruction. In Philip Baldi (ed.), *Patterns of change — change of patterns. Linguistic change and reconstruction methodology*, 55–70. Berlin: De Gruyter.

Goldberg, Adele E. 1995. *Constructions. A construction grammar approach to argument structure.* Chicago: University of Chicago Press.

Goto, Kazuhiko. 1961. Kagoshima/Miyazaki nanbu [Kagoshima and southern Miyazaki]. In Misao Tojo, Yoshimoto Endo, Teruo Hirayama, Tadatoshi Okubo, and Takeshi Shibata (eds.), *Kyūshū/Ryūkyū hōgen [Kyushu/Ryukyu dialects]* (*Hōgengaku kōza [Dialectology course]* 4), 268–293. Tokyo: Tokyodo Shuppan.

Hagège, Claude. 1990. Do the classical morphological types have clear-cut limits? In Wolfgang U. Dressler, Hans C. Luschützky, Oskar E. Pfeiffer and John R. Rennison (eds.), *Contemporary morphology*, 297–308. Berlin: De Gruyter.

doi   Hale, Kenneth. 1973. Deep-surface canonical disparities in relation to analysis and change: An Australian example. In Thomas A. Sebeok (ed.), *Diachronic, areal, and typological linguistics* (Current Trends in Linguistics 11), 401–458. The Hague: Mouton.

doi   Hall, T.A. 2011. Coronals. In Marc van Oostendorp, Colin J. Ewen, Elizabeth Hume, and Keren Rice (eds.), *The Blackwell companion to phonology*, 267–287. Oxford: Blackwell.

Halle, Morris. 1962. Phonology in generative grammar. *Word* 18. 54–72. Reprinted in Fodor, Jerry A., and Jerrold J. Katz (eds.). 1964. *The structure of language*, 334–352. Englewood Cliffs, NJ: Prentice-Hall.

Halle, Morris. 1973. Prolegomena to a theory of word formation. *Linguistic Inquiry* 4. 3–16.

Halle, Morris. 1997. Distributed morphology: Impoverishment and fission. In Benjamin Bruening, Yoonjung Kang, and Martha McGinnis (eds.), *PF: Papers at the interface* (MIT Working Papers in Linguistics 30), 425–449. Cambridge, MA: MITWPL.

Halle, Morris, and Alec Marantz. 1993. Distributed morphology and the pieces of inflection. In Kenneth Hale and Samuel J. Keyser (eds.), *The view from building 20. Essays in linguistics in honor of Sylvain Bromberger*, 111–176. Cambridge, MA: MIT Press.

Halle, Morris, and Alec Marantz. 1994. Some key features of distributed morphology. In Andrew Carnie and Heidi Harley (eds.), *Papers on phonology and morphology* (MIT Working Papers in Linguistics 21), 275–288. Cambridge, MA: MITWPL.

Harley, Heidi. 1995. Subjects, events and licensing. Doctoral dissertation, MIT.

Harley, Heidi. 2008. On the causative construction. In Shigeru Miyagawa and Mamoru Saito (eds.), *The Oxford handbook of Japanese linguistics*, 20–53. Oxford: Oxford University Press.

Harley, Heidi. 2009. The morphology of nominalizations and the syntax of vP*. In Anastasia Giannakidou and Monika Rathert (eds.), *Quantification, definiteness, and nominalization*, 321–343. Oxford: Oxford University Press.

Harley, Heidi. 2012. Lexical decomposition in modern syntactic theory. In Markus Werning, Wolfram Hinzen, and Edouard Machery (eds.), *The Oxford handbook of compositionality*, 328–350. Oxford: Oxford University Press.

doi   Harley, Heidi. 2015. The syntax-morphology interface. In Tibor Kiss and Artemis Alexiadou (eds.), *Syntax — theory and analysis*, vol. 2, 1128–1154. Berlin: De Gruyter.

Harley, Heidi, and Rolf Noyer. 1999. Distributed morphology. *Glot International* 4.4. 3–9.

doi   Harley, Heidi and Rolf Noyer. 2000. Formal versus encyclopedic properties of vocabulary: Evidence from nominalisations. In Bert Peeters (ed.), *The lexicon-encyclopedia interface*, 349–374. Leiden: Brill.

Harris, James W. 1974. Evidence from Portuguese for the "Elsewhere Condition" in phonology. *Linguistic Inquiry* 5. 61–80.

Hasegawa, Nobuko. 1999. *Seisei nihongogaku nyūmon* [*Introduction to the generative grammar of Japanese*]. Tokyo: Taishukan Shoten.

doi   Hasegawa, Nobuko. 2007. The possessor raising construction and the interpretation of the subject. In Simin Karimi, Vida Samiian, and Wendy K. Wilkins (eds.), *Phrasal and clausal architecture: Syntactic derivation and interpretation*, 66–92. Amsterdam: Benjamins.

doi   Haspelmath, Martin. 1996. Word-class-changing inflection and morphological theory. In Geert Booij and Jaap van Marle (eds.), *Yearbook of morphology 1995*, 43–66. Dordrecht: Kluwer.

Haspelmath, Martin. 2011. The indeterminacy of word segmentation and the nature of morphology and syntax. *Folia Linguistica* 45. 31–80.

Hattori, Shiro. 1955. Ryūkyūgo V: Bunpō. [Ryukyuan V: Grammar]. In Sanki Ichikawa and Shiro Hattori (eds.), *Sekai gengo gaisetsu [An introduction to the languages of the world]*, vol. 2, 328–353. Tokyo: Kenkyusha.

Hayes, Bruce, and James White. 2015. Saltation and the P-map. *Phonology* 32. 267–302.

Heinrich, Patrick, Shinsho Miyara, and Michinori Shimoji. 2015. Introduction: Ryukyuan languages and Ryukyuan linguistics. In Patrick Heinrich, Shinsho Miyara, and Michinori Shimoji (eds.), *Handbook of the Ryukyuan languages*, 1–10. Berlin: De Gruyter.

Hensey, Fritz G. 1972. Portuguese vowel alternation. In Jean Casagrande and Bohdan Saciuk (eds.), *Generative studies in Romance languages*, 285–292. Rowley, MA: Newbury House.

Hikosaka, Yoshinobu. 1999. Kyūshū ni okeru ichi/nidan katsuyō no godanka — "Kōgohō" kara GAJ e [The assimilation of unigrade and bigrade inflection to consonant-stem inflection in Kyushu — from the *Spoken usage survey report* to the GAJ]. In Takeyoshi Sato (ed.), *Goi/gohō no shinkenkyū [New research on lexicon and grammar]*, 277–292. Tokyo: Meiji Shoin.

Hippisley, Andrew, and Gregory Stump (eds.). 2016. *The Cambridge handbook of morphology*. Cambridge: Cambridge University Press.

Hirayama, Teruo. 1988. *Minami Ryūkyū no hōgen kiso goi [Basic vocabulary of southern Ryukyu dialects]*. Tokyo: Ofusha.

Hirayama, Teruo, and Masachie Nakamoto. 1964. *Ryūkyū Yonaguni hōgen no kenkyū [Research on the Ryukyu dialect of Yonaguni]*. Tokyo: Tokyodo Shuppan.

Hirayama, Teruo, and Ichiro Oshima. 1969. *Gotō rettō no hōgen [The dialects of the Goto archipelago]*. Tokyo: Tokyo Toritsu Daigaku Toshi Kenkyu Iinkai [Tokyo Metropolitan University Urban Research Committee].

Hirayama, Teruo, Ichiro Oshima, and Masachie Nakamoto. 1966. *Ryūkyū hōgen no sōgōteki kenkyū [Comprehensive research on Ryukyu dialects]*. Tokyo: Meiji Shoin.

Hirayama, Teruo, Ichiro Oshima, and Masachie Nakamoto. 1967. *Ryūkyū Sakishima hōgen no sōgōteki kenkyū [Comprehensive research on Ryukyu Sakishima dialects]*. Tokyo: Meiji Shoin.

Hirayama, Teruo, Ichiro Oshima, Makio Ono, Makoto Kuno, Mariko Kuno, and Takao Sugimura (eds.). 1992–1994. *Gendai Nihongo hōgen daijiten [Great dictionary of modern Japanese dialects]*, 9 vols. Tokyo: Meiji Shoin.

Hokama, Shuzen. 1960. Chūsei bunken ni arawareta Ryūkyū hōgen no dōshi [Ryukyu dialect verbs appearing in medieval documents]. *Kokugogaku* 41. 106–114. Reprinted in Inoue, Fumio, Koichi Shinozaki, Takashi Kobayashi, and Takuichiro Onishi (eds.). 2001. *Ryūkyū hōgen kō [Studies on Ryukyu dialects]* 2 (Nihon Rettō Hōgen Sōsho [Japanese Dialect Series] 29), 43–51. Tokyo: Yumani Shobo.

Hokama, Shuzen, and Masami Tamaki. 1980. *Nantō kayō taisei I: Okinawahen jō [Compilation of songs of the southern islands I: Okinawa book 1]*. Tokyo: Kadokawa Shoten.

Hokama, Shuzen et al. (eds.). 2011. *Okinawa kogo daijiten [Great historical dictionary of Okinawan]*, on-demand edition. Tokyo: Kadokawa Gakugei Shuppan.

Holton, David, Geoffrey Horrocks, Marjolijne Janssen, Tina Lendari, Io Manolessou, and Notis Toufexis. 2019. *The Cambridge grammar of medieval and early modern Greek*, 4 vols. Cambridge: Cambridge University Press.

Hooper, Joan B. 1979. Substantive principles in natural generative phonology. In Daniel A. Dinnsen (ed.), *Current approaches to phonological theory*, 106–125. Bloomington: Indiana University Press.

Hopper, Paul J., and Sandra A. Thompson. 1980. Transitivity in grammar and discourse. *Language* 56. 251–299.

Horrocks, Geoffrey. 1997. *Greek: A history of the language and its speakers*. London: Longman.

Householder, Fred W., Kostas Kazazis, and Andreas Koutsoudas. 1964. *Reference grammar of literary dhimotiki*. Bloomington: Indiana University.

Hyman, Larry. 2003. Suffix ordering in Bantu: A morphocentric approach. In Geert Booij and Jaap van Marle (eds.), *Yearbook of morphology 2002*, 245–281. Dordrecht: Kluwer.

Igartua, Iván. 2015. From cumulative to separative exponence in inflection: Reversing the morphological cycle. *Language* 91. 676–722.

Iha, Fuyu. 1933. Ryūkyū no hōgen [Ryukyu dialects]. In *Hōgengaku [Dialectology]* (*Kokugo kagaku kōza [Course in Japanese linguistics]* VII). Tokyo: Meiji Shoin. Reprinted in Hattori, Shiro, Seizen Nakasone, and Shuzen Hokama (eds.). 1975. *Iha Fuyū Zenshū [Collected writings of Iha Fuyu]*, vol. 8, 508–549. Tokyo: Heibonsha.

Iitoyo, Kiichi, Sukezumi Hino, and Ryoichi Sato (eds.). 1982–1986. *Kōza hōgengaku [Course in dialectology]*, 10 vols. Tokyo: Kokusho Kankokai.

Institute of Modern Greek Studies, Aristotle University of Thessaloniki. 1998. *Lexikó tis koinís Neoellenikís [Dictionary of Standard Modern Greek]*. https://www.greek-language.gr /greekLang/modern_greek/tools/lexica/triantafyllides/index.html

Ito, Chiyuki. 2010. Analogy and lexical restructuring in the development of nominal stem inflection from Middle to Contemporary Korean. *Journal of East Asian Linguistics* 19. 357–383.

Ito, Junko, and Armin Mester. 2004. Morphological contrast and merger: *ranuki* in Japanese. *Journal of Japanese Linguistics* 20. 1–18. Also in the Rutgers Optimality Archive, ROA-711.

Itoi, Kan'ichi. 1961. Ōita/Miyazaki hokubu [Oita and northern Miyazaki]. In Misao Tojo, Yoshimoto Endo, Teruo Hirayama, Tadatoshi Okubo, and Takeshi Shibata (eds.), *Kyūshū/Ryūkyū hōgen [Kyushu/Ryukyu dialects]* (*Hōgengaku kōza [Dialectology course]* 4), 239–267. Tokyo: Tokyodo Shuppan.

Itoi, Kan'ichi. 1983. Ōita-ken no hōgen [The dialects of Oita Prefecture]. In Kiichi Iitoyo, Sukezumi Hino, and Ryoichi Sato (eds.), *Kyūshū chihō no hōgen [The dialects of the Kyushu region]* (*Kōza hōgengaku [Course in dialectology]* 9), 237–266. Tokyo: Kokusho Kankokai.

Iwai, Ryusei. 1959. Ishikawa-ken Kanazawa-shi Hikozō ichibanchō. [(The dialect of) Hikozo ichibancho in Kanazawa, Ishikawa Prefecture]. In *Nihon hōgen no kijutsuteki kenkyū [Descriptive studies on Japanese dialects]*, 87–110. Tokyo: Kokuritsu Kokugo Kenkyujo.

Iwai, Ryusei. 1961. Toyama/Ishikawa. In Misao Tojo, Yoshimoto Endo, Teruo Hirayama, Tadatoshi Okubo, and Takeshi Shibata (eds.), *Seibu hōgen [Western dialects]* (*Hōgengaku kōza [Dialectology course]* 3), 84–110. Tokyo: Tokyodo Shuppan.

Iwasaki, Shoichi. 2013. *Japanese*, 2nd ed. Amsterdam: Benjamins.

Izuyama, Atsuko. 2012. Yonaguni. In Nicolas Tranter (ed.), *The languages of Japan and Korea*, 412–457. Abingdon: Routledge.

Jackendoff, Ray. 1975. Morphological and semantic regularities in the lexicon. *Language* 51. 639–671.

Jackendoff, Ray. 1997. *The architecture of the language faculty.* Cambridge, MA: MIT Press.

Jackendoff, Ray. 2002. *Foundations of language.* Oxford: Oxford University Press.

Jacobsen, Wesley M. 1982. Transitivity in the Japanese verbal system (Doctoral dissertation, University of Chicago). Bloomington: Indiana University Linguistics Club.

Jacobsen, Wesley M. 1992. *The transitive structure of events in Japanese.* Tokyo: Kurosio Publishers.

Jacobsen, Wesley M. 2017. Transitivity. In Masayoshi Shibatani, Shigeru Miyagawa, and Hisashi Noda (eds.), *Handbook of Japanese syntax,* 55–95. Berlin: De Gruyter.

Jinnouchi, Masataka. 1989. Hokubu kyūshū no shin-hōgen [New dialects of northern Kyushu]. In Mitsuo Okumura (ed.), *Kyūshū hōgen no shiteki kenkyū [Historical research on Kyushu dialects],* 331–347. Tokyo: Ofusha.

Jun, Jongho. 2010. Stem-final obstruent variation in Korean. *Journal of East Asian Linguistics* 19. 137–179.

Kageyama, Taro. 1999. Word formation. In Natsuko Tsujimura (ed.), *The handbook of Japanese linguistics,* 297–325. Oxford: Blackwell.

Kageyama, Taro, and Wesley M. Jacobsen (eds.). 2016. *Transitivity and valency alternations: Studies on Japanese and beyond.* Berlin: De Gruyter.

Kaisse, Ellen M., and Patricia A. Shaw. 1985. On the theory of lexical phonology. *Phonology* 2. 1–30.

Kamimura, Takaji. 1983. Kyūshū hōgen no gaisetsu [An outline of Kyushu dialects]. In Kiichi Iitoyo, Sukezumi Hino, and Ryoichi Sato (eds.), *Kyūshū chihō no hōgen [The dialects of the Kyushu region]* (*Kōza hōgengaku [Course in dialectology]* 9), 1–28. Tokyo: Kokusho Kankokai.

Karatsareas, Petros. 2011. A study of Cappadocian Greek nominal morphology from a diachronic and dialectological perspective. Doctoral dissertation, University of Cambridge.

Karimata, Shigehisa. 1997a. Miyako hōgen [Miyako dialects]. In Takashi Kamei, Rokuro Kono, and Eiichi Chino (eds.), *Nihon rettō no gengo (Gengogaku daijiten serekushon) [The languages of the Japanese archipelago (Selection from the Great dictionary of linguistics)],* 388–403. Tokyo: Sanseido.

Karimata, Shigehisa. 1997b. Yaeyama hōgen [Yaeyama dialects]. In Takashi Kamei, Rokuro Kono, and Eiichi Chino (eds.), *Nihon rettō no gengo (Gengogaku daijiten serekushon) [The languages of the Japanese archipelago (Selection from the Great dictionary of linguistics)],* 403–413. Tokyo: Sanseido.

Karimata, Shigehisa. 1999. Miyako shohōgen no dōshi "shūshikei" no seiritsu ni tsuite [On the formation of the verbal conclusive form in the dialects of Miyako]. *Nihon Tōyō Bunka Ronshū (Ryūkyū Daigaku Hōbungakubu Kiyō) [Japanese Papers on Eastern Culture (Bulletin of the Faculty of Law and Letters, University of the Ryukyus)]* 5. 27–51.

Karimata, Shigehisa. 2005. Okinawa-ken Miyakojima Hirara hōgen no foneemu [The phonemes of the dialect of Hirara, Miyakojima, Okinawa Prefecture]. *Nihon Tōyō Bunka Ronshū (Ryūkyū Daigaku Hōbungakubu Kiyō) [Japanese Papers on Eastern Culture (Bulletin of the Faculty of Law and Letters, University of the Ryukyus)]* 11. 67–113.

Karimata, Shigehisa. 2015. Ryukyuan languages: A grammar overview. In Patrick Heinrich, Shinsho Miyara, and Michinori Shimoji (eds.), *Handbook of the Ryukyuan languages,* 113–140. Berlin: De Gruyter.

Keino, Masaji. 1972. *Dōshi no kenkyū* [*Studies on verbs*]. Tokyo: Kasama Shoin.

Kenstowicz, Michael, and Charles Kisseberth. 1977. *Topics in phonological theory.* New York: Academic Press.

Kenstowicz, Michael, and Charles Kisseberth. 1979. *Generative phonology.* New York: Academic Press.

Kim, Heung-gyu, and Beom-mo Kang. 2000. *Frequency analysis of Korean morpheme and word usage* 1. Seoul: Institute of Korean Culture, Korea University.

Kiparsky, Paul. 1971. Historical linguistics. Lecture, University of Maryland. Published in Kiparsky, Paul. 1982. *Explanation in phonology,* 57–80. Dordrecht: Foris.

Kiparsky, Paul. 1972. Review of *Geschichte der indogermanischen Verbalflexion*, by Calvert Watkins. *Foundations of Language* 9. 277–286.

Kiparsky, Paul. 1973. Productivity in phonology. In Michael J. Kenstowicz and Charles W. Kisseberth (eds.), *Issues in phonological theory*, 169–176. The Hague: Mouton. Reprinted in Kiparsky, Paul. 1982. *Explanation in phonology,* 165–173. Dordrecht: Foris.

Kiparsky, Paul. 1982. Lexical morphology and phonology. In The Linguistic Society of Korea (ed.), *Linguistics in the morning calm*, 3–91. Seoul: Hanshin.

Kiparsky, Paul. 1996. Allomorphy or morphophonology? In Rajendra Singh (ed.), *Trubetzkoy's orphan*, 13–31. Amsterdam: Benjamins.

Kiparsky, Paul. 2003. The phonological basis of sound change. In Brian D. Joseph and Richard D. Janda (eds.), *The handbook of historical linguistics*, 313–342. Oxford: Blackwell.

Kiparsky, Paul. 2015. Stratal OT: A synopsis and FAQs. In Yuchau E. Hsiao and Lian-Hee Wee (eds.), *Capturing phonological shades within and across languages*, 2–44. Newcastle: Cambridge Scholars Publishing.

Kiparsky, Paul. 2020. Morphological units: Stems. In Rochelle Lieber (ed.), *The Oxford encyclopedia of morphology*, 33–52. Oxford: Oxford University Press.

Ko, Kwang-Mo. 1989. Cheeon kkeuth ui pyeonhwa *t > s* e taehan saeroun haeseok [A new interpretation of the noun-final change *t > s*]. *Eoneohak* [*Linguistics*] 11. 3–22.

Kobayashi, Takashi. 2004. *Hōgengakuteki Nihongoshi no hōhō* [*A dialectological approach to the history of the Japanese language*]. Tokyo: Hituzi Syobo.

Kokugo Chosa Iinkai [Japanese Language Survey Committee]. 1906. *Kōgohō chōsa hōkokusho* [*Report on the survey of spoken usage*], 2 vols. Tokyo: Monbusho.

Kokugo Gakkai [Society for Japanese Linguistics]. 1980. *Kokugogaku daijiten* [*Great dictionary of Japanese linguistics*]. Tokyo: Tokyodo Shuppan.

Kokuritsu Kokugo Kenkyujo [National Language Research Institute]. 1953. *Chiiki shakai no gengo seikatsu. Tsuruoka ni okeru jittai chōsa.* [*The linguistic life of regional society. A survey of Tsuruoka*]. Tokyo: Shuei Shuppan.

Kokuritsu Kokugo Kenkyujo [National Language Research Institute]. 1963. *Okinawa-go jiten* [*Dictionary of the Okinawan language*]. Tokyo: Okurasho Insatsukyoku.

Kokuritsu Kokugo Kenkyujo [National Language Research Institute]. 1966–1974. *Nihon gengo chizu* [*Linguistic atlas of Japan*], 6 vols. Tokyo: Okurasho Insatsukyoku.

Kokuritsu Kokugo Kenkyujo [National Language Research Institute]. 1989–2006. *Hōgen bunpō zenkoku chizu* [*Grammar atlas of Japanese dialects*], 6 vols. Tokyo: Kokuritsu Kokugo Kenkyujo. https://www2.ninjal.ac.jp/past-publications/publication/catalogue/gaj_map/

Komatsushiro, Yuichi. 1961. Iwate. In Misao Tojo, Yoshimoto Endo, Teruo Hirayama, Tadatoshi Okubo, and Takeshi Shibata (eds.), *Tōbu hōgen* [*Eastern dialects*] (*Hōgengaku kōza* [*Dialectology course*] 2), 177–203. Tokyo: Tokyodo Shuppan.

Konishi, Izumi. 2011. Izumo hōgen ni okeru "ichidan katsuyō no *ra*-gyō godanka" ni kansuru oboegaki [A note concerning "assimilation of vowel-stem to *r*-stem inflection" in the Izumo dialect]. *Ronsō Kokugo Kyōikugaku Fukkan* [*Papers on Japanese Language Education New Series*] 2. 49–60.

Konoshima, Masatoshi. 1961. Aomori. In Misao Tojo, Yoshimoto Endo, Teruo Hirayama, Tadatoshi Okubo, and Takeshi Shibata (eds.), *Tōbu hōgen* [*Eastern dialects*] (*Hōgengaku kōza* [*Dialectology course*] 2), 127–148. Tokyo: Tokyodo Shuppan.

Kubo, Miori. 1992. Japanese passives. *Hokkaidō Daigaku Gengobunkabu Kiyō* [*Bulletin of the Institute of Languages and Cultures, Hokkaido University*] 23. 231–302.

Kurisu, Kazutaka. 2001. The phonology of morpheme realization. Doctoral dissertation, University of California, Santa Cruz.

Kuroda, S.-Y. 1960. *Gengo no kijutsu* [*The description of language*]. Tokyo: Kenkyusha.

Kuroda, S.-Y. 1993. Lexical and productive causatives in Japanese: An examination of the theory of paradigmatic structure. *Journal of Japanese Linguistics* 15. 1–81.

Kuryłowicz, Jerzy. 1945–49. La nature des procès dits « analogiques ». *Acta Linguistica* V. 15–37. Reprinted in Hamp, Eric P., Fred W. Householder, and Robert Austerlitz (eds.). 1966. *Readings in linguistics II*, 158–174. Chicago: University of Chicago Press.

Kyushu Hogen Gakkai [Kyushu Dialect Society]. 1991. *Kyūshū hōgen no kisoteki kenkyū* [*Basic research on Kyushu dialects*], revised edition. Tokyo: Kazama Shobo.

Labov, William. 2001. *Principles of linguistic change,* vol. 2: *Social factors.* Oxford: Blackwell.

Labrune, Laurence. 2014. The phonology of Japanese /r/: A panchronic account. *Journal of East Asian Linguistics* 23. 1–25.

Lawrence, Wayne P. 2004. High vowels, glides, and Japanese phonology. *Gengo Kenkyu* 125. 1–30.

Lichtenberk, Frantisek, Jyotsna Vaid, and Hsin-Chin Chen. 2011. On the interpretation of alienable vs. inalienable possession: A psycholinguistic investigation. *Cognitive Linguistics* 22. 659–689.

Lieber, Rochelle. 1980. On the organization of the lexicon. Doctoral dissertation, MIT.

Lieber, Rochelle. 1992. *Deconstructing morphology. Word formation in syntactic theory.* Chicago: University of Chicago Press.

Lieber, Rochelle. 2004. *Morphology and lexical semantics.* Cambridge: Cambridge University Press.

Lieber, Rochelle (ed.). 2020. *The Oxford encyclopedia of morphology.* Oxford: Oxford University Press.

Lightner, Theodore. 1968. On the use of minor rules in Russian phonology. *Journal of Linguistics* 4. 69–72.

Lightner, Theodore. 1975. The role of derivational morphology in generative grammar. *Language* 51. 617–638.

Lombard, Alf. 1954. *Le verbe Roumain: Étude morphologique*, Tome I. Lund: C.W.K. Gleerup.

Lombardi, Linda. 2002. Coronal epenthesis and markedness. *Phonology* 19. 219–251.

Mackridge, Peter. 1985. *The modern Greek language*. Oxford: Oxford University Press.

Maiden, Martin. 2018. *The Romance verb*. Oxford: Oxford University Press.

Marantz, Alec. 1997. No escape from syntax: Don't try morphological analysis in the privacy of your own lexicon. *University of Pennsylvania Working Papers in Linguistics* 4. 201–225.

Marantz, Alec. 2005. Generative linguistics within the cognitive neuroscience of language. *The Linguistic Review* 22. 429–445.

Marantz, Alec. 2007. Phases and words. In Sook-Hee Choe (ed.), *Phases in the theory of grammar*, 191–222. Seoul: Dong In.

Marantz, Alec. 2013. Locality domains for contextual allomorphy across the interfaces. In Ora Matushansky and Alec Marantz (eds.), *Distributed morphology today*, 95–115. Cambridge, MA: MIT Press.

Marcus, Gary, Ursula Brinkmann, Harald Clahsen, Richard Wiese, and Steven Pinker. 1995. German inflection: The exception that proves the rule. *Cognitive Psychology* 29. 189–256.

Marcus, Gary, Steven Pinker, Michael Ullman, Michelle Hollander, T. John Rosen, Fei Xu and Harald Clahsen. 1992. Overregularization in language acquisition. *Monographs of the Society for Research in Child Development* 57.4. Chicago: University of Chicago Press.

Martin, Samuel E. 1966. Lexical evidence relating Korean to Japanese. *Language* 42. 185–251.

Martin, Samuel E. 1975. *A reference grammar of Japanese*. New Haven: Yale University Press.

Mateus, Maria Helena, and Ernesto d'Andrade. 2000. *The phonology of Portuguese*. Oxford: Oxford University Press.

Matsumaru, Michio. 2006. minai, miro [does not look, look!]. *Gengo* 35.12. 40–43.

Matsumoto, Yo. 2016. Phonological and semantic subregularities in noncausative-causative verb pairs in Japanese. In Taro Kageyama and Wesley M. Jacobsen (eds.), *Transitivity and valency alternations: Studies on Japanese and beyond*, 51–88. Berlin: De Gruyter.

Matsumura, Akira (ed.). 1971. *Nihon bunpō daijiten* [Great dictionary of Japanese grammar]. Tokyo: Meiji Shoin.

Matsumura, Akira (ed.). 1988. *Daijirin*. Tokyo: Sanseido.

Matsumura, Akira (ed.). 1995. *Daijirin*, 2nd ed. Tokyo: Sanseido.

Matthews, P. H. 1972. *Inflectional morphology*. Cambridge: Cambridge University Press.

McCarthy, John J. 2002. *A thematic guide to optimality theory*. Cambridge: Cambridge University Press.

McCarthy, John J., and Alan Prince. 1993. Generalized alignment. In Geert Booij and Jaap van Marle (eds.), *Yearbook of morphology 1993*, 79–153. Dordrecht: Kluwer.

McCawley, James D. 1968. *The phonological component of a grammar of Japanese*. The Hague: Mouton.

Melissaropoulou, Dimitra. 2013. Gradualness in analogical change as a complexification stage in a language simplification process: A case study from Modern Greek dialects. In Anna Giacalone Ramat, Caterina Mauri, and Piera Molinelli (eds.), *Synchrony and diachrony: A dynamic interface*, 125–150. Amsterdam: Benjamins.

doi Mester, Armin, and Junko Ito. 1989. Feature predictability and underspecification: Palatal prosody in Japanese mimetics. *Language* 65. 258–293.

doi Miyagawa, Shigeru. 1984. Blocking and Japanese causatives. *Lingua* 64. 177–207. Reprinted in Miyagawa, Shigeru. 2012. *Case, argument structure, and word order*, 169–194, 292 (notes). New York: Routledge.

doi Miyagawa, Shigeru. 1989. *Structure and case marking in Japanese.* San Diego: Academic Press.

doi Miyagawa, Shigeru. 1998. *(s)ase* as an elsewhere causative and the syntactic nature of words. *Journal of Japanese Linguistics* 16. 67–110.

Miyagawa, Shigeru. 1999. Causatives. In Natsuko Tsujimura (ed.), *The handbook of Japanese linguistics*, 236–268. Oxford: Blackwell.

Miyagawa, Shigeru. 2012. Blocking and causatives revisited. In Shigeru Miyagawa, *Case, argument structure, and word order*, 195–216. New York: Routledge.

Miyaji, Yutaka. 1969. *seru/saseru* (gendaigo) [*seru/saseru* (modern language)]. In Akira Matsumoto (ed.), *Kotengo/gendaigo joshi jodōshi shōsetsu* [*Detailed exposition of the particles and auxiliary verbs of the classical and modern language*], 89–96. Tokyo: Gakutosha.

Miyara, Shinsho. 1995. Minami Ryūkyū Yaeyama Ishigaki hōgen no bunpō [*The grammar of the Ishigaki dialect of Yaeyama, southern Ryukyus*]. Tokyo: Kurosio Publishers.

doi Miyara, Shinsho. 2015. Shuri Okinawan grammar. In Patrick Heinrich, Shinsho Miyara, and Michinori Shimoji (eds.), *Handbook of the Ryukyuan languages*, 379–404. Berlin: De Gruyter.

doi Moreton, Elliott, and Joe Pater. 2012a. Structure and substance in artificial-phonology learning, part I: Structure. *Language and Linguistics Compass* 6. 686–701.

doi Moreton, Elliott, and Joe Pater. 2012b. Structure and substance in artificial-phonology learning, part II: Substance. *Language and Linguistics Compass* 6. 702–718.

doi Morley, Rebecca L. 2018. Is phonological consonant epenthesis possible? A series of artificial grammar learning experiments. *Phonology* 35. 649–688.

Nakajima, Nobutaro (ed.). 1972. *Harima Kako-gun hokubu hōgen kiroku.* [*Records of the dialect of northern Kako county, Harima*]. Tokyo: Musashino Shoin.

Nakamoto, Masachie. 1990. *Nihon rettō gengoshi no kenkyū* [*Research on the linguistic history of the Japanese archipelago*]. Tokyo: Taishukan Shoten.

doi Nasukawa, Kuniya. 2010. No consonant-final stems in Japanese verb morphology. *Lingua* 120. 2336–2352.

doi Nevins, Andrew, and Bert Vaux. 2007. Underlying representations that do not minimize grammatical violations. In Sylvia Blaho, Patrik Bye, and Martin Krämer (eds.), *Freedom of analysis?*, 35–61. Berlin: De Gruyter.

Nguyễn, Đình-hoà. 1987. *Vietnamese.* Amsterdam: Benjamins.

Nihon kokugo daijiten dainihan henshu iinkai/Shogakukan kokugo jiten henshubu [Great dictionary of the Japanese language second edition editorial committee/Shogakukan Japanese dictionary editorial division] (eds.). 2000–2002. *Nihon kokugo daijiten* [*Great dictionary of the Japanese language*], 2nd ed. Tokyo: Shogakukan.

Nishio, Minoru, Etsutaro Iwabuchi, and Shizuo Mizutani (eds.). 2000. *Iwanami kokugo jiten* [*Iwanami dictionary of the Japanese language*], 6th ed. Tokyo: Iwanami Shoten.

Nishioka, Satoshi. 1993. Ryūka/Kumiodori-go ni okeru "nai" no katsuyō [The conjugation of "nai" in the language of the Ryuka and Kumiodori]. *Okinawa Bunka* 28.2. 27–39.

Nyrop, Kr. 1908. *Grammaire historique de la langue Française*, vol. 3. Copenhagen: Gyldendal.

Oehrle, Richard, and Hiroko Nishio. 1981. Adversity. In Ann Farmer and Chisato Kitagawa (eds.), *Proceedings of the Arizona conference on Japanese linguistics* (*Coyote Papers* 2), 163–187. Tucson, AZ: University of Arizona Linguistics Circle.

Ojeda, Almerindo E. 1982. Some constraints on deletion. Doctoral dissertation, University of Chicago.

Omodaka, Hisataka et al. (eds.). 1967. *Jidaibetsu kokugo daijiten, jōdaihen* [*Great historical dictionary of Japanese, Nara period*]. Tokyo: Sanseido.

Onishi, Takuichiro. 2006. Gengo chirigaku no saikidō [A new start for linguistic geography]. In Seiichi Nakai, Daniel Long, and Kenjiro Matsuda (eds.), *Nihon no fiirudo gengogaku* [*Field linguistics in Japan*], 80–93. Toyama: Katsura Shobo.

Onishi, Takuichiro (ed.). 2016a. *Shin Nihon gengo chizu* [*New linguistic atlas of Japan*]. Tokyo: Asakura Shoten.

Onishi, Takuichiro. 2016b. okiru [get up]. In Takuichiro Onishi (ed.), *Shin Nihon gengo chizu* [*New linguistic atlas of Japan*], 150–151. Tokyo: Asakura Shoten.

Onishi, Takuichiro. 2016c. okiro [get up!]. In Takuichiro Onishi (ed.), *Shin Nihon gengo chizu* [*New linguistic atlas of Japan*], 152–153. Tokyo: Asakura Shoten.

Ono, Susumu. 1953. Nihongo no dōshi no katsuyōkei no kigen ni tsuite [On the origin of the verbal inflectional forms of Japanese]. *Kokugo to Kokubungaku* 350. 47–56.

Ono, Susumu, Akihiro Satake, and Kingoro Maeda (eds.). 1974. Iwanami kogo jiten [*Iwanami historical dictionary of Japanese*]. Tokyo: Iwanami Shoten.

Ortmann, Albert. 1999. Affix repetition and non-redundancy in inflectional morphology. *Zeitschrift für Sprachwissenschaft* 18. 76–120.

Oseki, Yohei. 2017. Voice morphology in Japanese argument structures. MS, New York University. https://ling.auf.net/lingbuzz/003374

Oseki, Yohei. 2021. Bunsan keitairon to Nihongo no tadōsei kōtai [Distributed morphology and Japanese transitivity alternations]. In Hideki Kishimoto (ed.), *Rekishikon kenkyū no gendaiteki kadai* [*Current issues in lexicon research*], 1–23. Tokyo: Kurosio Publishers.

Oshima, David Y. 2014. On the morphological status of -*te*, -*ta*, and related forms in Japanese: Evidence from accent placement. *Journal of East Asian Linguistics* 23. 233–265.

Panagiotidis, Phoevos, Vassilios Spyropoulos, and Anthi Revithiadou. 2017. Little v as a categorizing verbal head: Evidence from Greek. In Roberta D'Alessandro, Irene Franco, and Ángel J. Gallego (eds.), *The verbal domain*, 29–48. Oxford: Oxford University Press.

Parsons, Terence. 1990. *Events in the semantics of English: A study in subatomic semantics*. Cambridge, MA: MIT Press.

Paul, Hermann. 1920. *Prinzipien der sprachgeschichte*, 5th ed. Halle: Niemeyer.

Payne, David L. 1981. *The phonology and morphology of Axininca Campa*. University of Texas, Arlington, and Summer Institute of Linguistics.

Payne, Doris, and Immanuel Barshi (eds.). 1999. *External possession*. Amsterdam: Benjamins.

Pellard, Thomas. 2009. Ōgami: Éléments de description d'un parler du Sud des Ryūkyū. Doctoral dissertation, École des Hautes Études en Sciences Sociales, Paris.

Pellard, Thomas. 2016. Nichiryū sogo no bunki nendai [The period of separation of Proto-Japanese-Ryukyuan]. In Yukinori Takubo, John Whitman, and Tatsuya Hirako (eds.), *Ryūkyū shogo to kodai Nihongo: Nichiryū sogo no saiken ni mukete* [*Ryukyuan and premodern Japanese: Toward the reconstruction of Proto-Japanese-Ryukyuan*], 99–124. Tokyo: Kurosio Publishers.

Pellard, Thomas, and Masahiro Yamada. 2017. Verb morphology and conjugation classes in Dunan (Yonaguni). In Ferenc Kiefer, James P. Blevins, and Huba Bartos (eds.), *Perspectives on morphological organization: Data and analyses*, 31–49. Leiden: Brill.

Penny, Ralph. 2002. *A history of the Spanish language*, 2nd ed. Cambridge: Cambridge University Press.

Perlmutter, David M. 1988. The split morphology hypothesis: Evidence from Yiddish. In Michael Hammond and Michael Noonan (eds.), *Theoretical morphology. Approaches in modern linguistics*, 79–100. San Diego: Academic Press.

Pinker, Steven. 2002. *The blank slate: The modern denial of human nature*. New York: Viking.

Pollard, Carl, and Ivan A. Sag. 1987. *Information-based syntax and semantics*, vol. 1. *Fundamentals*. Stanford: Center for the Study of Language and Information.

Pollard, Carl, and Ivan A. Sag. 1994. *Head-driven phrase structure grammar*. Chicago: University of Chicago Press.

Pross, Tillmann. 2019. What about lexical semantics if syntax is the only generative component of the grammar? A case study on word meaning in German. *Natural Language and Linguistic Theory* 37. 215–261.

Pylkkänen, Liina. 2002. Introducing arguments. Doctoral dissertation, MIT.

Pylkkänen, Liina. 2008. *Introducing arguments*. Cambridge, MA: MIT Press.

Ralli, Angela. 2000. A feature-based analysis of Greek nominal inflection. *Glossologia* 11–12. 201–227.

Ringe, Don. 2006. *From Proto-Indo-European to Proto-Germanic* (*A linguistic history of English*, vol. 1). Oxford: Oxford University Press.

Rizzi, Luigi. 2016. The concept of explanatory adequacy. In Ian Roberts (ed.), *The Oxford handbook of universal grammar*, 97–113. Oxford: Oxford University Press.

Rodriguez, Ioão. 1604–1608. *Arte da lingoa de Japam*. Nagasaki: Collegio de Iapão. Japanese translation by Doi Tadao published as Rodriguez, Ioão. 1955. *Nihon daibunten* [*Great Japanese grammar*]. Tokyo: Sanseido.

Sadakane, Kumi, and Masatoshi Koizumi. 1995. On the nature of the "dative" particle *ni* in Japanese. *Linguistics* 33. 5–33.

Sadock, Jerrold M. 1991. *Autolexical syntax*. Chicago: University of Chicago Press.

Sadock, Jerrold M. 1995. Review of *A-morphous morphology*, by Stephen R. Anderson. *Natural Language and Linguistic Theory* 13. 326–341.

Sakakura, Atsuyoshi. 1975. *Bunshō to hyōgen* [*Text and expression*]. Tokyo: Kadokawa Shoten.

Sakanashi, Ryuzo. 1982. Kindai no bunpō II (Kamigata-hen) [Grammar of the early modern period II (Kyoto-Osaka)]. In Hiroshi Tsukishima (ed.), *Bunpōshi* [*Grammatical history*] (*Kōza kokugoshi* [*Course in the history of Japanese*] 4), 467–536. Tokyo: Taishukan Shoten.

Sasaki, Kan. 2018. Hokkaidō hōgen ni okeru jihatsu gokei no yure [Variation in the spontaneous form in the Hokkaido dialect]. *KLS* 38 (*Proceedings of the 42nd annual meeting of the Kansai Linguistic Society*). 205–216.

Sasaki, Kan. 2019. *ra-gyō godanka no tayōsei* [The diversity of assimilation to *r*-stem conjugation]. In Taro Kageyama and Hideki Kishimoto (eds.), *Rekishikon kenkyū no arata na apuroochi* [*New approaches to lexicon research*], 201–228. Tokyo: Kurosio Publishers.

Sasaki, Kan, and Akie Yamazaki. 2006. Two types of detransitive constructions in the Hokkaido dialect of Japanese. In Werner Abraham and Larisa Leisiö (eds.), *Passivization and typology*, 352–372. Amsterdam: Benjamins.

Scalise, Sergio. 1984. *Generative morphology*. Dordrecht: Foris.

Schachter, Paul. 1987. Tagalog. In Bernard Comrie (ed.), *The world's major languages*, 936–958. Oxford: Oxford University Press.

Schachter, Paul, and Fe T. Otanes. 1972. *Tagalog reference grammar*. Berkeley: University of California Press.

Serafim, Leon A., and Rumiko Shinzato. 2021. *The language of the Old-Okinawan* Omoro Sōshi. Leiden: Brill.

Shibatani, Masayoshi. 1973. Semantics of Japanese causativization. *Foundations of Language* 9. 317–373.

Shibatani, Masayoshi. 1976. The grammar of causative constructions: A conspectus. In Masayoshi Shibatani (ed.), *The grammar of causative constructions*, 1–40. San Diego: Academic Press.

Shibatani, Masayoshi. 1977. Grammatical relations and surface cases. *Language* 53. 789–809.

Shimabukuro, Moriyo. 2007. *The accentual history of the Japanese and Ryukyuan languages: A reconstruction*. Folkestone: Global Oriental.

Shimabukuro, Yukiko. 1997. Okinawa hokubu hōgen [Dialects of northern Okinawa]. In Takashi Kamei, Rokuro Kono, and Eiichi Chino (eds.), *Nihon rettō no gengo (Gengogaku daijiten serekushon)* [*The languages of the Japanese archipelago (Selection from the Great dictionary of linguistics)*], 354–369. Tokyo: Sanseido.

Shinmura, Izuru (ed.). 1991. *Kōjien*, 4th ed. Tokyo: Iwanami Shoten.

Shinmura, Izuru (ed.). 1998. *Kōjien*, 5th ed. Tokyo: Iwanami Shoten.

Siddiqi, Daniel. 2014. The morphology–syntax interface. In Andrew Carnie, Yosuke Sato, and Daniel Siddiqi (eds.), *The Routledge handbook of syntax*, 345–364. Abingdon: Routledge.

Sihler, Andrew L. 1995. *New comparative grammar of Greek and Latin*. Oxford: Oxford University Press.

Siloni, Tal. 2019. Event structure and syntax. In Robert Truswell (ed.), *The Oxford handbook of event structure*, 456–489. Oxford: Oxford University Press.

Skoruppa, Katrin, Anna Lambrechts, and Sharon Peperkamp. 2011. The role of phonetic distance in the acquisition of phonological alternations. *North Eastern Linguistic Society* (*NELS*) 39. 717–729.

Sorace, Antonella. 2000. Gradients in auxiliary selection with intransitive verbs. *Language* 76. 859–890.

Sotiropoulos, Dimitri. 1972. *Noun morphology of modern demotic Greek*. The Hague: Mouton.

Sowell, Thomas. 1987. *A conflict of visions: Ideological origins of political struggles*. New York: Quill.

Stephany, Ursula. 1982. Inflectional and lexical morphology — A linguistic continuum. *Glossologia* 1. 27–55.

Steriade, Donca. 2016. The morphome vs similarity-based syncretism: Latin *t*-stem derivatives. In Ricardo Bermúdez-Otero and Ana R. Luís (eds.), *The morphome debate*, 112–171. Oxford: Oxford University Press.

Stump, Gregory T. 2001. *Inflectional morphology*. Cambridge: Cambridge University Press.

Suzuki, Kazuhiko. 1977. Bunpō no utsurikawari [Grammatical change]. In Atsuyoshi Sakakura (ed.), *Nihongo no rekishi* [*The history of Japanese*] (*Nihongo kōza* [*Course in Japanese*] 6), 197–242. Tokyo: Taishukan Shoten.

Takahashi, Toshizo. 1987a. *Ryūkyū no hōgen* [*Ryukyu dialects*] 11 (*Yaeyama: Yonaguni-jima*). Tokyo: Hosei Daigaku Okinawa Bunka Kenkyujo.

Takahashi, Toshizo. 1987b. *Ryūkyū no hōgen* [*Ryukyu dialects*] 12 (*Yaeyama: Yonaguni-jima*). Tokyo: Hosei Daigaku Okinawa Bunka Kenkyujo.

Takahashi, Toshizo. 1991a. *Omoro Saushi no dōshi no kenkyū* [*Research on the verbs of the Omoro Soshi*]. Tokyo: Musashino Shoin.

Takahashi, Toshizo. 1991b. *Omoro Saushi no kokugogakuteki kenkyū* [*Linguistic research on the Omoro Soshi*]. Tokyo: Musashino Shoin.

Takahashi, Toshizo. 1997a. Koten Ryūkyūgo [Classical Ryukyuan]. In Takashi Kamei, Rokuro Kono, and Eiichi Chino (eds.) *Nihon rettō no gengo (Gengogaku daijiten serekushon)* [*The languages of the Japanese archipelago (Selection from the Great dictionary of linguistics)*], 422–431. Tokyo: Sanseido.

Takahashi, Toshizo. 1997b. Yonaguni hōgen [The Yonaguni dialect]. In Takashi Kamei, Rokuro Kono, and Eiichi Chino (eds.) *Nihon rettō no gengo (Gengogaku daijiten serekushon)* [*The languages of the Japanese archipelago (Selection from the Great dictionary of linguistics)*], 413–422. Tokyo: Sanseido.

Thorpe, Maner L. 1983. Ryūkūan language history. Doctoral dissertation, University of Southern California.

Thumb, Albert. 1910. *Handbuch der neugriechischen Volkssprache*, 2nd ed. Strassburg: Trübner. English translation by S. Angus published as Thumb, Albert. 1912. *Handbook of the modern Greek vernacular*. Edinburgh: Clark.

Tiersma, Peter. 1978. Bidirectional leveling as evidence for relational rules. *Lingua* 45. 67–77.

Tiersma, Peter. 1982. Local and general markedness. *Language* 58. 832–849.

Tojo, Misao (ed.). 1951. *Zenkoku hōgen jiten* [*Nationwide dialect dictionary*]. Tokyo: Tokyodo Shuppan.

Tojo, Misao, Yoshimoto Endo, Teruo Hirayama, Tadatoshi Okubo, and Takeshi Shibata (eds.). 1961. *Hōgengaku kōza* [*Dialectology course*], 4 vols. Tokyo: Tokyodo Shuppan.

Toyama, Nana. 2013a. Okinawa-ken Shuri hōgen ni okeru shiekibun no imikōzō [The semantic structure of causative sentences in the Shuri dialect of Okinawa Prefecture]. *Nihongo Bunpō* 13. 105–121.

Toyama, Nana. 2013b. Okinawa Shuri hōgen no shieki dōshi to tadōsei [Causative verbs and transitivity in the Shuri dialect of Okinawa]. *Ryūkyū-Ajia Shakaibunka Kenkyū* [*Ryukyu/Asia Sociocultural Research*] 16. 113–130.

Toyama, Nana. 2015. Okinawa Shuri hōgen ni okeru voisu to riekisei no kijutsu bunpō kenkyū [Descriptive grammatical study of voice and benefactivity in the Shuri dialect of Okinawa]. Doctoral dissertation, University of the Ryukyus.

Triandaphyllidis, Manolis A. 1949. *Mikrí Neoellinikí grammatikí*. Athens. English translation by John B. Burke published as Triandaphyllidis, Manolis A. 2004. *Concise Modern Greek grammar*. Aristotle University of Thessaloniki.

Tsuda, Katsumi. 2000. Ōitaben ni okeru hukanō hyōgen ni tsuite [On expressions of impossibility in the Oita dialect]. *Nippon Bunri Daigaku Kiyō [Bulletin of Nippon Bunri University]* 28. 116–126.

Tsuhako, Toshiko. 1997. Okinawa chūnanbu hōgen [Dialects of central and southern Okinawa]. In Takashi Kamei, Rokuro Kono, and Eiichi Chino (eds.) *Nihon rettō no gengo (Gengogaku daijiten serekushon) [The languages of the Japanese archipelago (Selection from the Great dictionary of linguistics)]*, 369–388. Tokyo: Sanseido.

Uchima, Chokujin. 1980. Yonaguni hōgen no katsuyō to sono seiritsu [Conjugation of the Yonaguni dialect and its formation]. In Kuroshio Bunka no Kai [Kuroshio Cultural Association] (ed.), *Kuroshio no minzoku, bunka, gengo [The peoples, cultures, and languages of the Kuroshio current]*, 447–490. Tokyo: Kadokawa Shoten.

Uchima, Chokujin. 1982. Ha-gyō yodankei dōshi no katsuyō no tsūjiteki kōsatsu [Diachronic observations on the conjugation of *w*-stems]. In Kyugakkai Rengo Amami Chosa Iinkai [Union of Nine Learned Societies Amami Survey Committee] (ed.), *Amami: Shizen, bunka, shakai [Amami: Nature, culture, society]*, 300–308. Tokyo: Kobundo.

Uchima, Chokujin. 1984a. Miyako shotō no hōgen [The dialects of the Miyako island group]. In Kiichi Iitoyo, Sukezumi Hino, and Ryoichi Sato (eds.), *Okinawa/Amami chihō no hōgen [The dialects of the Okinawa/Amami region] (Kōza hōgengaku [Course in dialectology]* 10), 251–287. Tokyo: Kokusho Kankokai.

Uchima, Chokujin. 1984b. Ryūkyū hōgen bunpō no kenkyū [*Research on the grammar of Ryukyu dialects*]. Tokyo: Kasama Shoin.

Uchima, Chokujin, and Mitsuyoshi Nohara. 2006. *Okinawa-go jiten [Okinawan dictionary]*. Tokyo: Kenkyusha.

Uemura, Yukio. 1961. Okinawa hontō [The main island of Okinawa]. In Misao Tojo, Yoshimoto Endo, Teruo Hirayama, Tadatoshi Okubo, and Takeshi Shibata (eds.), *Kyūshū/Ryūkyū hōgen [Kyushu and Ryukyu dialects] (Hōgengaku kōza [Dialectology course]* 4), 334–357. Tokyo: Tokyodo Shuppan.

Uemura, Yukio. 1963. Shuri hōgen no bunpō [A grammar of the Shuri dialect]. In Kokuritsu Kokugo Kenkyujo [National Language Research Institute], *Okinawa-go jiten [Dictionary of the Okinawan language]*, 58–86. Tokyo: Okurasho Insatsukyoku. English translation by Wayne P. Lawrence in Uemura, Yukio. 2003. *The Ryukyuan language*, 124–161. Osaka: Osaka Gakuin Daigaku Joho Gakubu.

Uemura, Yukio. 1997. Sōsetsu [Introduction]. In Takashi Kamei, Rokuro Kono, and Eiichi Chino (eds.), *Nihon rettō no gengo (Gengogaku daijiten serekushon) [The languages of the Japanese archipelago (Selection from the Great dictionary of linguistics)]*, 311–354. Tokyo: Sanseido. English translation by Wayne P. Lawrence in Uemura, Yukio. 2003. *The Ryukyuan language*, 1–110. Osaka: Osaka Gakuin Daigaku Joho Gakubu.

Umegaki, Minoru. 1962. Mie-ken hōgen [The dialects of Mie Prefecture]. In Minoru Umegaki (ed.), *Kinki hōgen no sōgōteki kenkyū* [*A comprehensive study of the Kinki dialects*], 91–157. Tokyo: Sanseido.

Unger, J. Marshall. 1977. Studies in early Japanese morphophonemics (Doctoral dissertation, Yale University). Bloomington: Indiana University Linguistics Club.

Unger, J. Marshall. 2000. Reconciling comparative and internal reconstruction: The case of Old Japanese /ti, ri, ni/. *Language* 76: 655–681.

Vance, Timothy J. 1987. *An introduction to Japanese phonology*. Albany: State University of New York Press.

Vance, Timothy J. 2008. *The sounds of Japanese*. Cambridge: Cambridge University Press.

Vaux, Bert. 2001. Consonant insertion and hypercorrection. Paper presented at the LSA Annual Meeting, Washington, DC. https://www.academia.edu/300593/Consonant_Epenthesis_and_Hypercorrection

Vaux, Bert. 2008. Why the phonological component must be serial and rule-based. In Bert Vaux and Andrew Nevins (eds.), *Rules, constraints, and phonological phenomena*, 20–60. Oxford: Oxford University Press.

Vazou, Elli, and George J. Xydopoulos. 2007. Towards an account of acronyms/initialisms in Greek. *Selected Papers on Theoretical and Applied Linguistics* (Aristotle University of Thessaloniki) 17. 233–243.

Vennemann, Theo. 1972. Rule inversion. *Lingua* 29. 209–242.

Vennemann, Theo. 1974. Words and syllables in natural generative grammar. In Anthony Bruck, Robert A. Fox, and Michael W. LaGaly (eds.), *Papers from the parasession on natural phonology*, 346–374. Chicago: Chicago Linguistic Society.

Volpe, Mark. 2005. Japanese morphology and its theoretical consequences: Derivational morphology in distributed morphology. Doctoral dissertation, Stony Brook University.

Vovin, Alexander. 2010. *Koreo-Japonica*. Honolulu: University of Hawai'i Press.

Whitman, John. 1985. The phonological basis for the comparison of Japanese and Korean. Doctoral dissertation, Harvard University.

Whitman, John. 2008. The source of the bigrade conjugation and stem-shape in pre-Old Japanese. In Bjarke Frellesvig and John Whitman (eds.), *Proto-Japanese*, 159–173. Amsterdam: Benjamins.

Whitman, John. 2012. The relationship between Japanese and Korean. In Nicolas Tranter (ed.), *The languages of Japan and Korea*, 24–38. London: Routledge.

Whitman, John. 2016. Nichiryū sogo no on'in taikei to rentaikei/izenkei no kigen [The vowel system of Proto-Japanese-Ryukyuan and the origin of the adnominal/realis forms]. In Yukinori Takubo, John Whitman, and Tatsuya Hirako (eds.), *Ryūkyū shogo to kodai Nihongo: Nichiryū sogo no saiken ni mukete* [*Ryukyuan and premodern Japanese: Toward the reconstruction of Proto-Japanese-Ryukyuan*], 21–38. Tokyo: Kurosio Publishers.

Whitney, William Dwight. 1889. *Sanskrit grammar*, 2nd ed. Cambridge, MA: Harvard University Press.

Williams, Edwin B. 1938. *From Latin to Portuguese*. Philadelphia: University of Pennsylvania Press.

Yamada, Masahiro. 2016. Dunan(Yonaguni)go no dōshi keitairon [The verbal morphology of Dunan (Yonaguni)]. In Yukinori Takubo, John Whitman, and Tatsuya Hirako (eds.), *Ryūkyū shogo to kodai Nihongo: Nichiryū sogo no saiken ni mukete* [*Ryukyuan and premodern Japanese: Toward the reconstruction of Proto-Japanese-Ryukyuan*], 259–289. Tokyo: Kurosio Publishers.

Yamada, Masahiro, Thomas Pellard and Michinori Shimoji. 2015. Dunan grammar (Yonaguni Ryukyuan). In Patrick Heinrich, Shinsho Miyara, and Michinori Shimoji (eds.), *Handbook of the Ryukyuan languages*, 449–478. Berlin: De Gruyter.

Yamaguchi, Akiho, and Morihide Akimoto (eds.). 2001. *Nihongo bunpō daijiten* [*Great dictionary of Japanese grammar*]. Tokyo: Meiji Shoin.

Yoshikawa, Toshiaki. 1972. Toyohashi chihō no hōgen [The dialect of the Toyohashi region]. In Toshiaki Yoshikawa and Yukihiro Yamaguchi, *Toyohashi chihō no hōgen* [*The dialect of the Toyohashi region*], 15–283. Toyohashi: Toyohashi Bunka Kyokai.

Zuraw, Kie. 2000. Patterned exceptions in phonology. Doctoral dissertation, University of California, Los Angeles.

Name index

Subject index

I

idiomatization 81–82, 98–100 *see also* lexicalization
idioms 96, 98–100, 102, 107–108, 109–114
inalienable possession 107–108, 110–111
inferential theories of morphology 1, 18
inflection, inflectional morphology
   category-changing 84
   contextual 11, 13
   inherent 2, 11–14
   syntactic nature of 4–14
   see also affixes, inflectional
inflectional affixes *see* affixes, inflectional
innovative *r*-suffixes 134–139, 149–152, 163, 166, 172–173, 175–176, 211, 213–214, 216–219, 231n8
interference mechanisms in analogy 226n6
internal suffixes 70–72, 74–76
irregularity, grammatical characterization of 124–125, 190
irregularity, psychological interpretation of 125, 190
isolating languages 9
isolation forms 182, 192–193
isoradical relations 55–60, 62–63, 65–68, 72, 77, 86–87, 96, 191n4
isoradical sets 58–59, 62, 64, 65n10, 66n11, 66n12, 68, 72
Italian 84
iterativity 30

J

Japonic family 21, 176–177, 215

K

Kamigata-go 115, 137, 228
Korean 85, 129n1, 182, 187–194, 196–197, 204
Kumiodori 164, 167

L

language acquisition 177, 235
late insertion 4, 14, 31, 120
Latin 54, 118, 183
leveling

as loss of irregularity 125, 227
   cases lacking proportional motivation 226–227
   of C/V polarity alternations 230
   of the bigrade alternation 211–214
   of the Inferential alternation 223–231
   phonological distance in 221–223
   regulated by the Regularization Priority Principle (RPP) 223–227
   typology of alternations and 125–126
levels of adequacy *see* descriptive adequacy; explanatory adequacy; observational adequacy
lexical causatives 15, 68n14, 81, 86, 97–117
lexical conditioning 32, 48
lexical diffusion 194
Lexical (Morphology and) Phonology 3
lexical redundancy rules 1, 3, 5, 50–51, 85–86, 90, 236
Lexical-Functional Grammar 3
lexicalization 72, 81–83, 102–103, 112–113 *see also* idiomatization
listed representations, stems and inflectional affixes as units with 6, 119, 122, 153, 233
little a 67, 76
little n 50, 64
little v
   causative (v_c) 13, 51, 60–69, 76, 85–86
   in Modern Greek 234–235
   inchoative (v_i) 51, 60–69, 70–71, 74–76, 85–86
   trapped 67
   Voice-little v split 69–76
Livisi dialect (Modern Greek) noun inflection Table 5, 203
loanwords 142n11, 169, 190, 200
local markedness 215
low attachment vs. high attachment analyses 90–94, 118, 120

M

Maori 181–182, 208
Merge operation 10
Minimal Divergence Principle (MDP) 204–206, 209–210
Minimalist Program 4, 180
Miyako 21, 159–160, 162n11, 163
   failure to adopt Analysis A 16, 176–177, 197–198, 232
Modern Greek 124, 198–206, 208, 234–236
monophthongization 19, 141, 143–144, 160, 171, 223–227
morphemes, functional/grammatical 2, 51
morphological conditioning 46, 47, 48, 208n14
morphomes 22–25
morphosyntactic conditioning, as a factor determining whether an alternation is rule-governed 24
morphosyntactic fusion 19–21

N

narrow syntax 11
Natural Generative Phonology 182
Network Morphology 4
neutralization 47, 101, 122–123, 165, 178, 182, 185–195
neutralizing choices of underlying representations 178, 185–195
nominalization 50, 64
nonagentive subjects 32, 95
nonautomatic alternations 123–126, 182
nonbasic morpheme alternants 124–125, 130, 182–183, 185
Northern Ryukyuan 21, 174n20
   adoption of Analysis A 16, 175–176

O

observational adequacy 179, 197
Okinawan 21, 31n6, 35
   Shuri dialect 15, 35, 154–160, 162–175
Old English 125, 221–222
Old Japanese 55, 57, 72, 74, 81, 82, 92, 100, 102, 103, 118, 161, 212
Omoro Soshi 162–167, 168n17